Yu-Gi-Oh!
Millennium World

Vol. 3

THE RETURN OF BAKURA

STORY AND ART BY
KAZUKI TAKAHASHI

KATSUYA
JONOUCHI

OBASA   ANZU MAZAKI   HIROTO HONDA

YUGI MUTOU

THE STORY SO FAR...

Shy 10th grader Yugi spent most of his time alone playing games…until he solved the Millennium Puzzle, a mysterious Egyptian artifact. Possessed by the puzzle, Yugi developed an alter ego: Yu-Gi-Oh, the King of Games, the soul of a pharaoh from ancient Egypt!

Discovering that the collectible card game "Duel Monsters" was of Ancient Egyptian origin, Yu-Gi-Oh collected the three Egyptian God Cards—Slifer the Sky Dragon, the God of the Obelisk, and the Sun Dragon Ra—and used them to travel into the "world of memories" of his own life 3,000 years ago. There, he found that he was the pharaoh, served by six priests who used the Millennium Items to summon *ka*—spirits and monsters—from people's souls.

But all was not well in Ancient Egypt. Bakura, a fiendish tomb-robber, attacked the palace. With his powerful spirit Diabound, Bakura was undefeatable, until Yugi summoned the God of the Obelisk. But Bakura escaped, and then ambushed and killed the priest Mahado, stealing the Millennium Ring.

Meanwhile, with the help of the Egyptian mystic Bobasa, Yugi and his friends followed Yu-Gi-Oh into the "world of memories" in order to find the pharaoh's forgotten name. But a sinister hitchhiker has gone with them into the past…

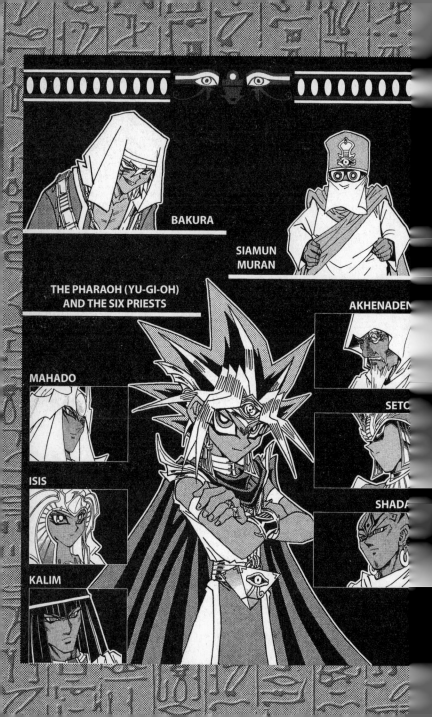

BAKURA

SIAMUN
MURAN

THE PHARAOH (YU-GI-OH)
AND THE SIX PRIESTS

AKHENADEN

MAHADO

SETO

ISIS

SHADA

KALIM

Yu-Gi-Oh! Millennium World

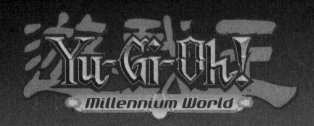

Vol. 3

CONTENTS

Duel 19: Bakura Lives!

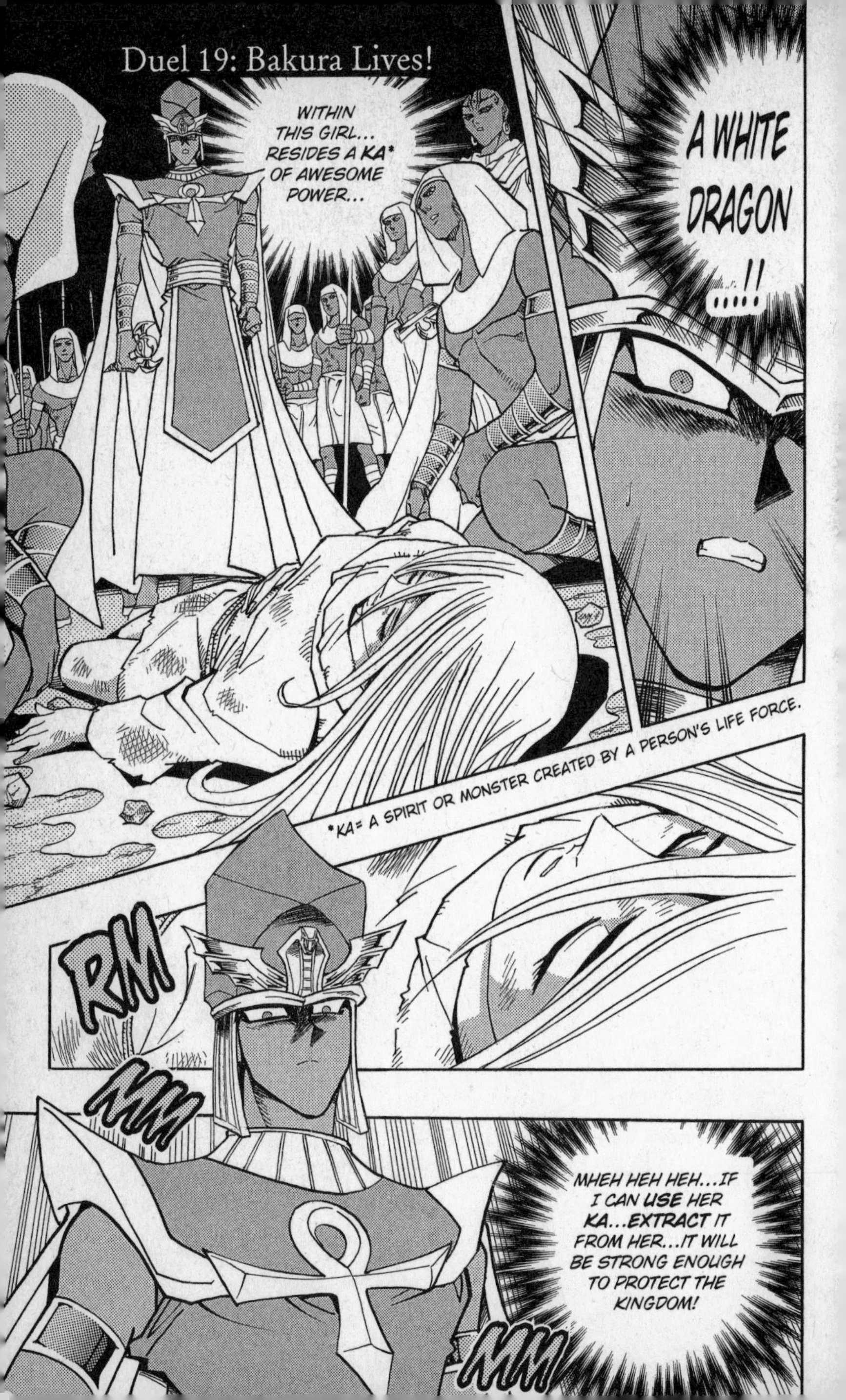
A WHITE DRAGON ......!!
WITHIN THIS GIRL... RESIDES A KA* OF AWESOME POWER...
*KA= A SPIRIT OR MONSTER CREATED BY A PERSON'S LIFE FORCE.
RM
MM
MHEH HEH HEH...IF I CAN USE HER KA...EXTRACT IT FROM HER...IT WILL BE STRONG ENOUGH TO PROTECT THE KINGDOM!
MM

Duel 19: Bakura Lives!

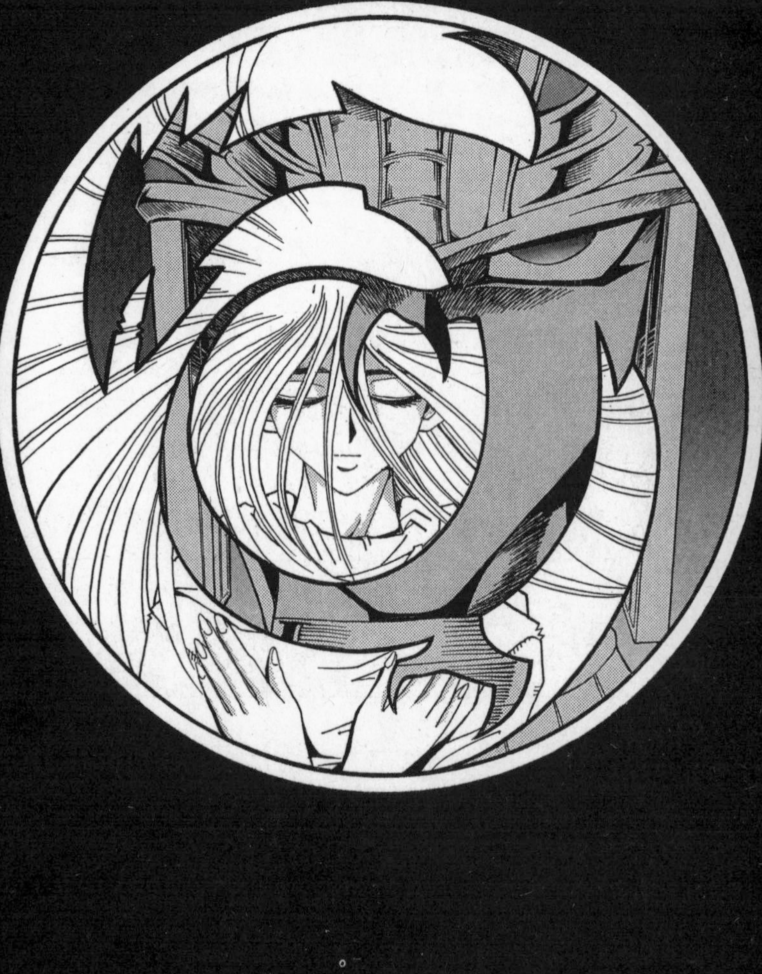

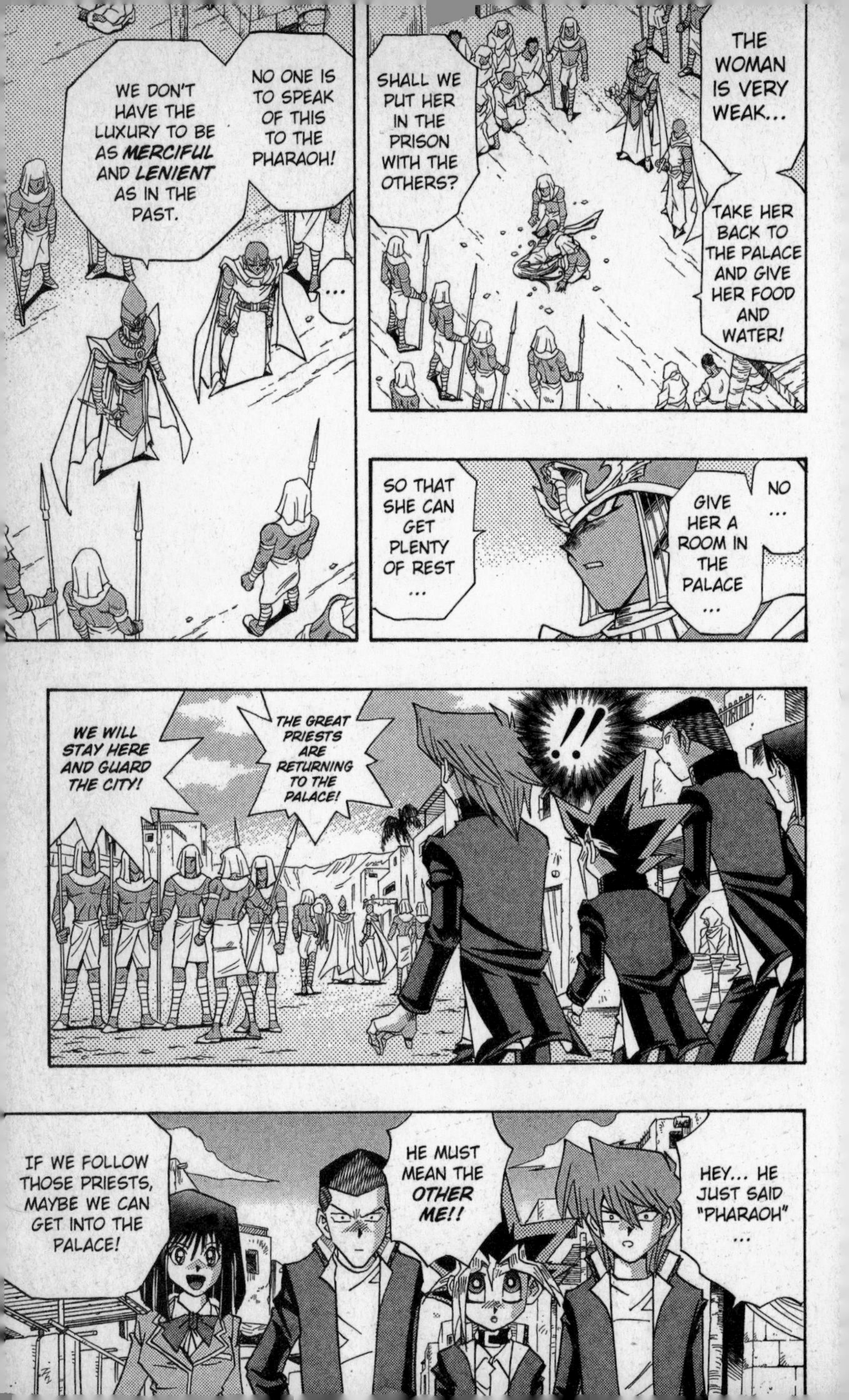
THE WOMAN IS VERY WEAK...
TAKE HER BACK TO THE PALACE AND GIVE HER FOOD AND WATER!
SHALL WE PUT HER IN THE PRISON WITH THE OTHERS?
NO ...
GIVE HER A ROOM IN THE PALACE ...
SO THAT SHE CAN GET PLENTY OF REST ...
NO ONE IS TO SPEAK OF THIS TO THE PHARAOH!
WE DON'T HAVE THE LUXURY TO BE AS *MERCIFUL* AND *LENIENT* AS IN THE PAST.
...
!!
THE GREAT PRIESTS ARE RETURNING TO THE PALACE!
WE WILL STAY HERE AND GUARD THE CITY!
HEY... HE JUST SAID "PHARAOH" ...
HE MUST MEAN THE *OTHER ME!!*
IF WE FOLLOW THOSE PRIESTS, MAYBE WE CAN GET INTO THE PALACE!

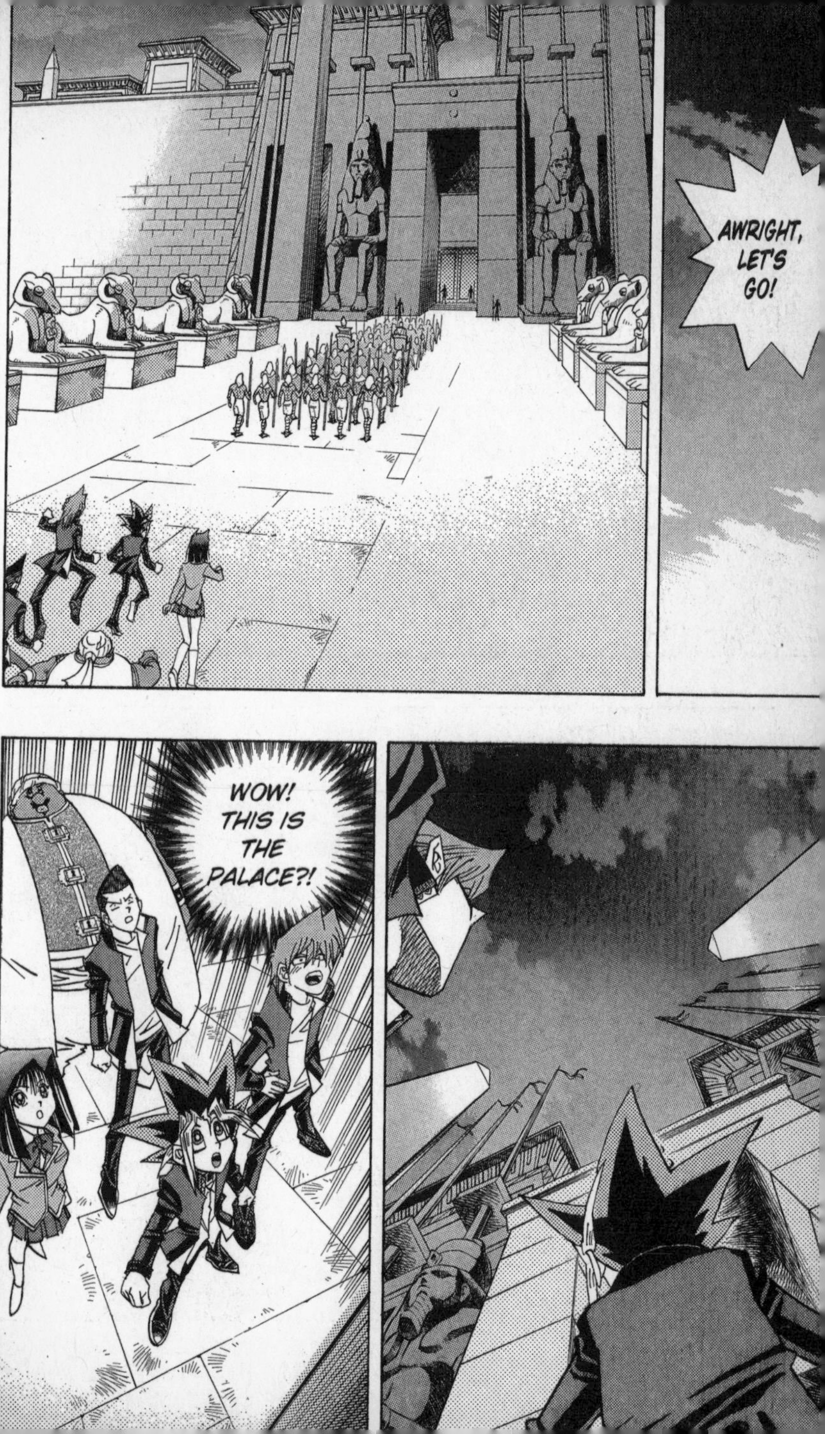
AWRIGHT, LET'S GO!
WOW! THIS IS THE PALACE?!

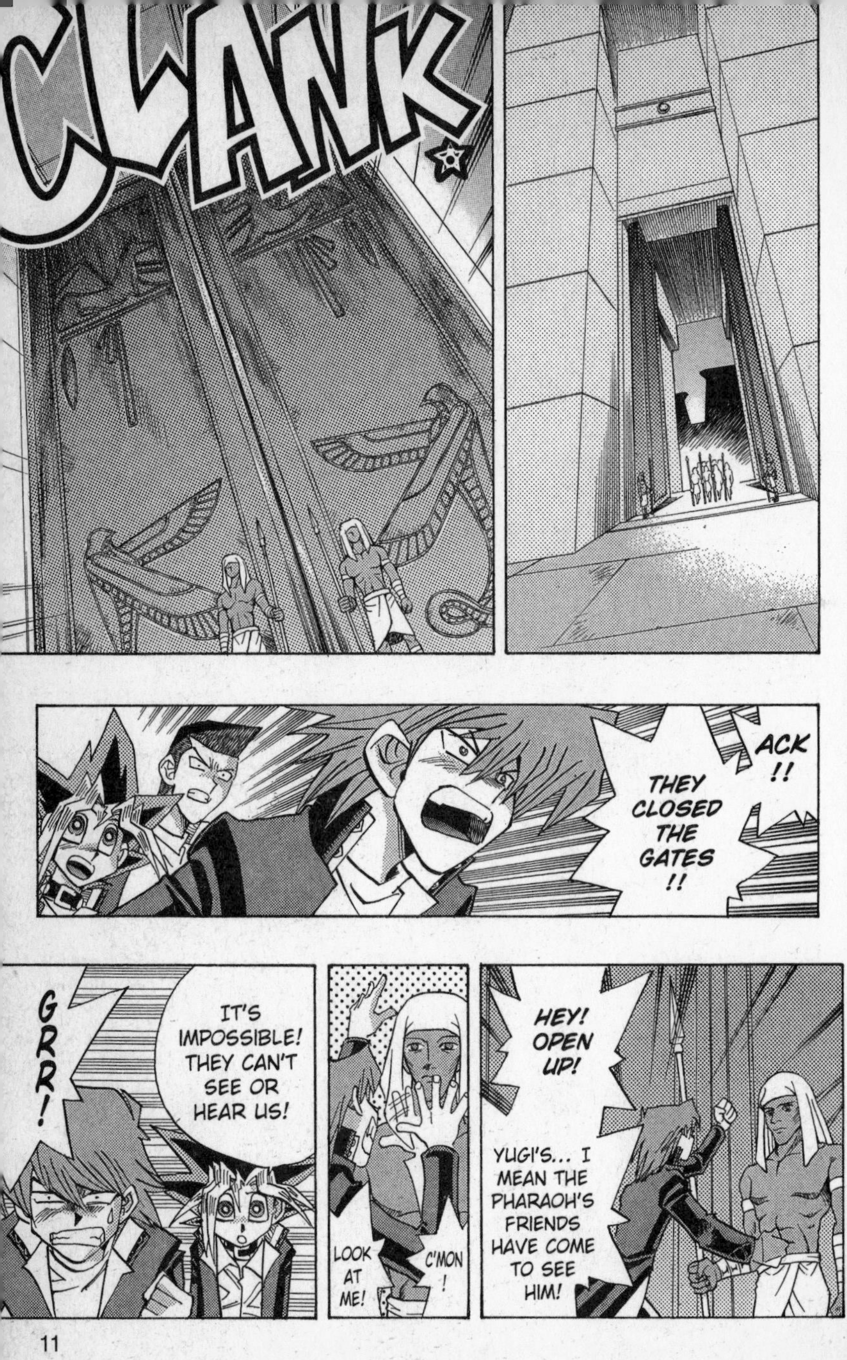
CLANK
ACK!!
THEY CLOSED THE GATES!!
HEY! OPEN UP!
YUGI'S... I MEAN THE PHARAOH'S FRIENDS HAVE COME TO SEE HIM!
C'MON!
LOOK AT ME!
IT'S IMPOSSIBLE! THEY CAN'T SEE OR HEAR US!
GRRR!

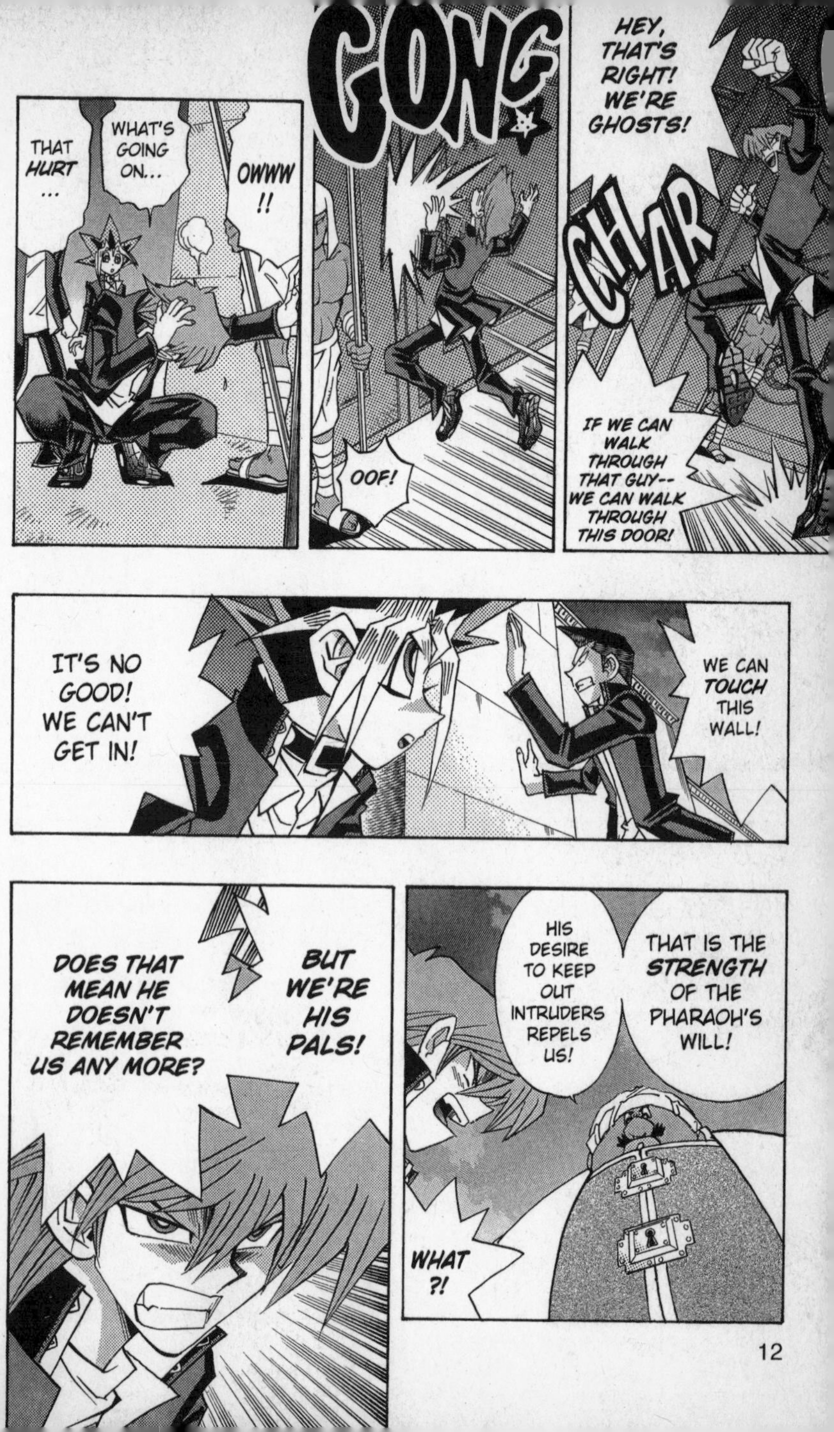

HEY, THAT'S RIGHT! WE'RE GHOSTS!
CHAR
IF WE CAN WALK THROUGH THAT GUY-- WE CAN WALK THROUGH THIS DOOR!
GONG
OOF!
OWWW!!
WHAT'S GOING ON...
THAT HURT...
WE CAN TOUCH THIS WALL!
IT'S NO GOOD! WE CAN'T GET IN!
THAT IS THE STRENGTH OF THE PHARAOH'S WILL!
HIS DESIRE TO KEEP OUT INTRUDERS REPELS US!
WHAT?!
BUT WE'RE HIS PALS!
DOES THAT MEAN HE DOESN'T REMEMBER US ANY MORE?

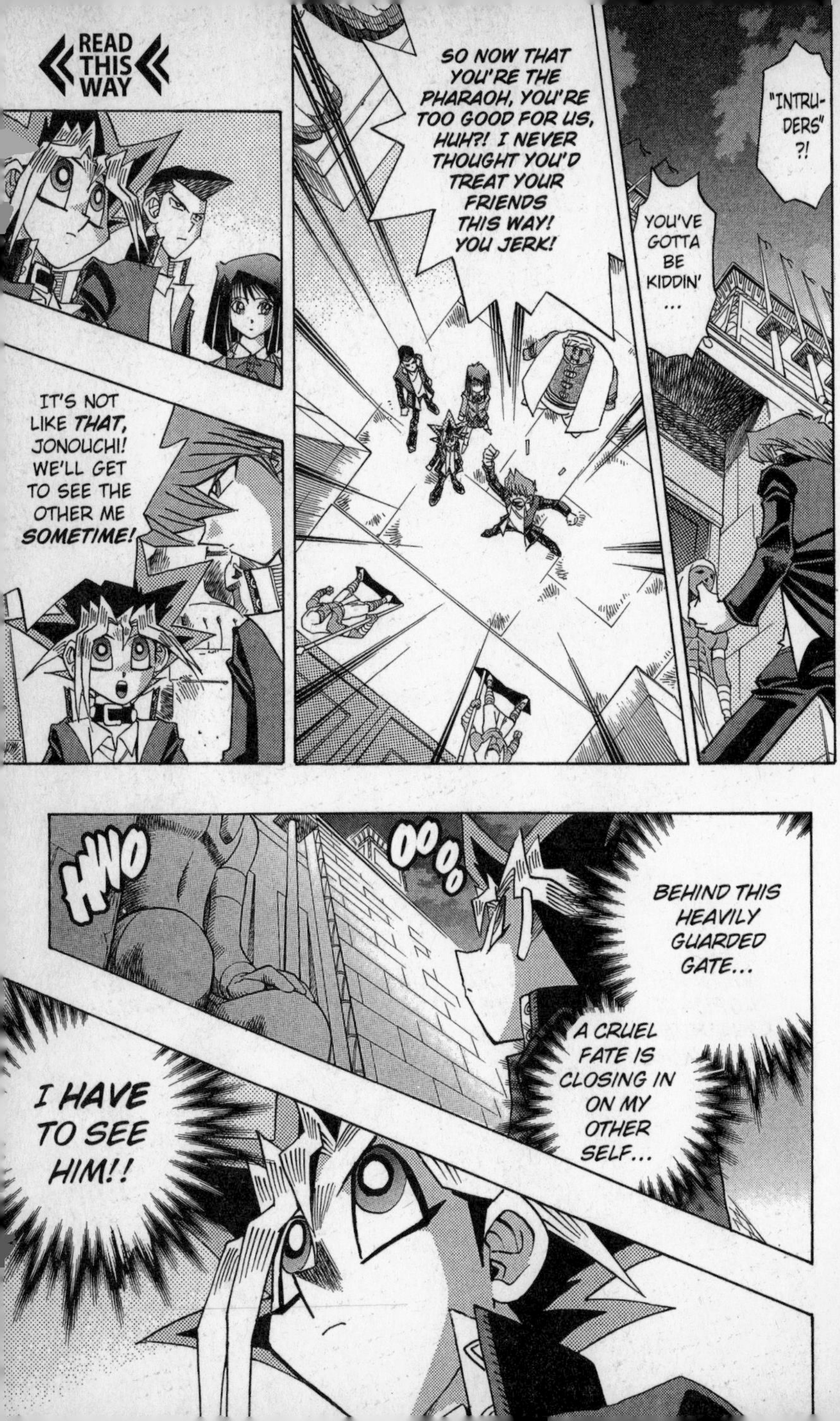
READ THIS WAY
"INTRU-DERS" ?!
YOU'VE GOTTA BE KIDDIN' ...
SO NOW THAT YOU'RE THE PHARAOH, YOU'RE TOO GOOD FOR US, HUH?! I NEVER THOUGHT YOU'D TREAT YOUR FRIENDS THIS WAY! YOU JERK!
IT'S NOT LIKE THAT, JONOUCHI! WE'LL GET TO SEE THE OTHER ME SOMETIME!
HWOOOO
BEHIND THIS HEAVILY GUARDED GATE...
A CRUEL FATE IS CLOSING IN ON MY OTHER SELF...
I HAVE TO SEE HIM!!

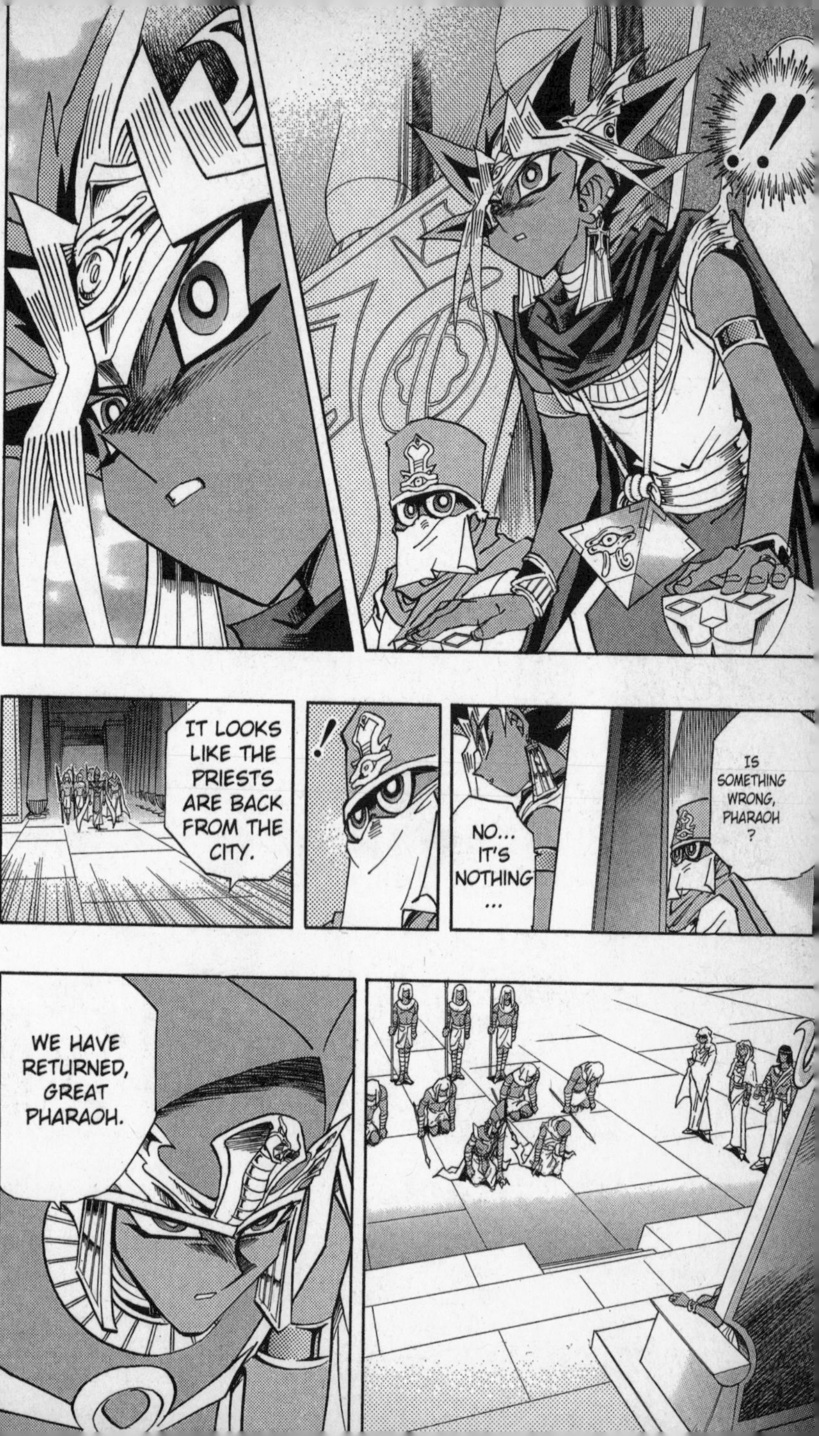
!!
IS SOMETHING WRONG, PHARAOH?
NO... IT'S NOTHING...
!
IT LOOKS LIKE THE PRIESTS ARE BACK FROM THE CITY.
WE HAVE RETURNED, GREAT PHARAOH.

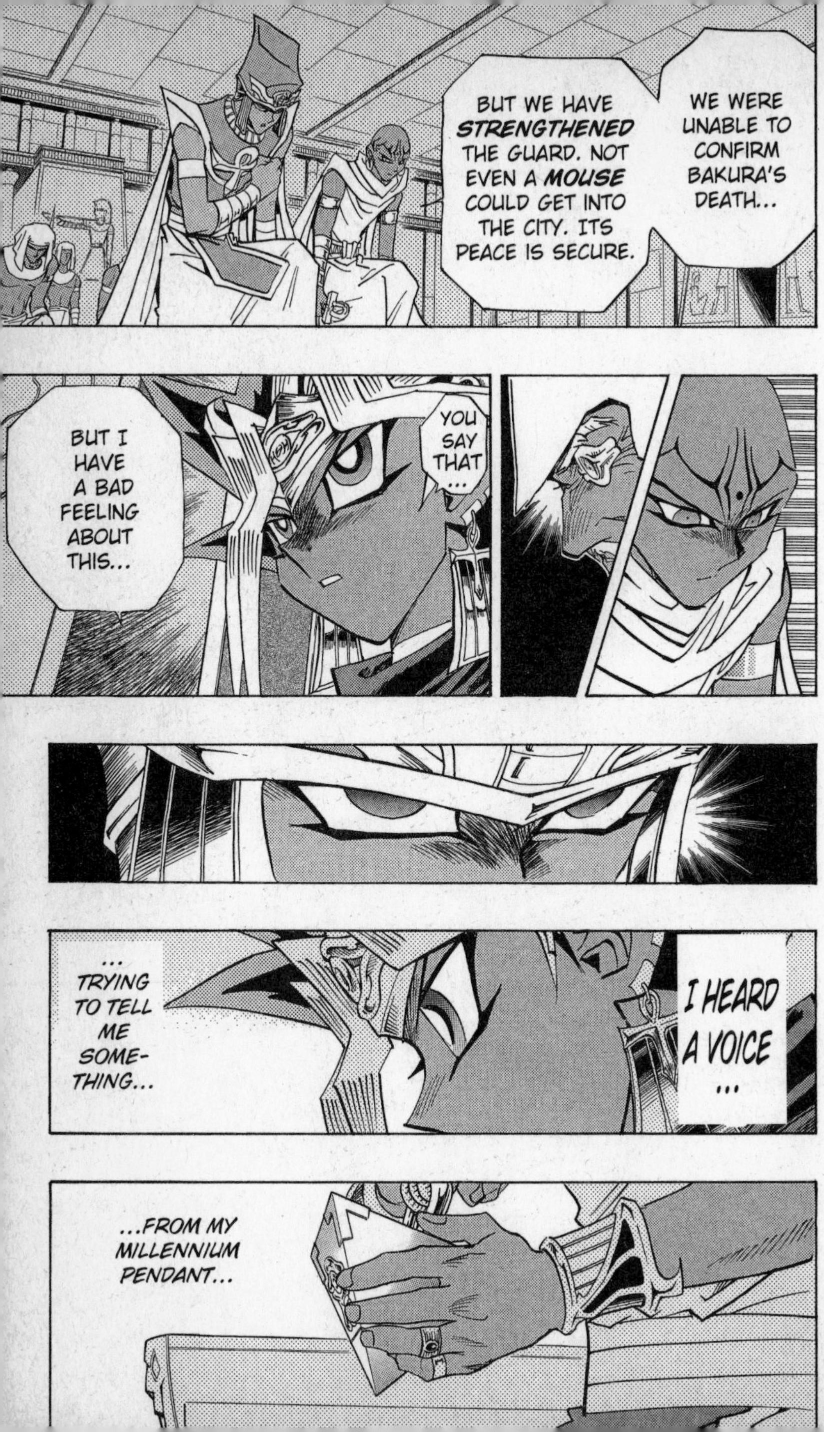
WE WERE UNABLE TO CONFIRM BAKURA'S DEATH...
BUT WE HAVE STRENGTHENED THE GUARD. NOT EVEN A MOUSE COULD GET INTO THE CITY. ITS PEACE IS SECURE.
YOU SAY THAT...
BUT I HAVE A BAD FEELING ABOUT THIS...
I HEARD A VOICE...
...TRYING TO TELL ME SOME-THING...
...FROM MY MILLENNIUM PENDANT...

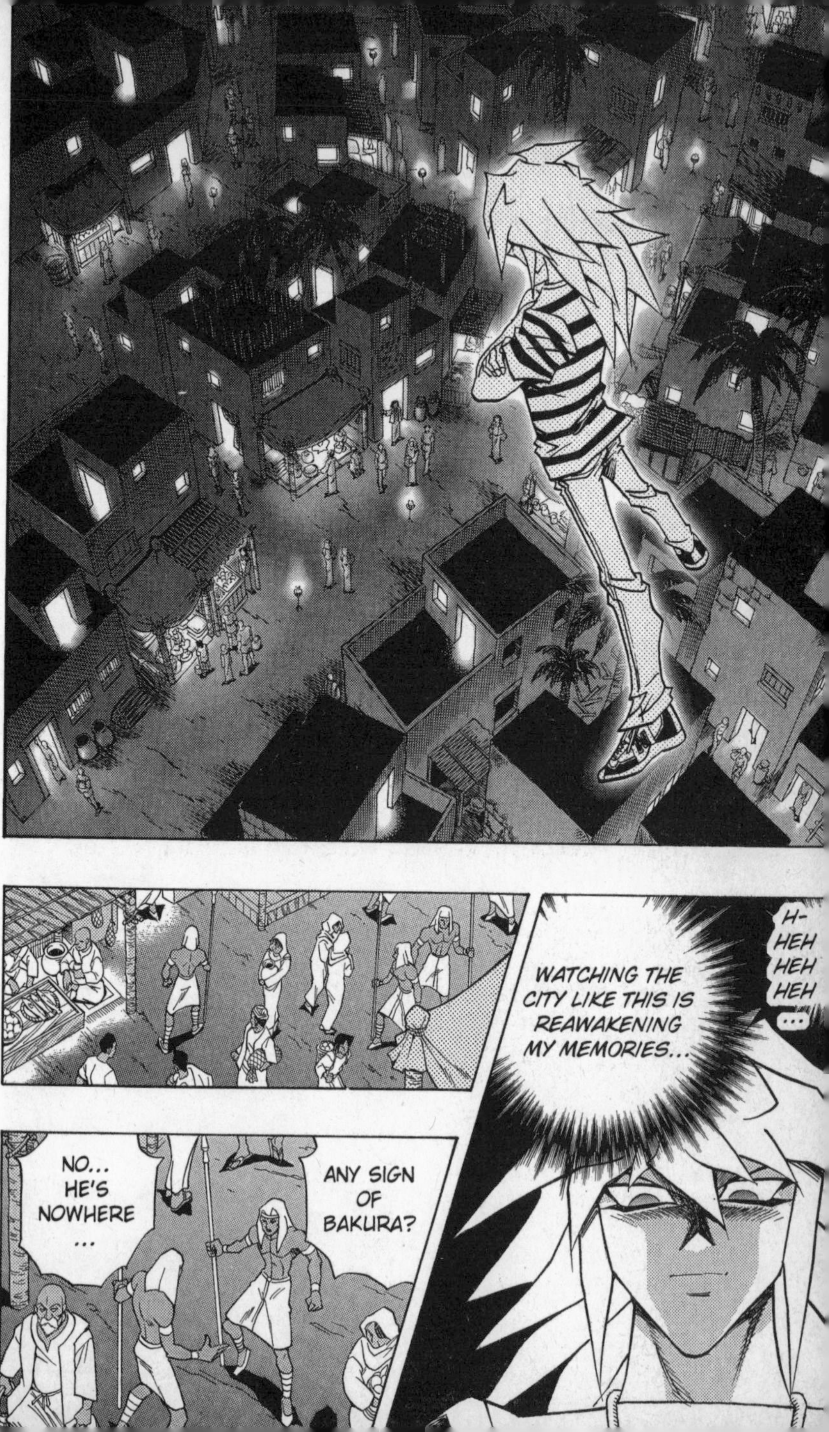
H-HEH HEH HEH...
WATCHING THE CITY LIKE THIS IS REAWAKENING MY MEMORIES...
ANY SIGN OF BAKURA?
NO... HE'S NOWHERE ...

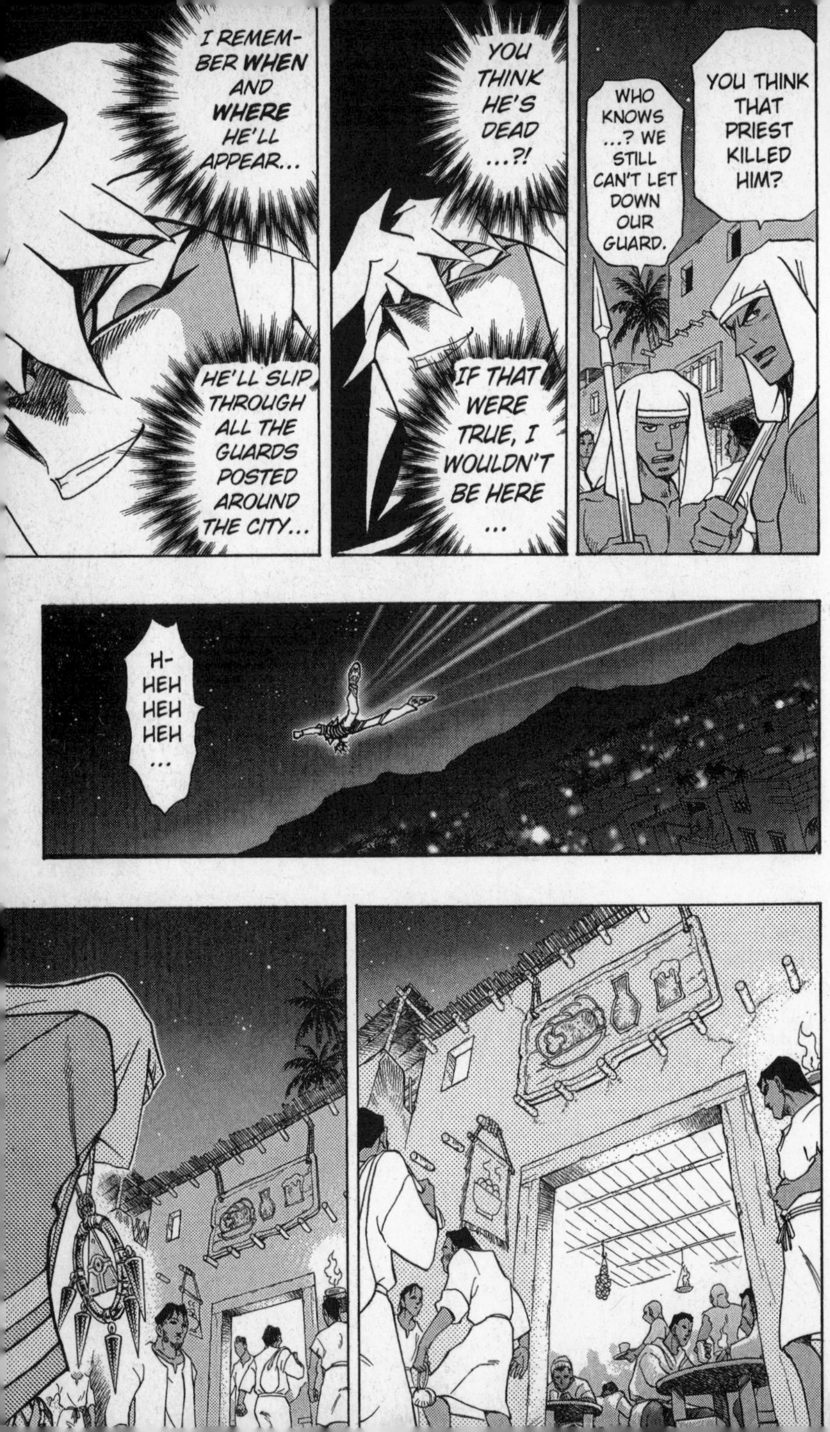
YOU THINK THAT PRIEST KILLED HIM?
WHO KNOWS ...? WE STILL CAN'T LET DOWN OUR GUARD.
YOU THINK HE'S DEAD ...?!
IF THAT WERE TRUE, I WOULDN'T BE HERE ...
I REMEMBER WHEN AND WHERE HE'LL APPEAR...
HE'LL SLIP THROUGH ALL THE GUARDS POSTED AROUND THE CITY...
H-HEH HEH HEH ...

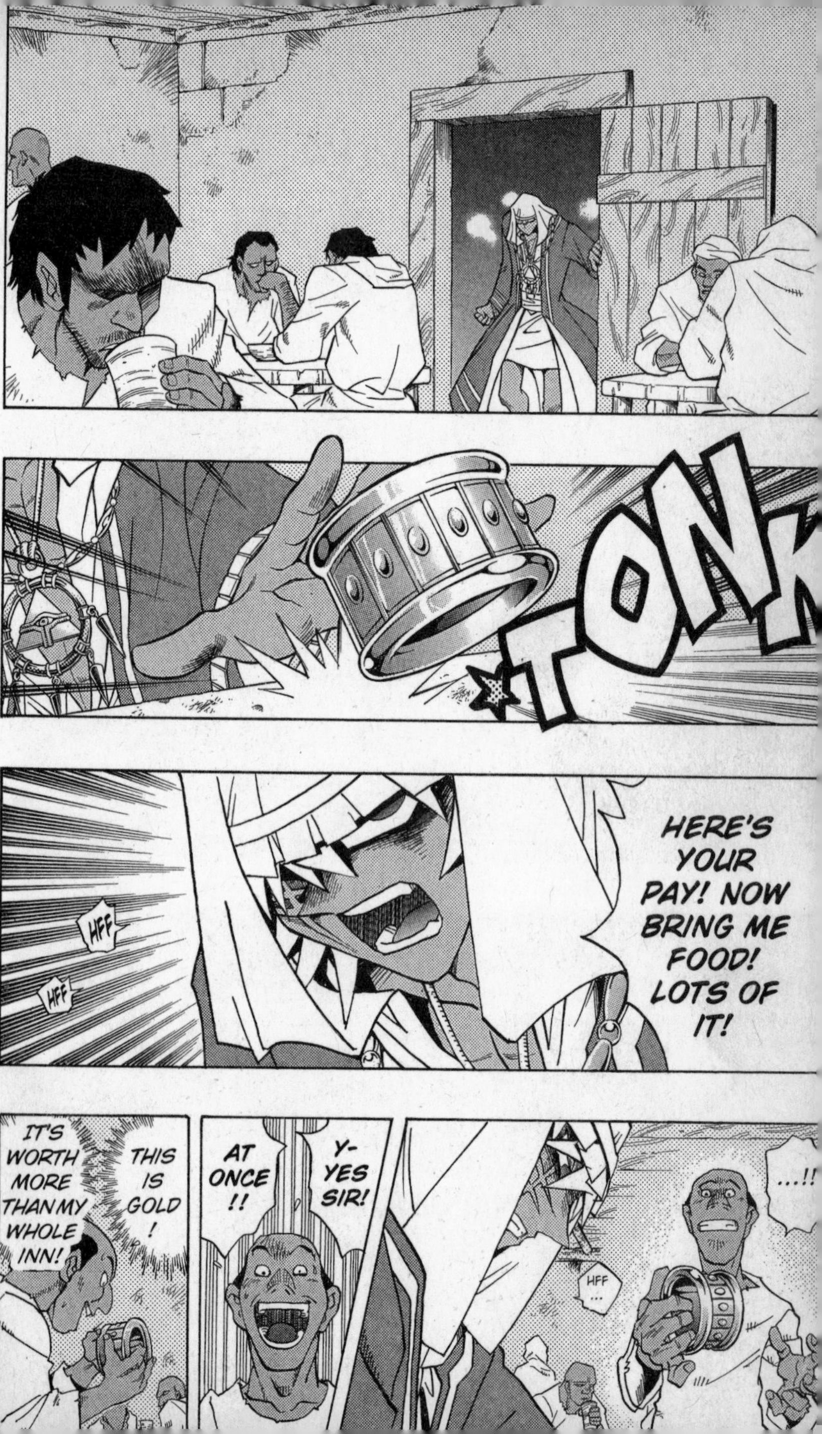
TONK
HERE'S YOUR PAY! NOW BRING ME FOOD! LOTS OF IT!
HFF
HFF
...!!
HFF ...
Y-YES SIR!
AT ONCE!!
THIS IS GOLD!
IT'S WORTH MORE THAN MY WHOLE INN!

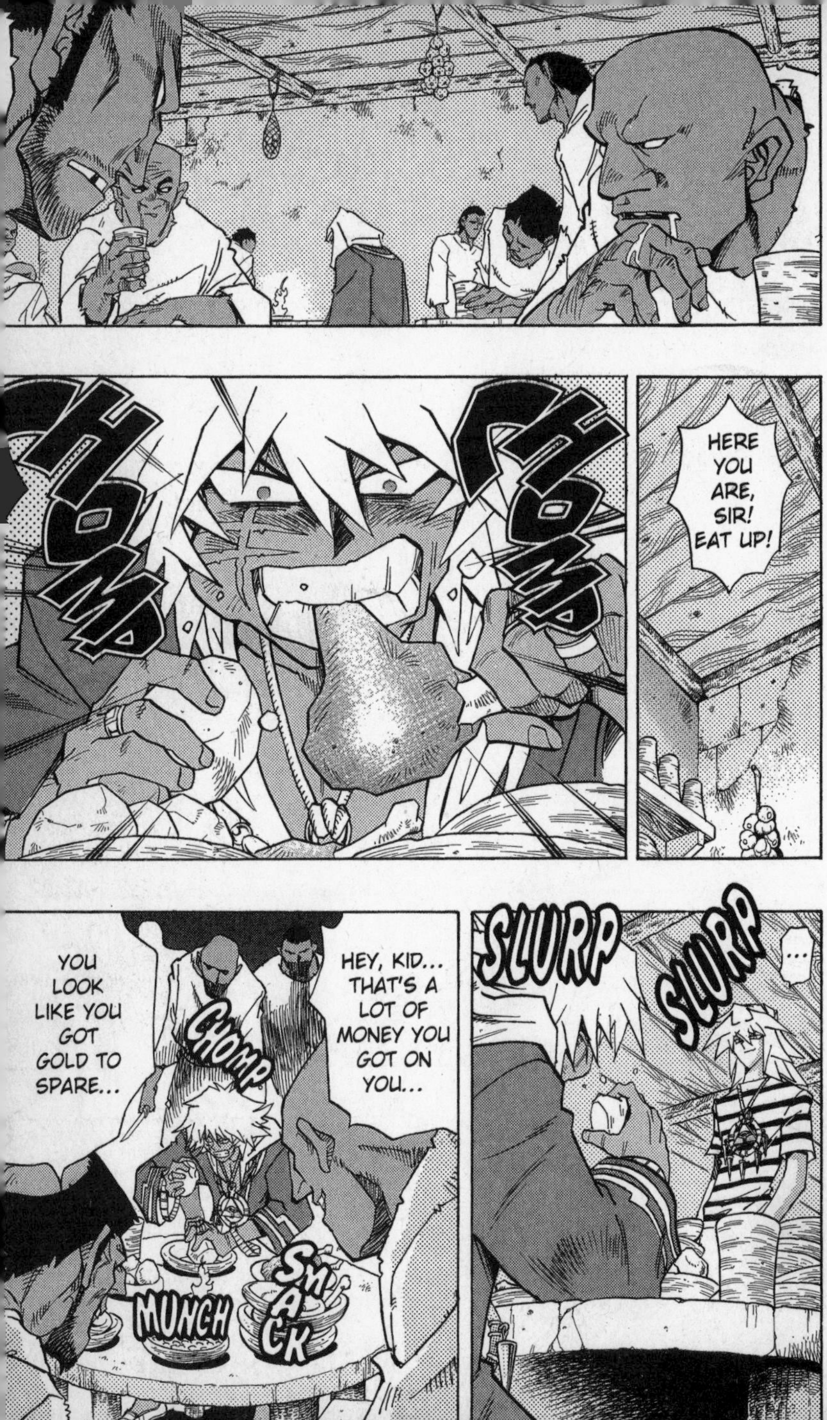
HERE YOU ARE, SIR! EAT UP!
CHOMP
CHOMP
...
SLURP
SLURP
HEY, KID... THAT'S A LOT OF MONEY YOU GOT ON YOU...
YOU LOOK LIKE YOU GOT GOLD TO SPARE...
CHOMP
SMACK
MUNCH

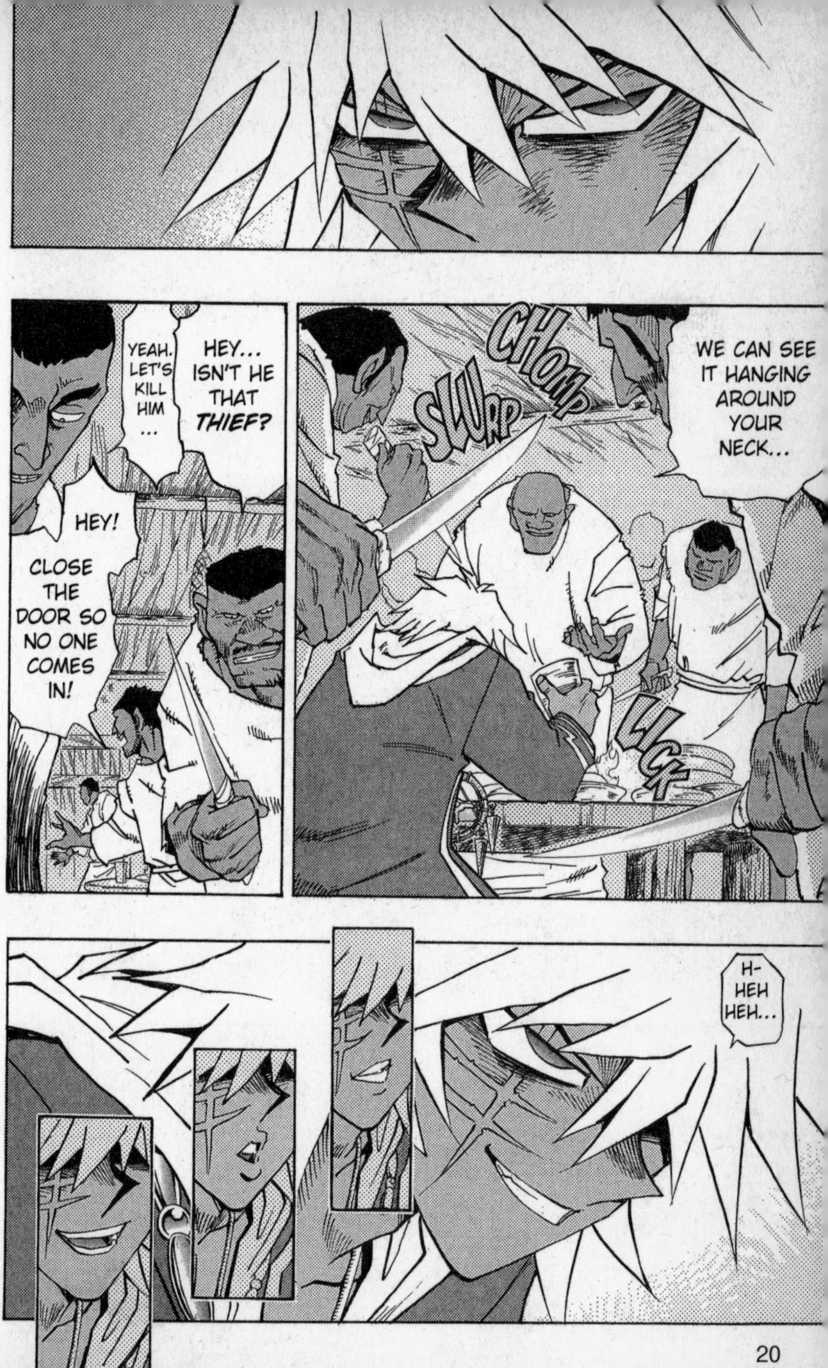

WE CAN SEE IT HANGING AROUND YOUR NECK...
CHOMP
SLURP
LICK
HEY... ISN'T HE THAT *THIEF?*
YEAH. LET'S KILL HIM ...
HEY!
CLOSE THE DOOR SO NO ONE COMES IN!
H-HEH HEH...

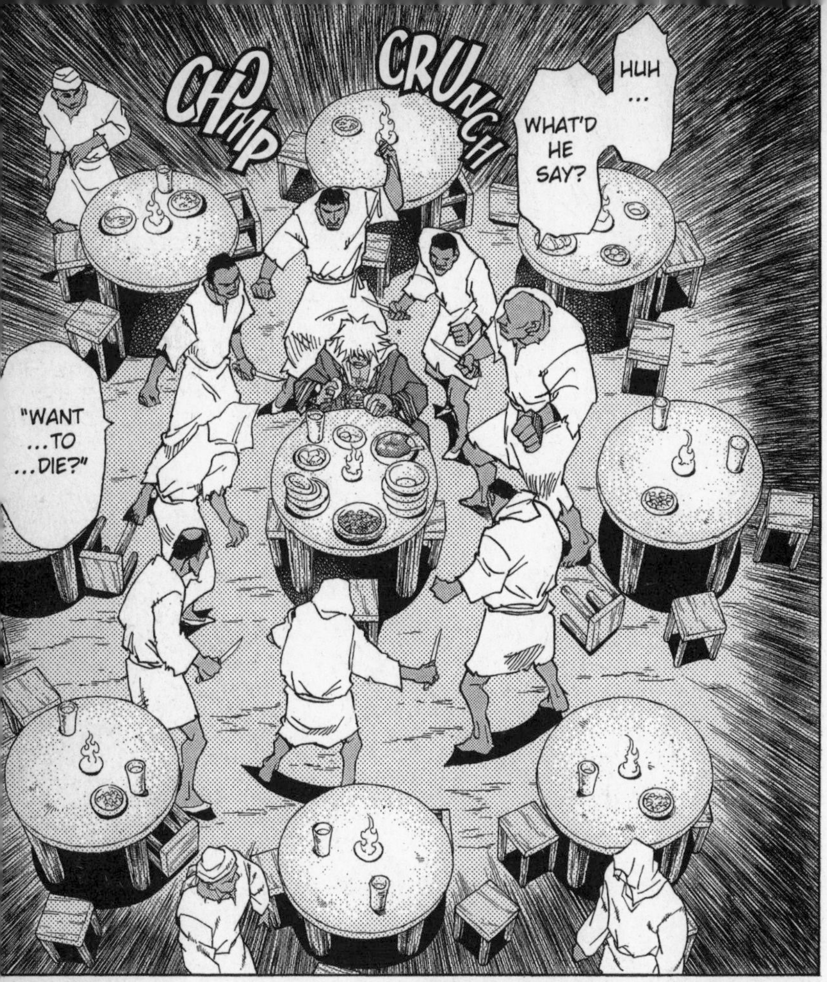
HUH ... WHAT'D HE SAY?
CRUNCH
CHOMP
"WANT ... TO ... DIE?"

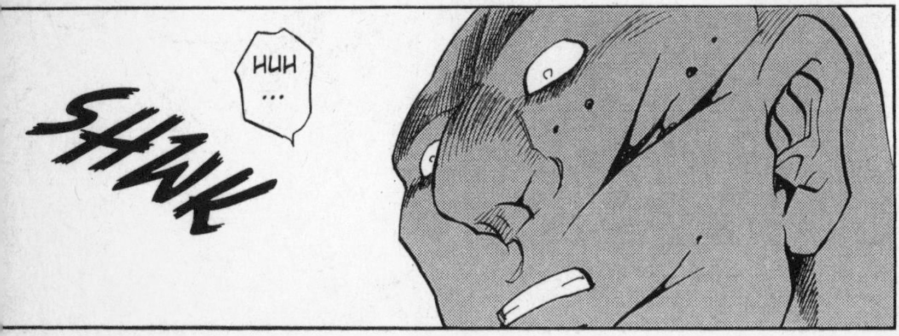
HUH ...
SHNK

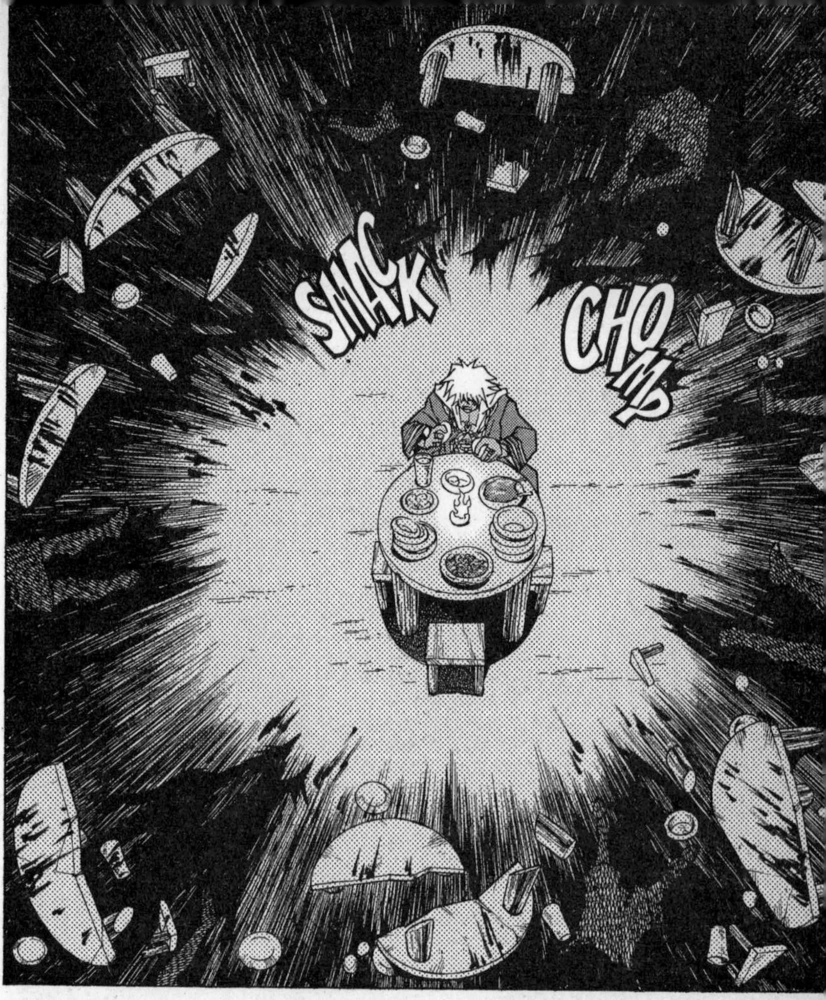
CHOMP
SMACK

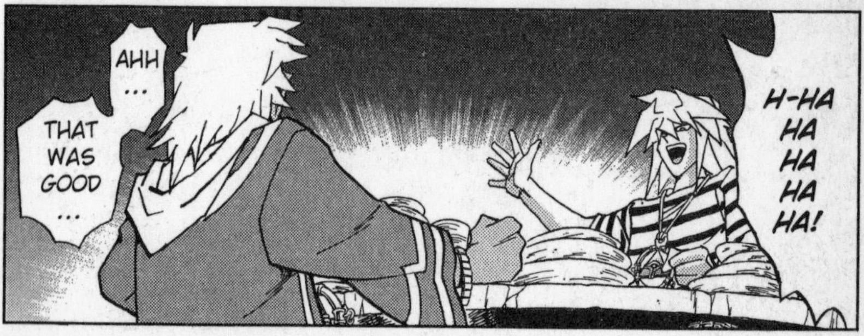
H-HA HA HA HA HA HA!
AHH ...
THAT WAS GOOD ...

READ THIS WAY

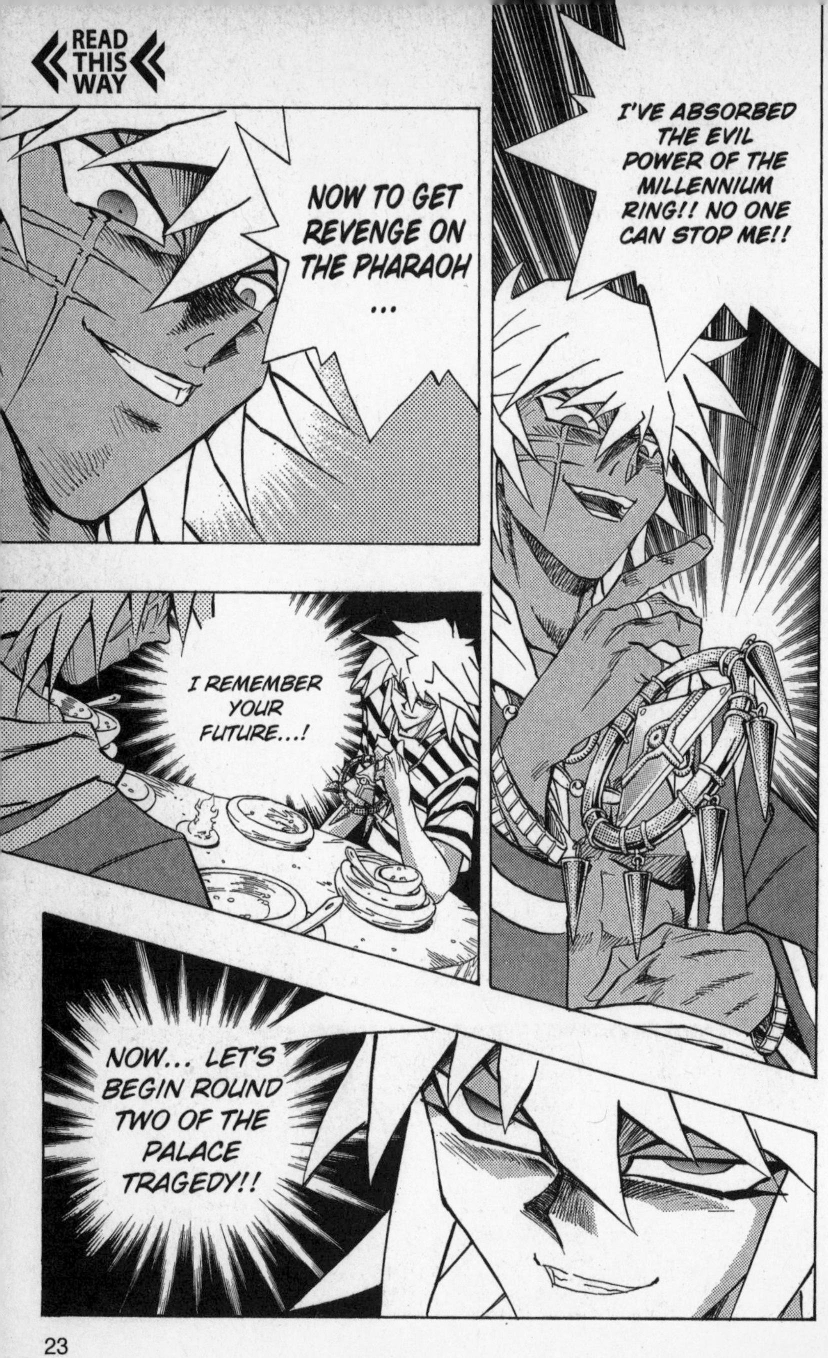
I'VE ABSORBED THE EVIL POWER OF THE MILLENNIUM RING!! NO ONE CAN STOP ME!!
NOW TO GET REVENGE ON THE PHARAOH ...
I REMEMBER YOUR FUTURE...!
NOW... LET'S BEGIN ROUND TWO OF THE PALACE TRAGEDY!!

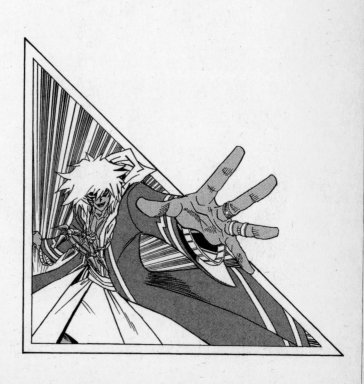

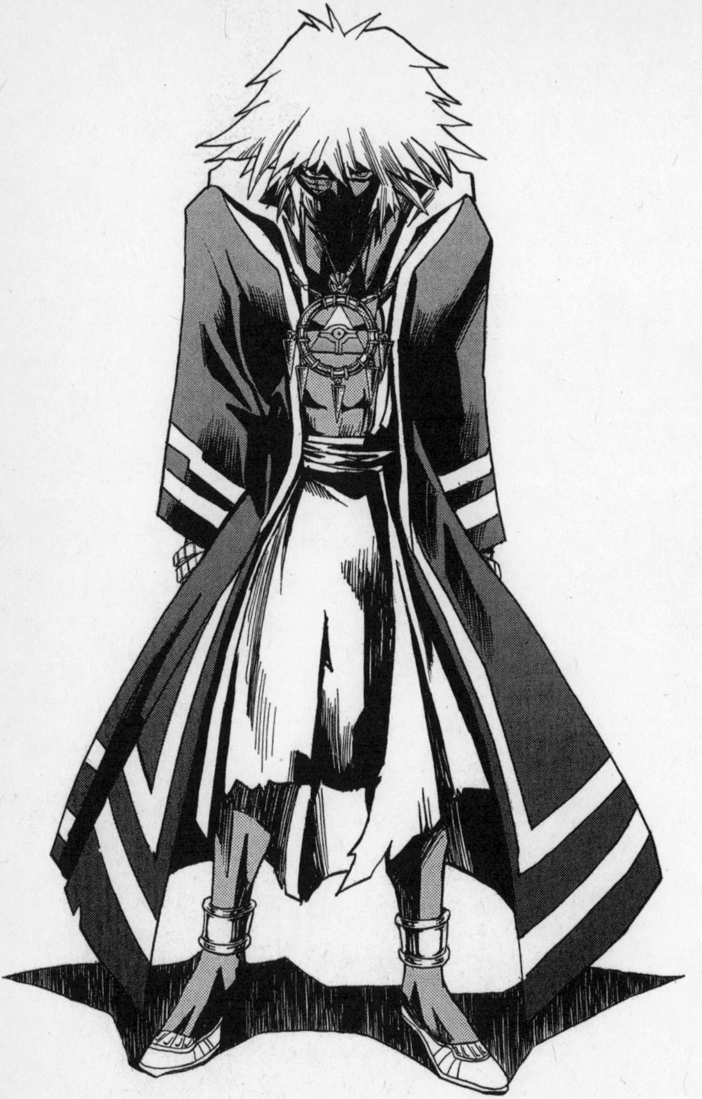

Duel 20: Out of the Darkness

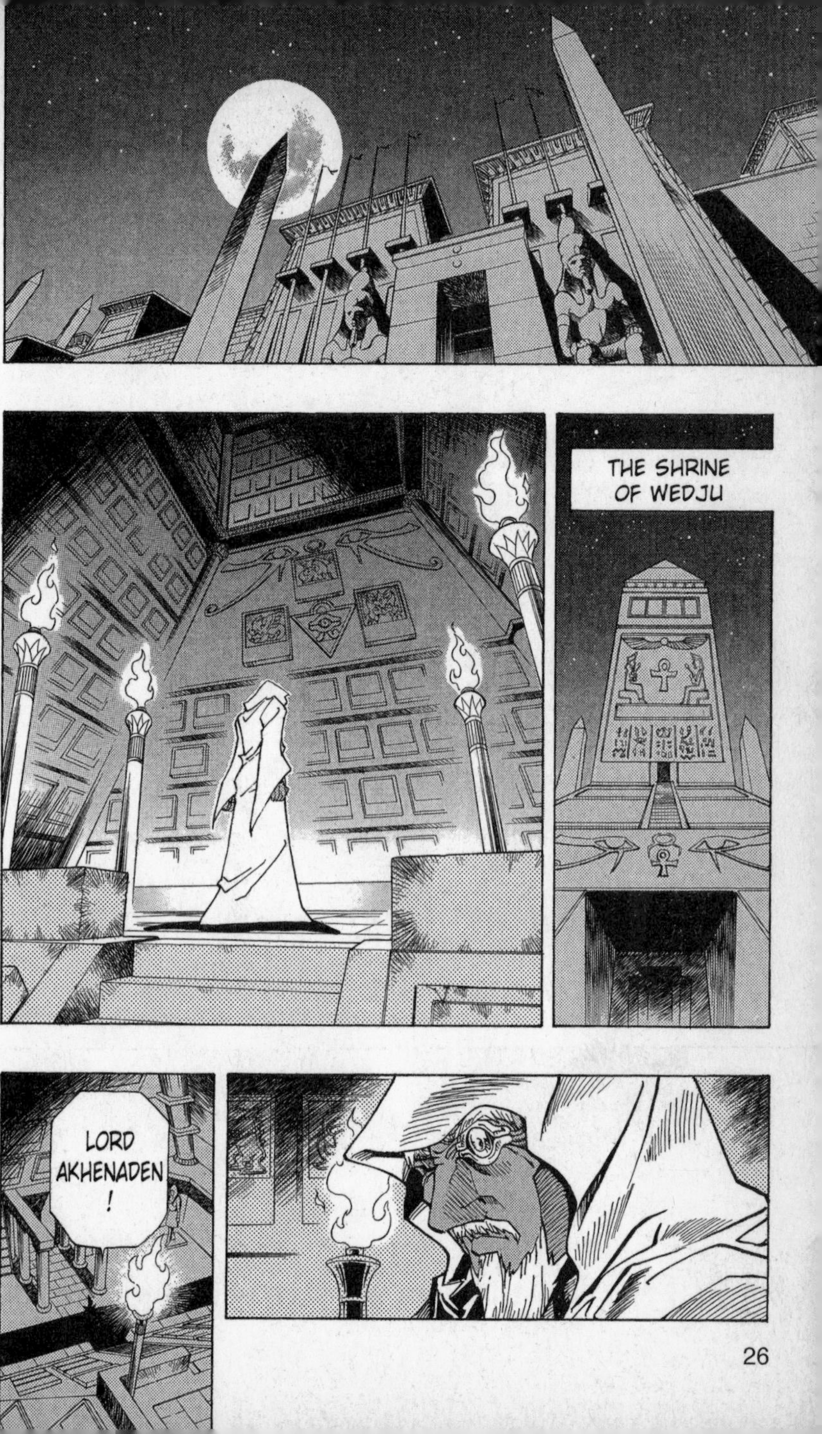
THE SHRINE OF WEDJU
LORD AKHENADEN!

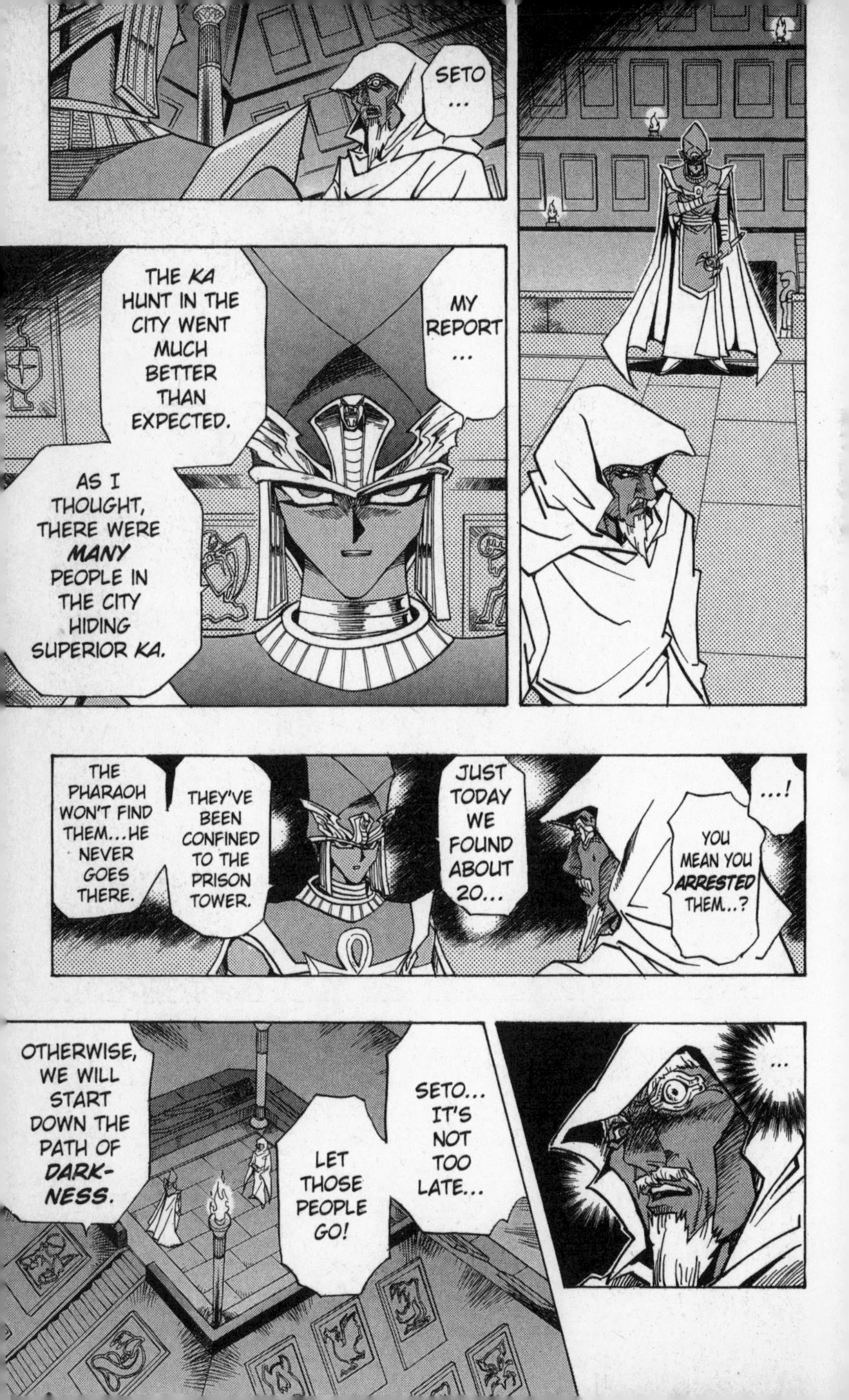
SETO ...
MY REPORT ...
THE KA HUNT IN THE CITY WENT MUCH BETTER THAN EXPECTED.
AS I THOUGHT, THERE WERE MANY PEOPLE IN THE CITY HIDING SUPERIOR KA.
...!
YOU MEAN YOU ARRESTED THEM...?
JUST TODAY WE FOUND ABOUT 20...
THEY'VE BEEN CONFINED TO THE PRISON TOWER.
THE PHARAOH WON'T FIND THEM...HE NEVER GOES THERE.
...
SETO... IT'S NOT TOO LATE...
LET THOSE PEOPLE GO!
OTHERWISE, WE WILL START DOWN THE PATH OF DARK-NESS.

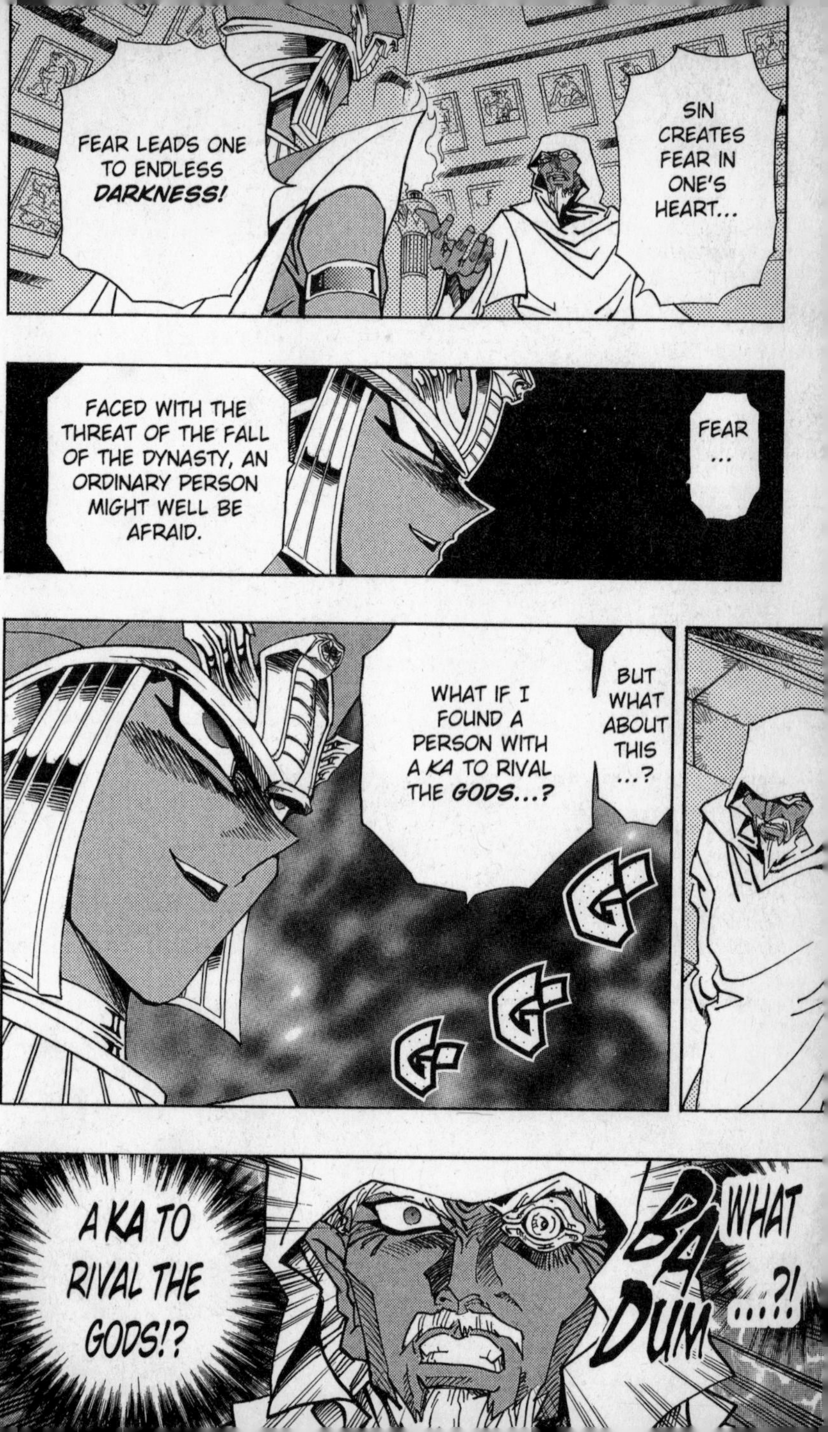
SIN CREATES FEAR IN ONE'S HEART...
FEAR LEADS ONE TO ENDLESS **DARKNESS!**
FEAR...
FACED WITH THE THREAT OF THE FALL OF THE DYNASTY, AN ORDINARY PERSON MIGHT WELL BE AFRAID.
BUT WHAT ABOUT THIS...?
WHAT IF I FOUND A PERSON WITH A *KA* TO RIVAL THE **GODS...?**
G G G
WHAT ...?!
BA DUM
A *KA* TO RIVAL THE GODS!?

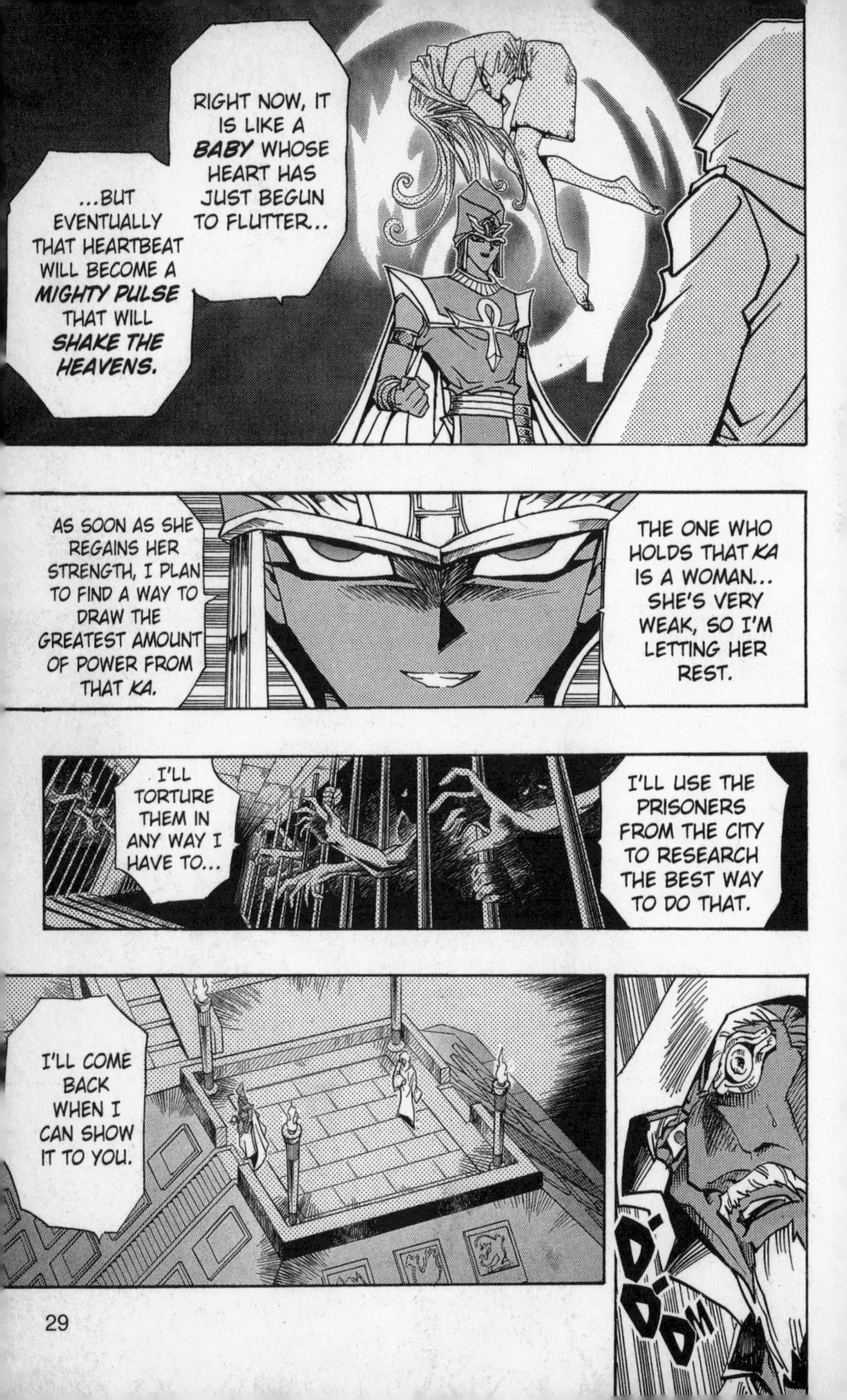
RIGHT NOW, IT IS LIKE A *BABY* WHOSE HEART HAS JUST BEGUN TO FLUTTER...
...BUT EVENTUALLY THAT HEARTBEAT WILL BECOME A *MIGHTY PULSE* THAT WILL *SHAKE THE HEAVENS.*
THE ONE WHO HOLDS THAT *KA* IS A WOMAN... SHE'S VERY WEAK, SO I'M LETTING HER REST.
AS SOON AS SHE REGAINS HER STRENGTH, I PLAN TO FIND A WAY TO DRAW THE GREATEST AMOUNT OF POWER FROM THAT *KA*.
I'LL USE THE PRISONERS FROM THE CITY TO RESEARCH THE BEST WAY TO DO THAT.
I'LL TORTURE THEM IN ANY WAY I HAVE TO...
D-D-DM
I'LL COME BACK WHEN I CAN SHOW IT TO YOU.

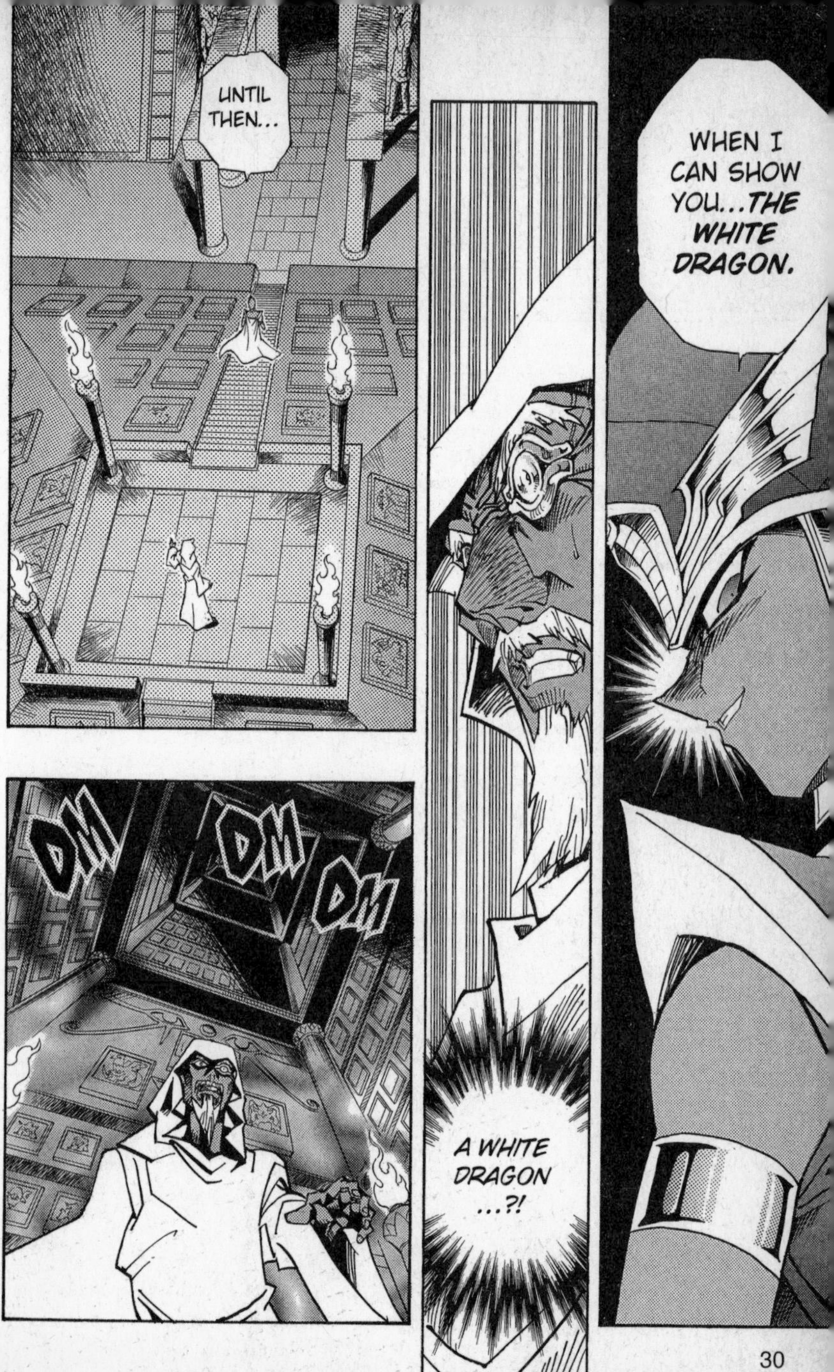
WHEN I CAN SHOW YOU...*THE WHITE DRAGON.*
A WHITE DRAGON ...?!
UNTIL THEN...
DM
DM
DM

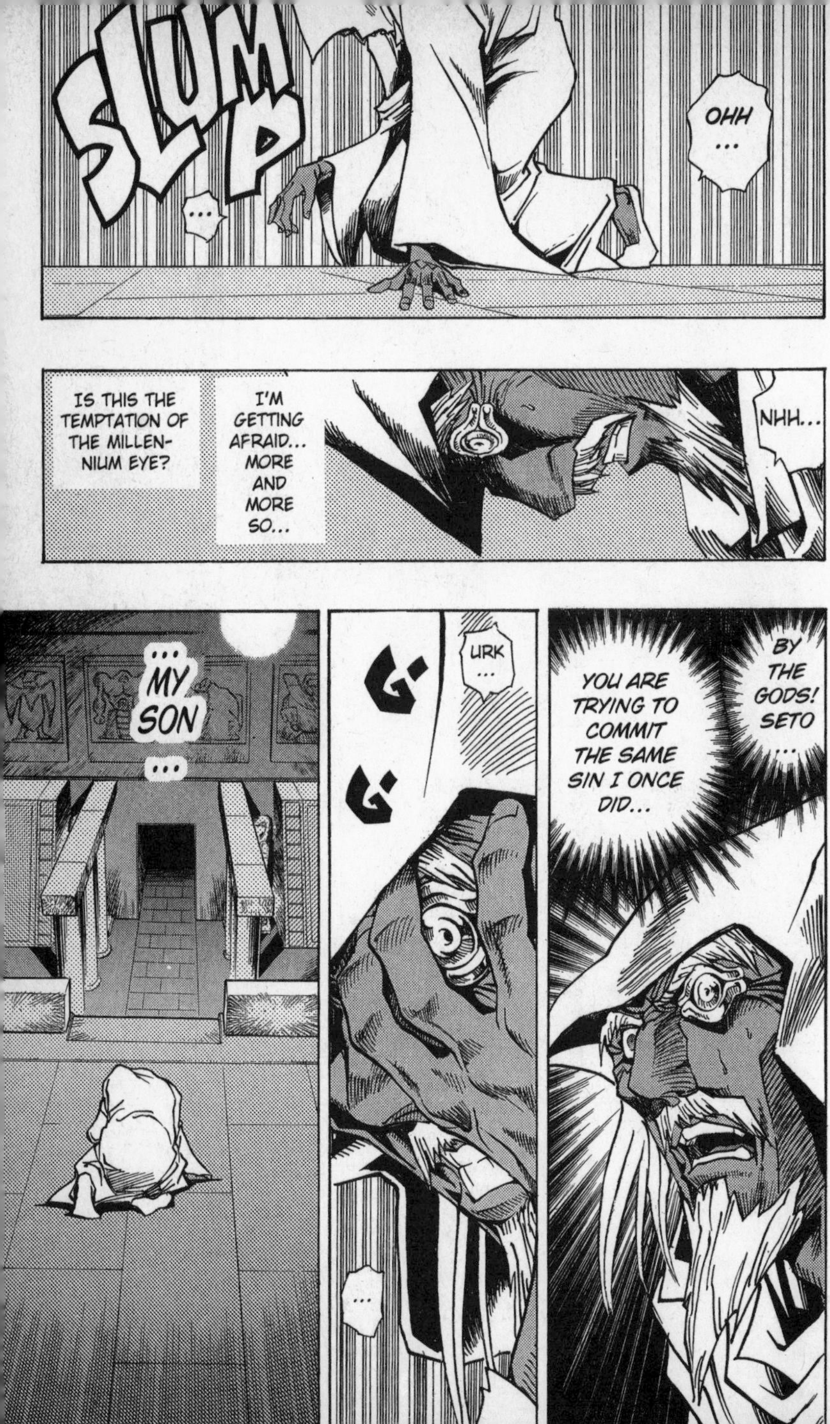
OHH ...
SLUMP
...
NHH...
I'M GETTING AFRAID... MORE AND MORE SO...
IS THIS THE TEMPTATION OF THE MILLEN-NIUM EYE?
BY THE GODS! SETO ...
YOU ARE TRYING TO COMMIT THE SAME SIN I ONCE DID...
URK ...
G
G
...
... MY SON ...

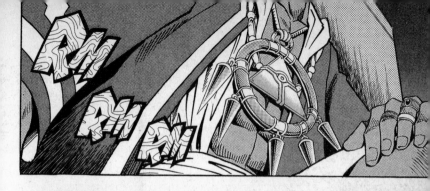

THIS TIME I ATTACK AT *NIGHT*...

LIKE A THIEF *SHOULD* ...

READ THIS WAY

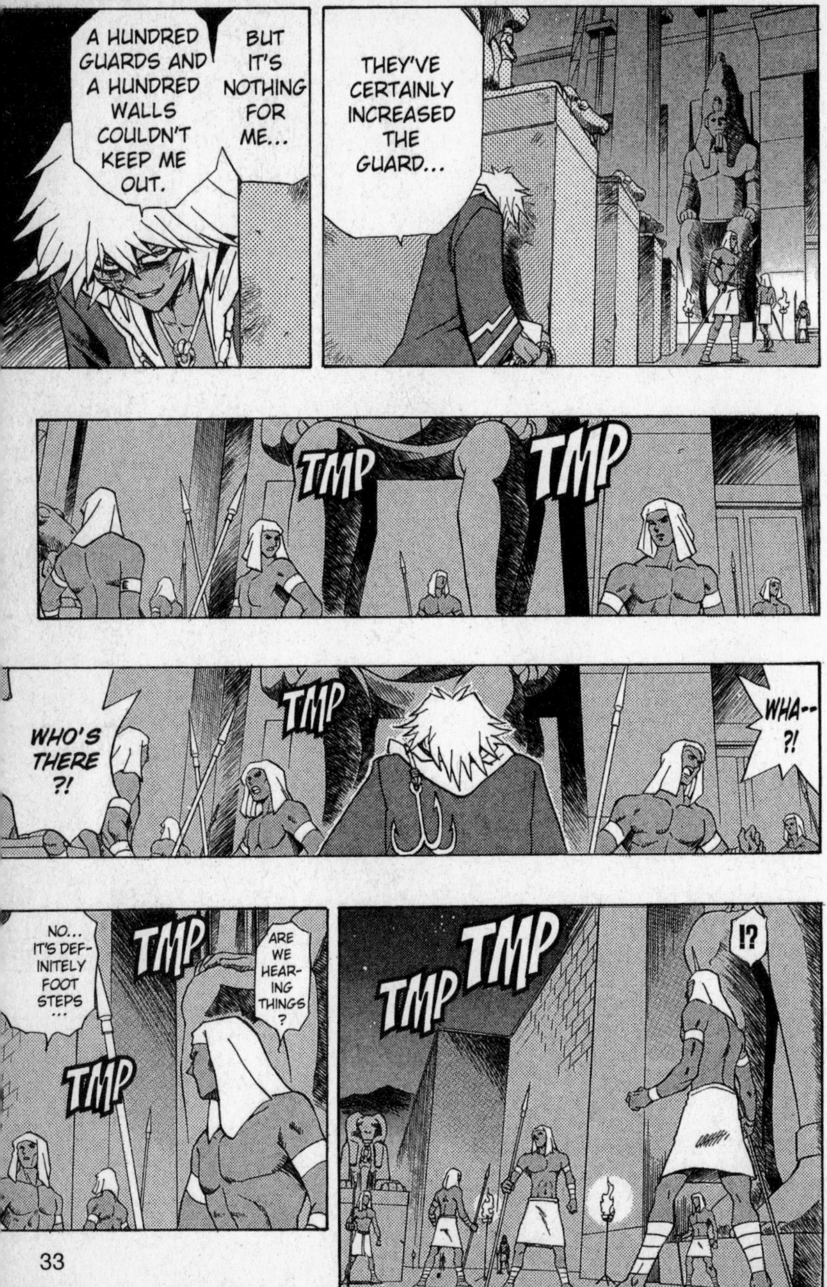
THEY'VE CERTAINLY INCREASED THE GUARD...
BUT IT'S NOTHING FOR ME...
A HUNDRED GUARDS AND A HUNDRED WALLS COULDN'T KEEP ME OUT.
TMP
TMP
WHA-- ?!
TMP
WHO'S THERE ?!
!?
TMP
TMP
ARE WE HEAR-ING THINGS ?
TMP
NO... IT'S DEF-INITELY FOOT STEPS ...
TMP

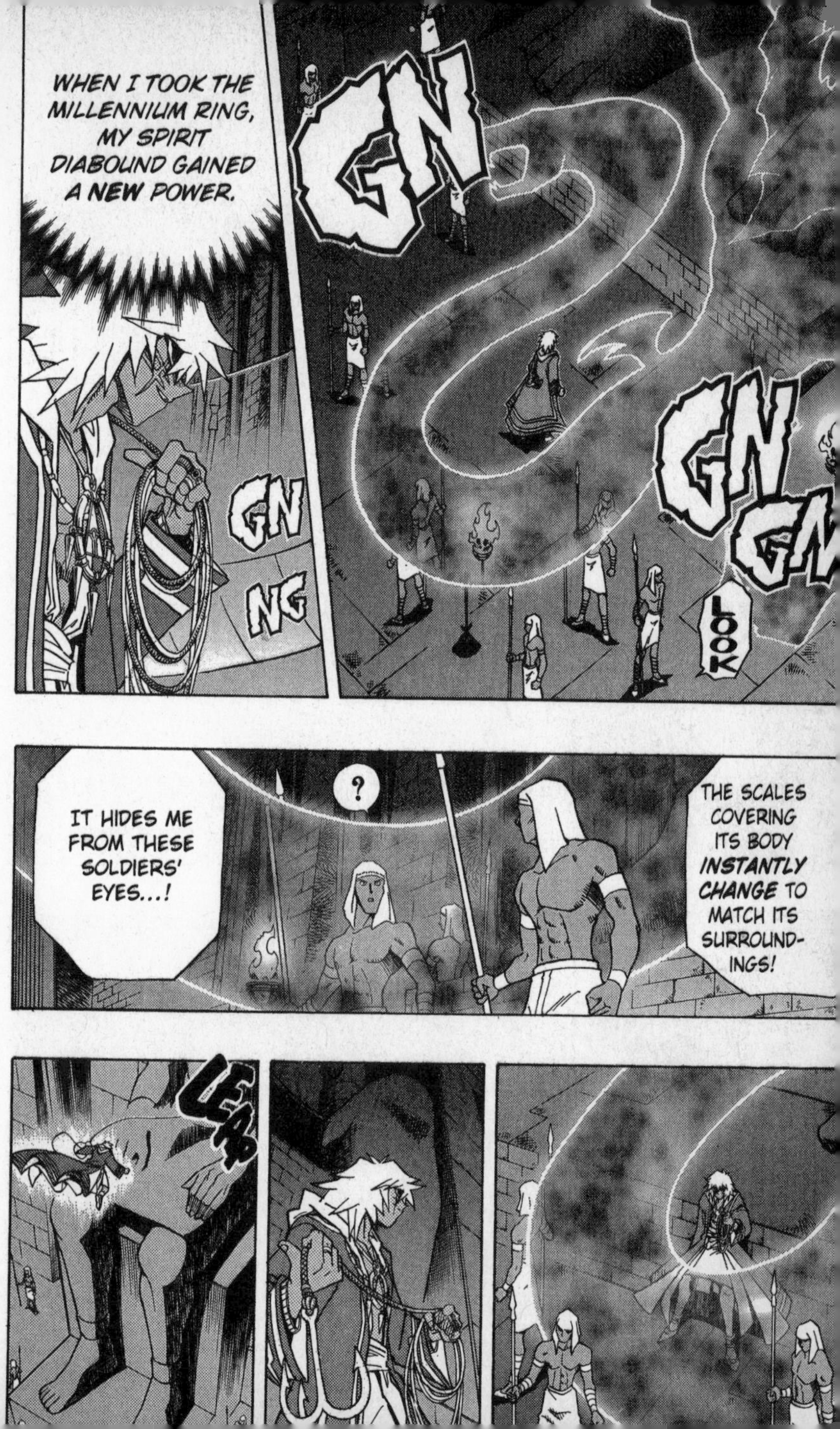
GN
GN
GN
LOOK
WHEN I TOOK THE MILLENNIUM RING, MY SPIRIT DIABOUND GAINED A NEW POWER.
GN
NG
THE SCALES COVERING ITS BODY INSTANTLY CHANGE TO MATCH ITS SURROUND-INGS!
?
IT HIDES ME FROM THESE SOLDIERS' EYES...!
LEAP

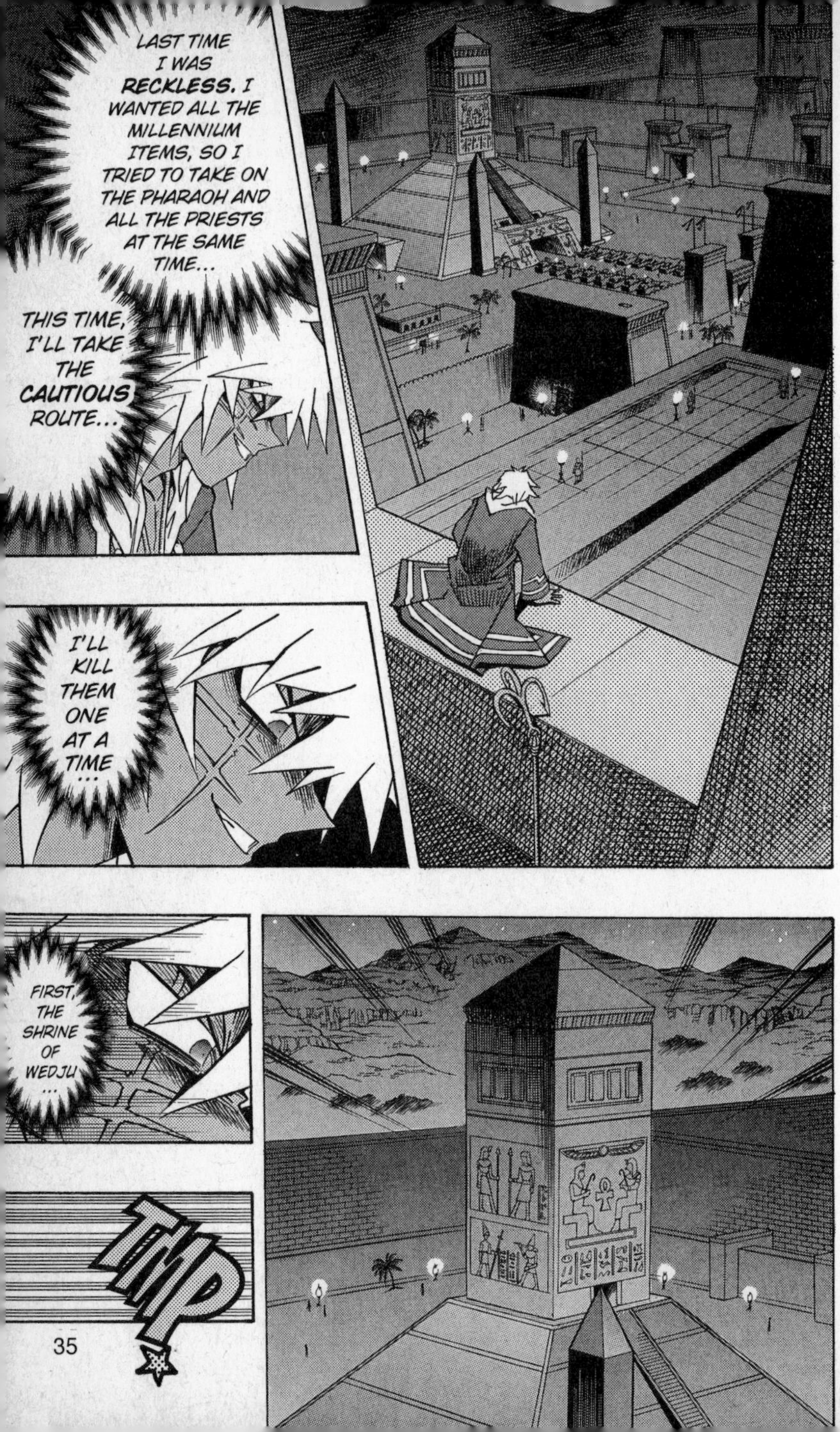
LAST TIME I WAS **RECKLESS.** I WANTED ALL THE MILLENNIUM ITEMS, SO I TRIED TO TAKE ON THE PHARAOH AND ALL THE PRIESTS AT THE SAME TIME...
THIS TIME, I'LL TAKE THE **CAUTIOUS** ROUTE...
I'LL KILL THEM ONE AT A TIME...
FIRST, THE SHRINE OF WEDJU...
THP

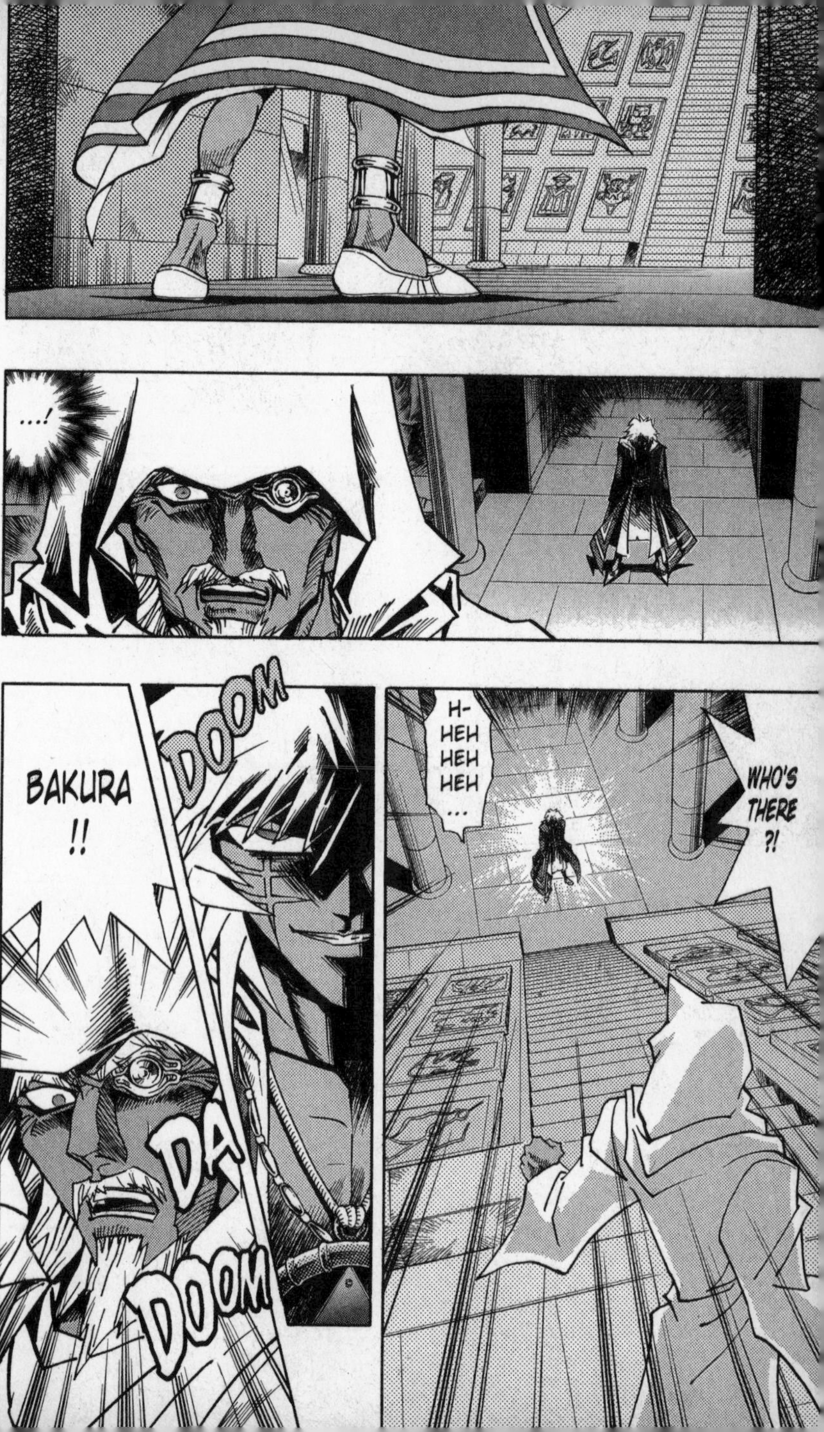
...!
H-HEH HEH HEH...
WHO'S THERE?!
DOOM
BAKURA!!
DA
DOOM

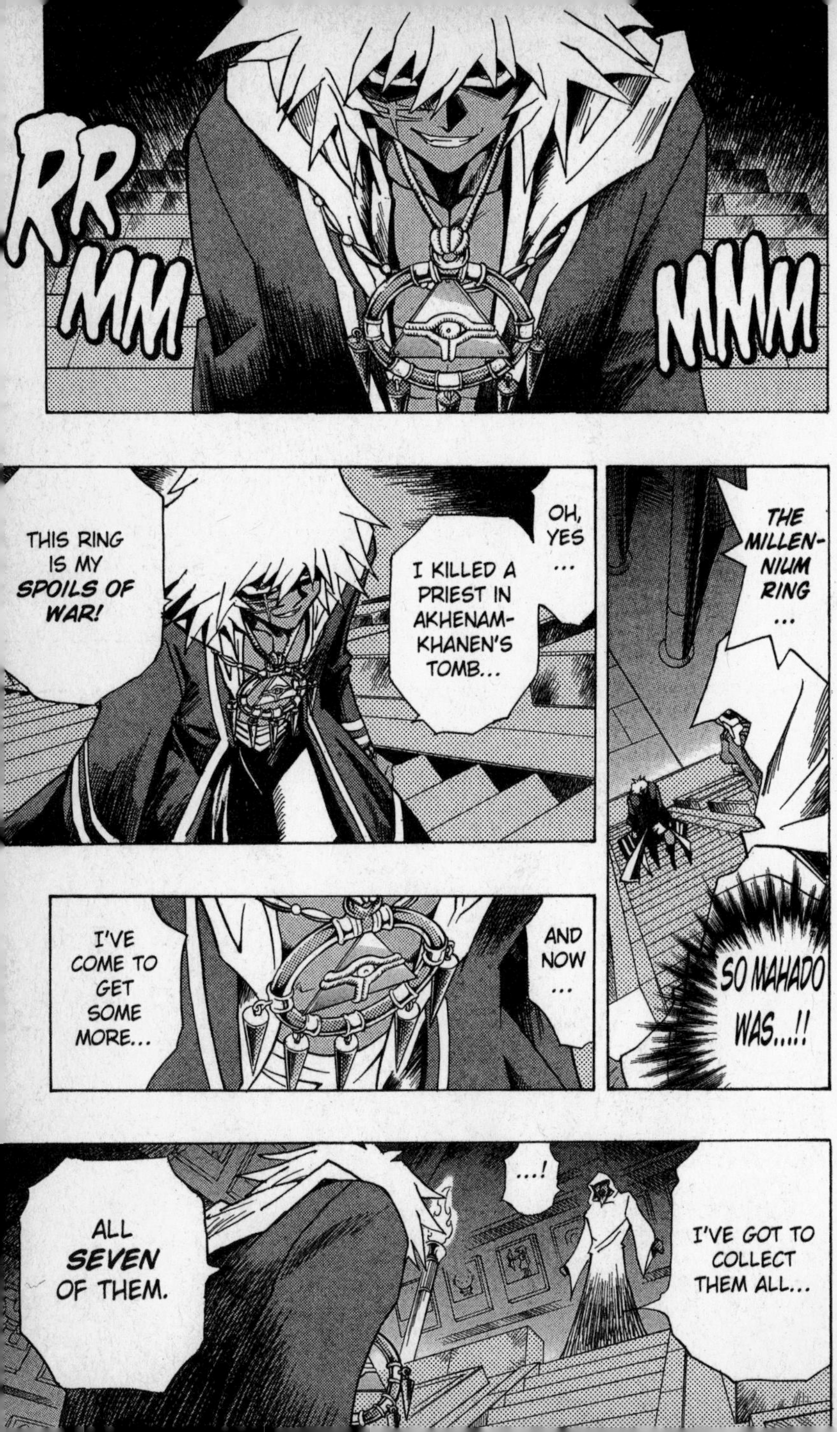
RR MM
MMM
THE MILLEN-NIUM RING ...
SO MAHADO WAS...!!
OH, YES ...
I KILLED A PRIEST IN AKHENAM-KHANEN'S TOMB...
THIS RING IS MY SPOILS OF WAR!
AND NOW ...
I'VE COME TO GET SOME MORE...
...!
I'VE GOT TO COLLECT THEM ALL...
ALL SEVEN OF THEM.

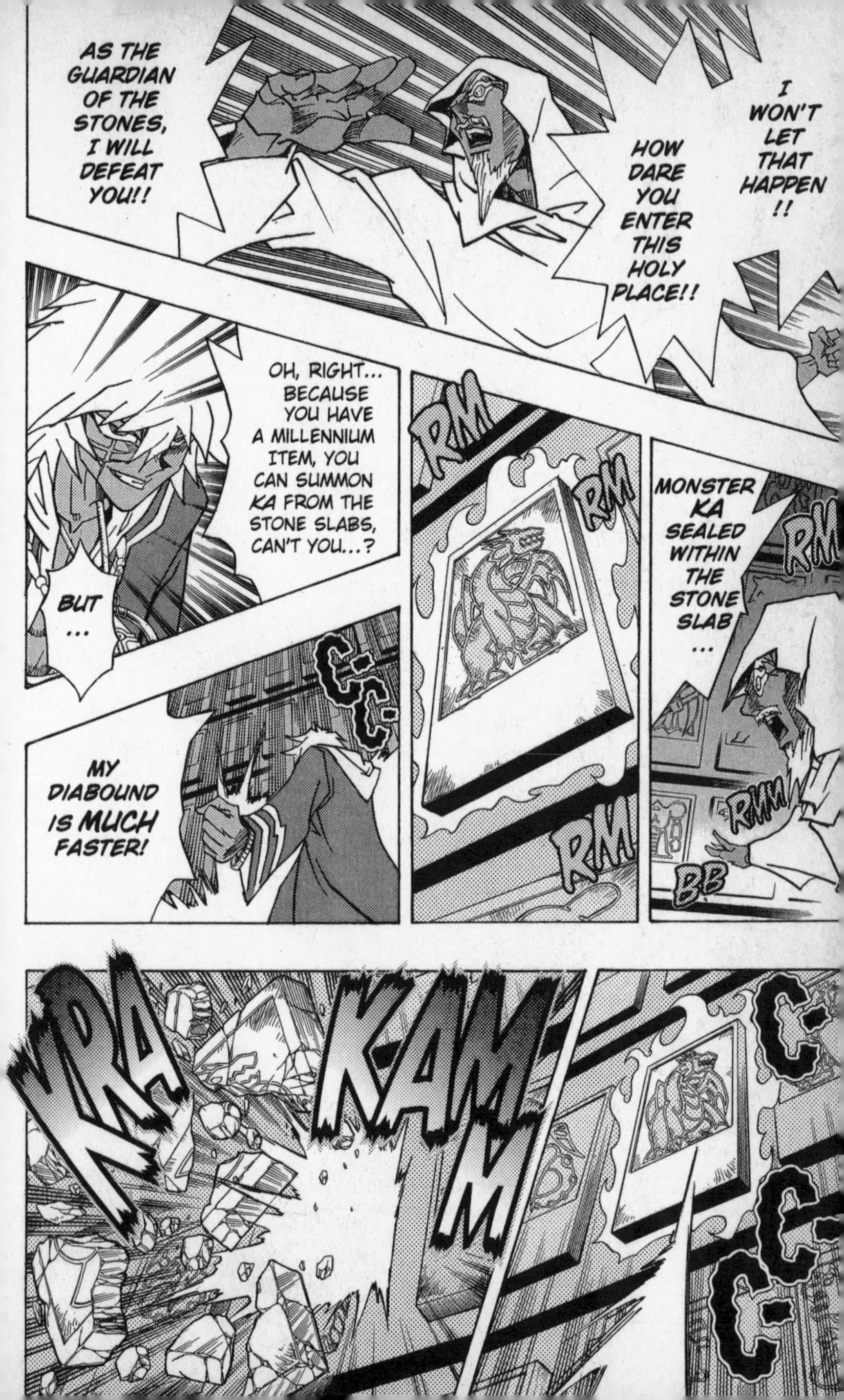
I WON'T LET THAT HAPPEN!!
HOW DARE YOU ENTER THIS HOLY PLACE!!
AS THE GUARDIAN OF THE STONES, I WILL DEFEAT YOU!!
MONSTER KA SEALED WITHIN THE STONE SLAB...
RM
RMM
BB
RM
RM
RM
OH, RIGHT... BECAUSE YOU HAVE A MILLENNIUM ITEM, YOU CAN SUMMON KA FROM THE STONE SLABS, CAN'T YOU...?
BUT...
C-C-
MY DIABOUND IS MUCH FASTER!
C-C-
C-C-
KAM
M
KRA

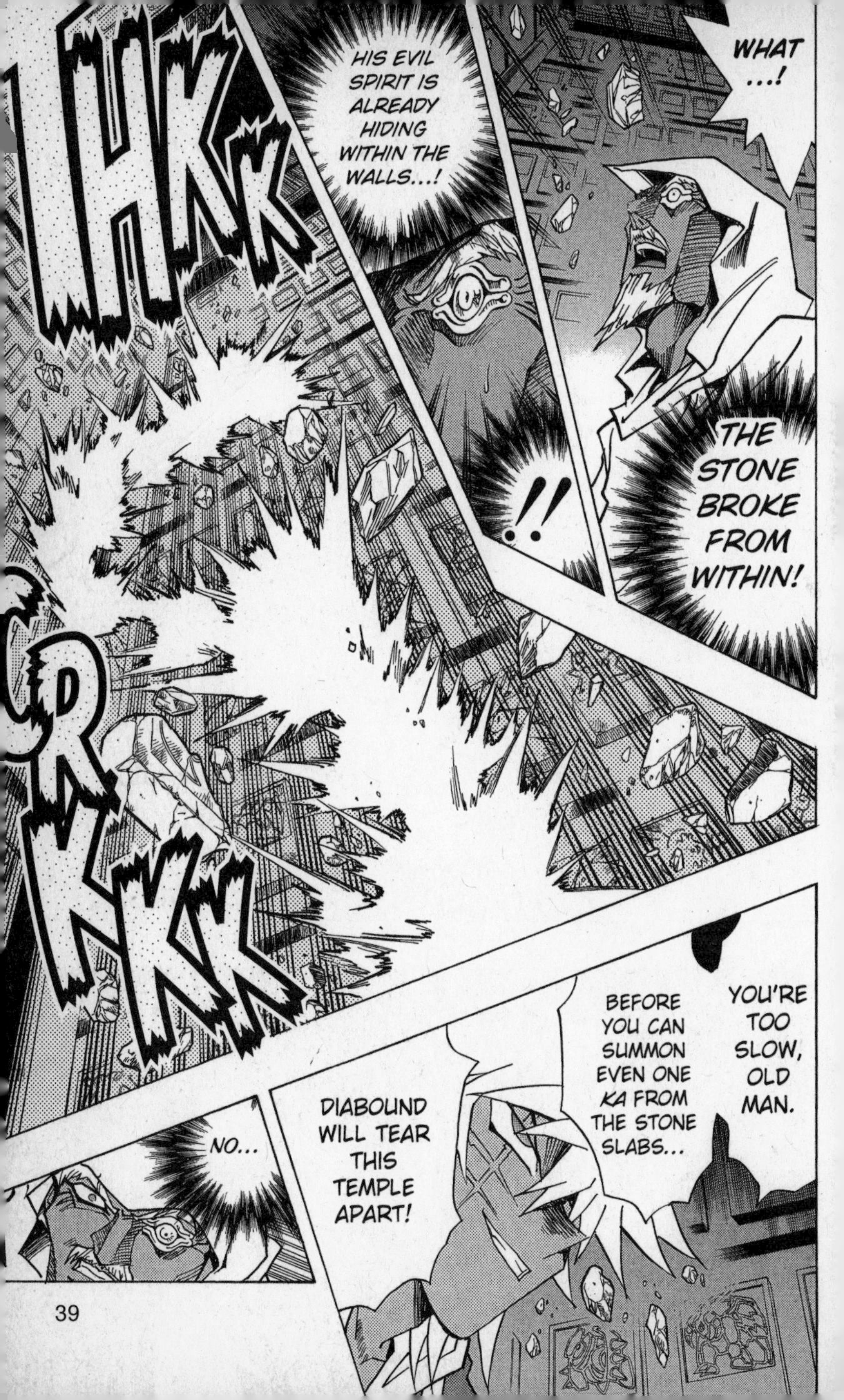
WHAT ...!
THE STONE BROKE FROM WITHIN!
HIS EVIL SPIRIT IS ALREADY HIDING WITHIN THE WALLS...!
!!
YOU'RE TOO SLOW, OLD MAN.
BEFORE YOU CAN SUMMON EVEN ONE *KA* FROM THE STONE SLABS...
DIABOUND WILL TEAR THIS TEMPLE APART!
NO...

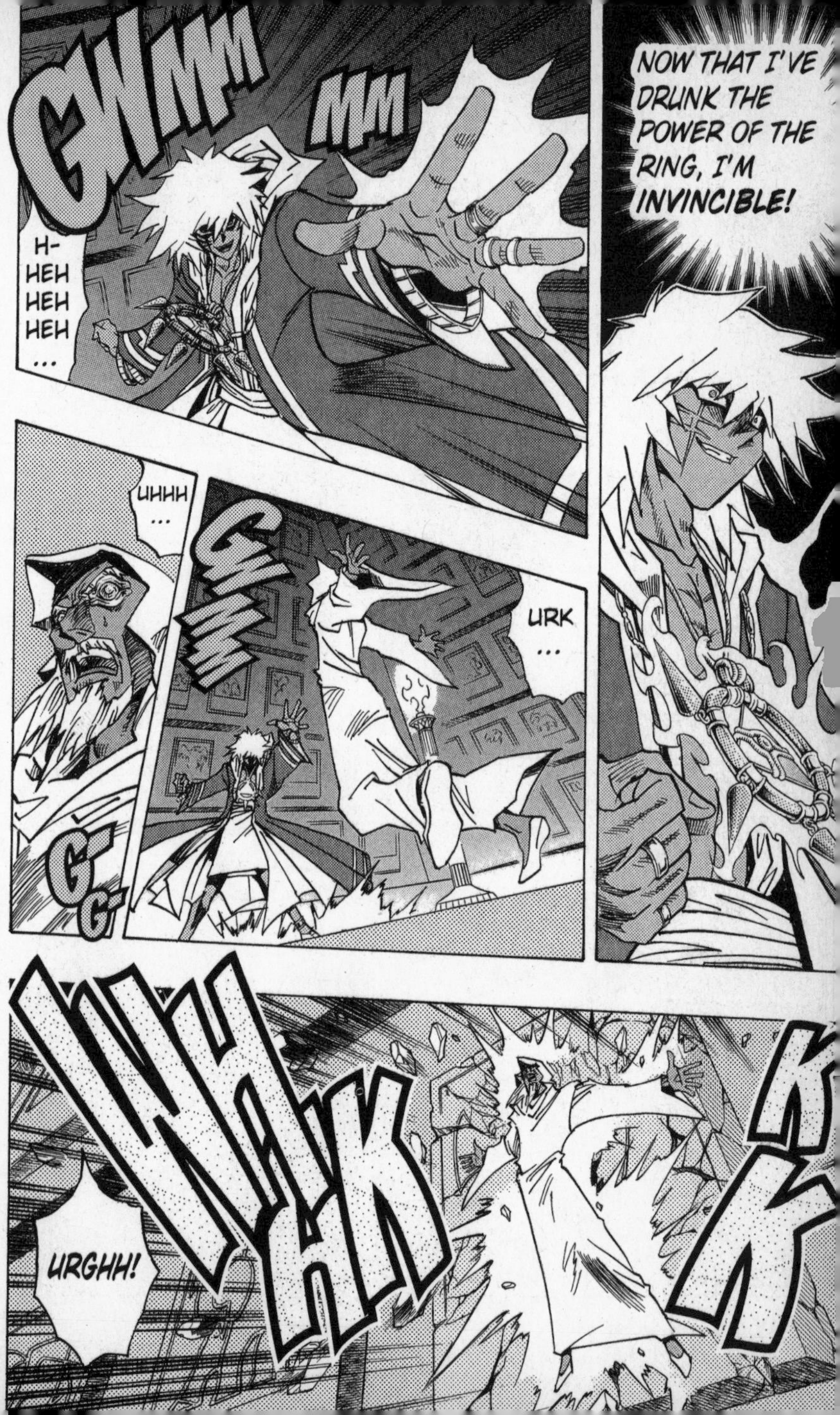
NOW THAT I'VE DRUNK THE POWER OF THE RING, I'M INVINCIBLE!
GWMMM
MM
H-HEH HEH HEH...
URK...
GWMM
UHHH...
GG-
WHAKK
KK
URGHH!

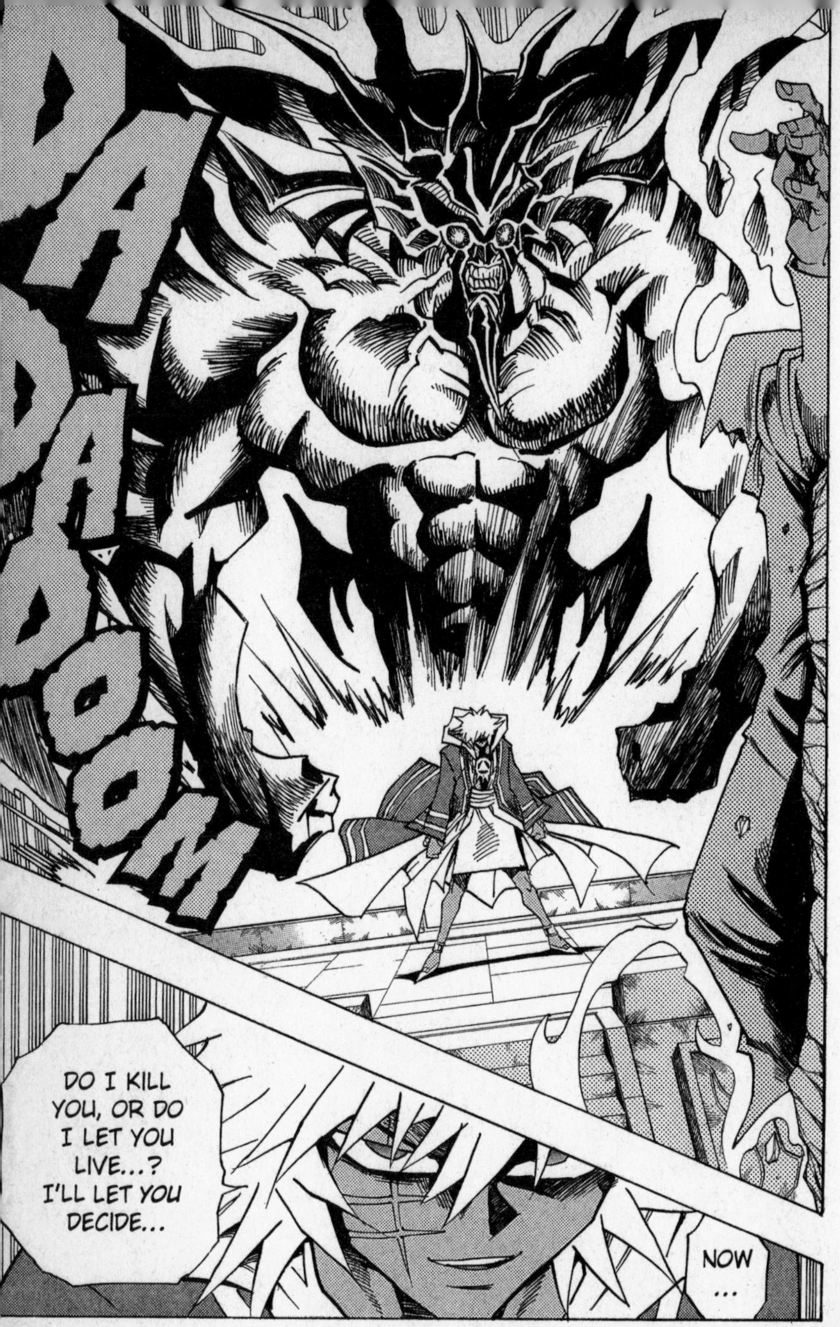
DADOOM
NOW
...
DO I KILL YOU, OR DO I LET YOU LIVE...? I'LL LET YOU DECIDE...

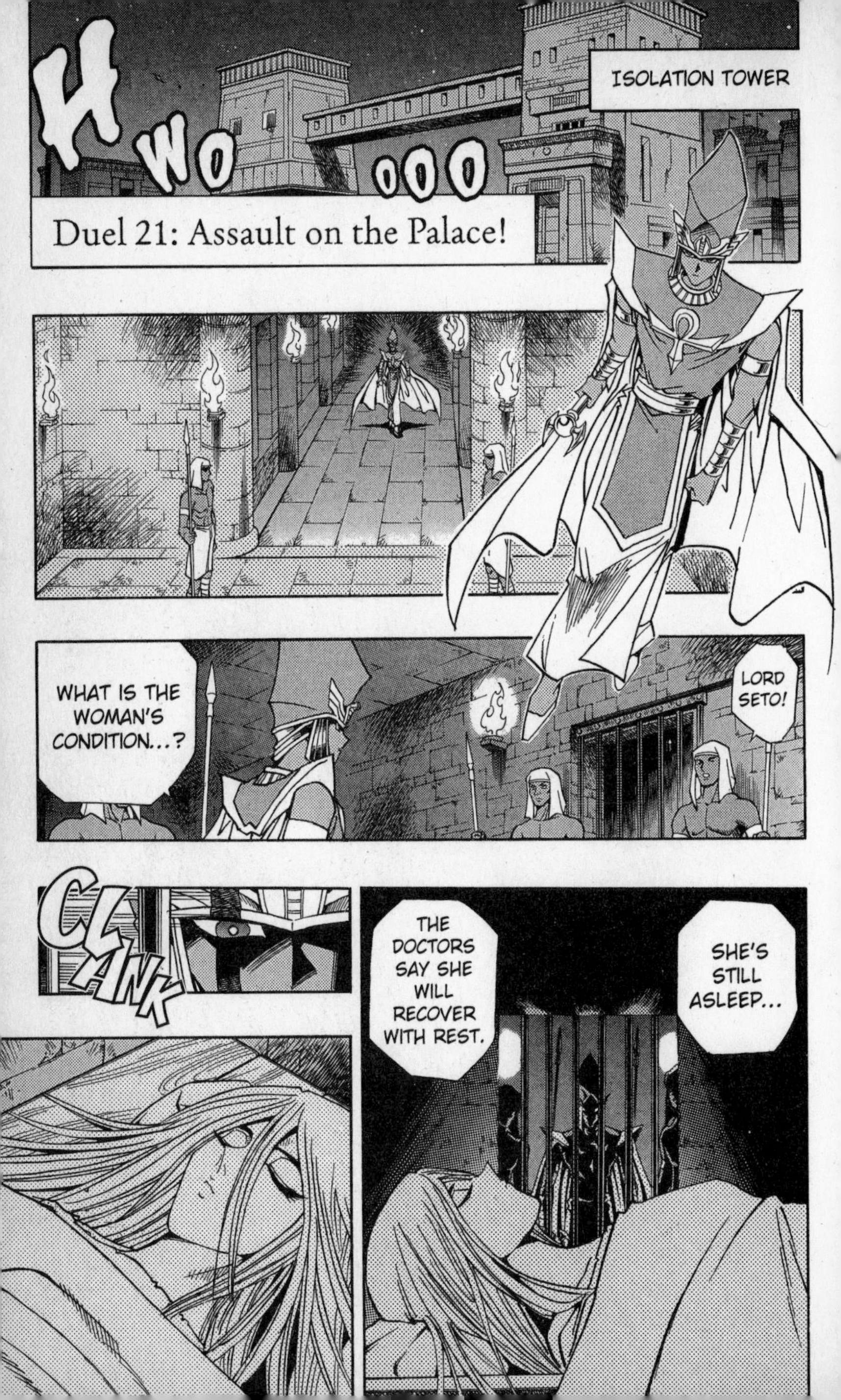
ISOLATION TOWER
HWOOOO
Duel 21: Assault on the Palace!
LORD SETO!
WHAT IS THE WOMAN'S CONDITION...?
SHE'S STILL ASLEEP...
THE DOCTORS SAY SHE WILL RECOVER WITH REST.
CLANK

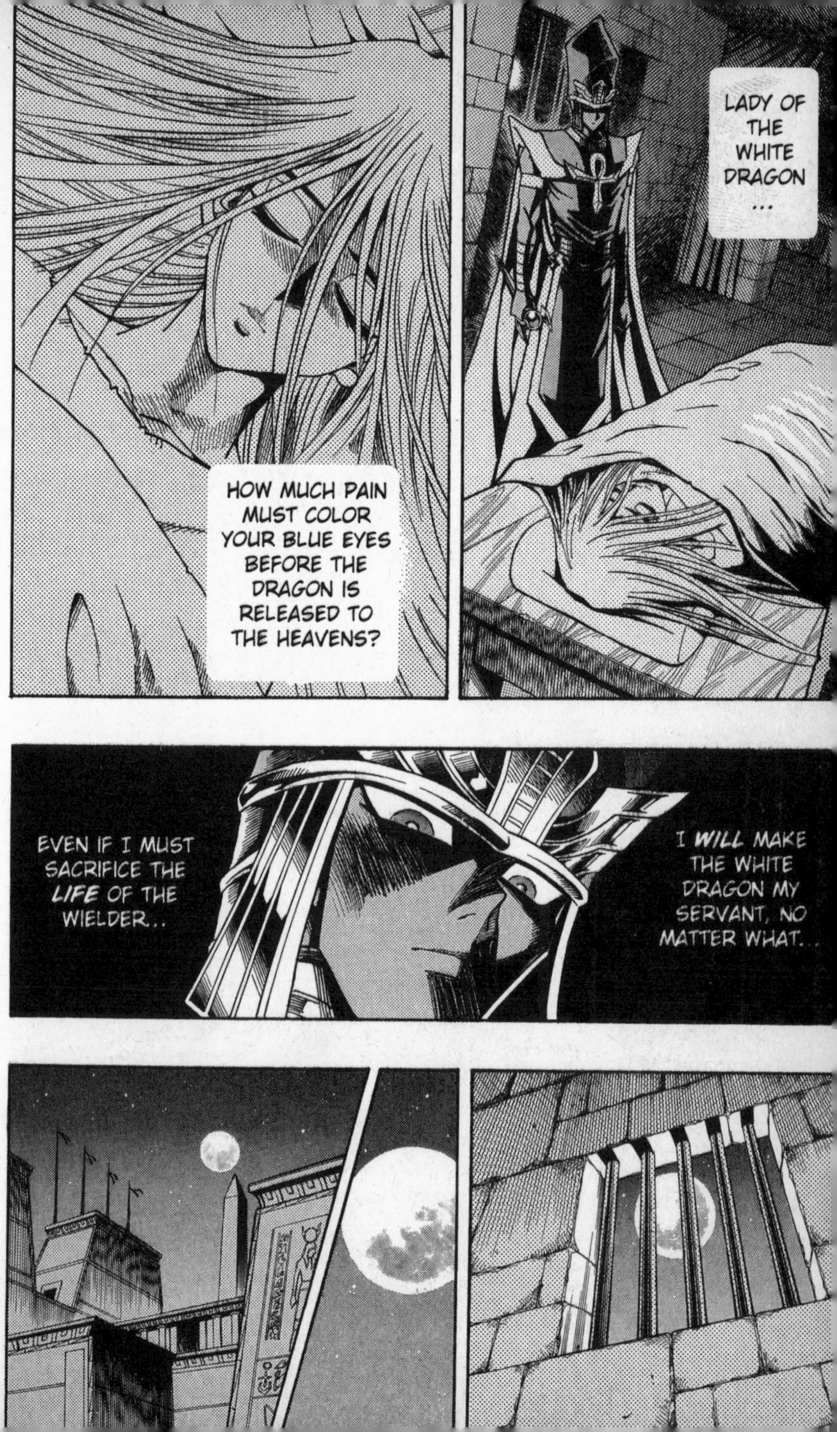
LADY OF THE WHITE DRAGON ...
HOW MUCH PAIN MUST COLOR YOUR BLUE EYES BEFORE THE DRAGON IS RELEASED TO THE HEAVENS?
I WILL MAKE THE WHITE DRAGON MY SERVANT, NO MATTER WHAT...
EVEN IF I MUST SACRIFICE THE LIFE OF THE WIELDER...

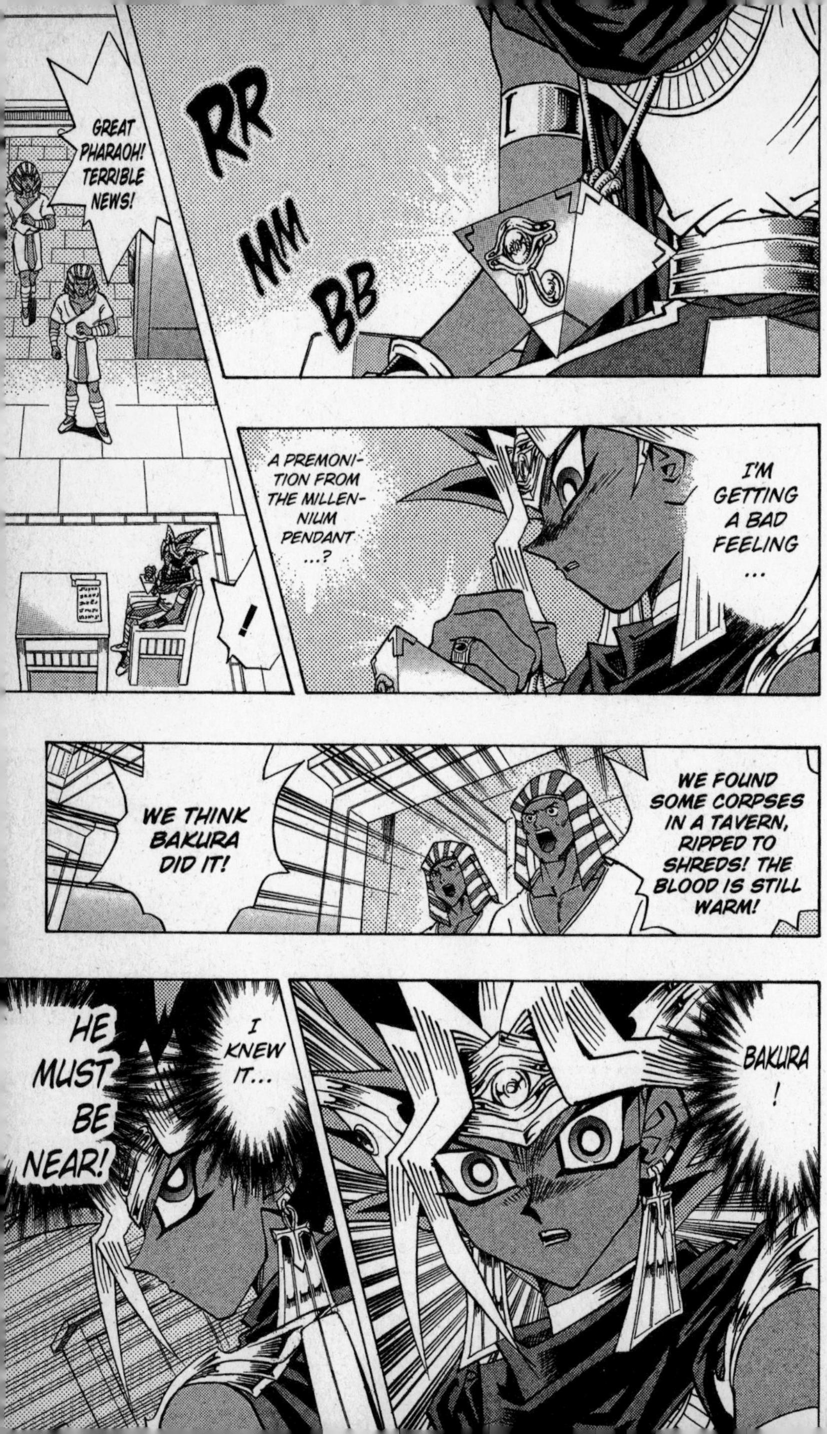
RR
MM
BB
I'M GETTING A BAD FEELING...
A PREMONITION FROM THE MILLENNIUM PENDANT...?
GREAT PHARAOH! TERRIBLE NEWS!
!
WE FOUND SOME CORPSES IN A TAVERN, RIPPED TO SHREDS! THE BLOOD IS STILL WARM!
WE THINK BAKURA DID IT!
BAKURA!
I KNEW IT...
HE MUST BE NEAR!

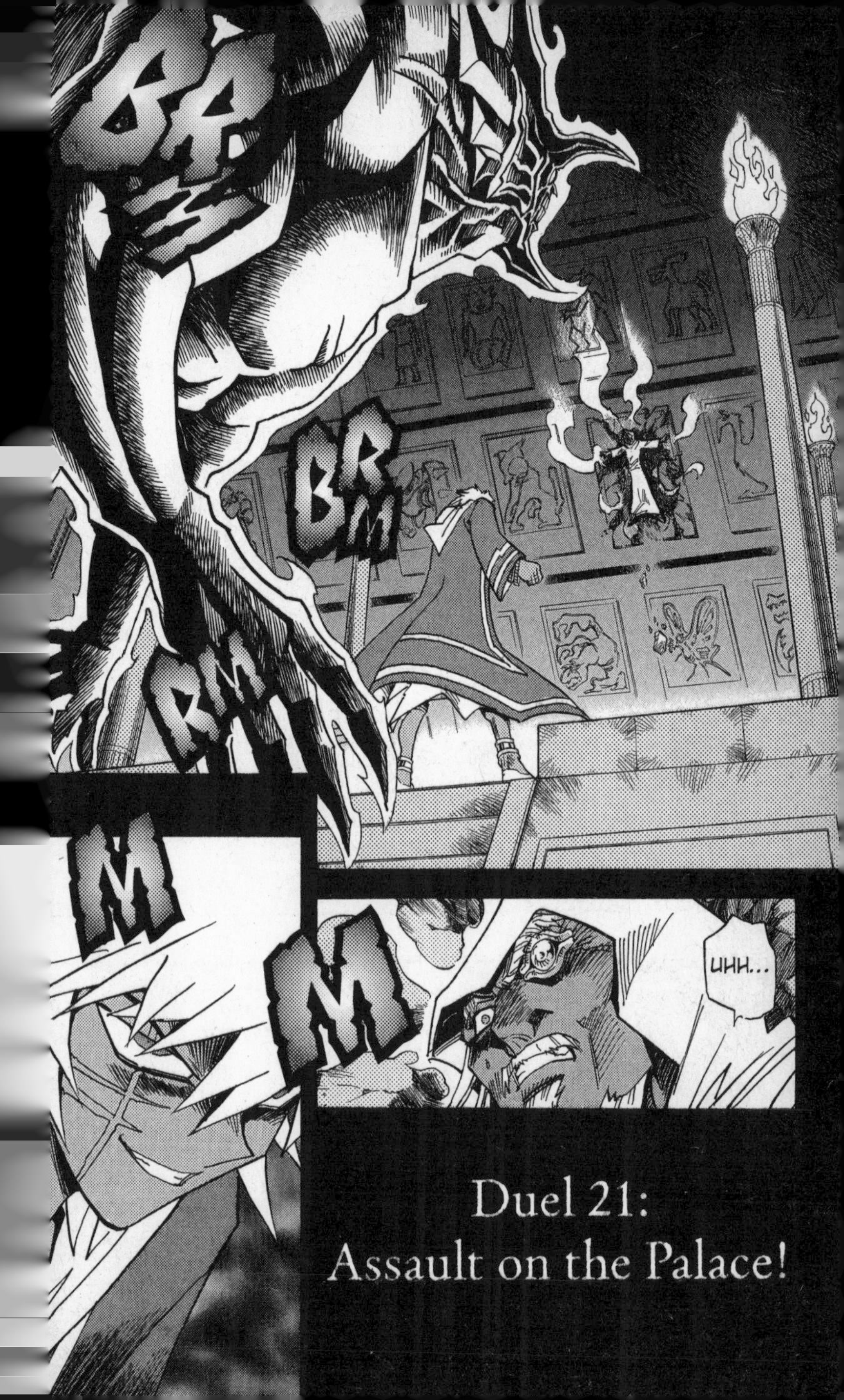
BA
BRM
RM
M
M
UHH...

Duel 21: Assault on the Palace!

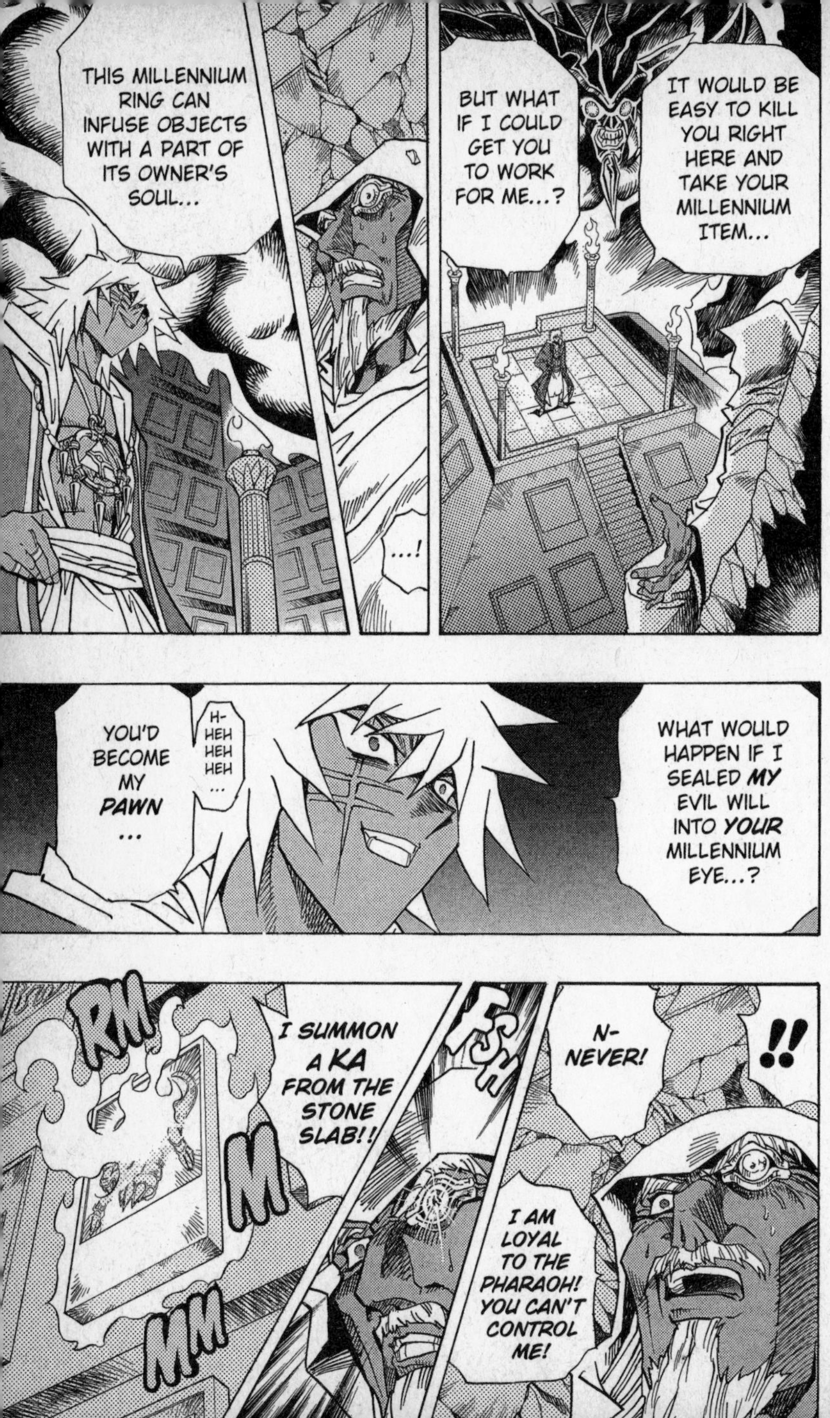
IT WOULD BE EASY TO KILL YOU RIGHT HERE AND TAKE YOUR MILLENNIUM ITEM...
BUT WHAT IF I COULD GET YOU TO WORK FOR ME...?
...!
THIS MILLENNIUM RING CAN INFUSE OBJECTS WITH A PART OF ITS OWNER'S SOUL...
WHAT WOULD HAPPEN IF I SEALED *MY* EVIL WILL INTO *YOUR* MILLENNIUM EYE...?
H-HEH HEH HEH...
YOU'D BECOME MY *PAWN*...
!!
N-NEVER!
I AM LOYAL TO THE PHARAOH! YOU CAN'T CONTROL ME!
FSH
I SUMMON A **KA** FROM THE STONE SLAB!!
RM
M
MM

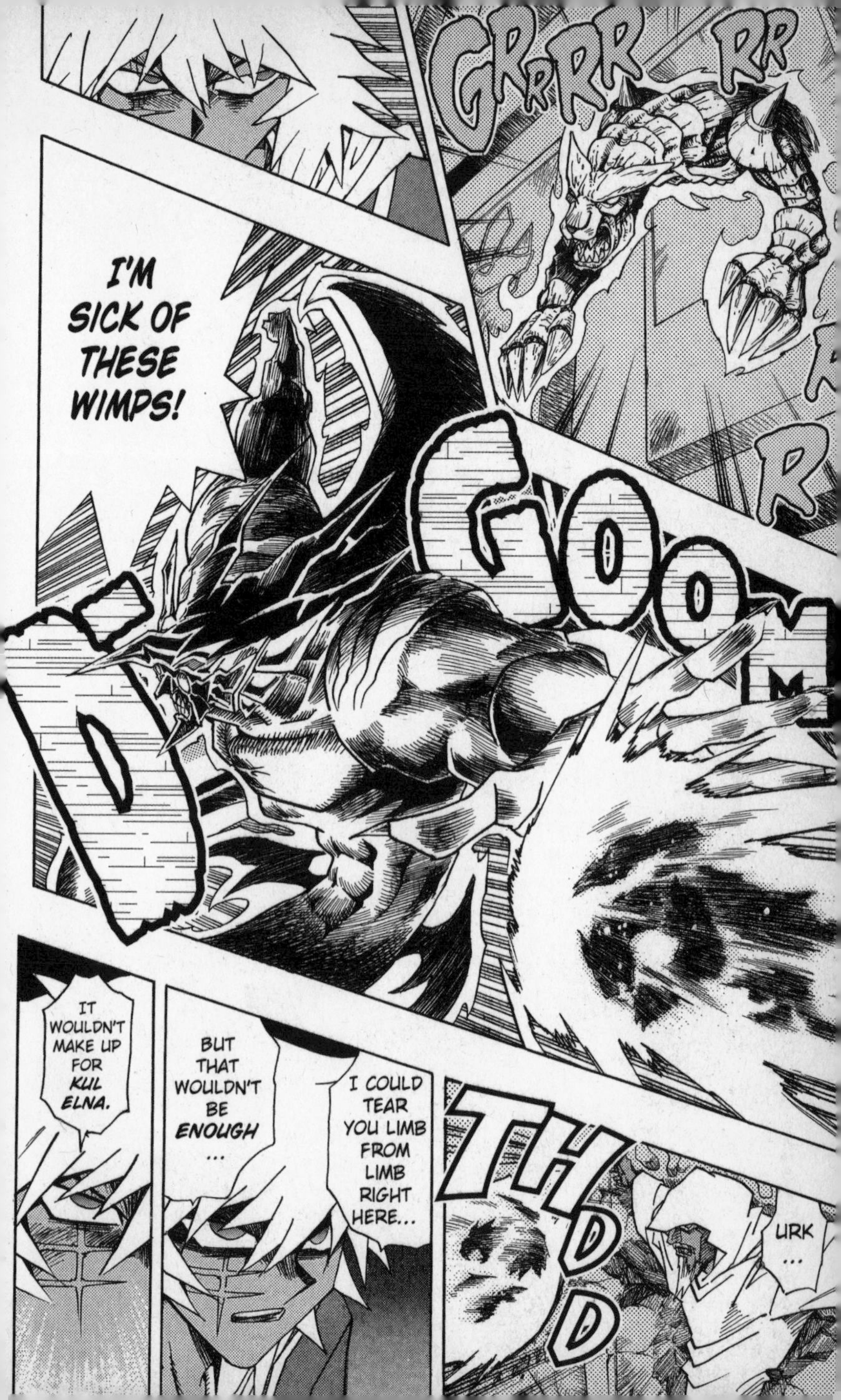
GRRRR RR
RRR
I'M SICK OF THESE WIMPS!
DOOOM
THDDD
URK ...
I COULD TEAR YOU LIMB FROM LIMB RIGHT HERE...
BUT THAT WOULDN'T BE *ENOUGH* ...
IT WOULDN'T MAKE UP FOR *KUL ELNA.*

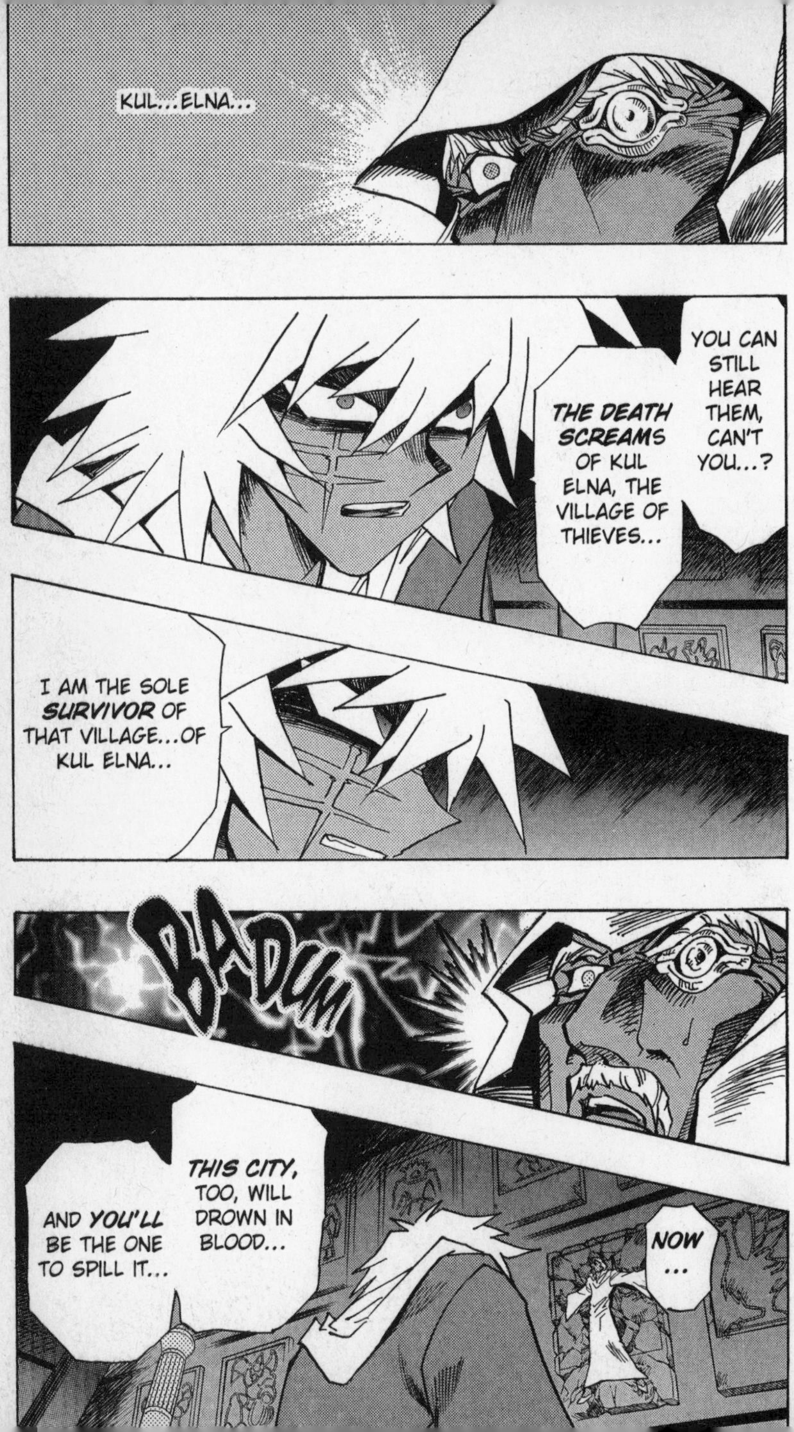
KUL...ELNA...
YOU CAN STILL HEAR THEM, CAN'T YOU...?
THE DEATH SCREAMS OF KUL ELNA, THE VILLAGE OF THIEVES...
I AM THE SOLE *SURVIVOR* OF THAT VILLAGE...OF KUL ELNA...
BA-DUM
NOW...
THIS CITY, TOO, WILL DROWN IN BLOOD...
AND *YOU'LL* BE THE ONE TO SPILL IT...

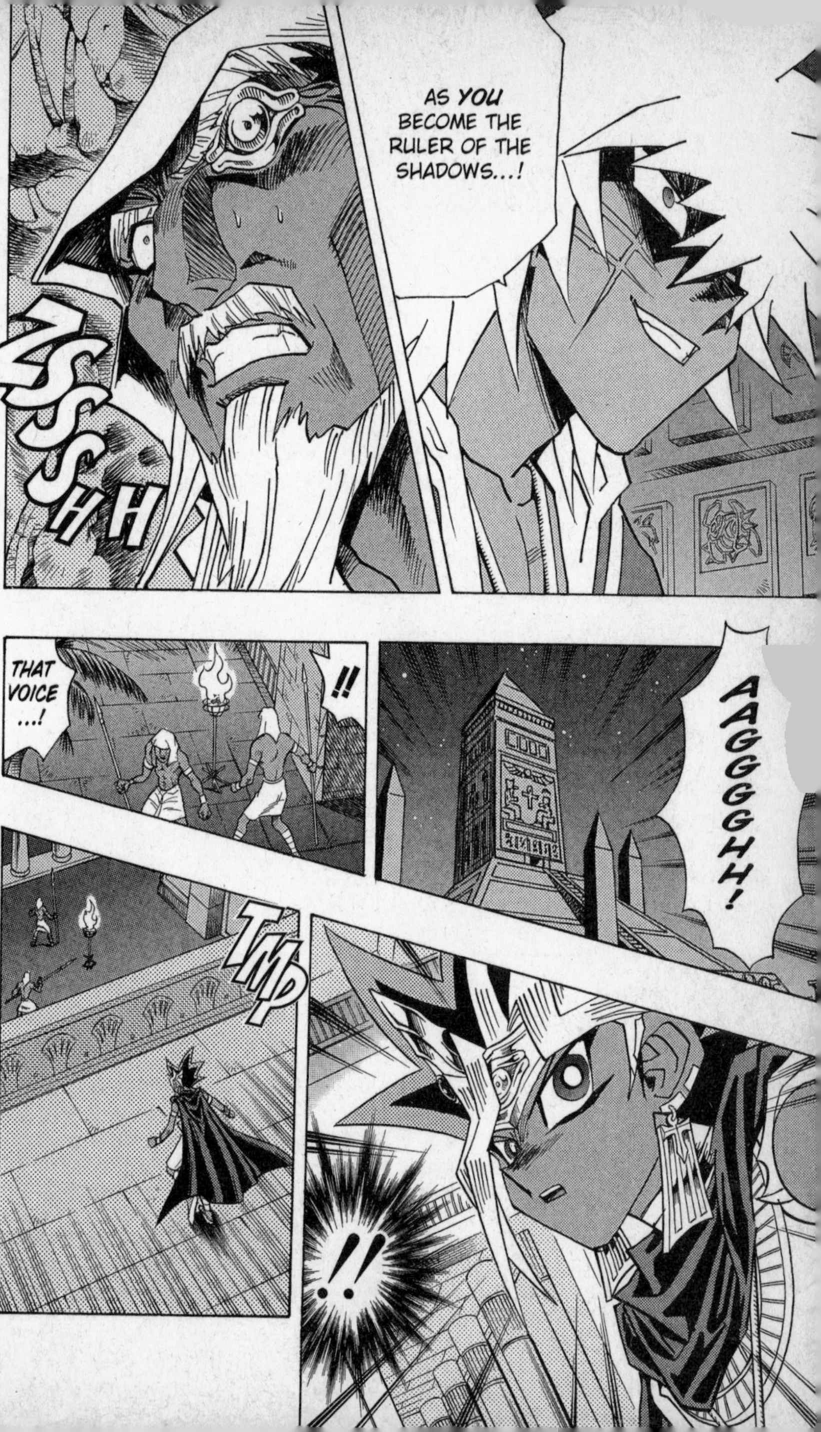
AS *YOU* BECOME THE RULER OF THE SHADOWS...!
ZSSSHH
AAGGGGH!
!!
THAT VOICE ...!
!!
TMP

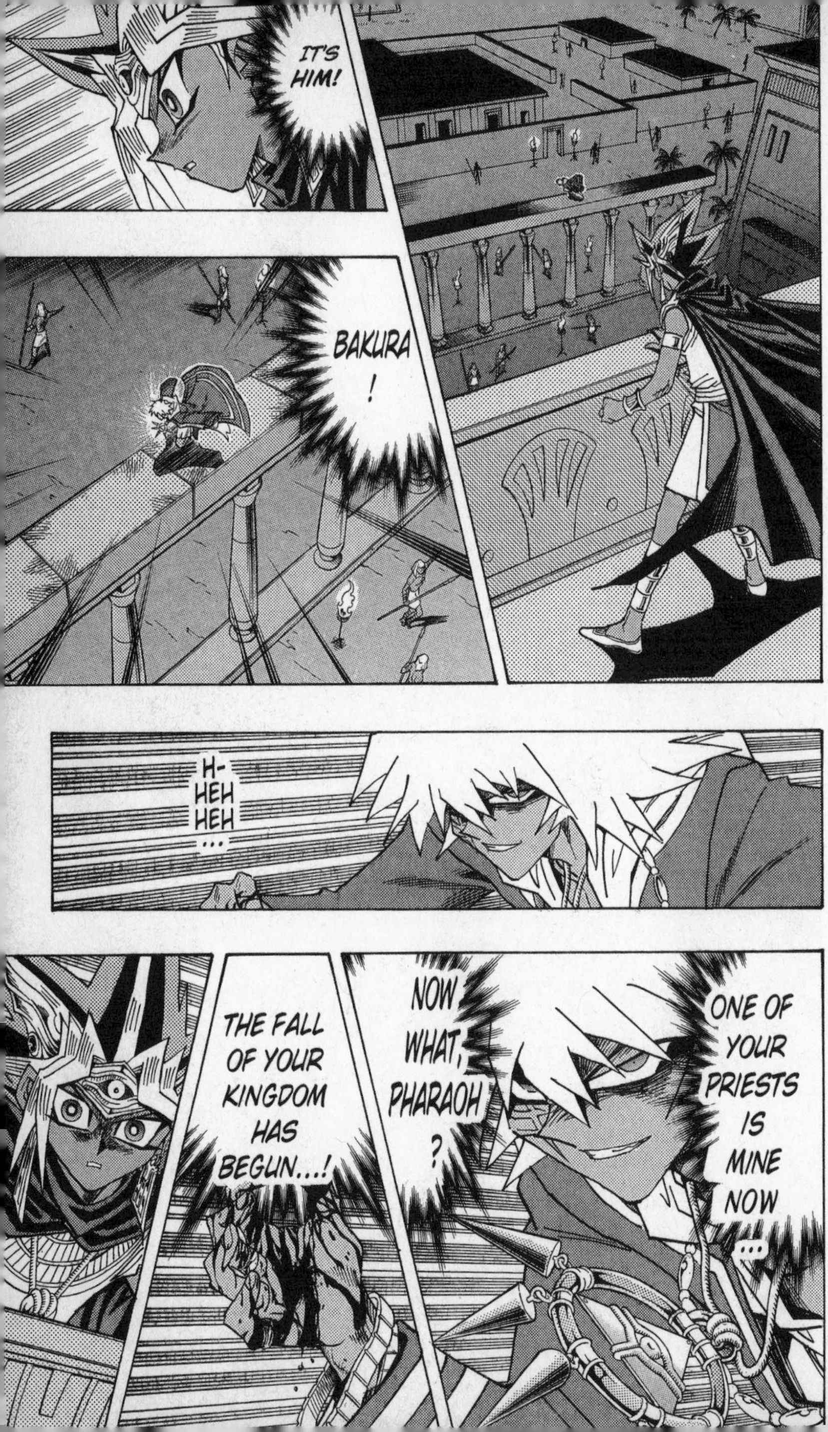
IT'S HIM!
BAKURA!
H-HEH HEH...
ONE OF YOUR PRIESTS IS MINE NOW...
NOW WHAT, PHARAOH?
THE FALL OF YOUR KINGDOM HAS BEGUN...!

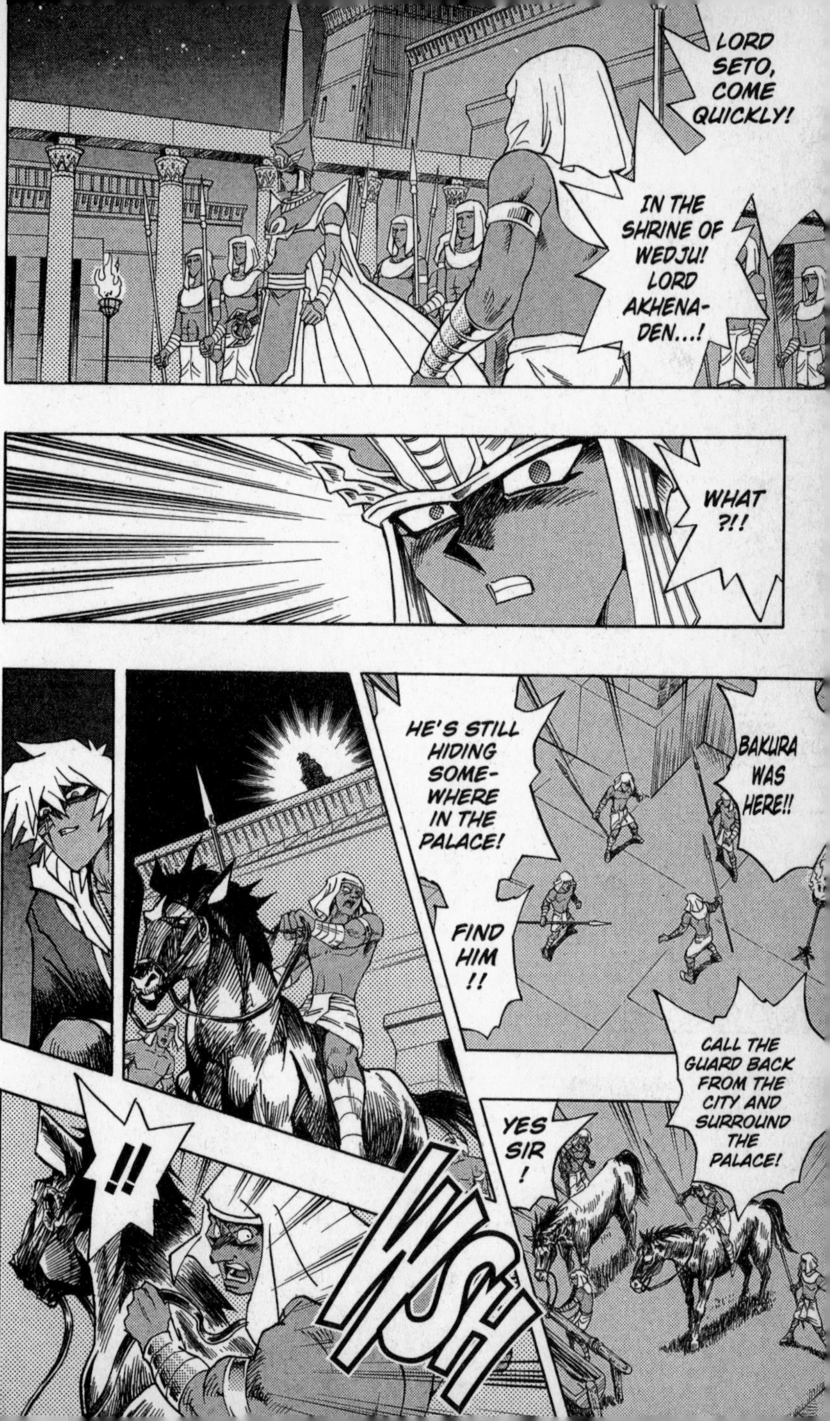
LORD SETO, COME QUICKLY!
IN THE SHRINE OF WEDJU! LORD AKHENADEN...!
WHAT ?!!
BAKURA WAS HERE!!
HE'S STILL HIDING SOMEWHERE IN THE PALACE!
FIND HIM !!
CALL THE GUARD BACK FROM THE CITY AND SURROUND THE PALACE!
YES SIR !
!!
WHSH

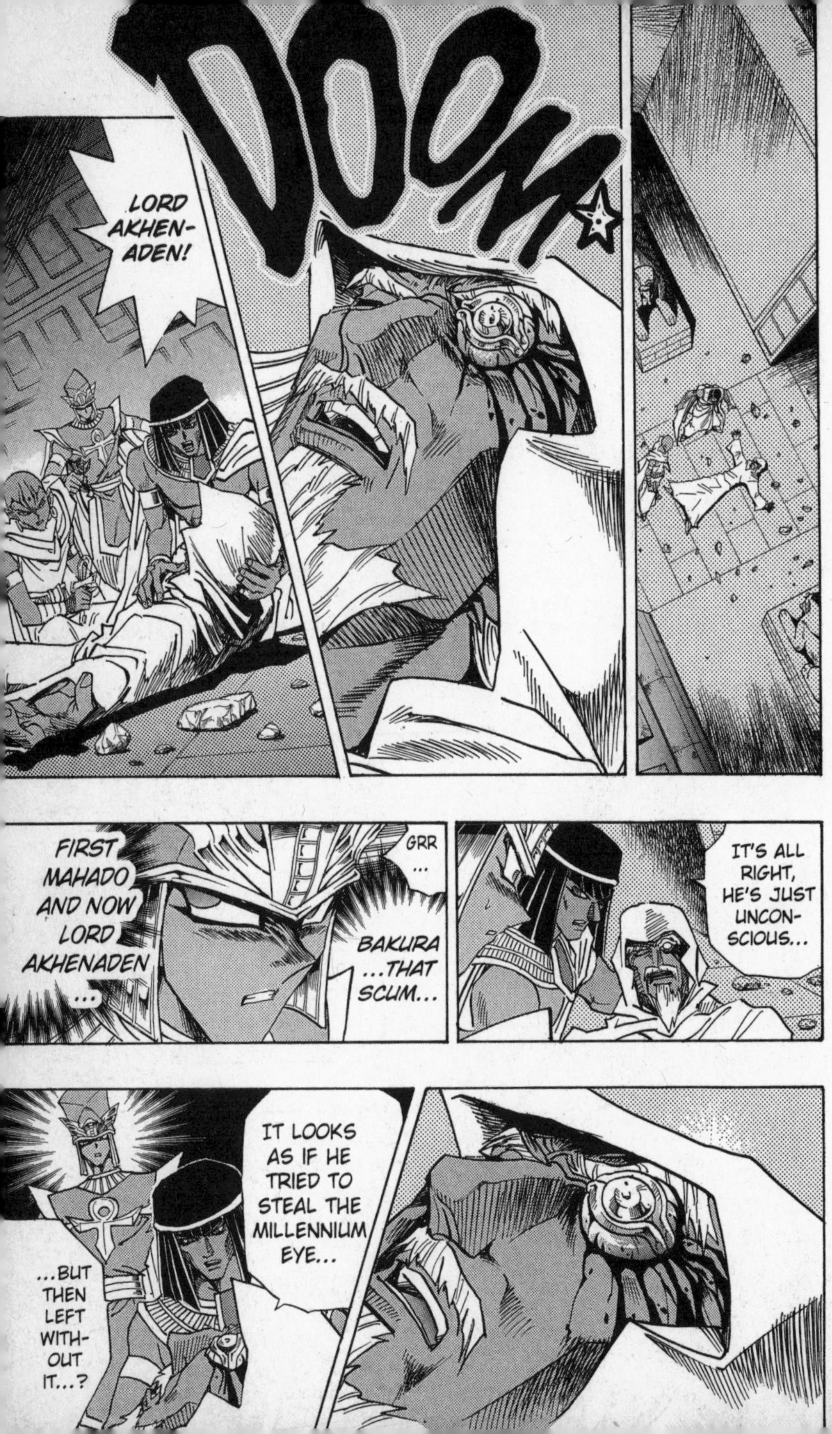
DOOM
LORD AKHEN-ADEN!
IT'S ALL RIGHT, HE'S JUST UNCON-SCIOUS...
GRR ...
BAKURA ...THAT SCUM...
FIRST MAHADO AND NOW LORD AKHENADEN ...
IT LOOKS AS IF HE TRIED TO STEAL THE MILLENNIUM EYE...
...BUT THEN LEFT WITH-OUT IT...?

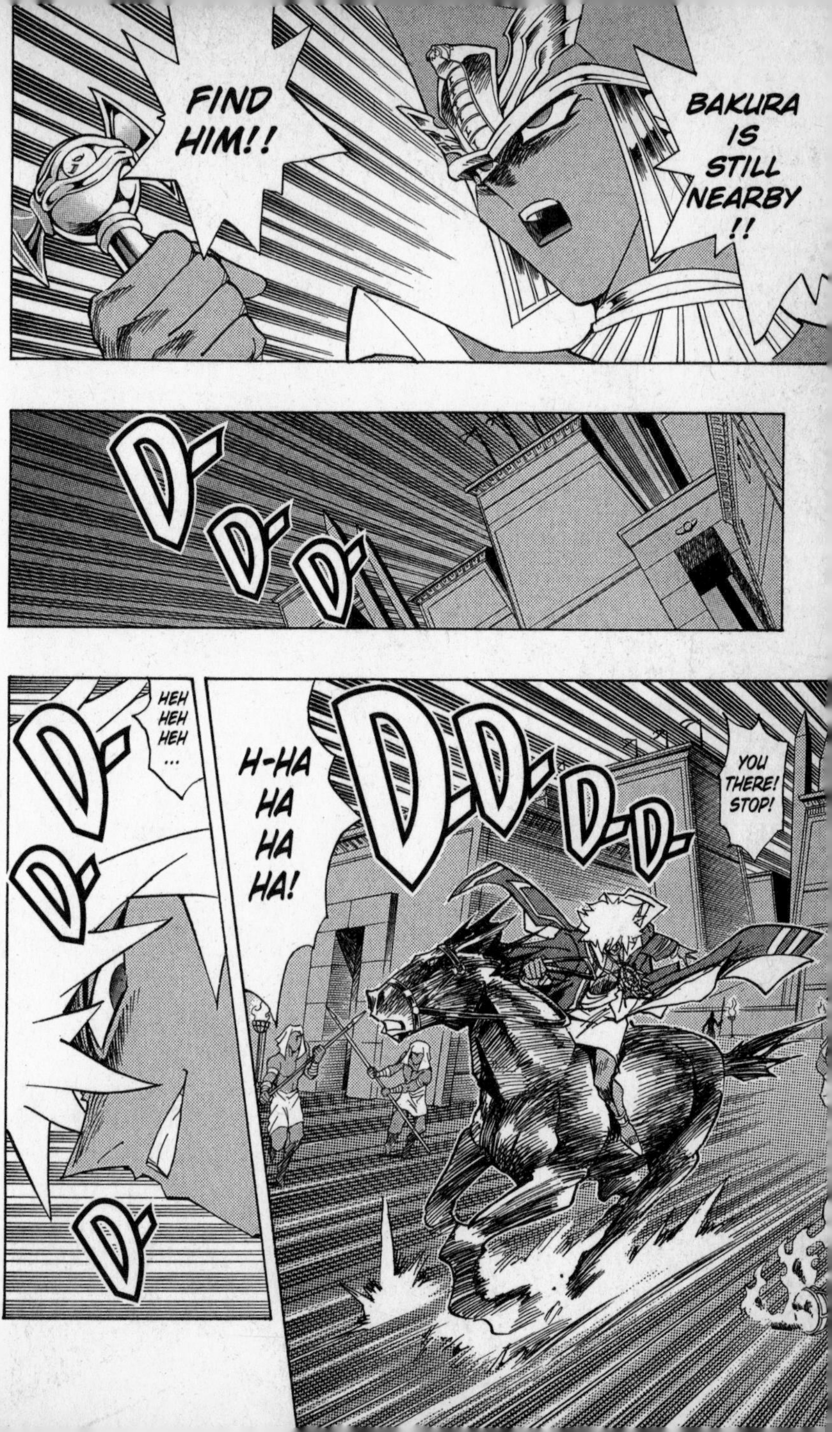
BAKURA IS STILL NEARBY!!
FIND HIM!!
D-D-D
YOU THERE! STOP!
D-D-D-D-D
H-HA HA HA HA!
HEH HEH HEH...
D-D-D

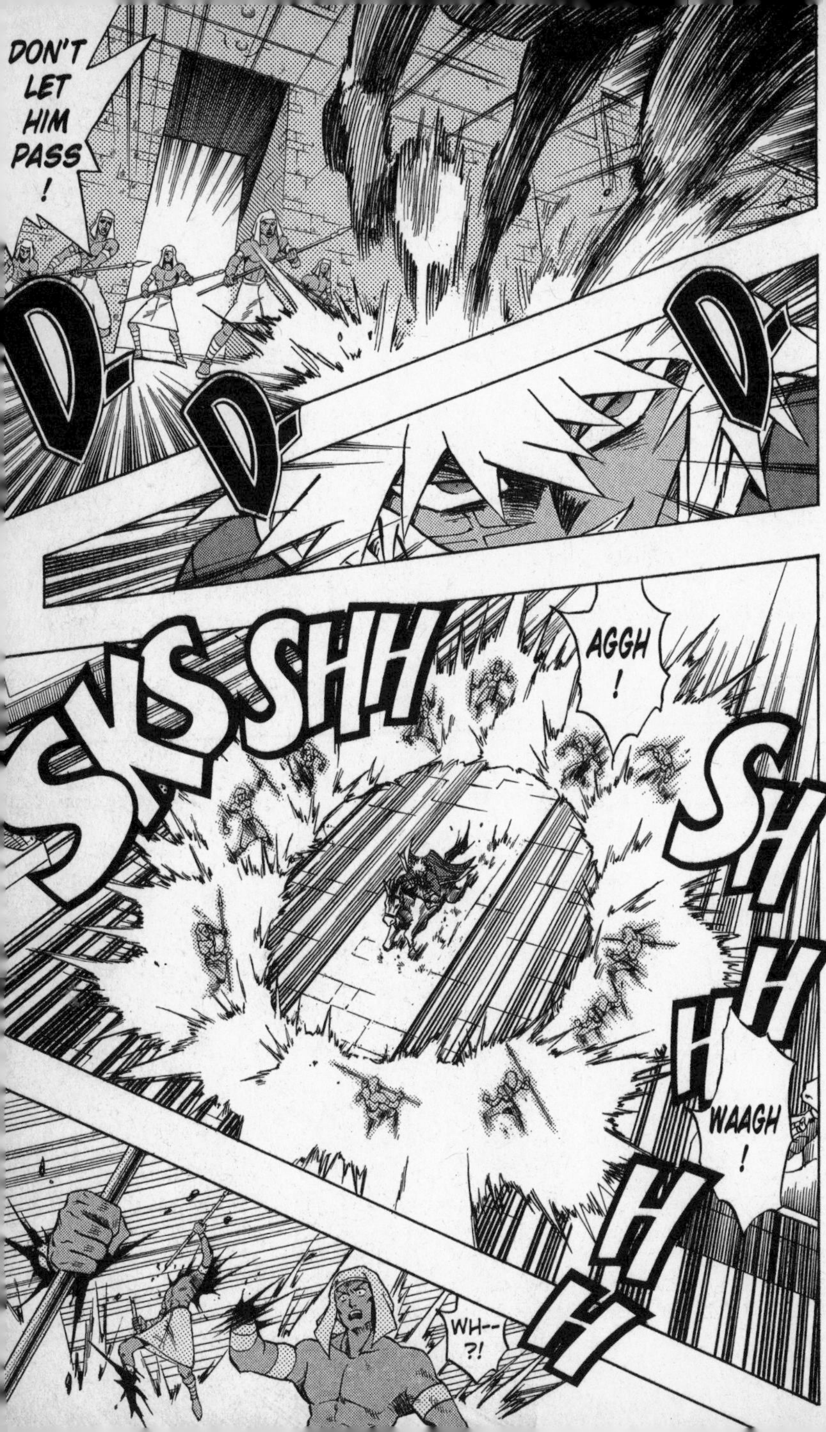

DON'T LET HIM PASS!
D
D
D
AGGH!
S'S SHH
SHHHHHH
WAAGH!
WH-- ?!

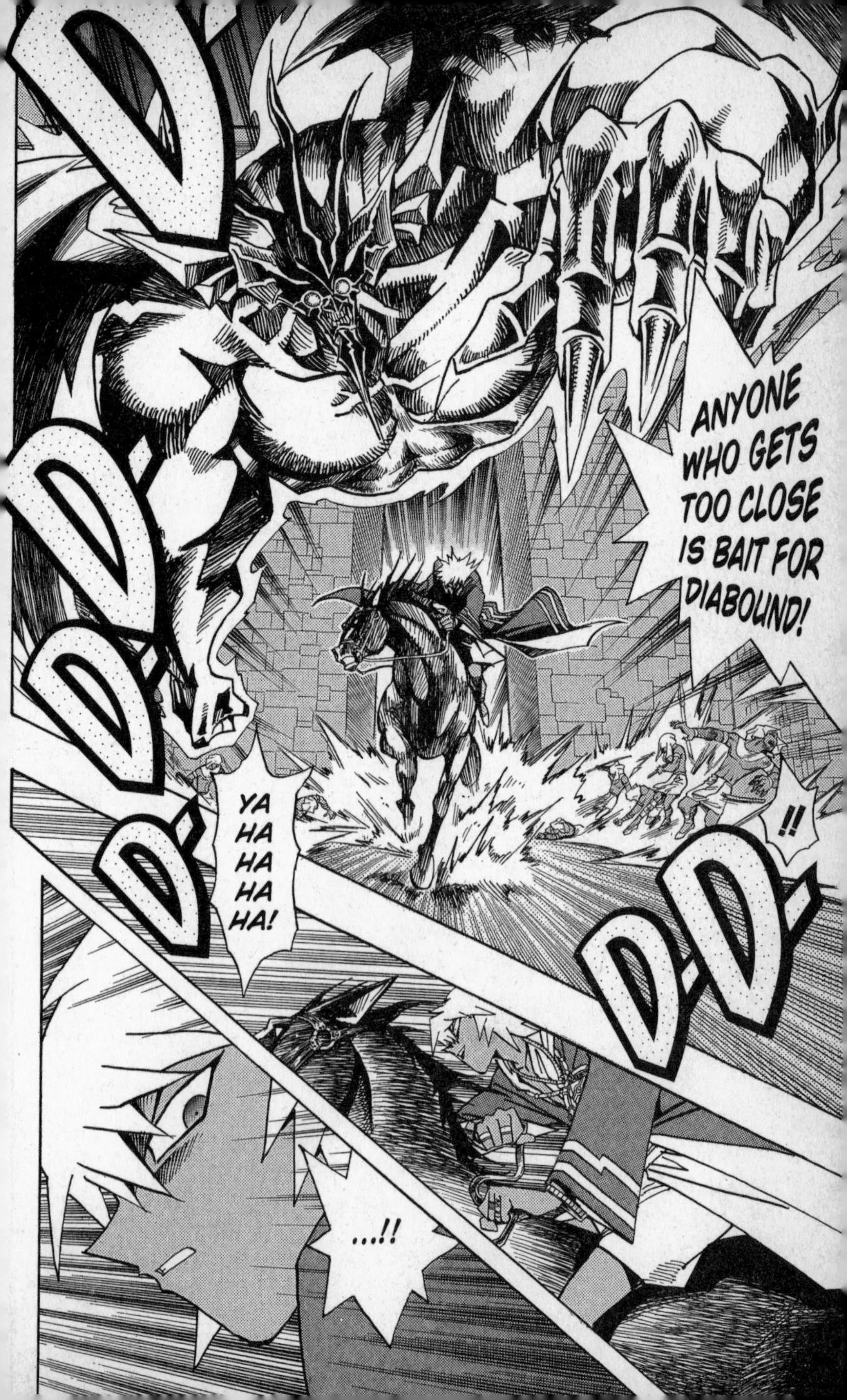
ANYONE WHO GETS TOO CLOSE IS BAIT FOR DIABOUND!
!!
DD
YA HA HA HA HA!
DDDD
...!!

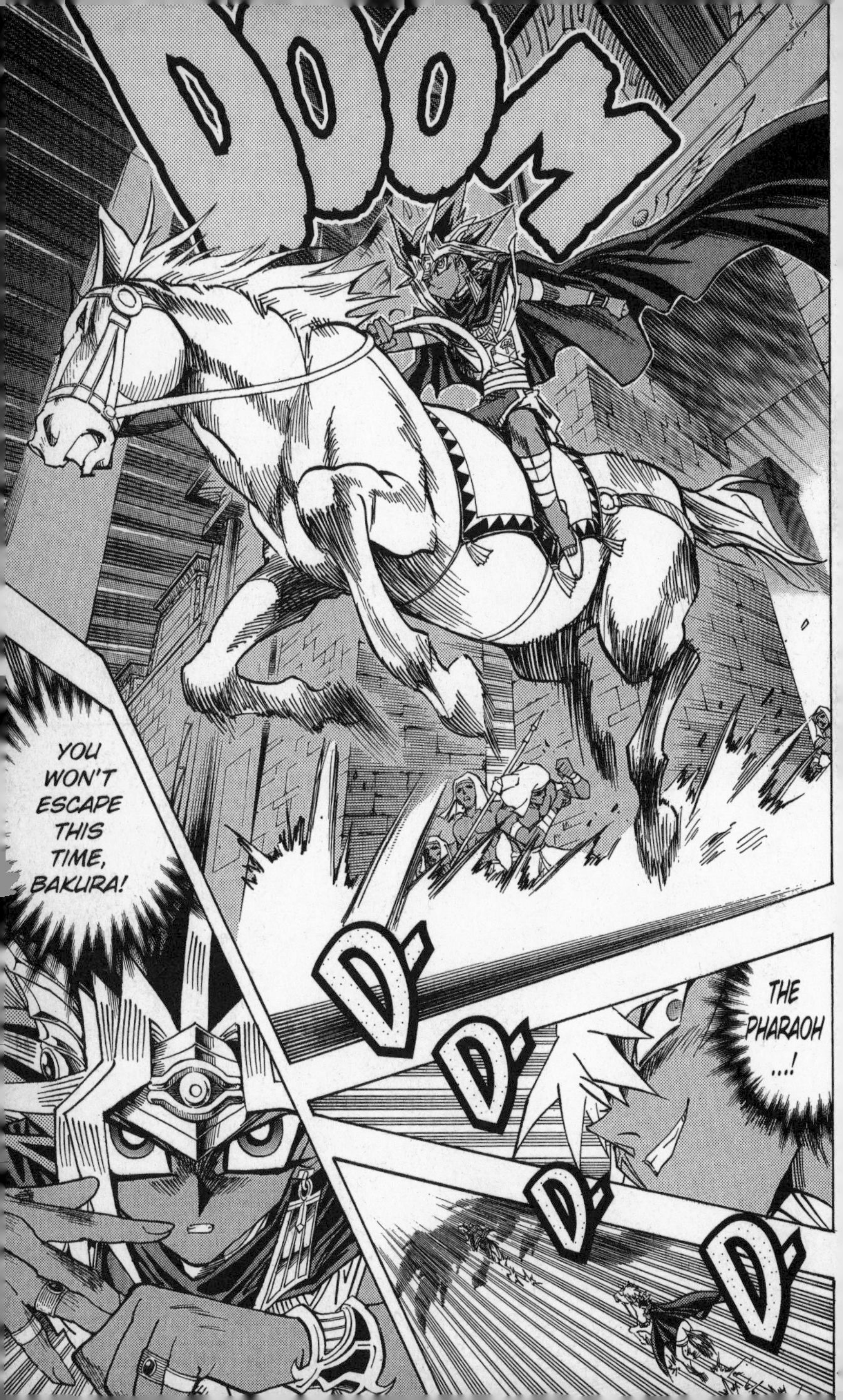
THE PHARAOH ...!
D
D
D
D
YOU WON'T ESCAPE THIS TIME, BAKURA!

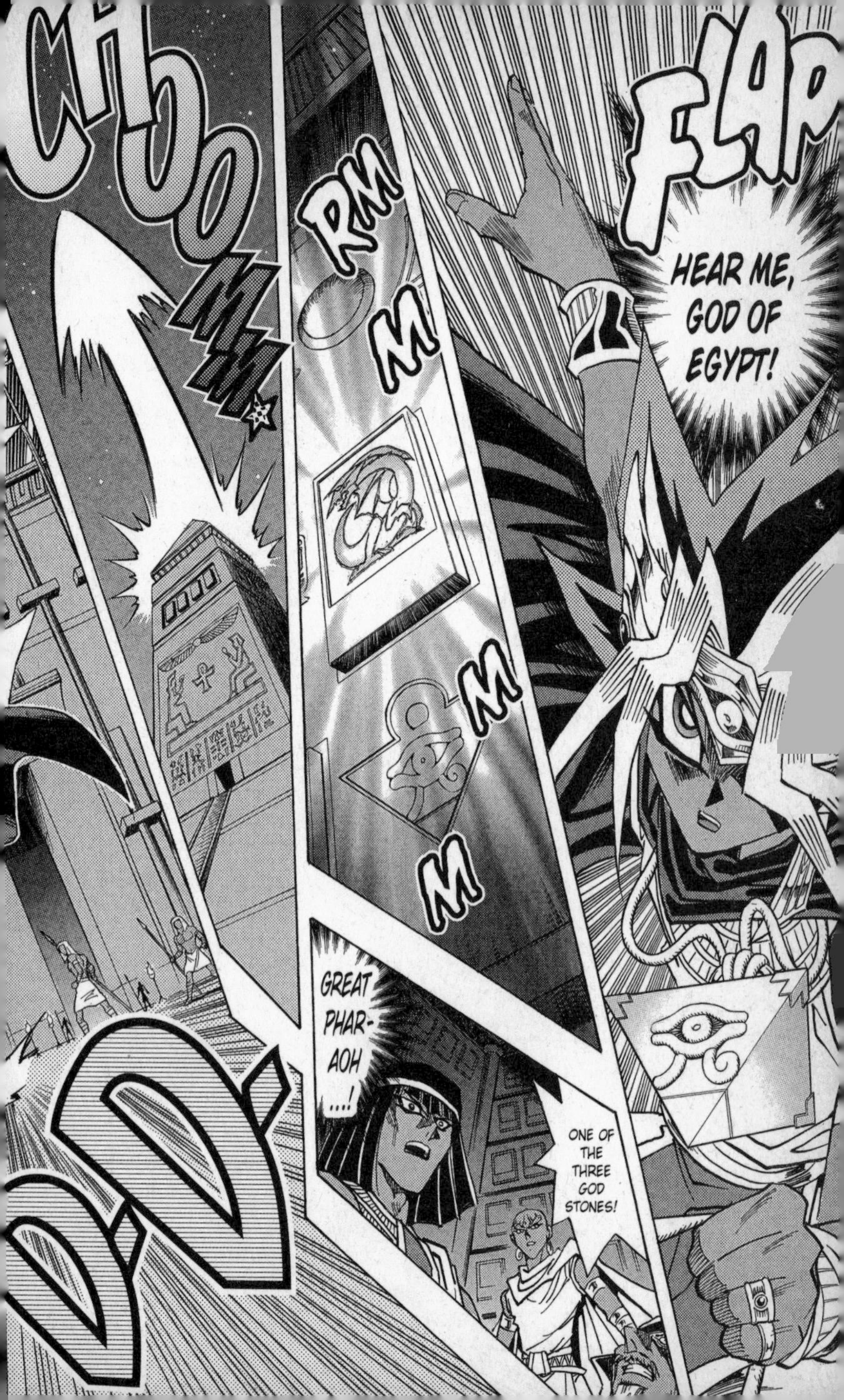
FLAP
HEAR ME, GOD OF EGYPT!
RMMMM
CHOOMMM
ONE OF THE THREE GOD STONES!
GREAT PHAR-AOH ...!

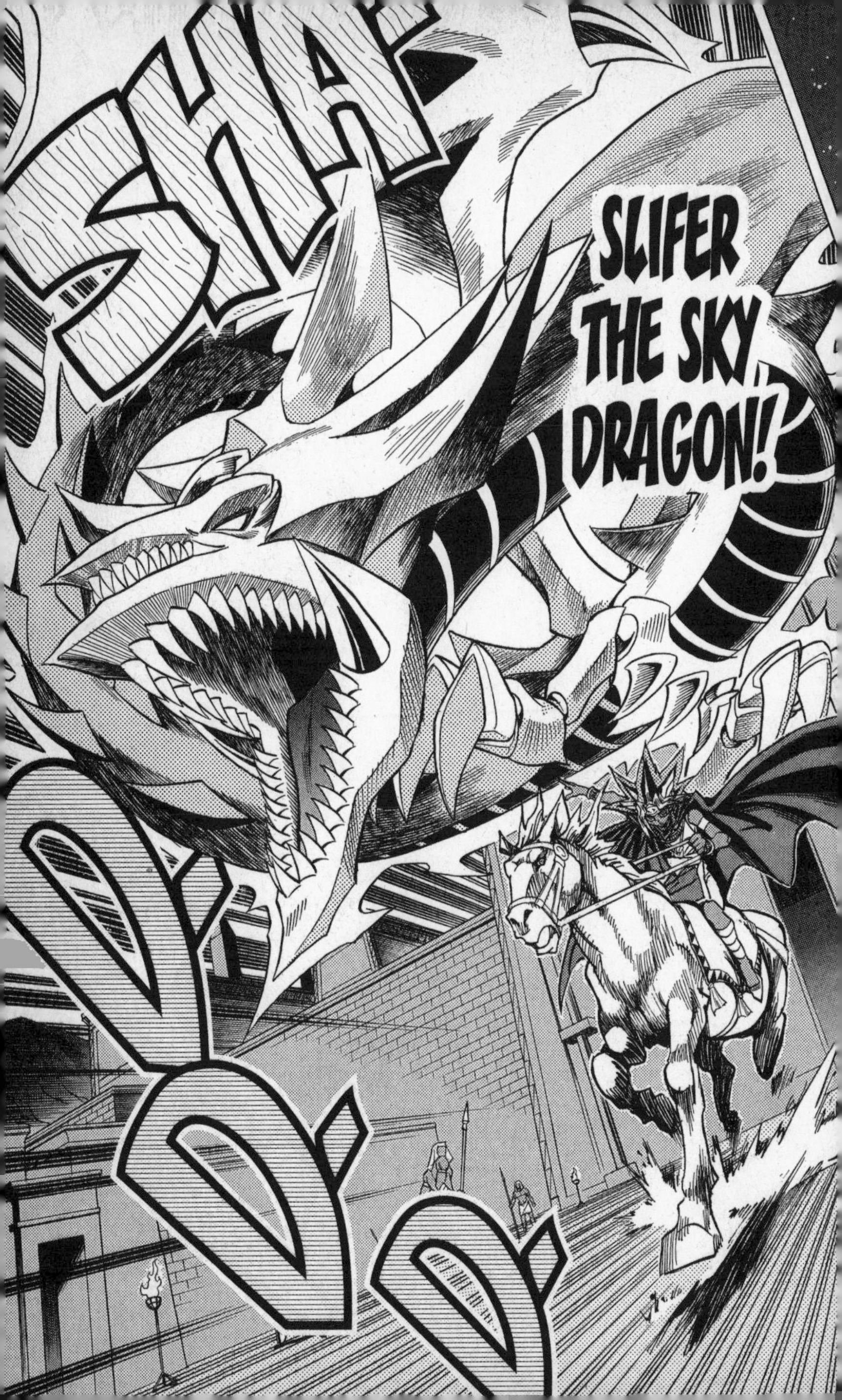
SHA
SLIFER THE SKY DRAGON!?

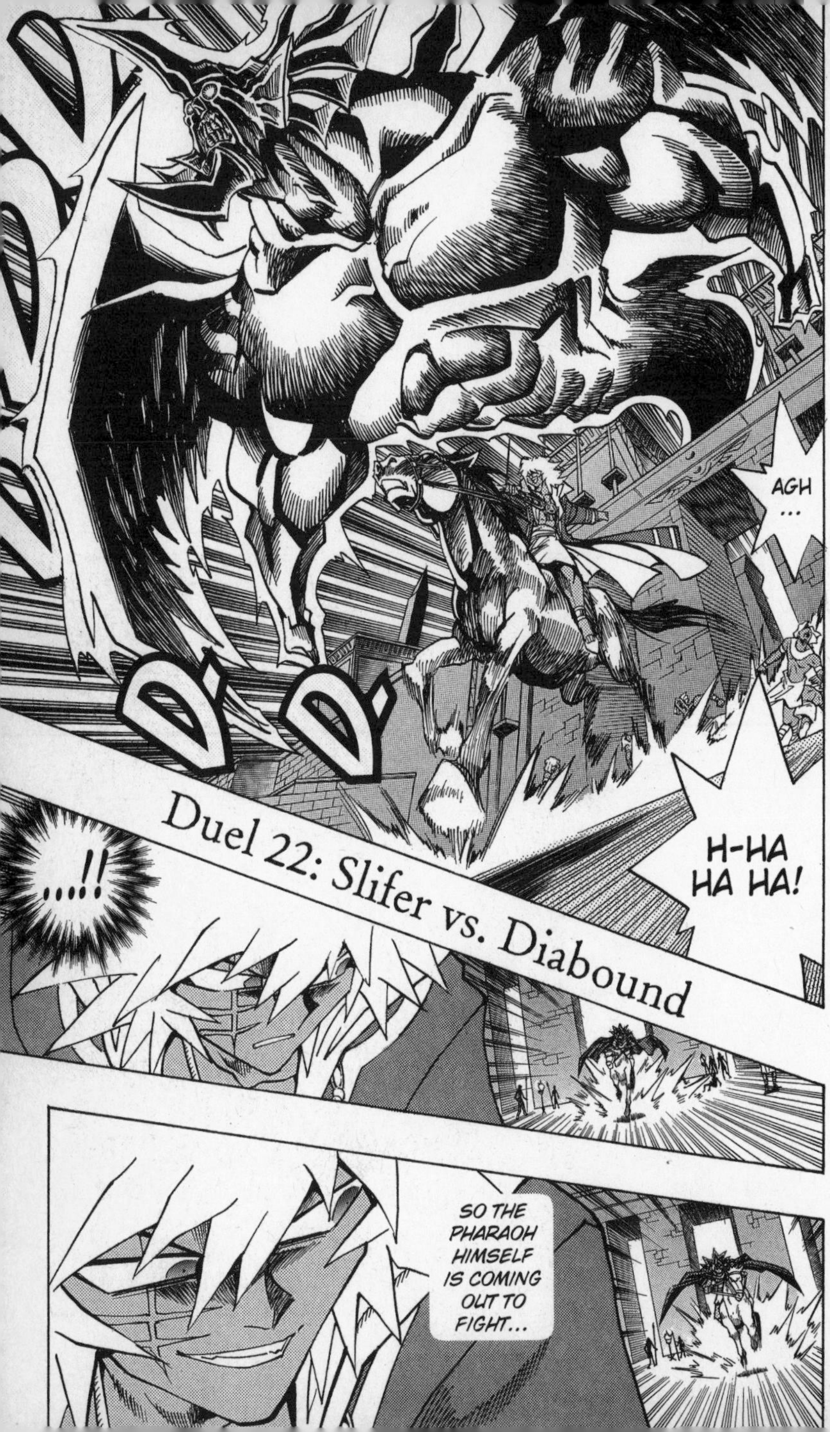
AGH ...
H-HA HA HA!
Duel 22: Slifer vs. Diabound
...!!
SO THE PHARAOH HIMSELF IS COMING OUT TO FIGHT...

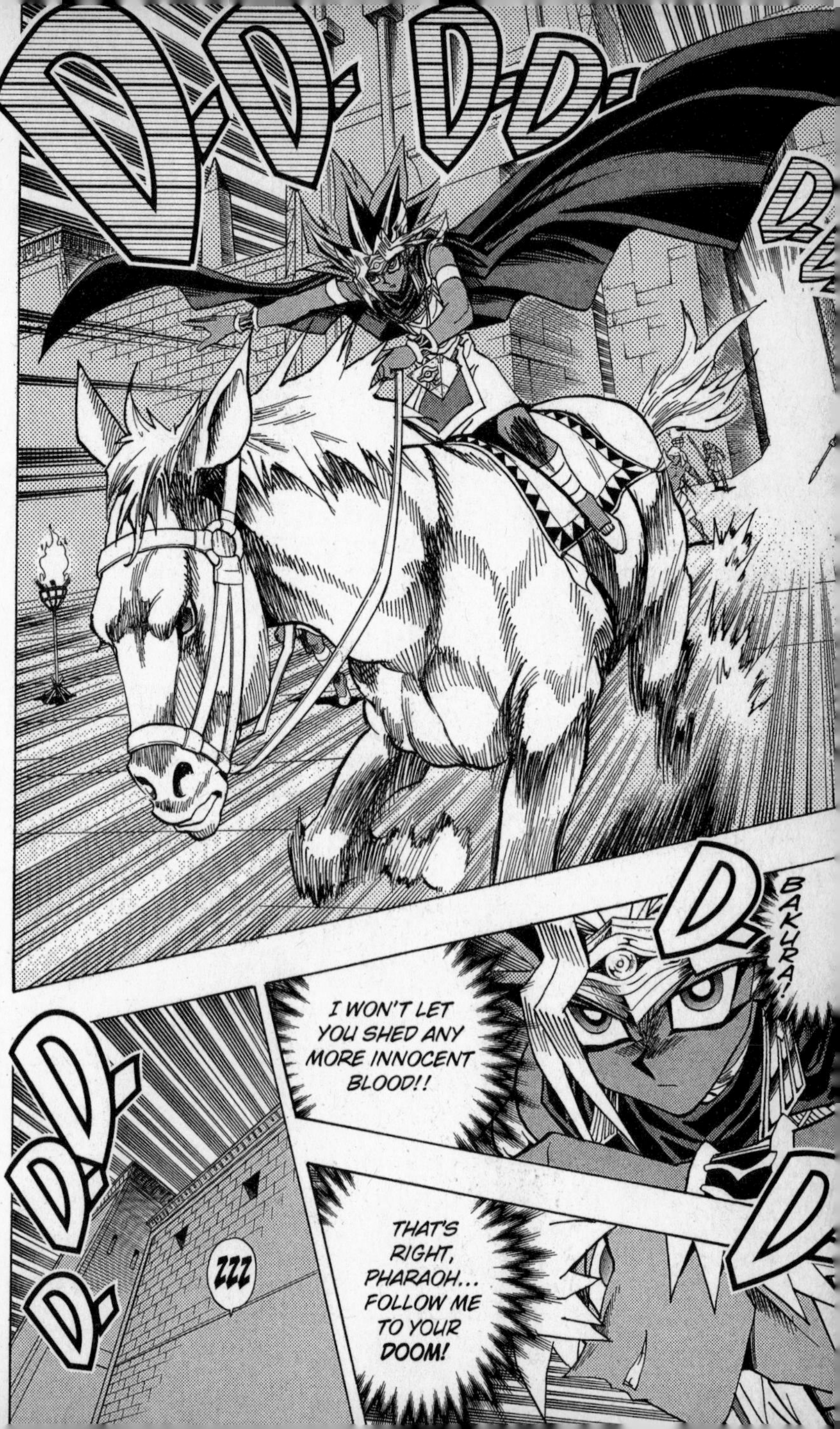
D-D-D-D-
D-D-
D
BAKURA!
I WON'T LET YOU SHED ANY MORE INNOCENT BLOOD!!
D
THAT'S RIGHT, PHARAOH... FOLLOW ME TO YOUR DOOM!
D-D-D-
ZZZ

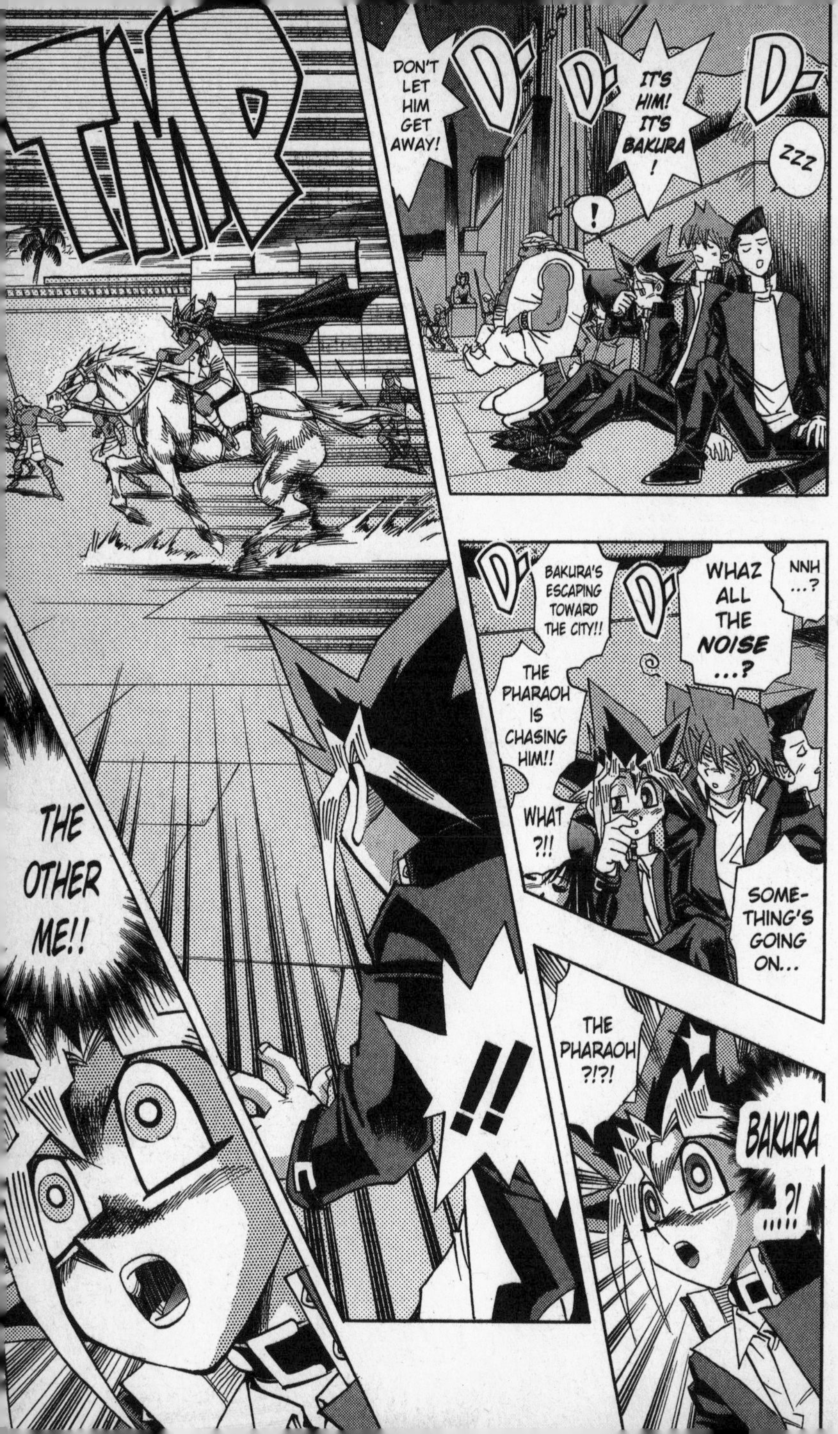

D-
ZZZ
D-
IT'S HIM! IT'S BAKURA!
D-
DON'T LET HIM GET AWAY!
!
TMP
NNH ...?
WHAZ ALL THE NOISE ...?
D
D
BAKURA'S ESCAPING TOWARD THE CITY!!
THE PHARAOH IS CHASING HIM!!
WHAT ?!!
SOME-THING'S GOING ON...
THE PHARAOH ?!?!
BAKURA ...?!
!!
THE OTHER ME!!

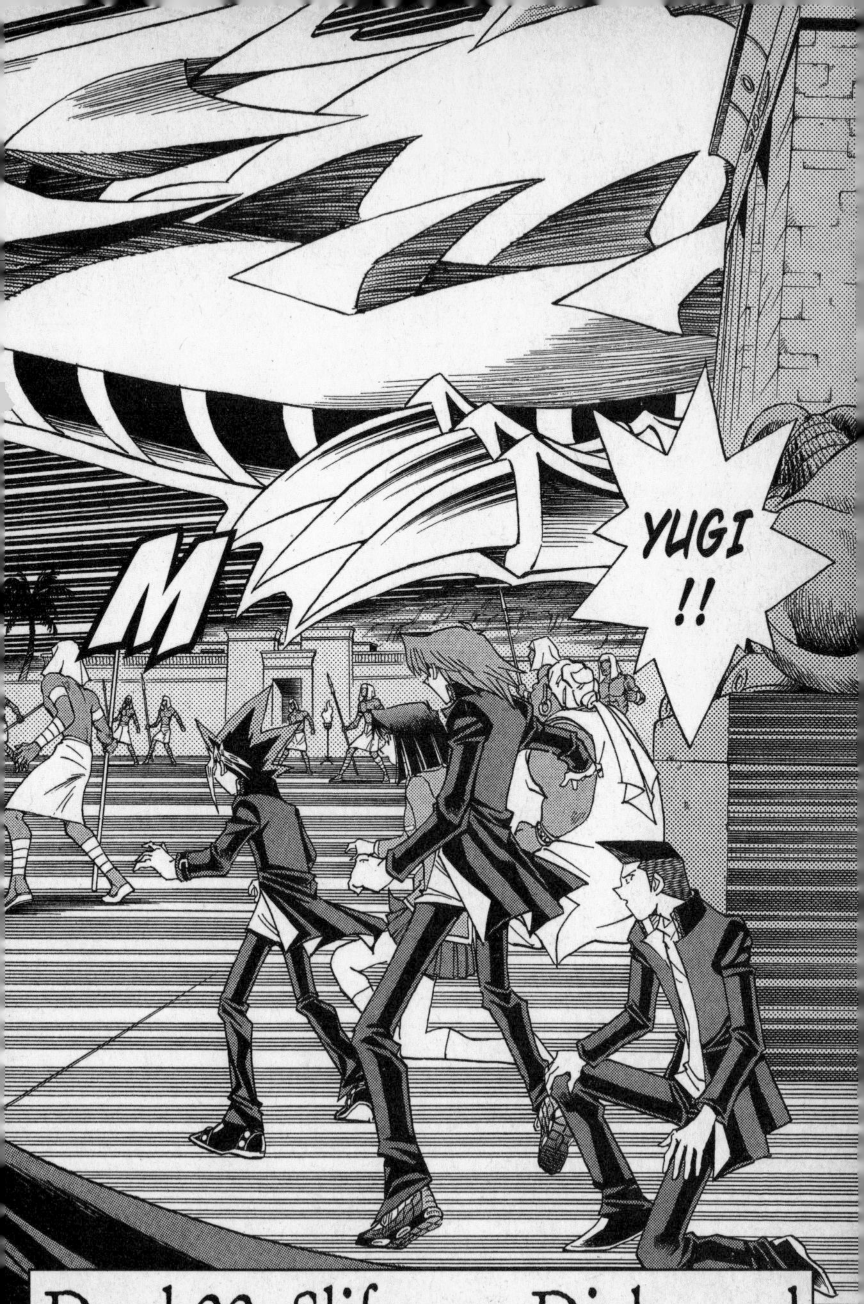
YUGI !!
M

Duel 22: Slifer vs. Diabound

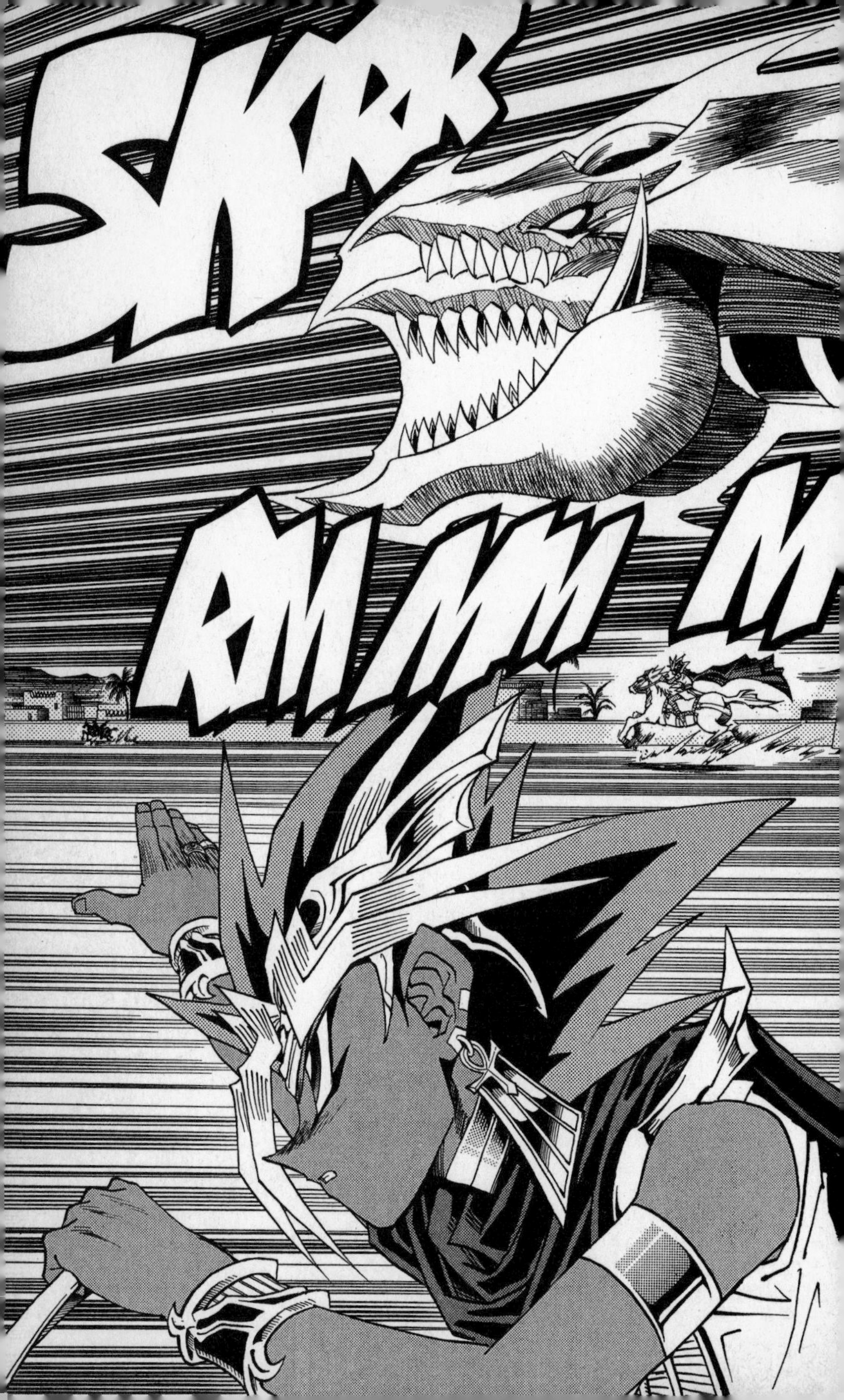
SKRAK

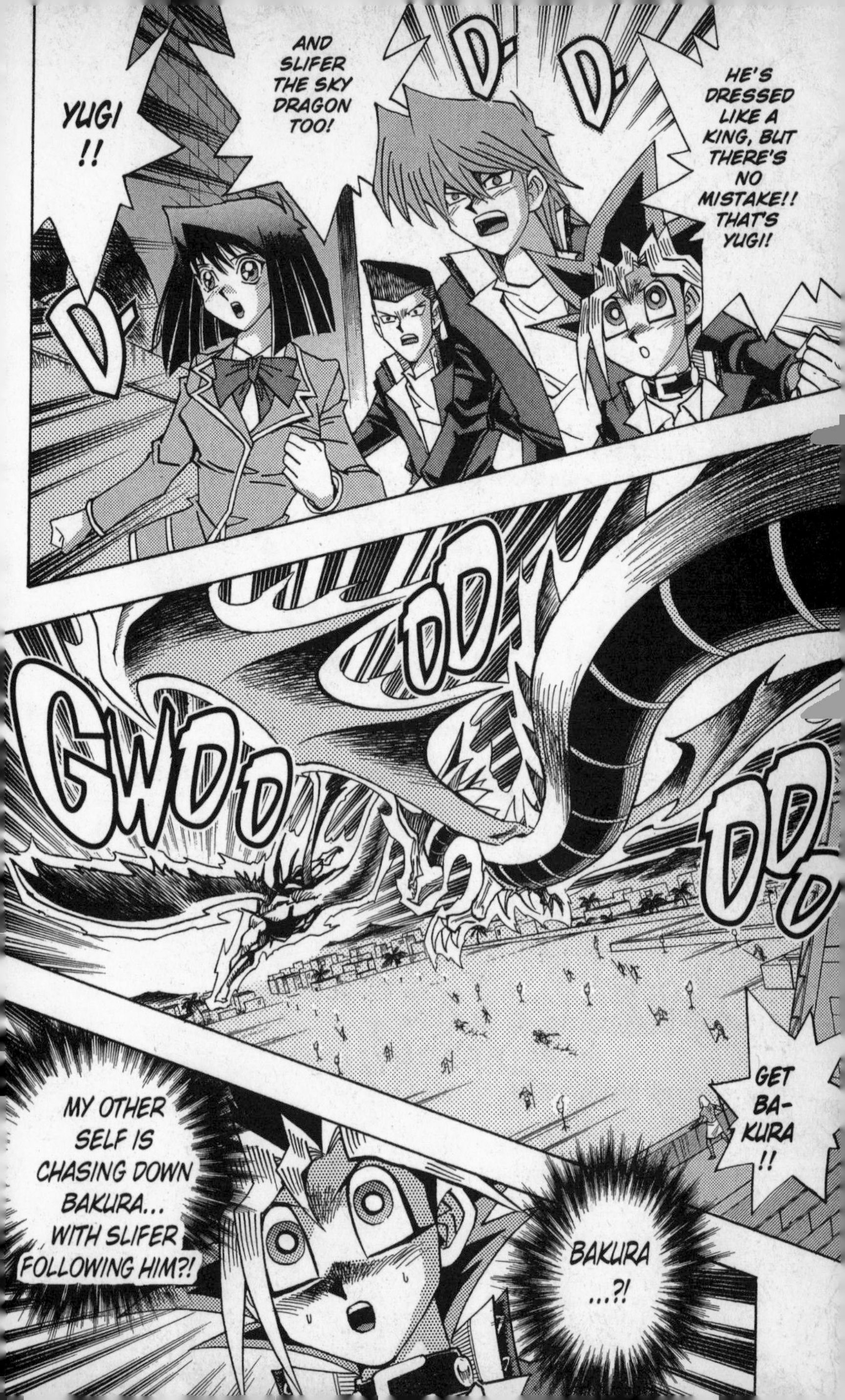
HE'S DRESSED LIKE A KING, BUT THERE'S NO MISTAKE!! THAT'S YUGI!
D D
AND SLIFER THE SKY DRAGON TOO!
YUGI !!
D
DDDD
DD
GWDDD
GET BAKURA !!
BAKURA ...?!
MY OTHER SELF IS CHASING DOWN BAKURA... WITH SLIFER FOLLOWING HIM?!

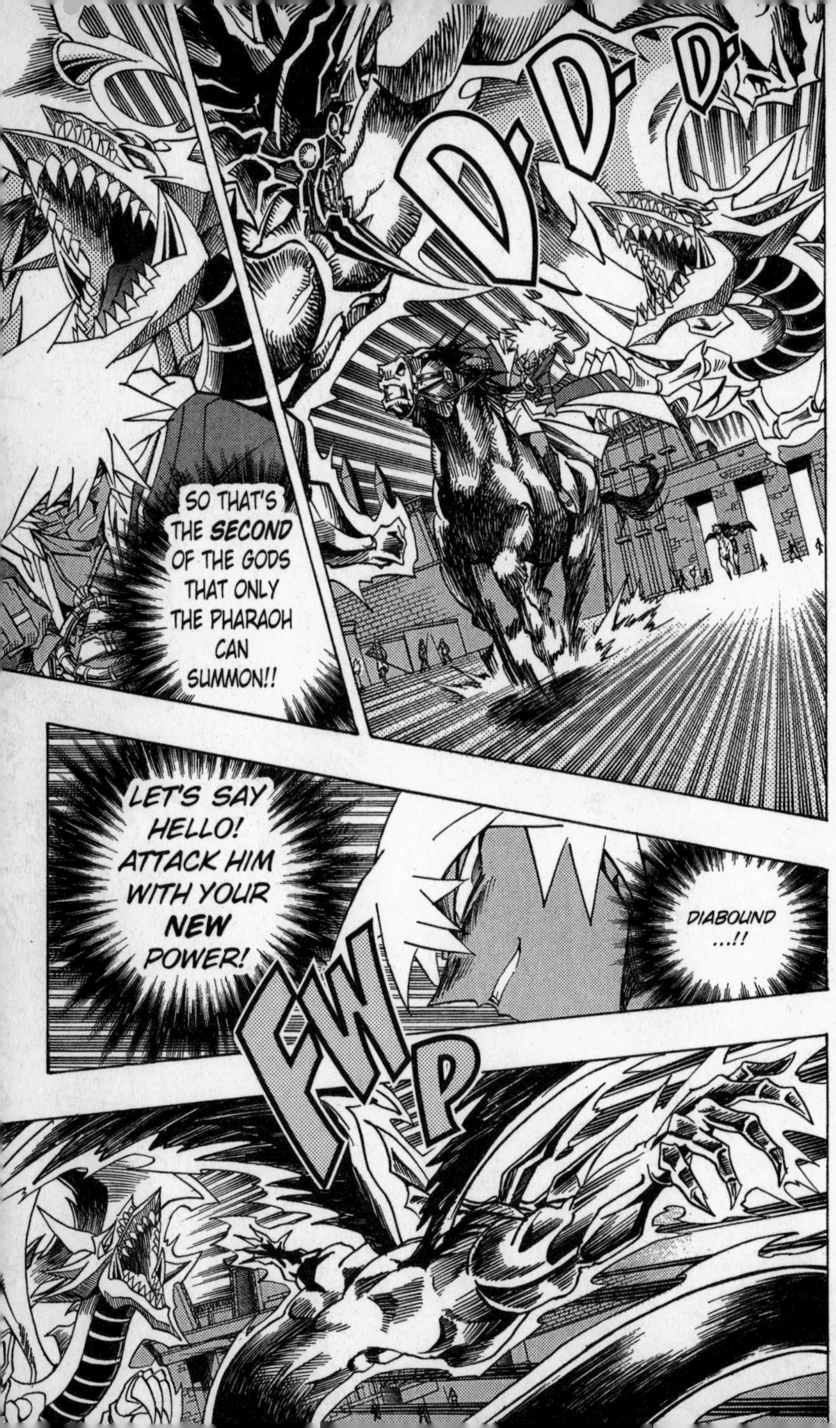
D-D-D
SO THAT'S THE SECOND OF THE GODS THAT ONLY THE PHARAOH CAN SUMMON!!
DIABOUND ...!!
LET'S SAY HELLO! ATTACK HIM WITH YOUR NEW POWER!
FWP

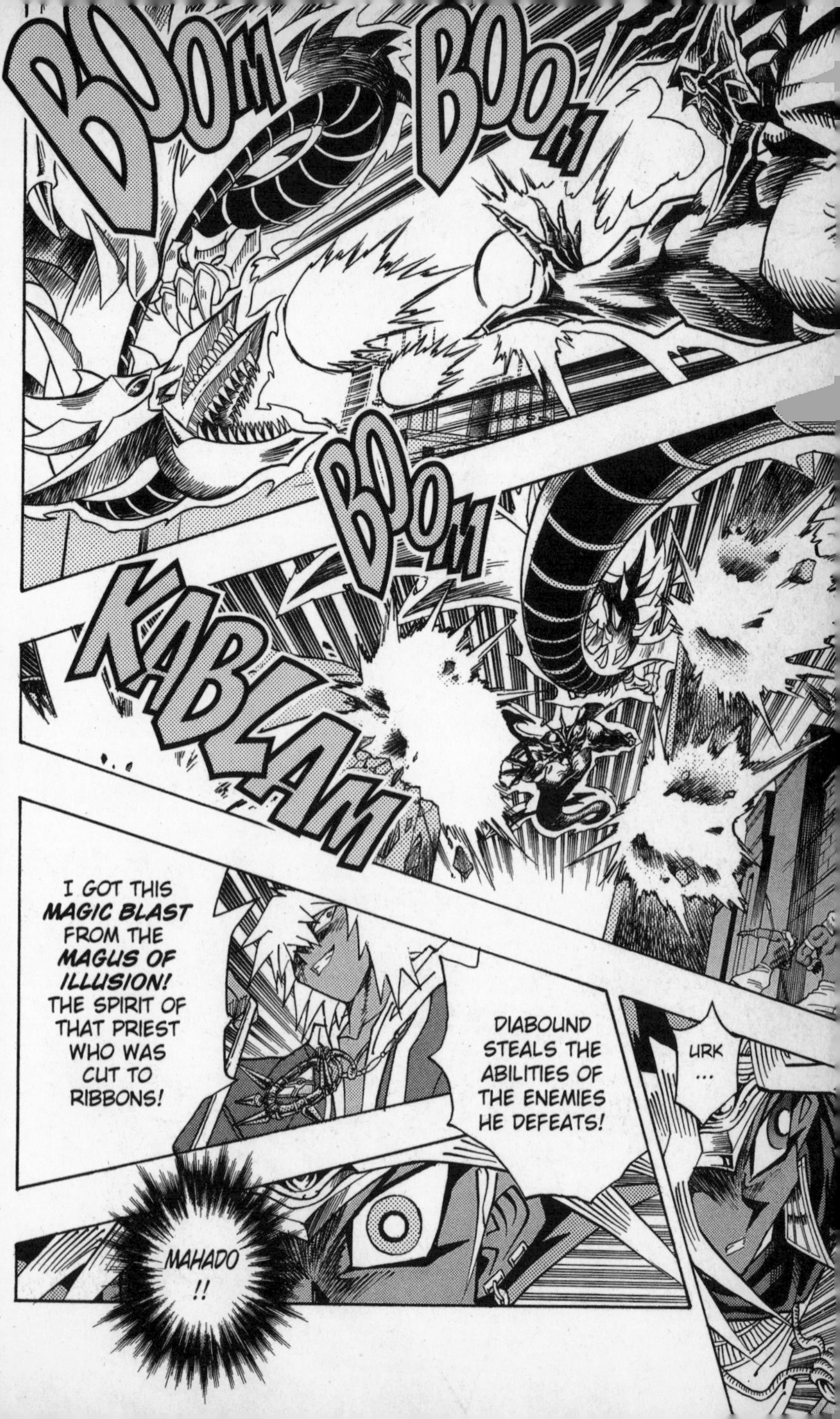
BOOM
BOOM
BOOM
KABLAM
I GOT THIS *MAGIC BLAST* FROM THE *MAGUS OF ILLUSION!* THE SPIRIT OF THAT PRIEST WHO WAS CUT TO RIBBONS!
DIABOUND STEALS THE ABILITIES OF THE ENEMIES HE DEFEATS!
URK ...
MAHADO !!

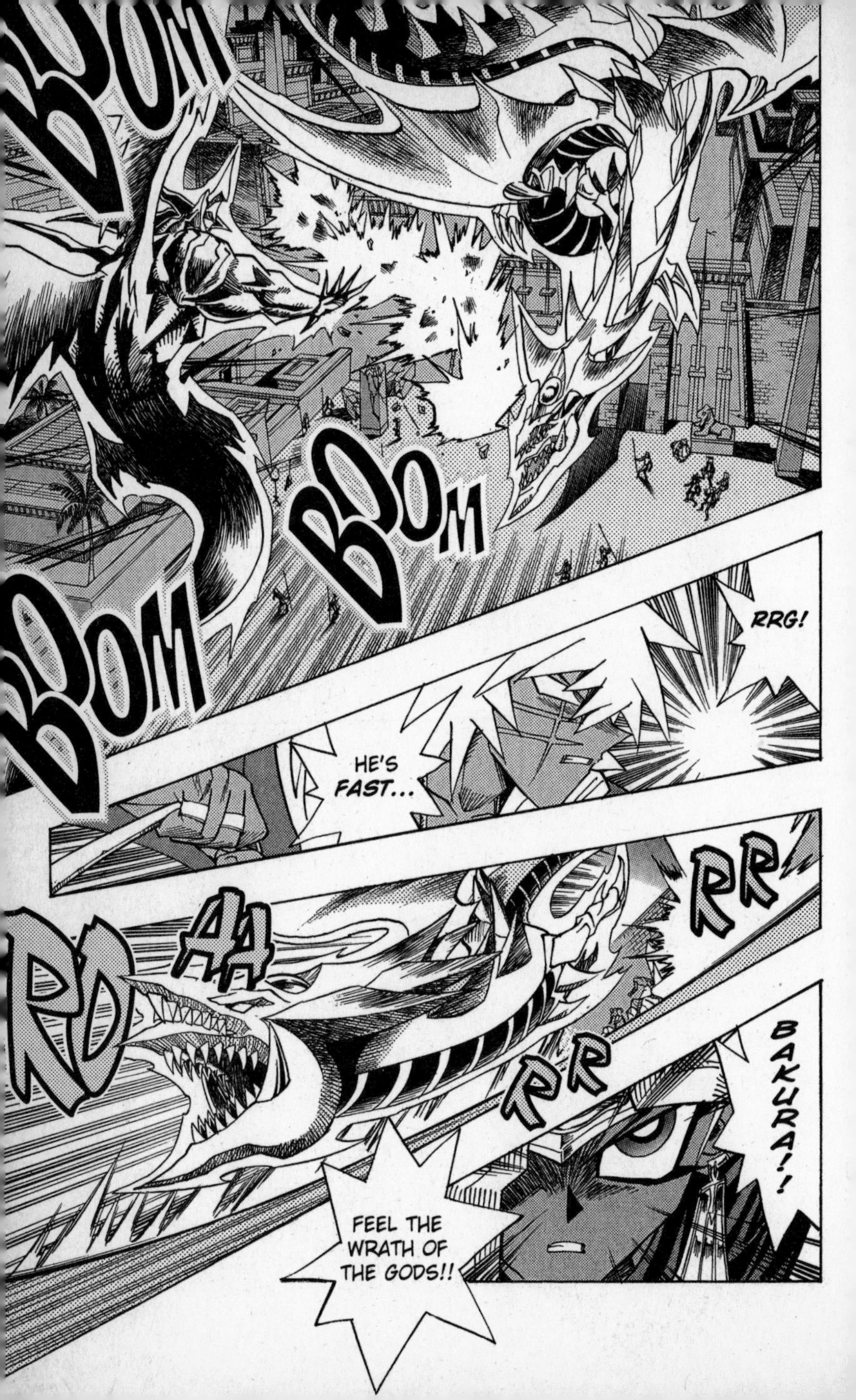
BOOM
BOOM
BOOM
RRG!
HE'S FAST...
RR
RR
BAKURA!!
FEEL THE WRATH OF THE GODS!!

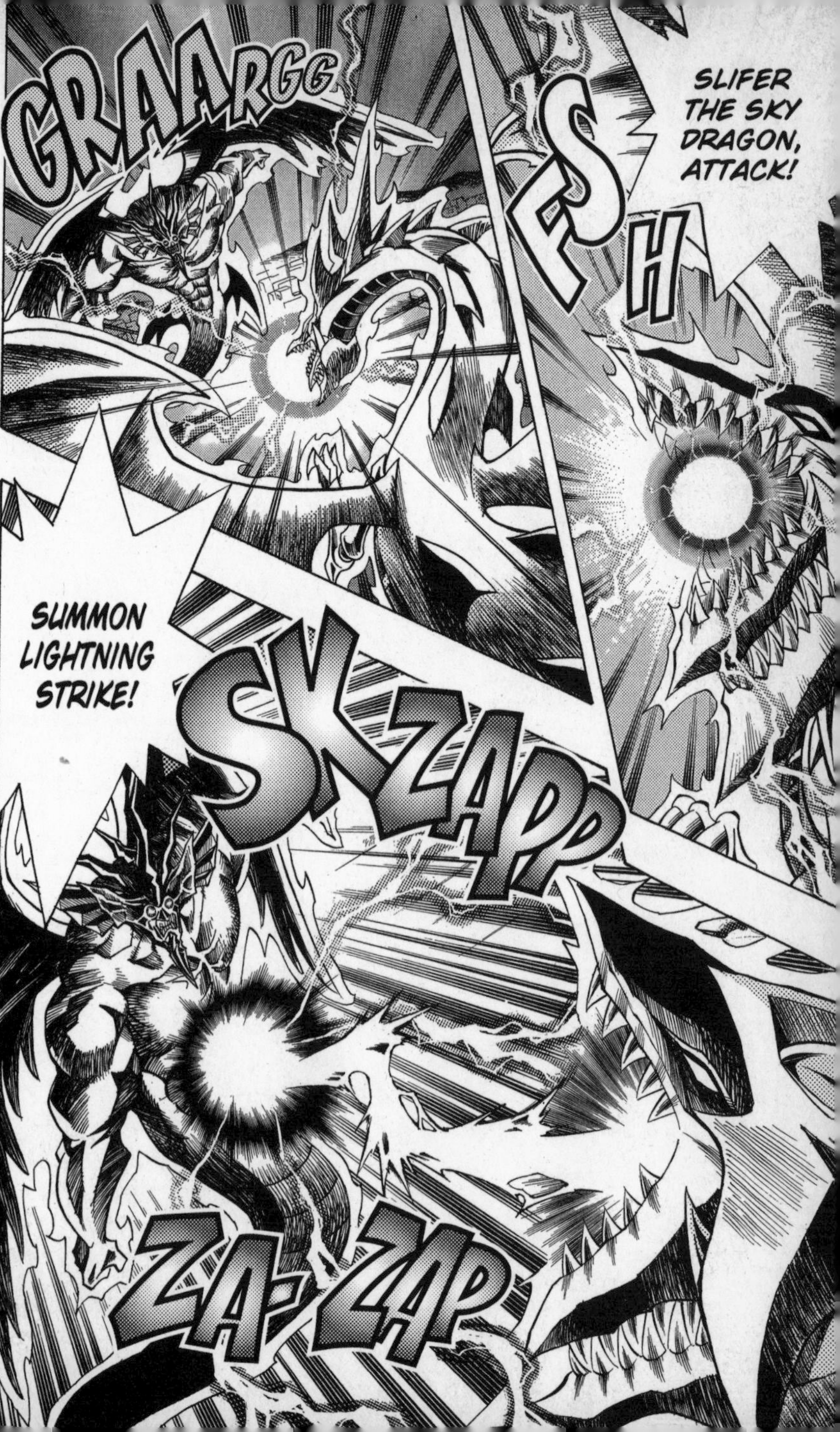
SLIFER THE SKY DRAGON, ATTACK!
FSSH
GRAARGG
SUMMON LIGHTNING STRIKE!
SKZAPP
ZA-ZAP

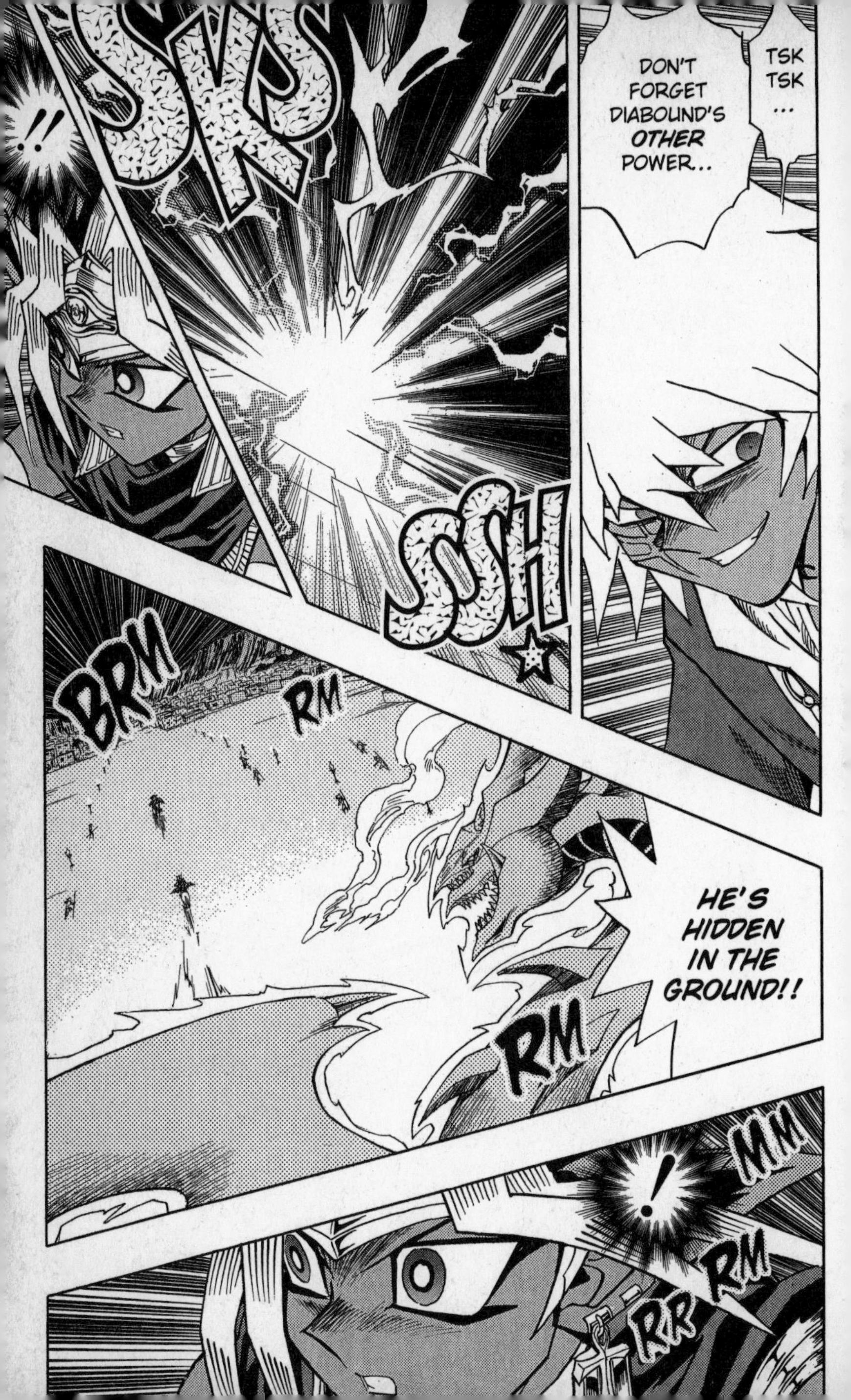
TSK TSK ...
DON'T FORGET DIABOUND'S OTHER POWER...
!!
SSH
BRM
RM
HE'S HIDDEN IN THE GROUND!!
RM
MM
!
RM
RR

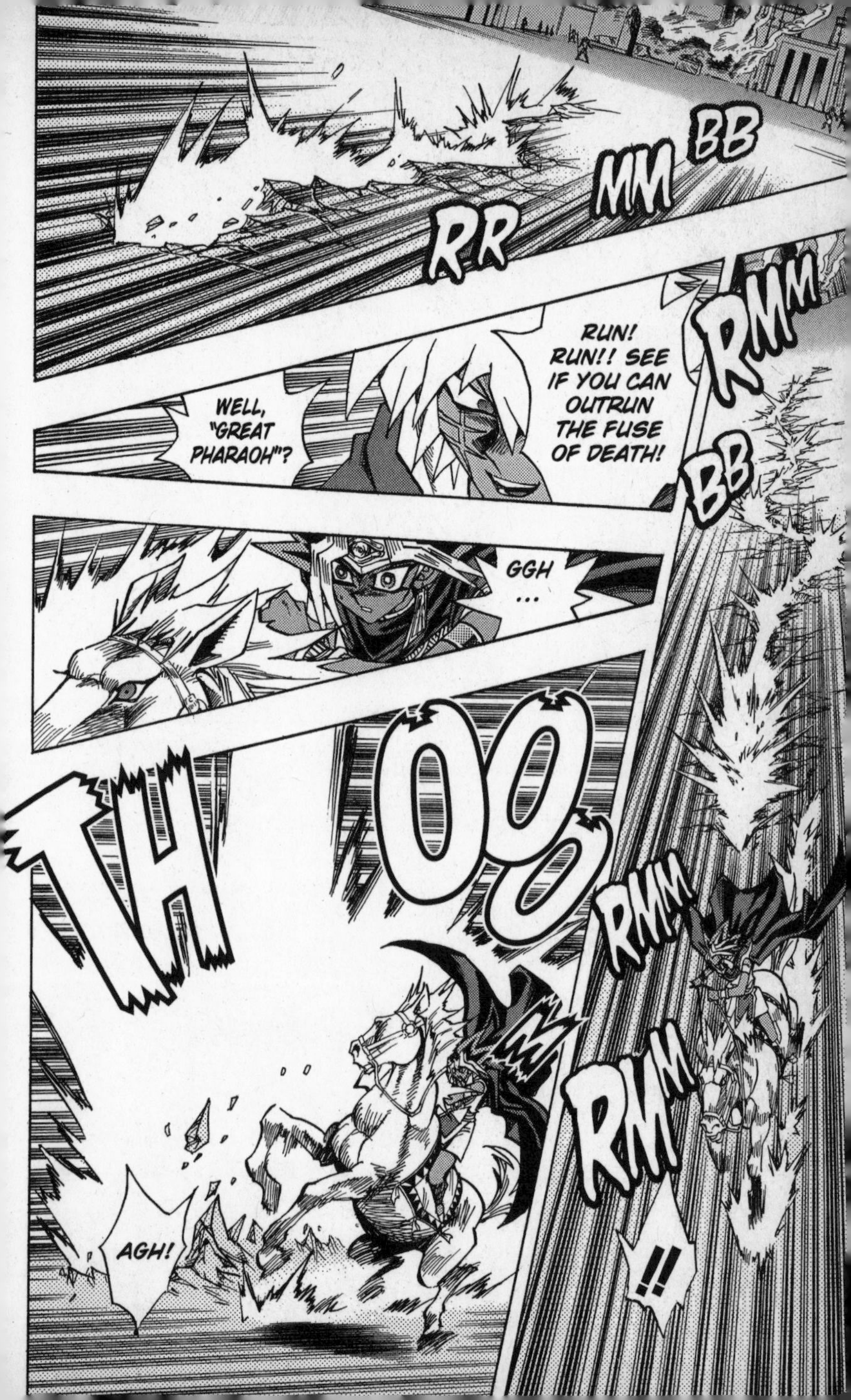
RR MM BB
RMM BB
RUN! RUN!! SEE IF YOU CAN OUTRUN THE FUSE OF DEATH!
WELL, "GREAT PHARAOH"?
GGH ...
THOOOM
RMM
RMM
!!
AGH!

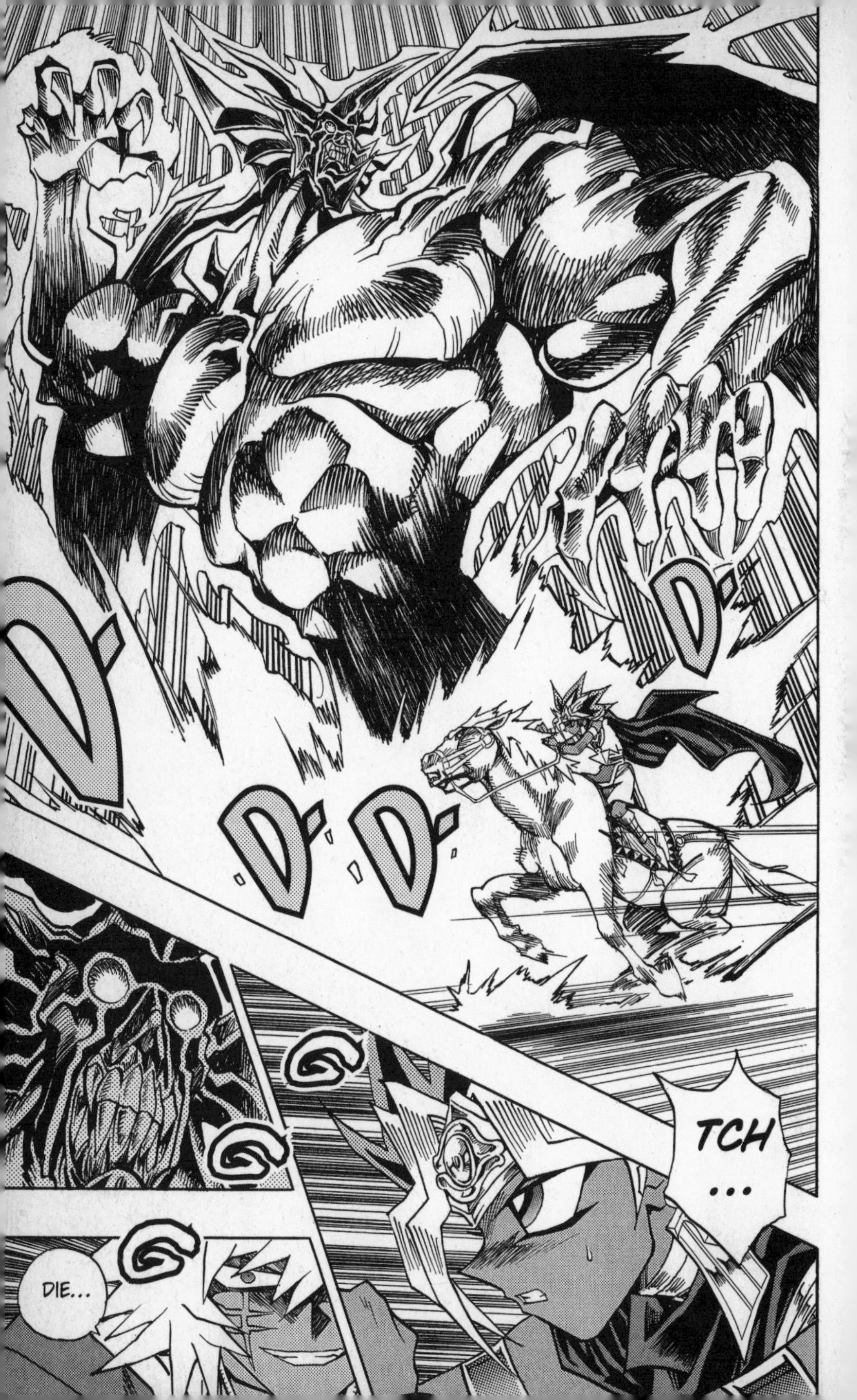
TCH ...
DIE...

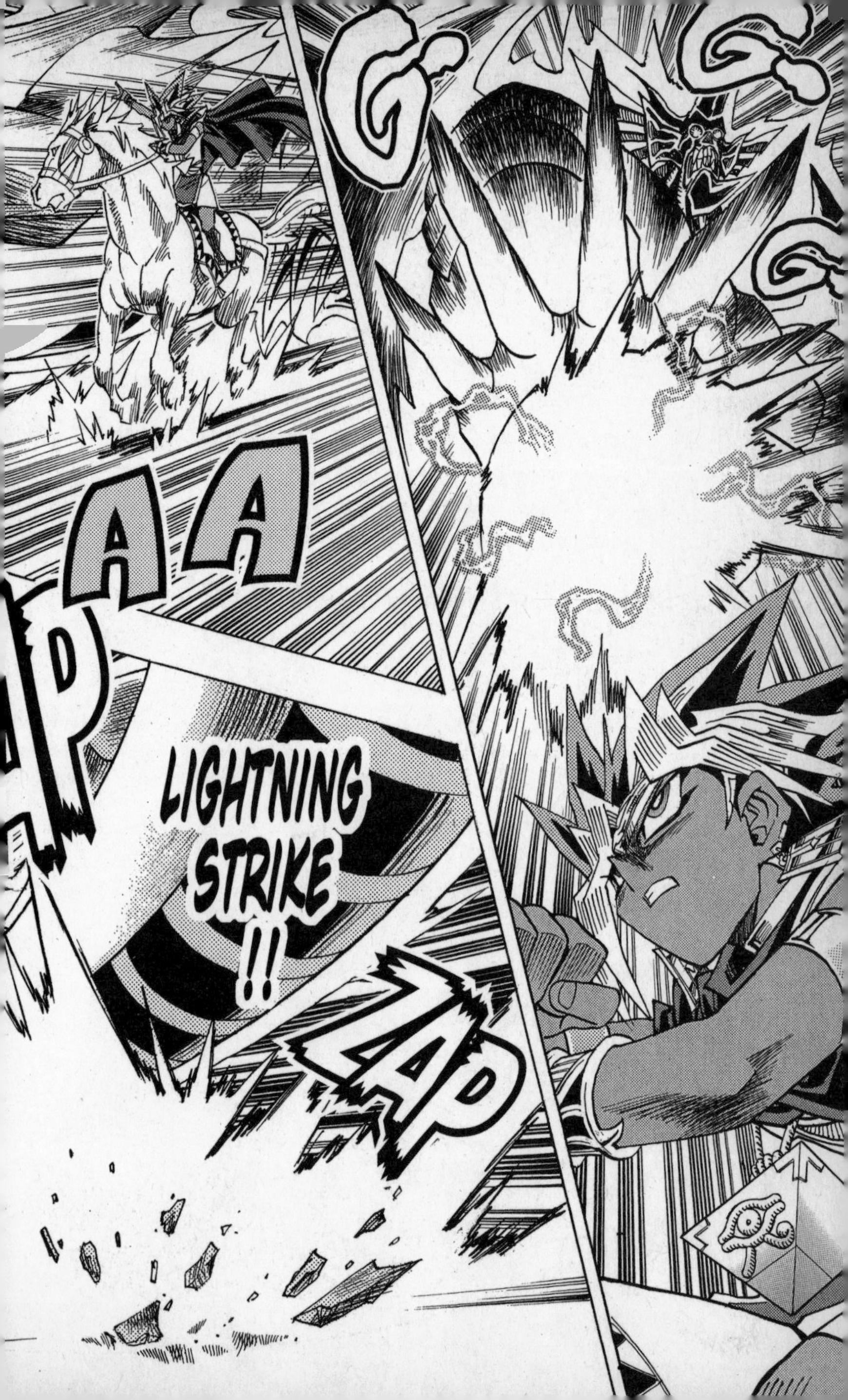
G
G
G
AP
A A
LIGHTNING STRIKE !!
ZAP

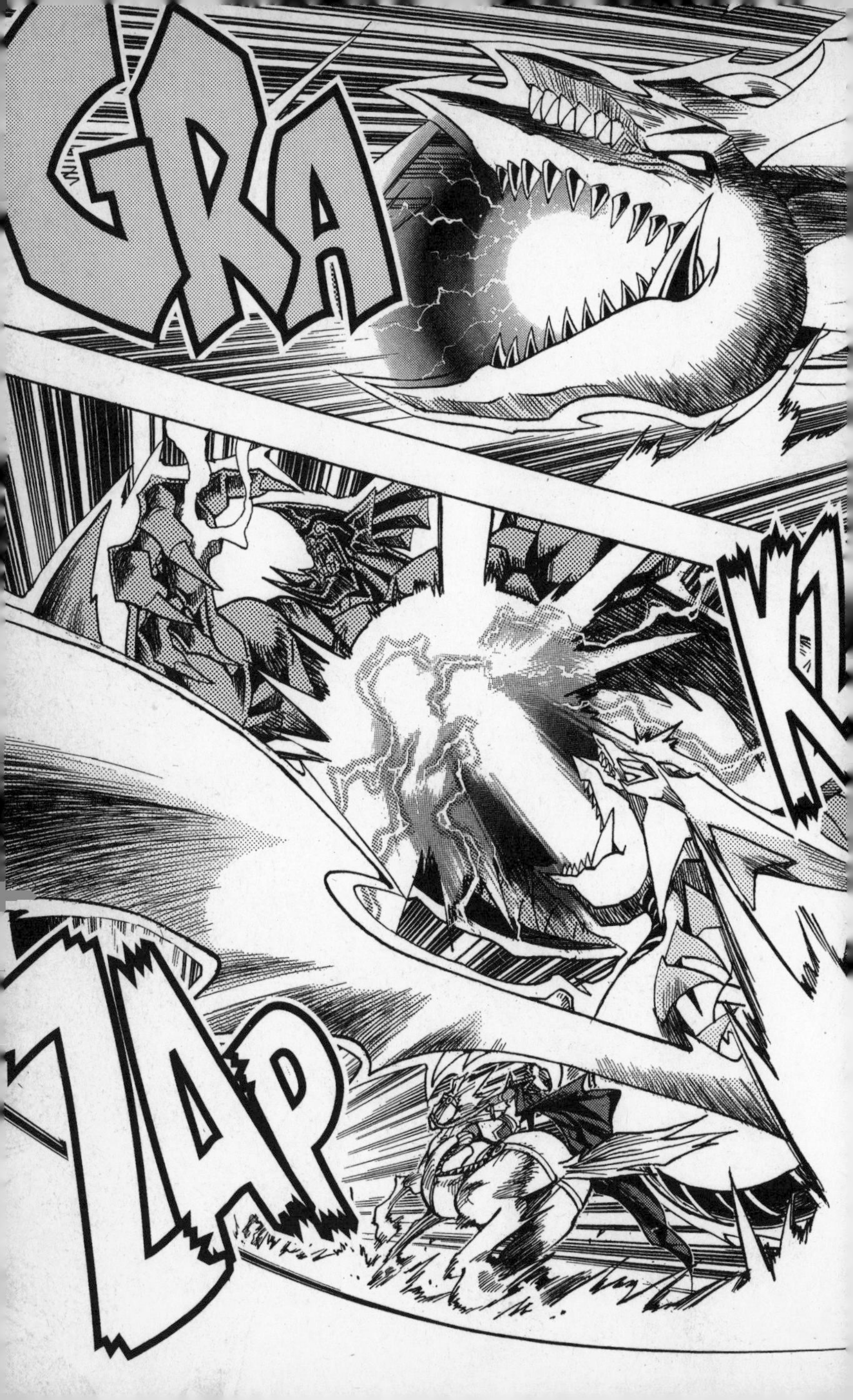
GRA
ZAP

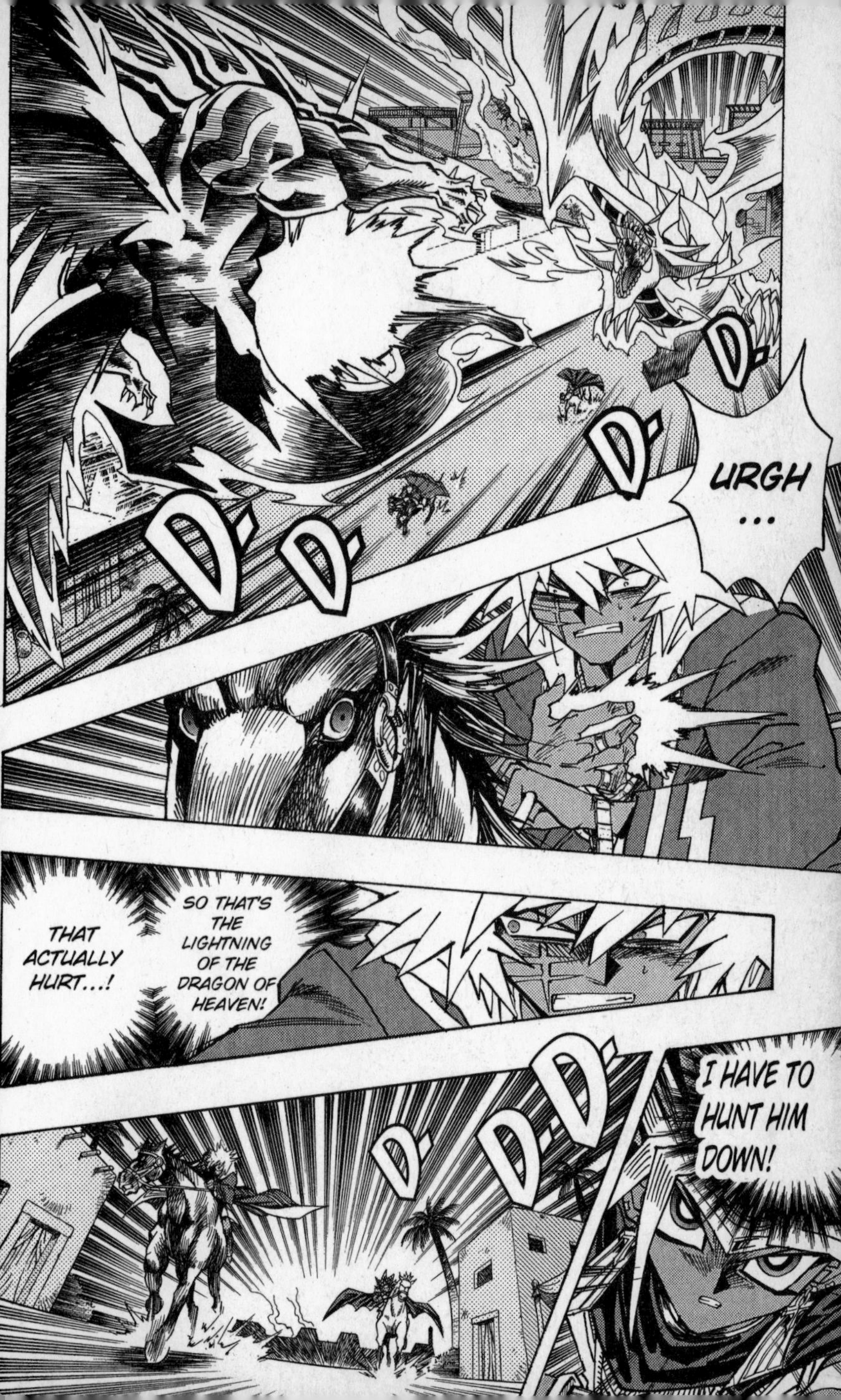
URGH...
SO THAT'S THE LIGHTNING OF THE DRAGON OF HEAVEN!
THAT ACTUALLY HURT...!
I HAVE TO HUNT HIM DOWN!

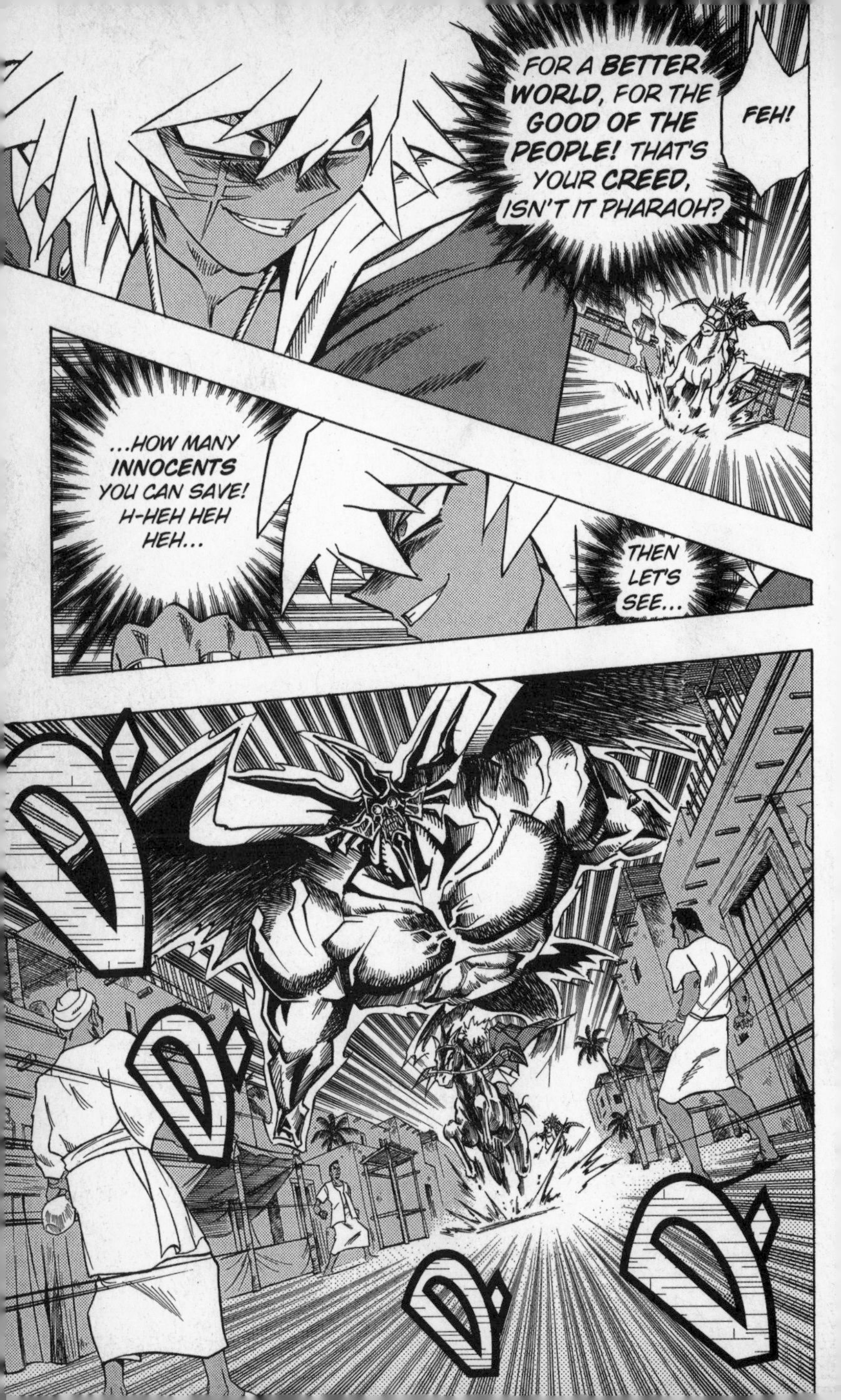
FEH!
FOR A BETTER WORLD, FOR THE GOOD OF THE PEOPLE! THAT'S YOUR CREED, ISN'T IT PHARAOH?
THEN LET'S SEE...
...HOW MANY INNOCENTS YOU CAN SAVE! H-HEH HEH HEH...

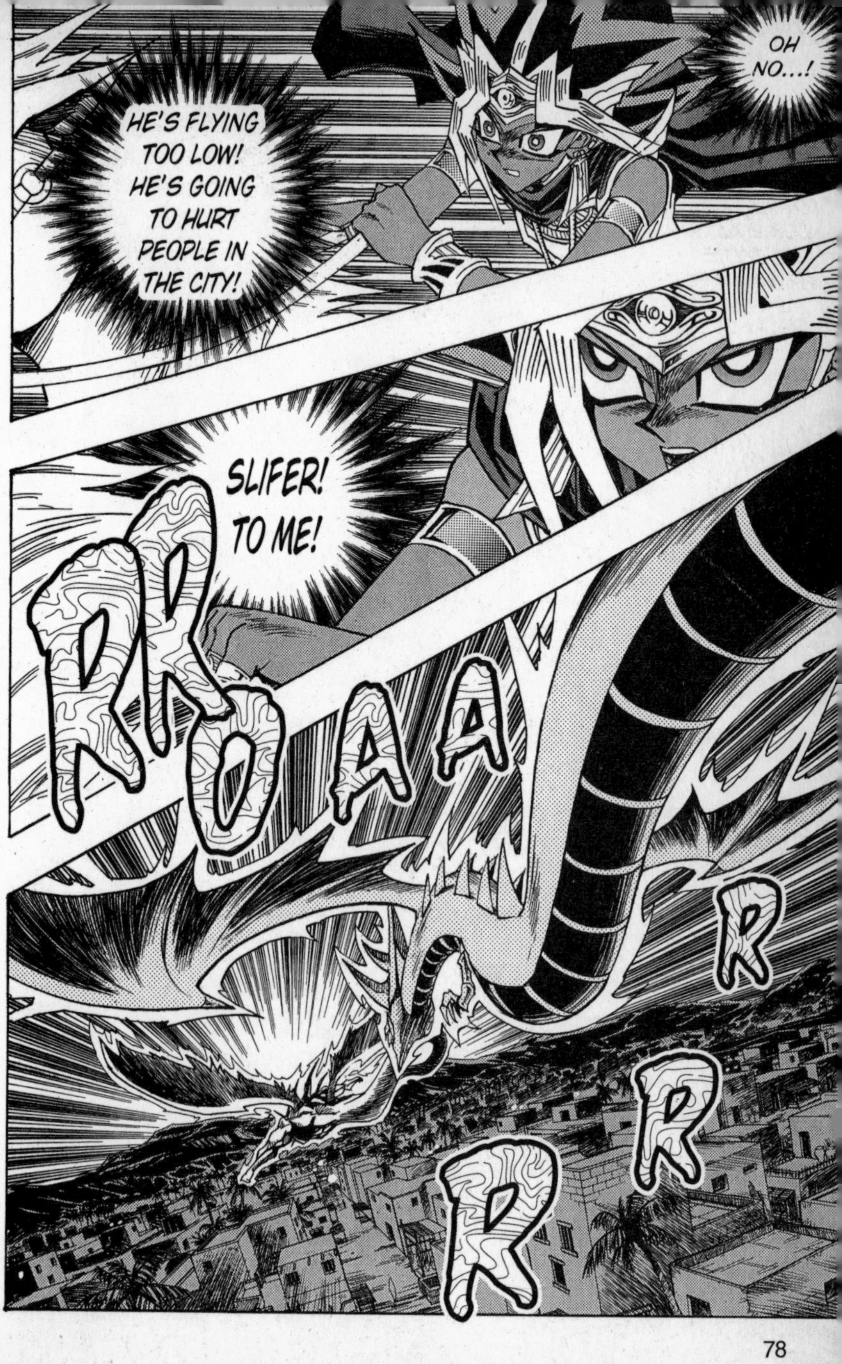
OH NO...!
HE'S FLYING TOO LOW! HE'S GOING TO HURT PEOPLE IN THE CITY!
SLIFER! TO ME!
RROAARRR

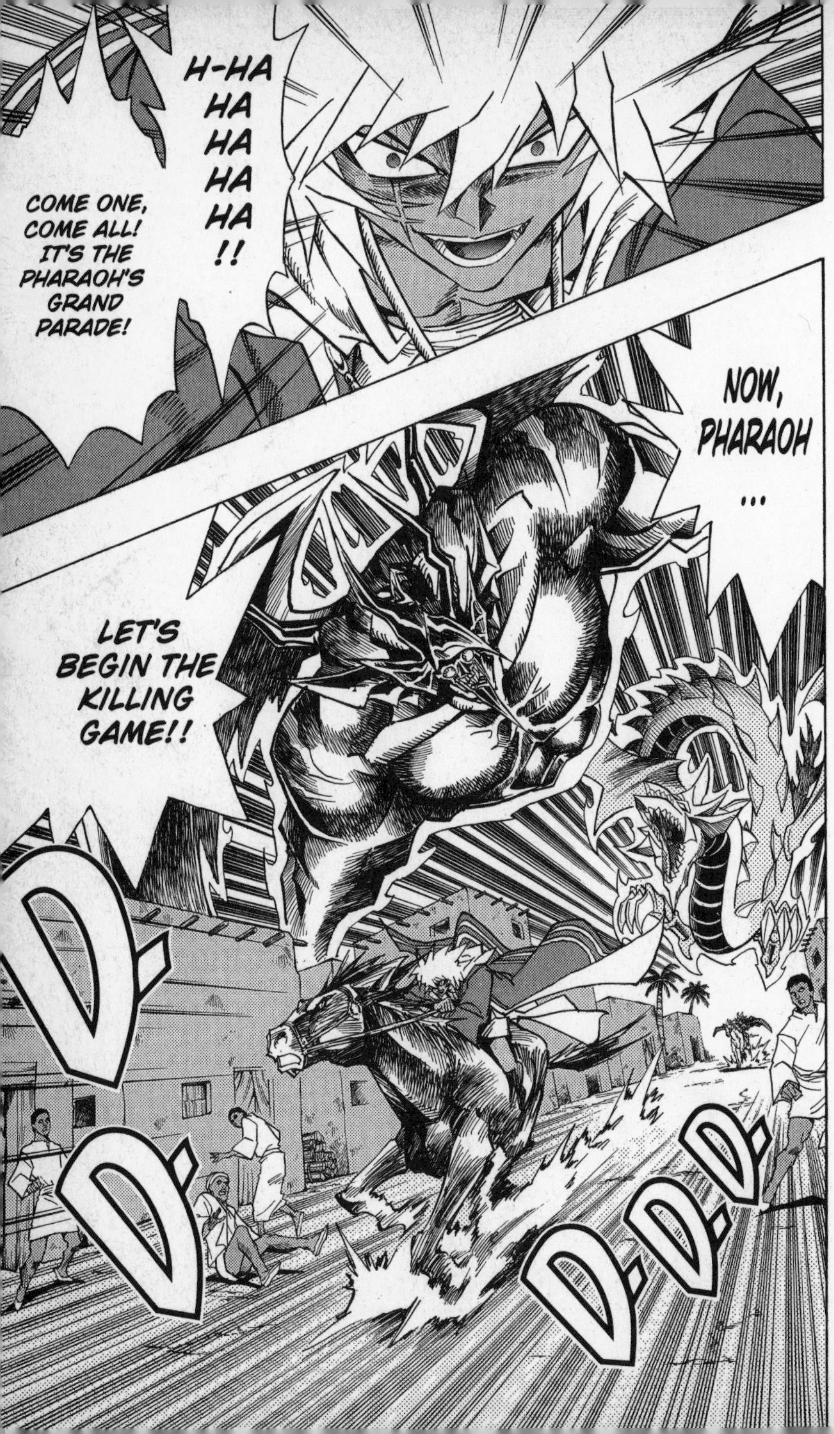
H-HA HA HA HA HA!!
COME ONE, COME ALL! IT'S THE PHARAOH'S GRAND PARADE!
NOW, PHARAOH...
LET'S BEGIN THE KILLING GAME!!
D.D.D.
D.
D.

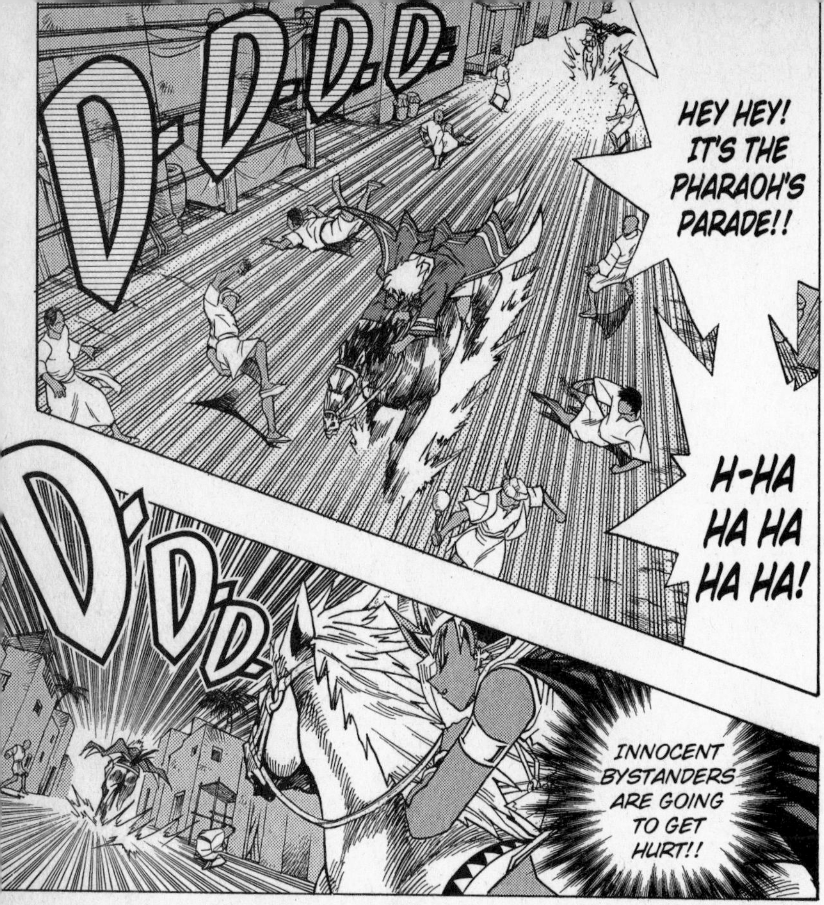
HEY HEY! IT'S THE PHARAOH'S PARADE!!
D-D-D-D
H-HA HA HA HA HA!
INNOCENT BYSTANDERS ARE GOING TO GET HURT!!
D-D-D

Duel 23: Divine Light, Divine Shadow

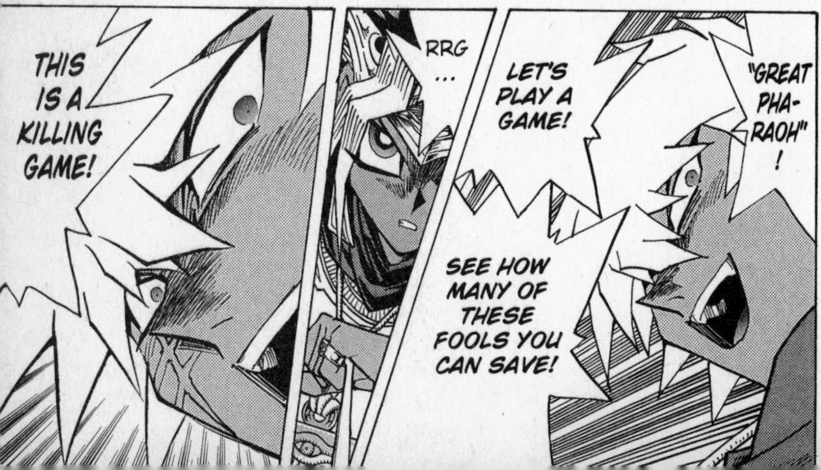
"GREAT PHARAOH"!
LET'S PLAY A GAME!
SEE HOW MANY OF THESE FOOLS YOU CAN SAVE!
RRG...
THIS IS A KILLING GAME!

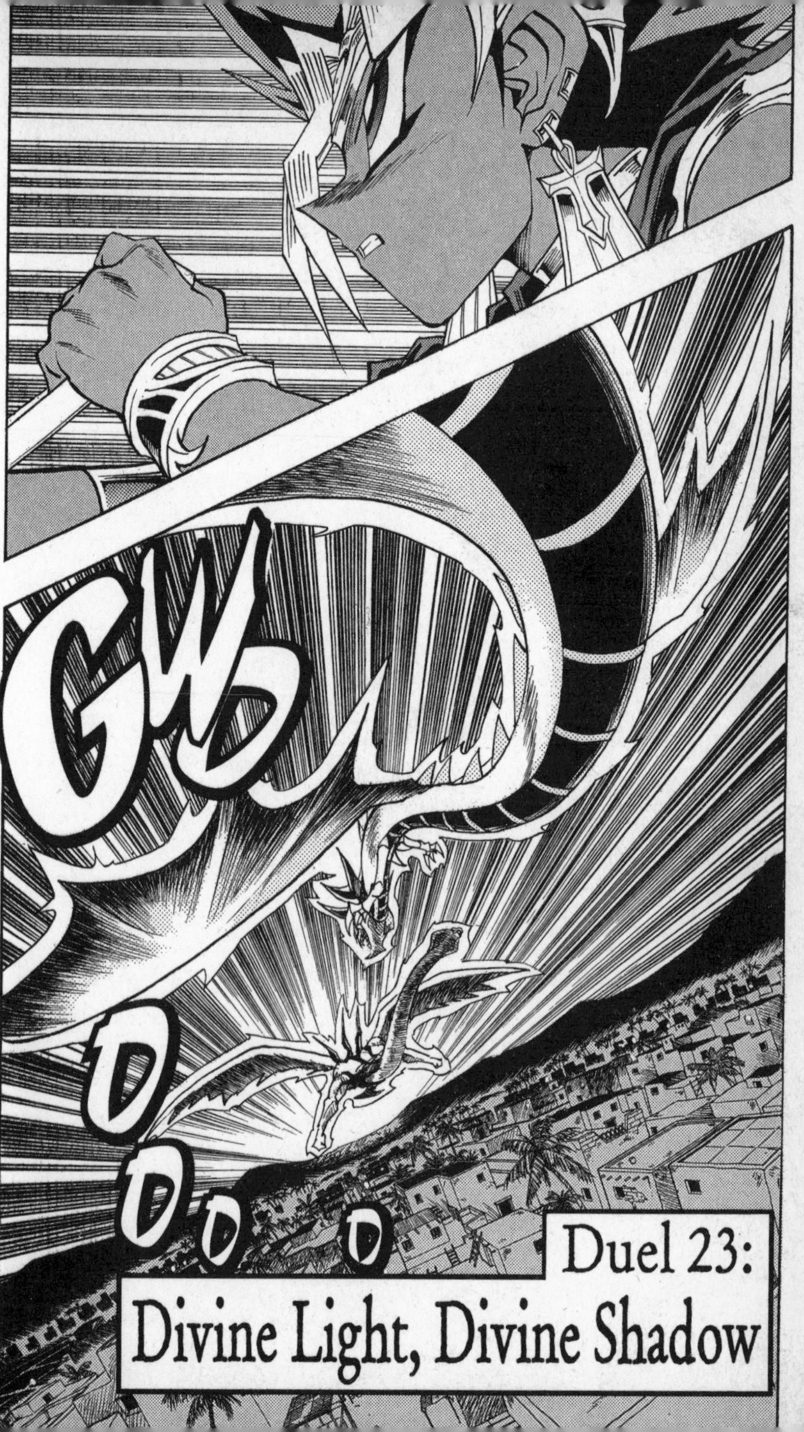
GW
D D D D D

Duel 23: Divine Light, Divine Shadow

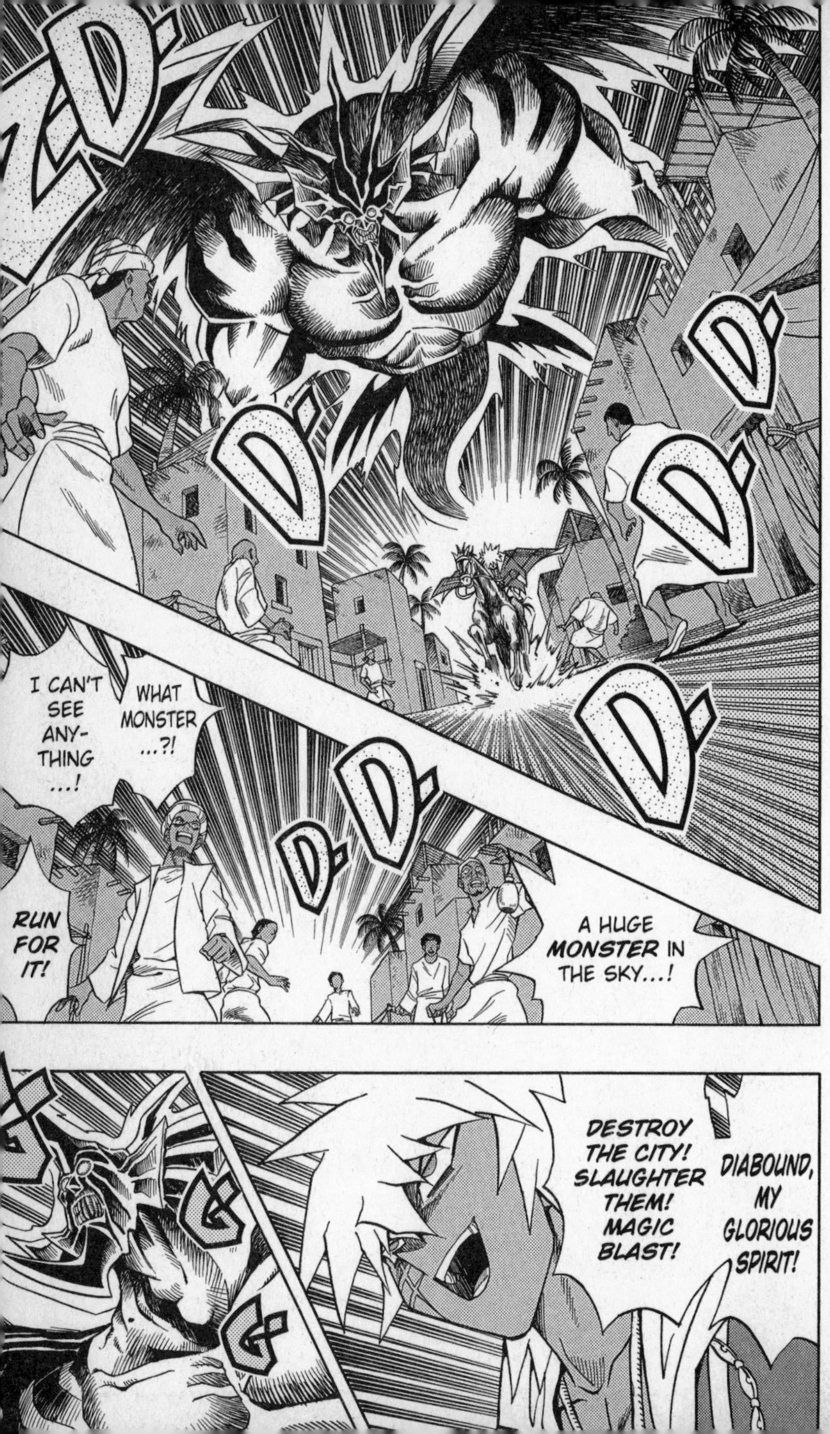

A HUGE MONSTER IN THE SKY...!
WHAT MONSTER ...?!
I CAN'T SEE ANYTHING ...!
RUN FOR IT!
DIABOUND, MY GLORIOUS SPIRIT!
DESTROY THE CITY! SLAUGHTER THEM! MAGIC BLAST!

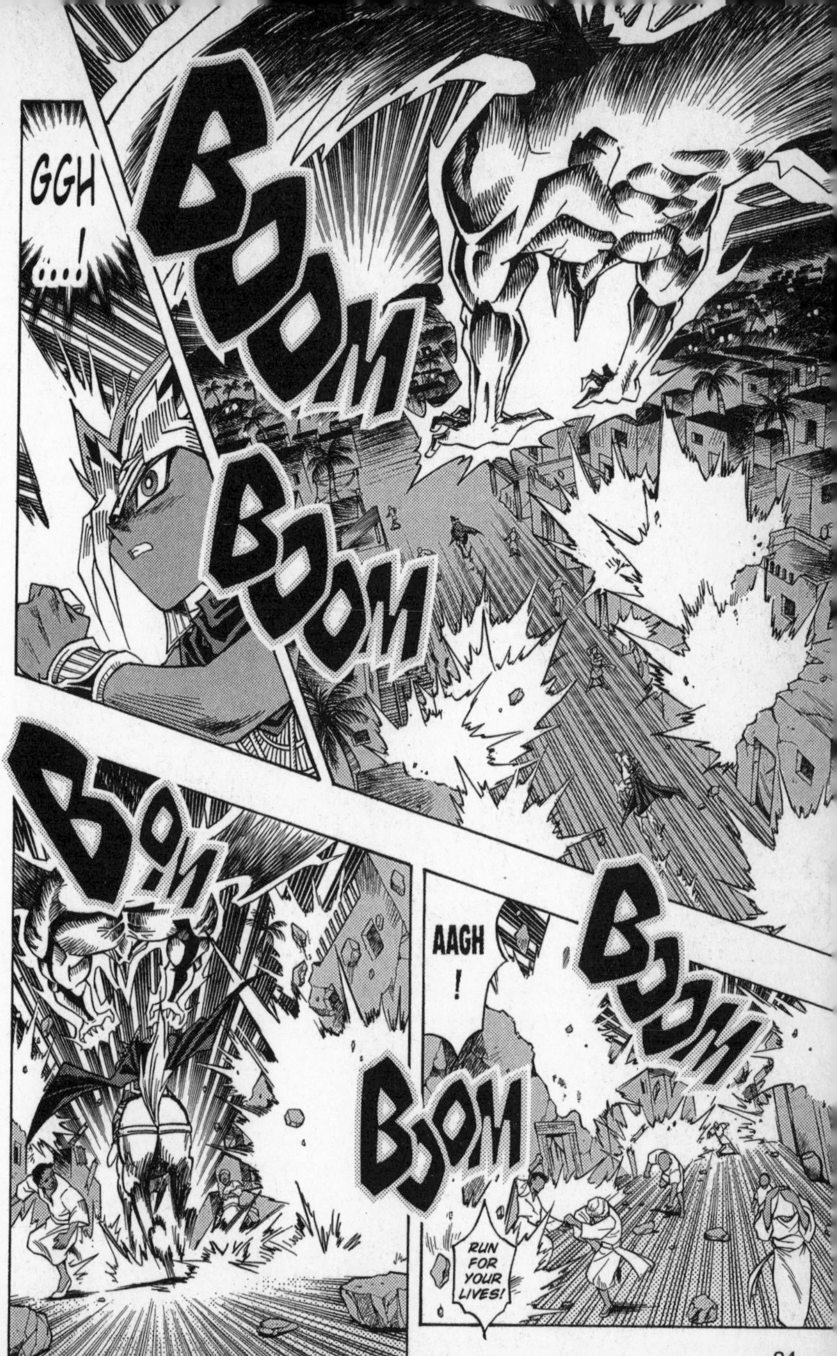
BOOM
BOOM
GGH...!
AAGH!
BOOM
BOOM
RUN FOR YOUR LIVES!
BOOM

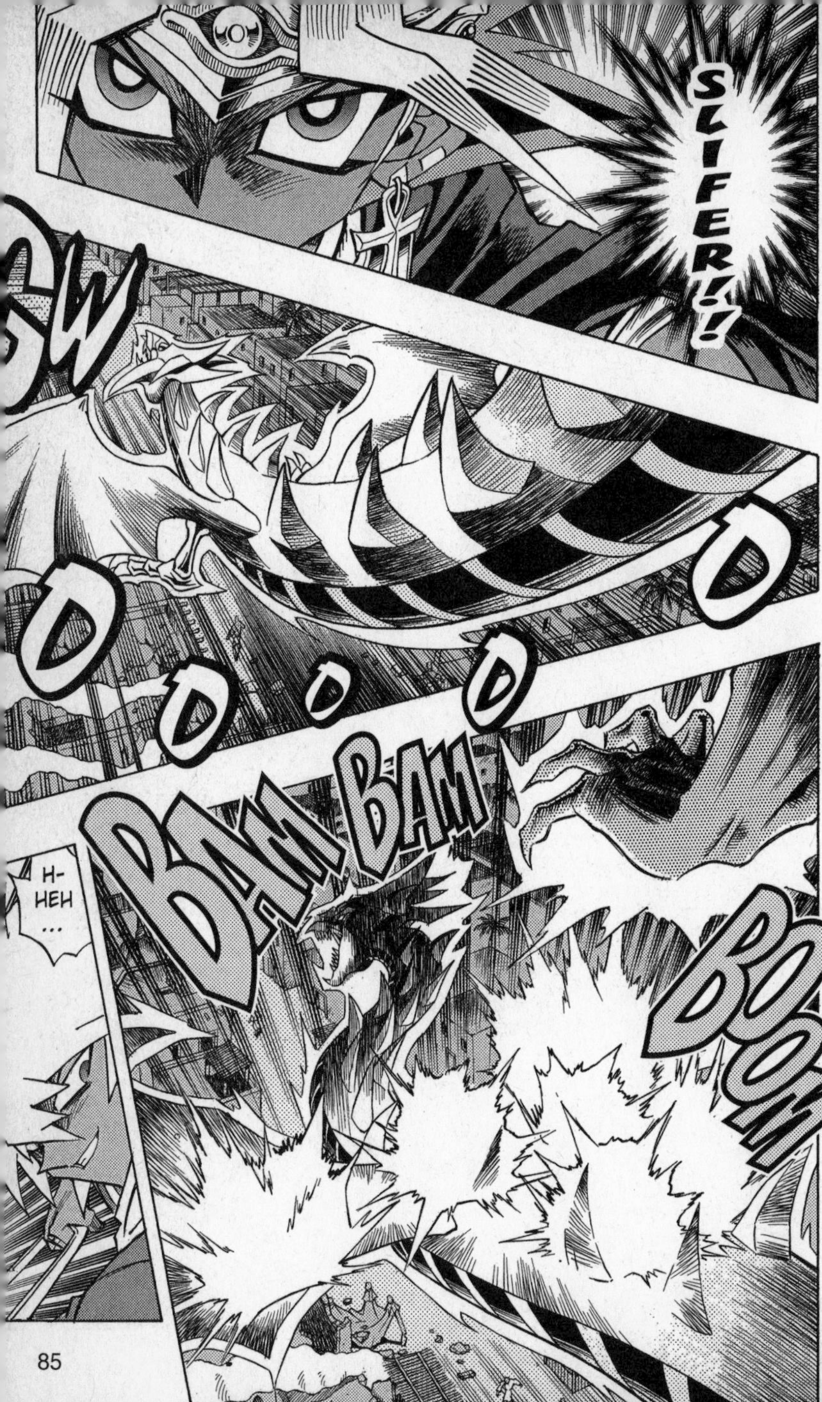
SLIFER!!
GW
D
D
D
D
D
BOOM
BAM
BAM
H-HEH ...

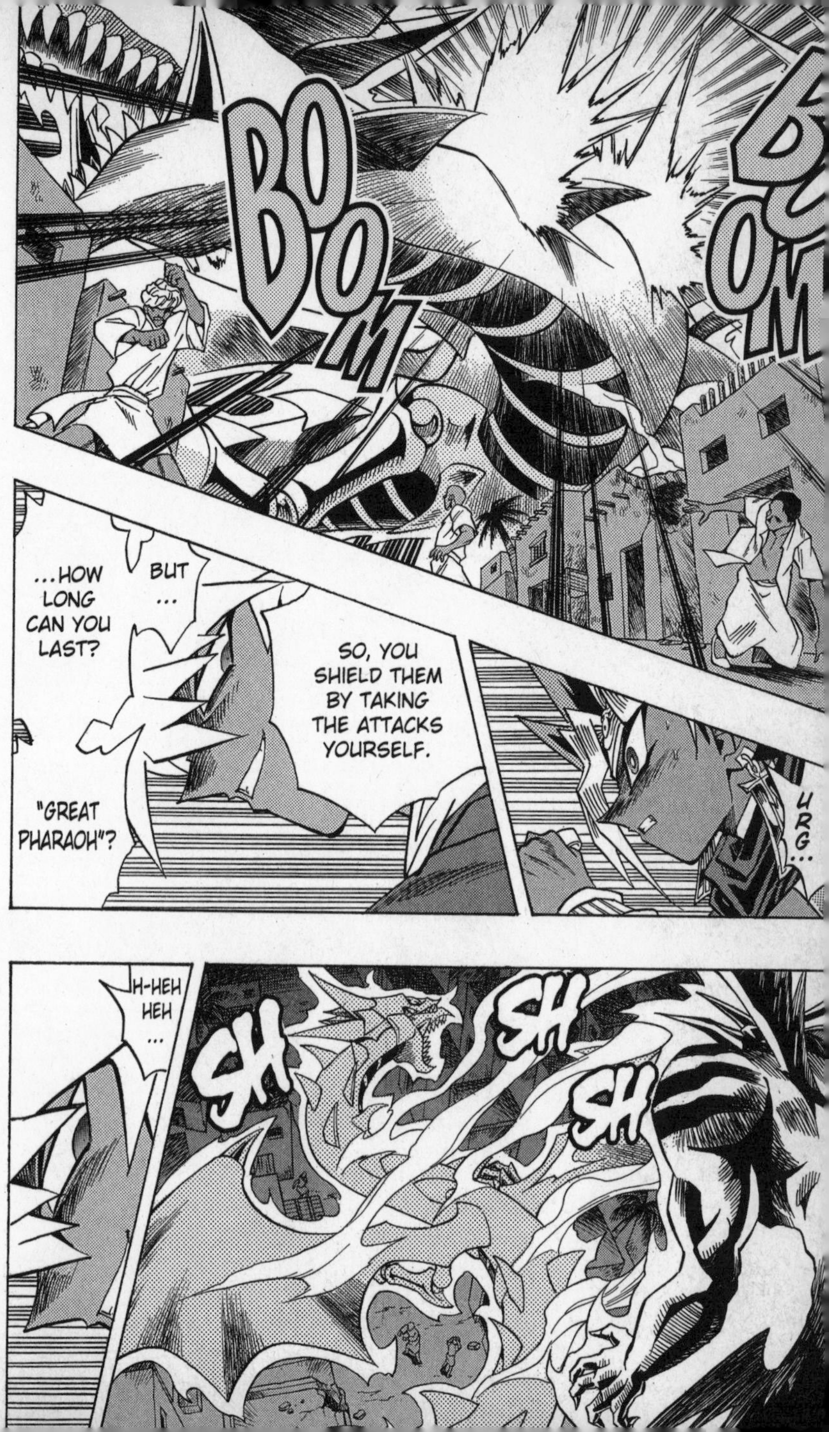
BOOM
BOOM
URG...
SO, YOU SHIELD THEM BY TAKING THE ATTACKS YOURSELF.
BUT ...
...HOW LONG CAN YOU LAST?
"GREAT PHARAOH"?
SH
SH
SH
H-HEH HEH ...

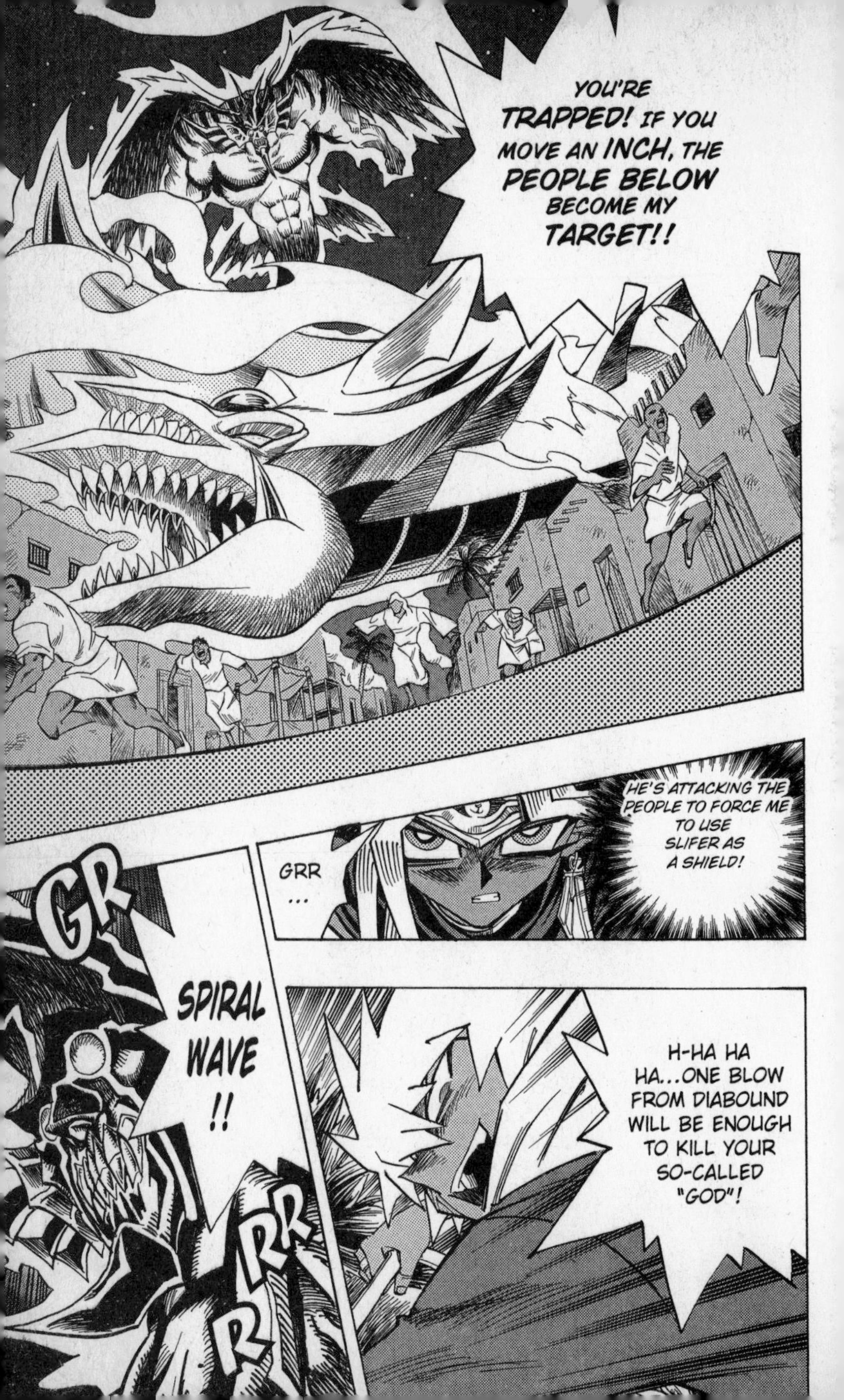
YOU'RE TRAPPED! IF YOU MOVE AN INCH, THE PEOPLE BELOW BECOME MY TARGET!!
HE'S ATTACKING THE PEOPLE TO FORCE ME TO USE SLIFER AS A SHIELD!
GRR ...
H-HA HA HA...ONE BLOW FROM DIABOUND WILL BE ENOUGH TO KILL YOUR SO-CALLED "GOD"!
GR
SPIRAL WAVE !!
RRR

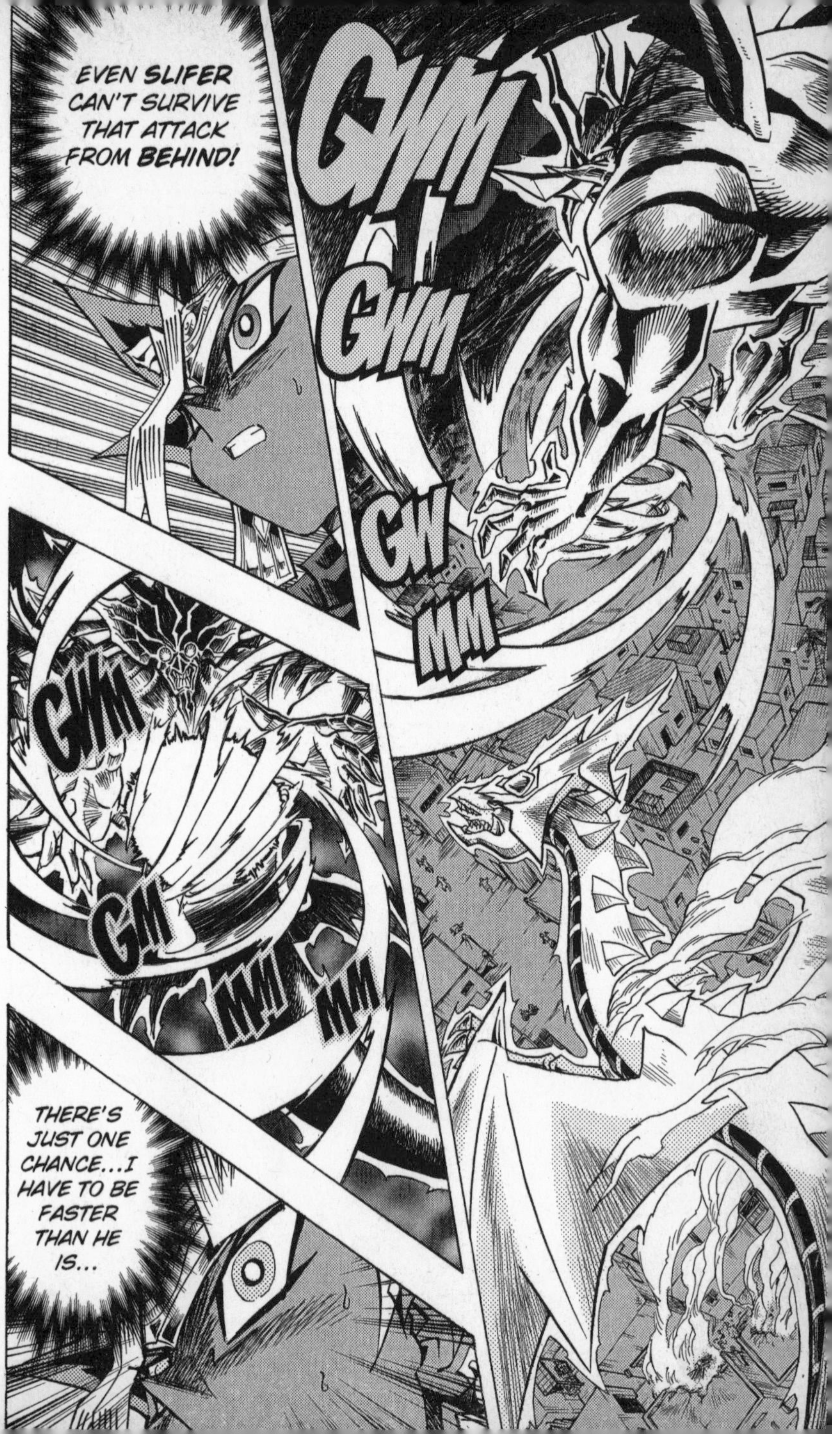

GWM
GWM
GW
MM
EVEN SLIFER CAN'T SURVIVE THAT ATTACK FROM BEHIND!
GWM
GM
MM
MM
THERE'S JUST ONE CHANCE...I HAVE TO BE FASTER THAN HE IS...

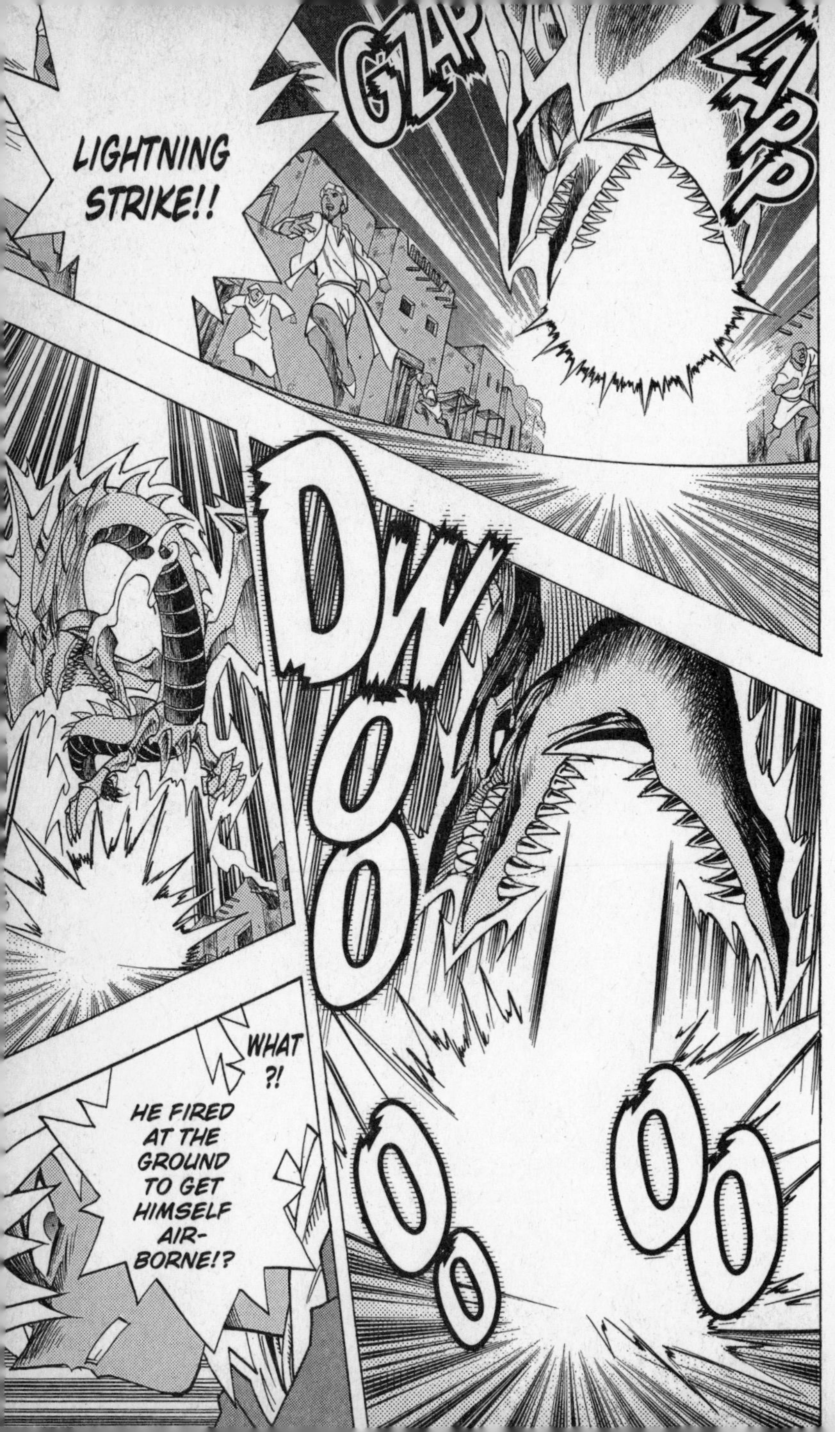
ZAPP
GZAP
LIGHTNING STRIKE!!
DWOOOOOO
WHAT ?!
HE FIRED AT THE GROUND TO GET HIMSELF AIR-BORNE!?

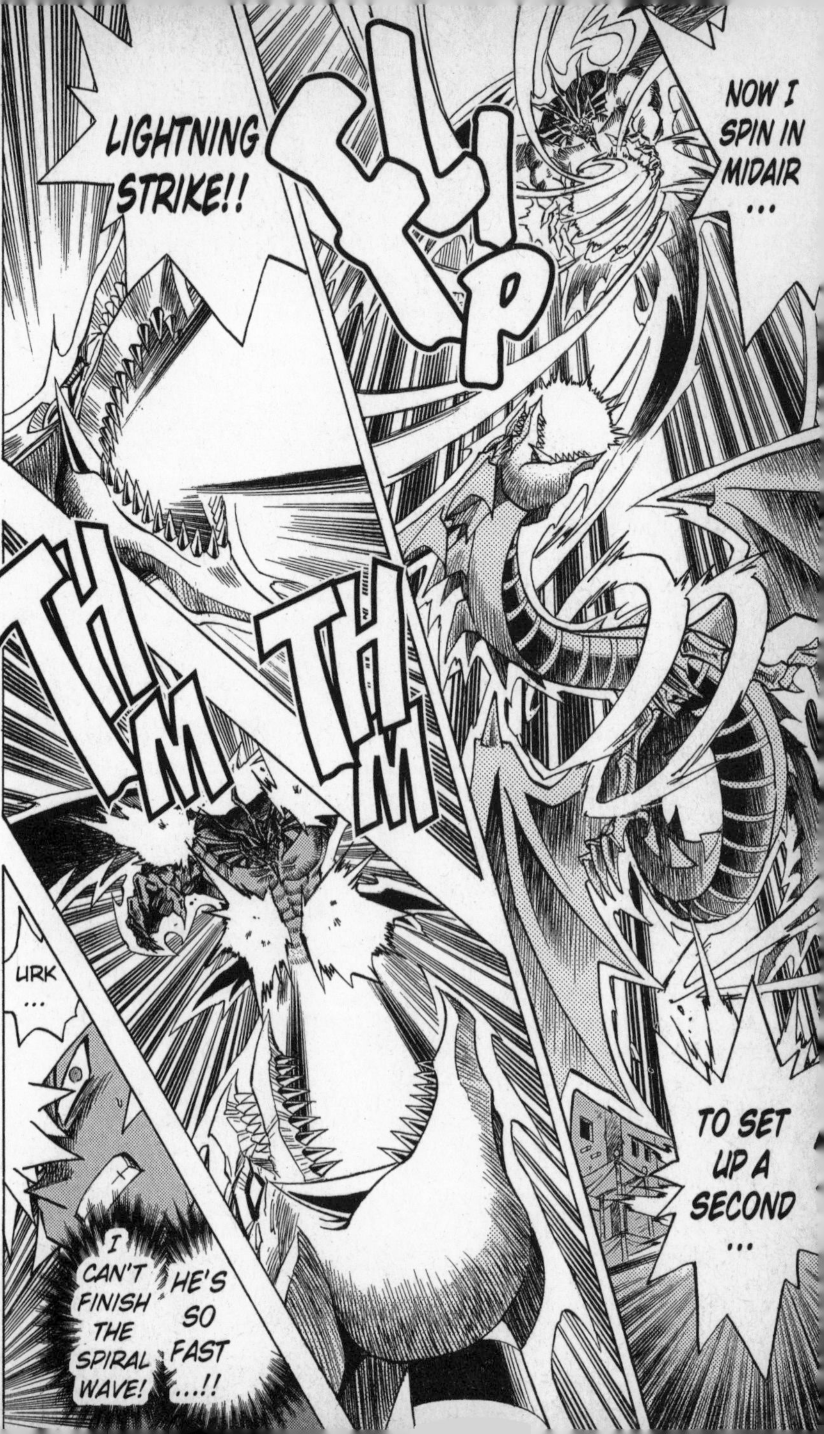
NOW I SPIN IN MIDAIR ...
FLIP
LIGHTNING STRIKE!!
THM
THM
TO SET UP A SECOND ...
URK ...
HE'S SO FAST ...!!
I CAN'T FINISH THE SPIRAL WAVE!

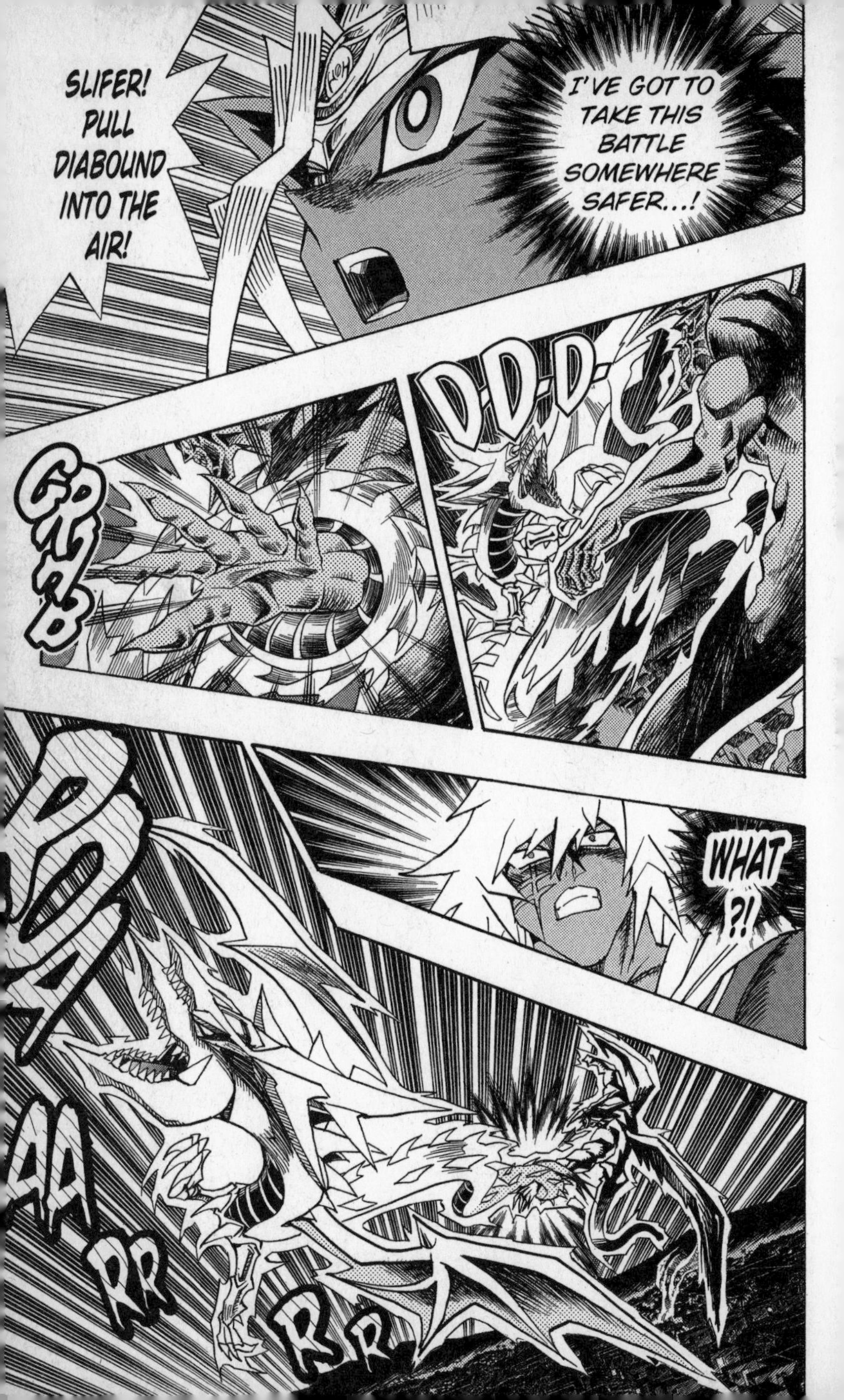
I'VE GOT TO TAKE THIS BATTLE SOMEWHERE SAFER...!
SLIFER! PULL DIABOUND INTO THE AIR!
D-D-D-
GRAB
WHAT ?!

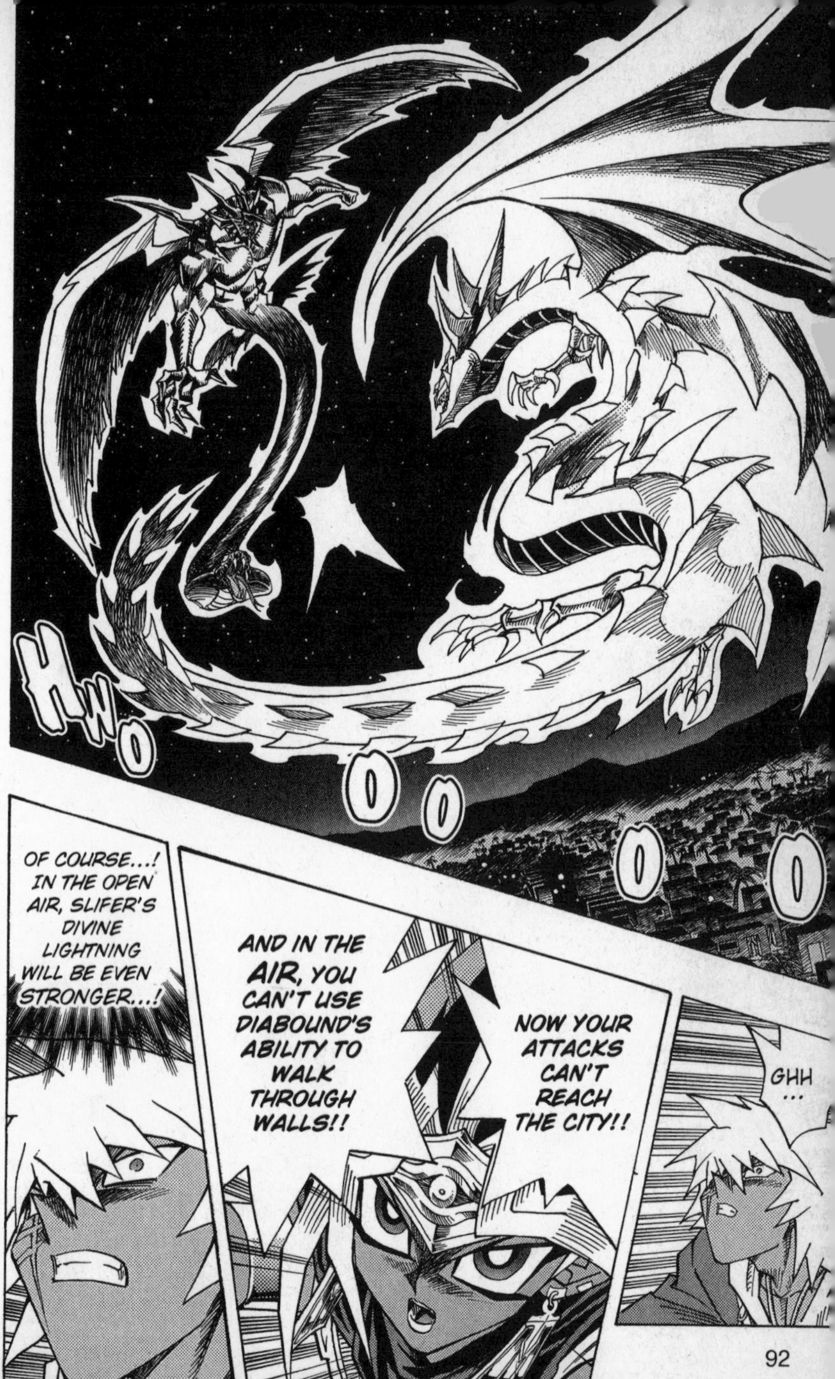
HWOOOOO
GHH...
NOW YOUR ATTACKS CAN'T REACH THE CITY!!
AND IN THE AIR, YOU CAN'T USE DIABOUND'S ABILITY TO WALK THROUGH WALLS!!
OF COURSE...! IN THE OPEN AIR, SLIFER'S DIVINE LIGHTNING WILL BE EVEN STRONGER...!

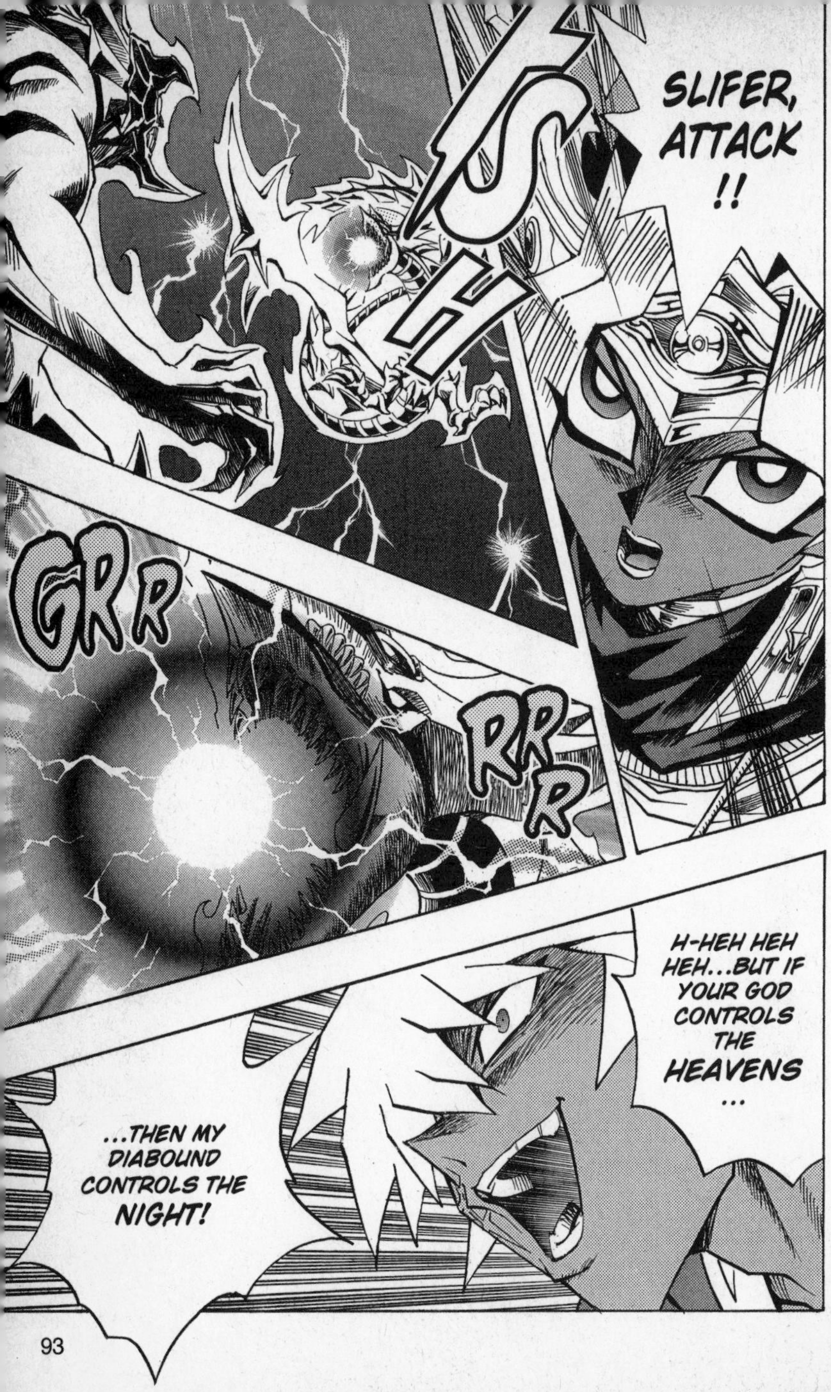
SLIFER, ATTACK!!
SH
GRR
RRR
H-HEH HEH HEH...BUT IF YOUR GOD CONTROLS THE HEAVENS...
...THEN MY DIABOUND CONTROLS THE NIGHT!

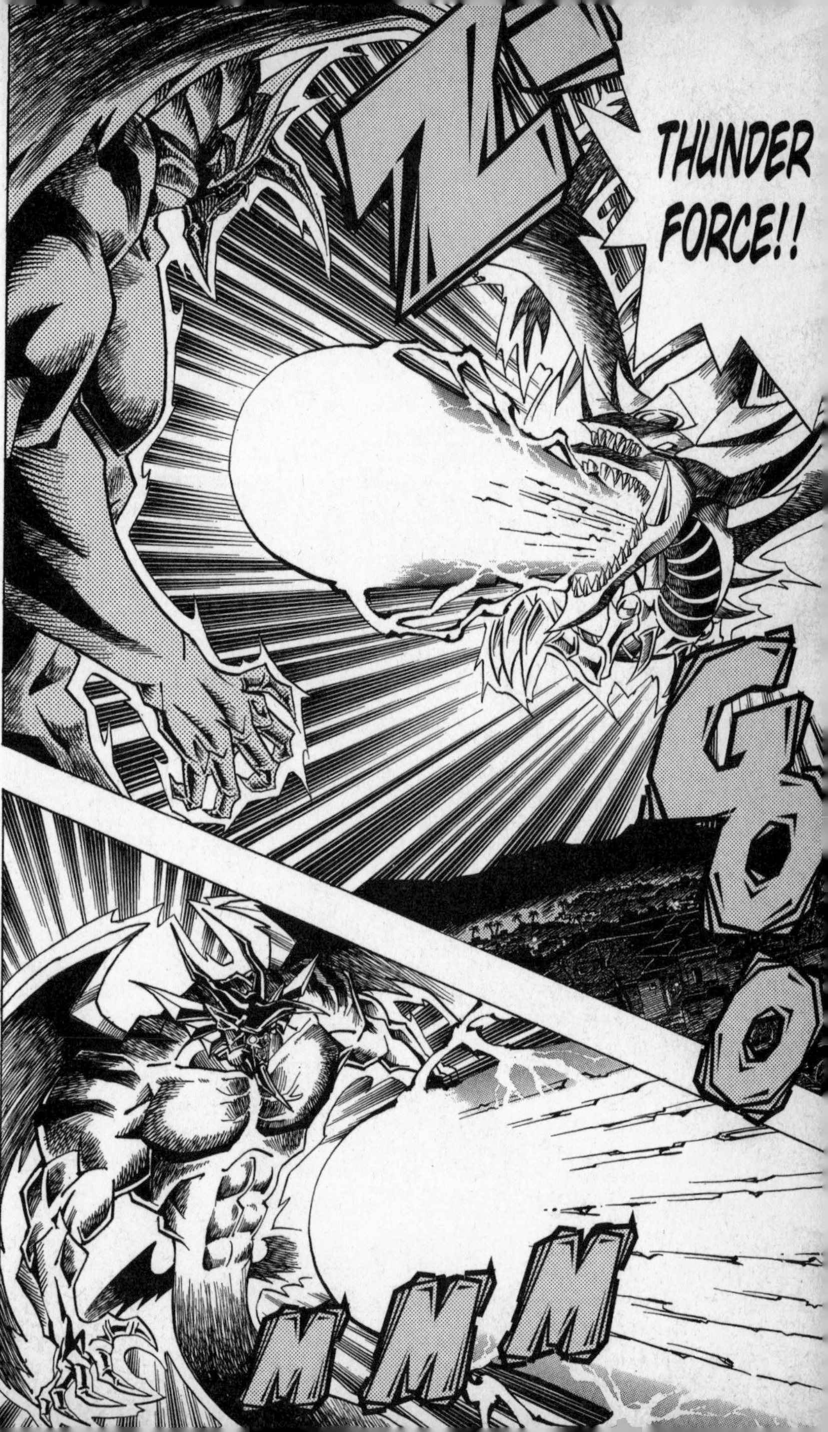
THUNDER FORCE!!
GO
MMM

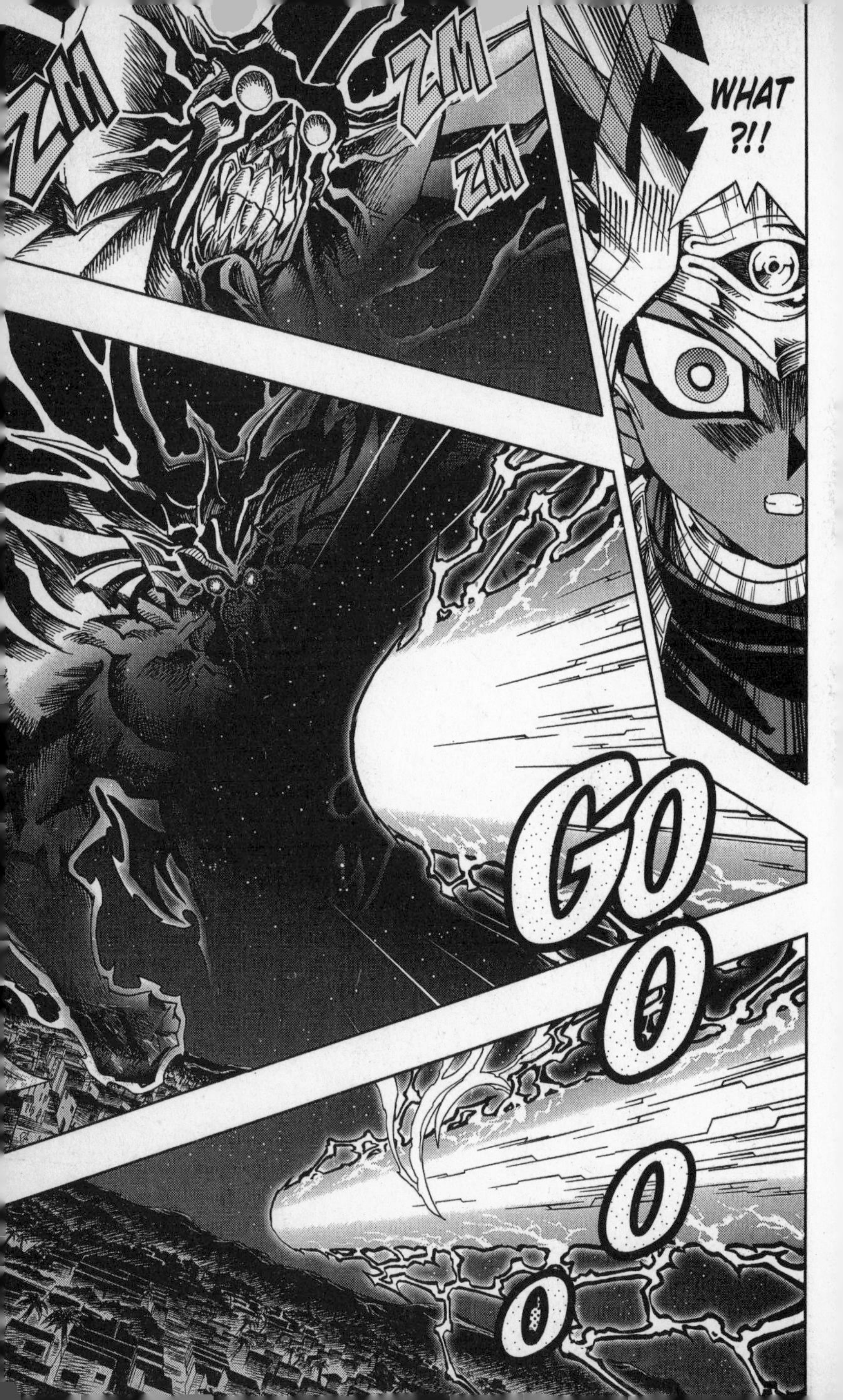
WHAT ?!!
Z-M
ZM
ZM
GOOOO

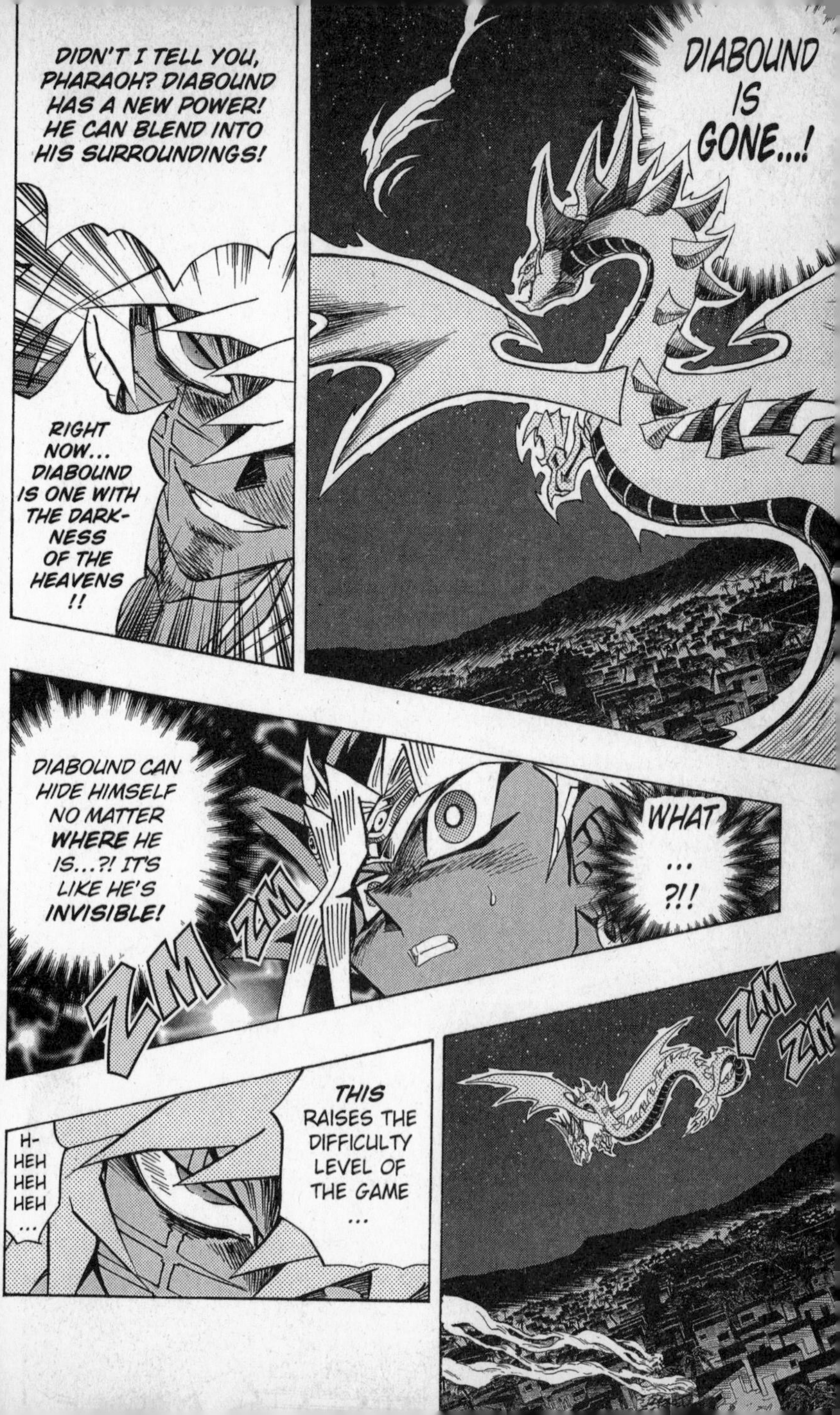
DIABOUND IS GONE...!
DIDN'T I TELL YOU, PHARAOH? DIABOUND HAS A NEW POWER! HE CAN BLEND INTO HIS SURROUNDINGS!
RIGHT NOW... DIABOUND IS ONE WITH THE DARKNESS OF THE HEAVENS!!
WHAT...?!!
DIABOUND CAN HIDE HIMSELF NO MATTER WHERE HE IS...?! IT'S LIKE HE'S INVISIBLE!
ZM
ZM
ZM
ZM
ZM
THIS RAISES THE DIFFICULTY LEVEL OF THE GAME...
H-HEH HEH HEH...

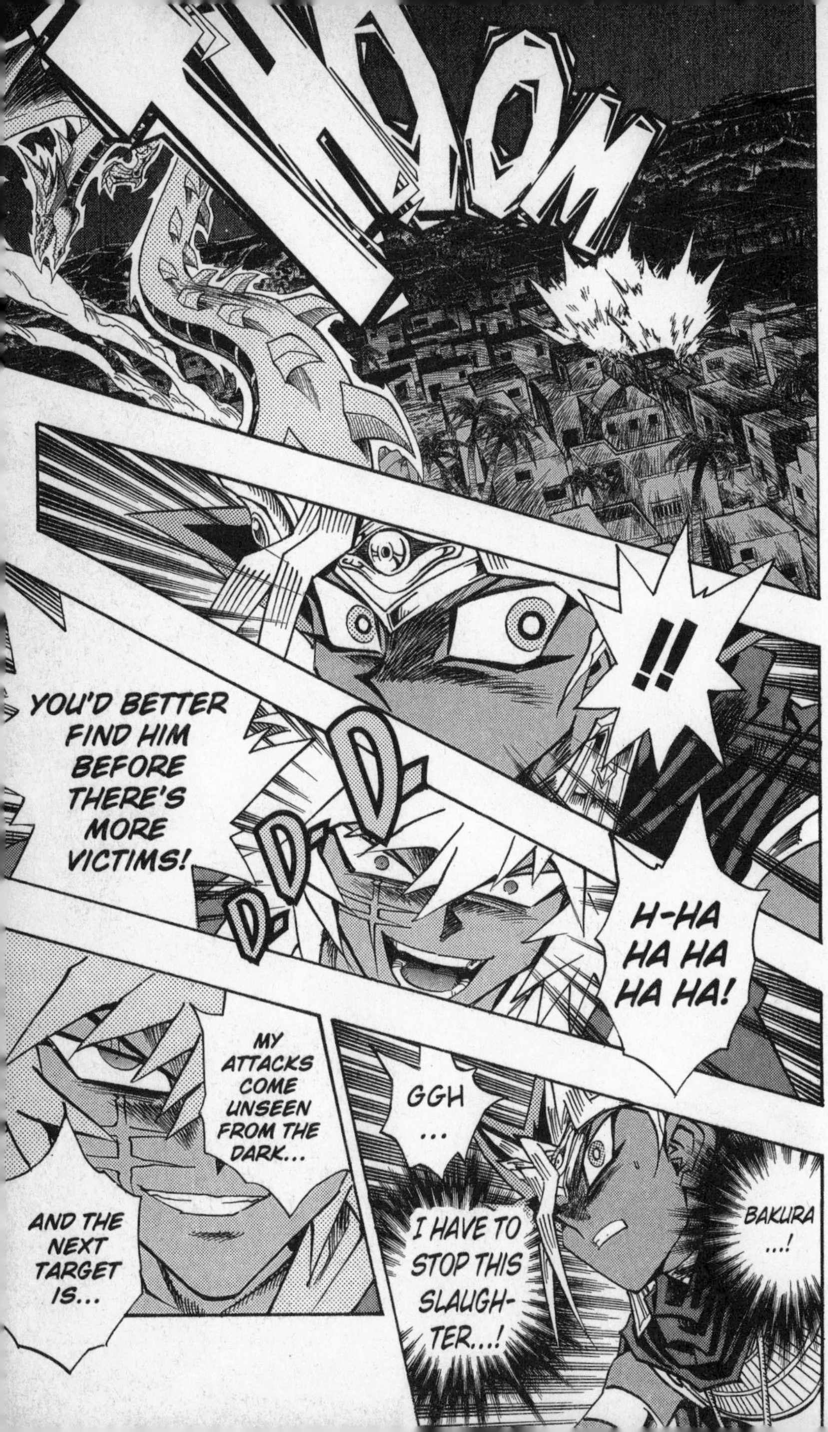
THOOM
!!
YOU'D BETTER FIND HIM BEFORE THERE'S MORE VICTIMS!
H-HA HA HA HA HA!
GGH ...
BAKURA ...!
I HAVE TO STOP THIS SLAUGH-TER...!
MY ATTACKS COME UNSEEN FROM THE DARK...
AND THE NEXT TARGET IS...

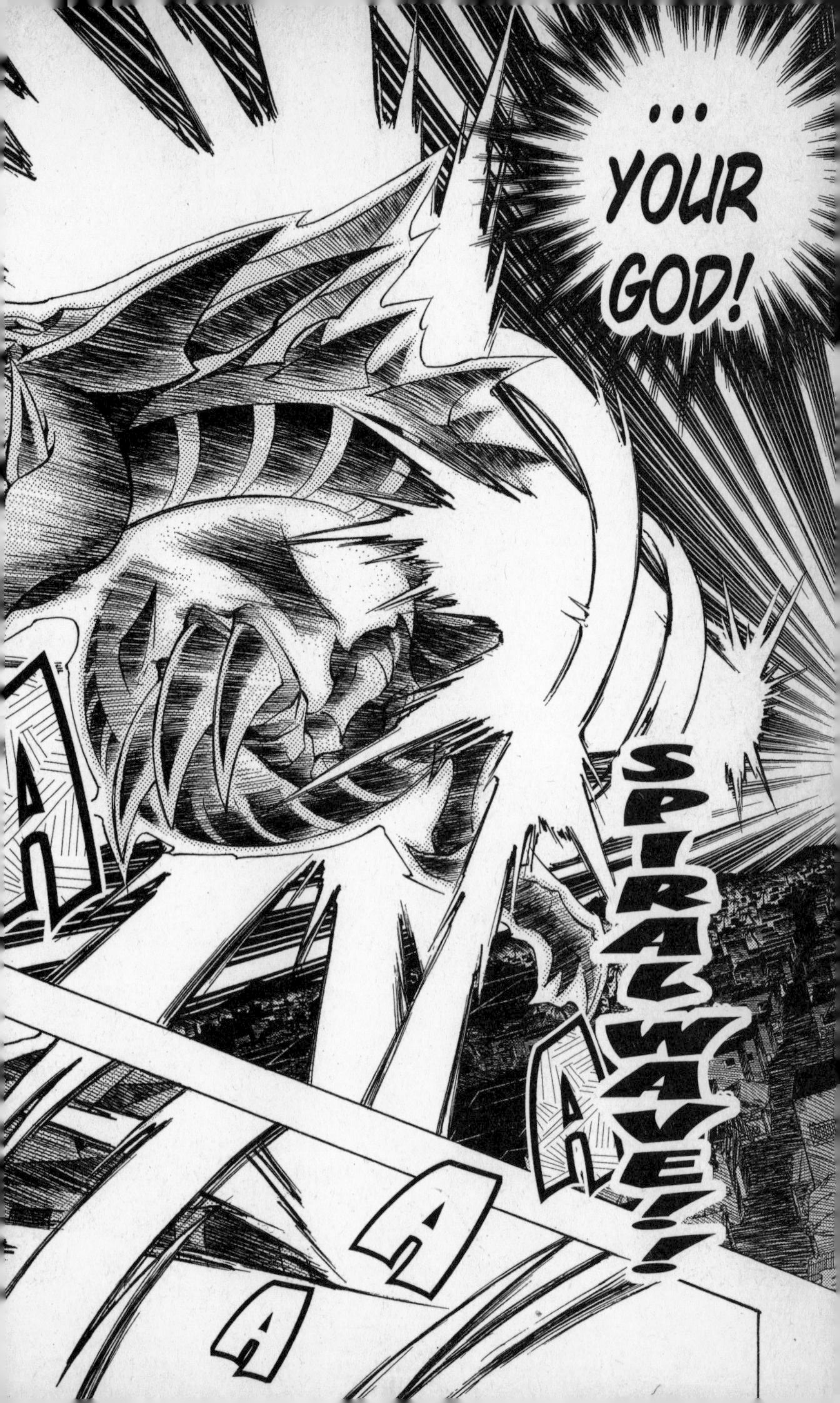

... YOUR GOD!
SPIRAL WAVE!!
AAAAA

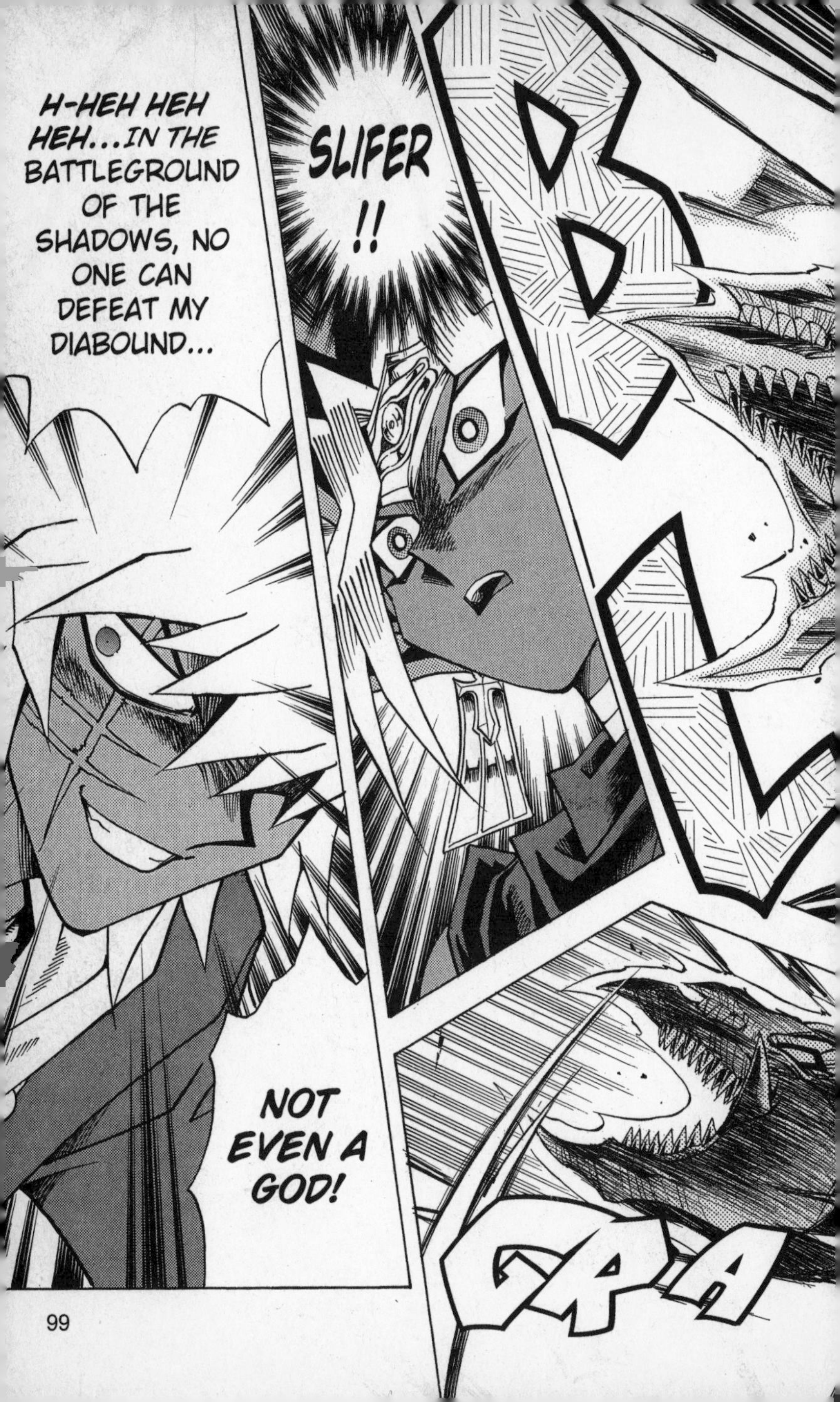
SLIFER !!
CRA
H-HEH HEH HEH...IN THE BATTLEGROUND OF THE SHADOWS, NO ONE CAN DEFEAT MY DIABOUND...
NOT EVEN A GOD!

Duel 24: Surprise Attack! Power Attack!

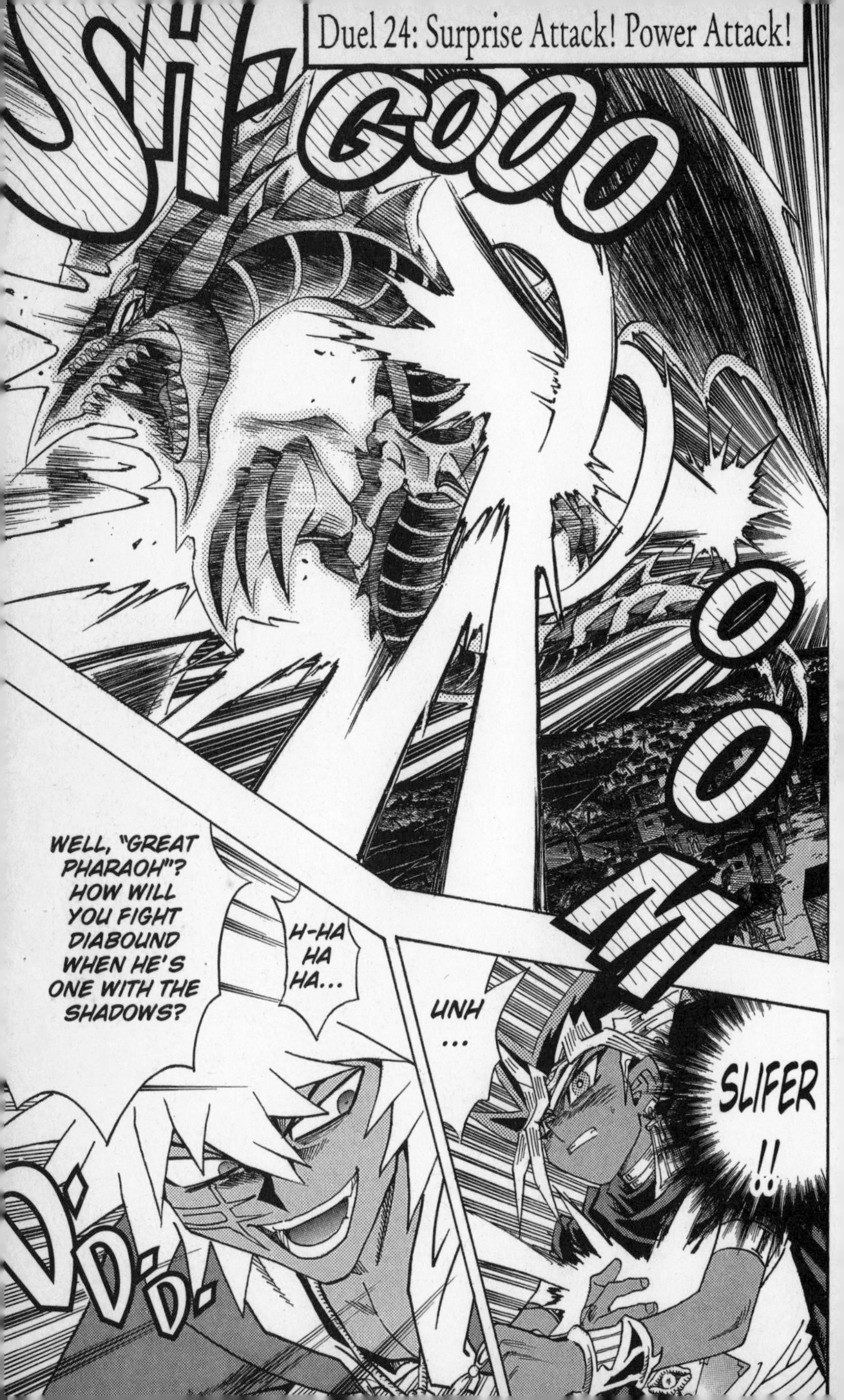

SHGOOOOOOM
WELL, "GREAT PHARAOH"? HOW WILL YOU FIGHT DIABOUND WHEN HE'S ONE WITH THE SHADOWS?
H-HA HA HA...
UNH ...
SLIFER !!

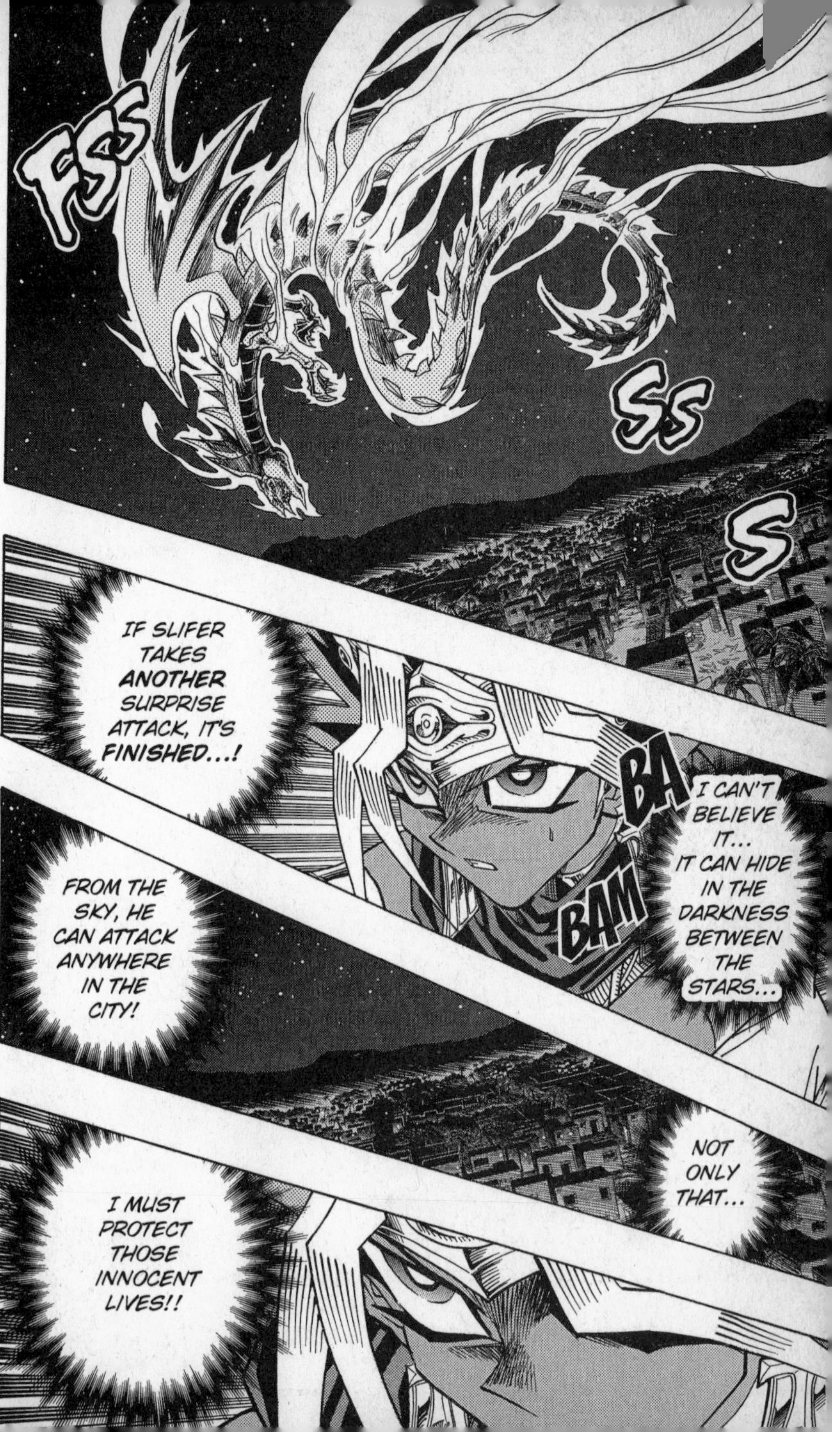
FSS
Ss
S
BA
BAM
I CAN'T BELIEVE IT... IT CAN HIDE IN THE DARKNESS BETWEEN THE STARS...
IF SLIFER TAKES ANOTHER SURPRISE ATTACK, IT'S FINISHED...!
FROM THE SKY, HE CAN ATTACK ANYWHERE IN THE CITY!
NOT ONLY THAT...
I MUST PROTECT THOSE INNOCENT LIVES!!

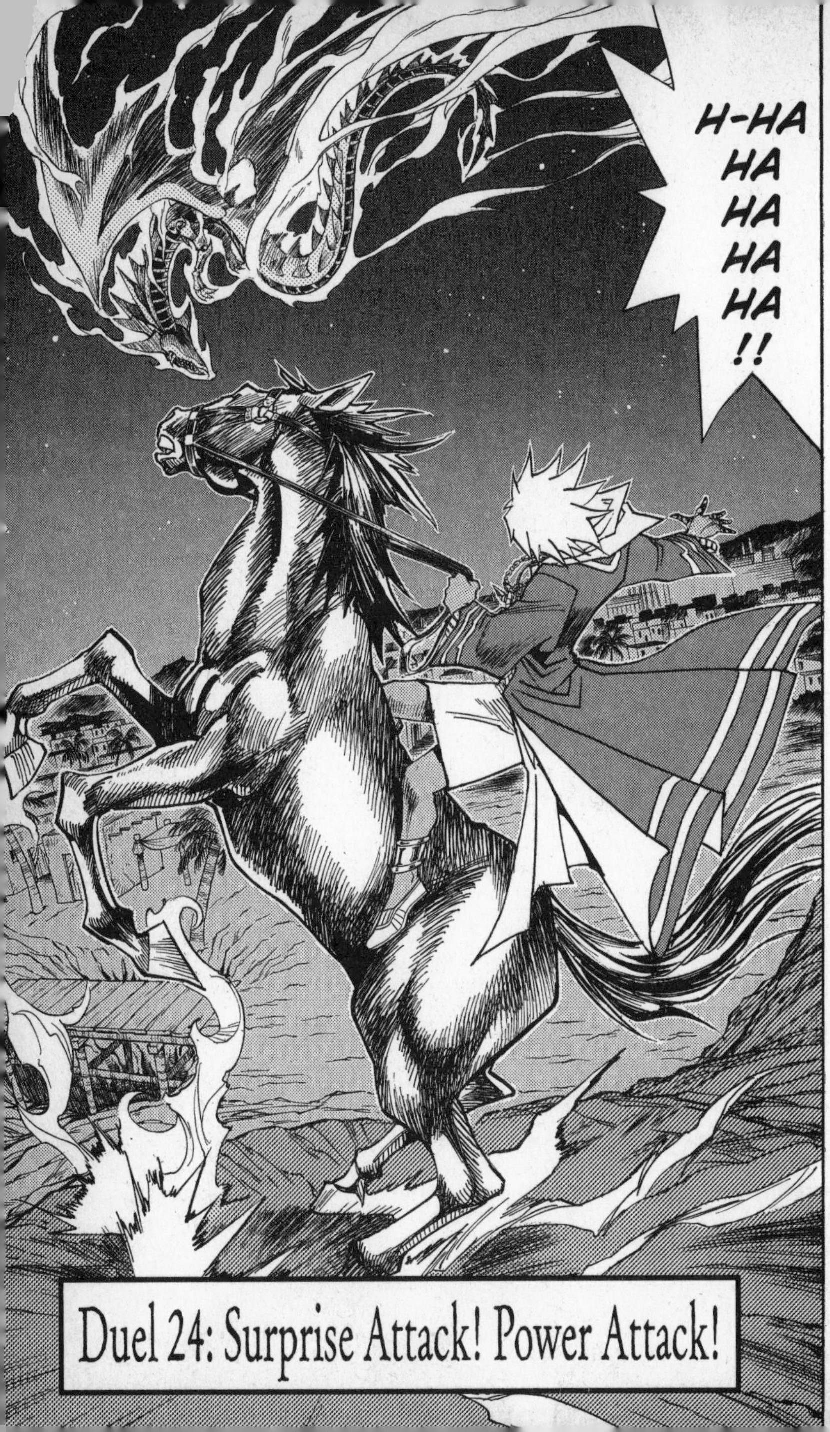
H-HA HA HA HA HA!!

Duel 24: Surprise Attack! Power Attack!

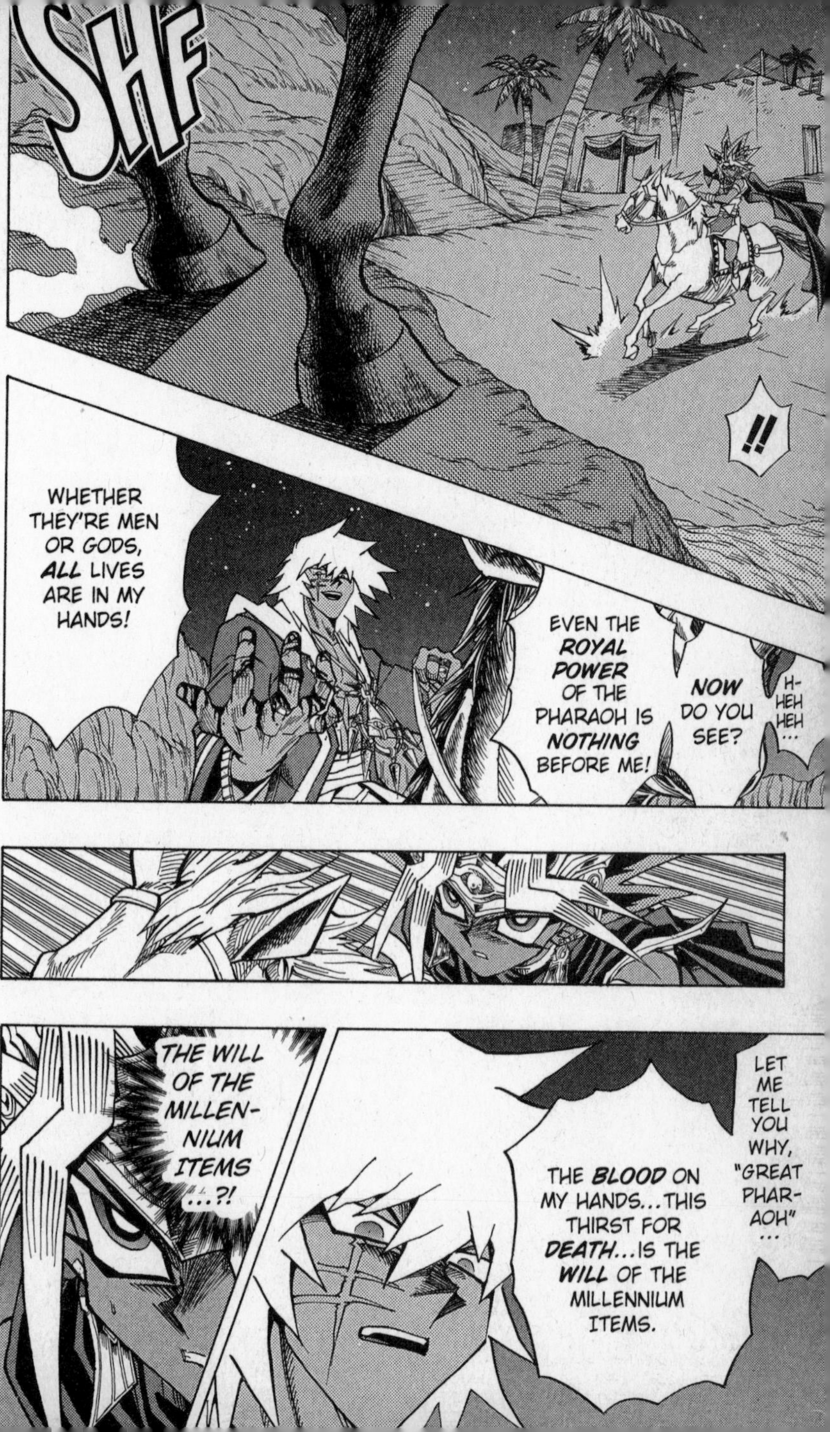
SHF
!!
H-HEH HEH...
NOW DO YOU SEE?
EVEN THE ROYAL POWER OF THE PHARAOH IS NOTHING BEFORE ME!
WHETHER THEY'RE MEN OR GODS, ALL LIVES ARE IN MY HANDS!
LET ME TELL YOU WHY, "GREAT PHARAOH"...
THE BLOOD ON MY HANDS...THIS THIRST FOR DEATH...IS THE WILL OF THE MILLENNIUM ITEMS.
THE WILL OF THE MILLENNIUM ITEMS ...?!

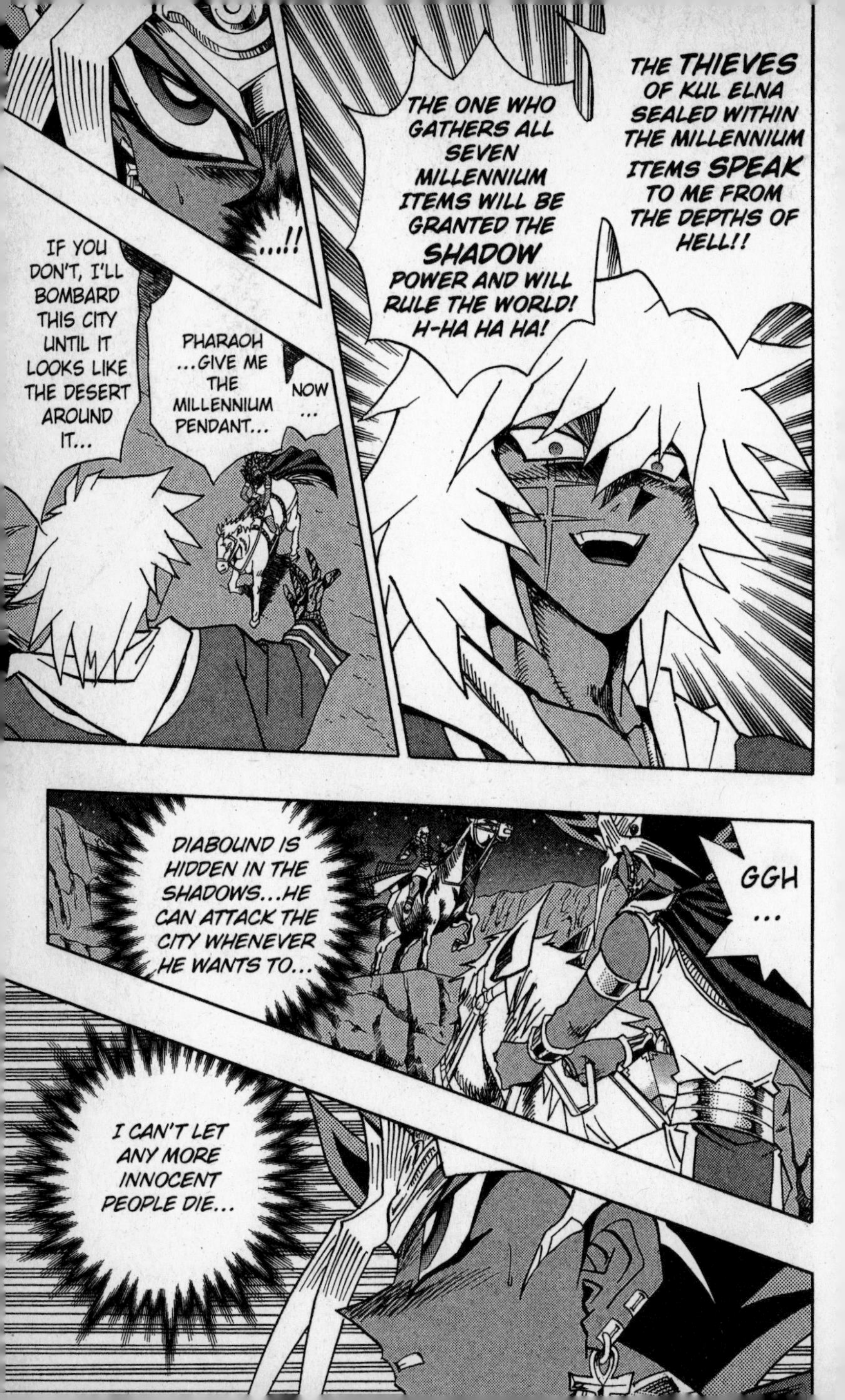
THE THIEVES OF KUL ELNA SEALED WITHIN THE MILLENNIUM ITEMS SPEAK TO ME FROM THE DEPTHS OF HELL!!
THE ONE WHO GATHERS ALL SEVEN MILLENNIUM ITEMS WILL BE GRANTED THE SHADOW POWER AND WILL RULE THE WORLD! H-HA HA HA!
...!!
NOW ...
PHARAOH ...GIVE ME THE MILLENNIUM PENDANT...
IF YOU DON'T, I'LL BOMBARD THIS CITY UNTIL IT LOOKS LIKE THE DESERT AROUND IT...
GGH ...
DIABOUND IS HIDDEN IN THE SHADOWS...HE CAN ATTACK THE CITY WHENEVER HE WANTS TO...
I CAN'T LET ANY MORE INNOCENT PEOPLE DIE...

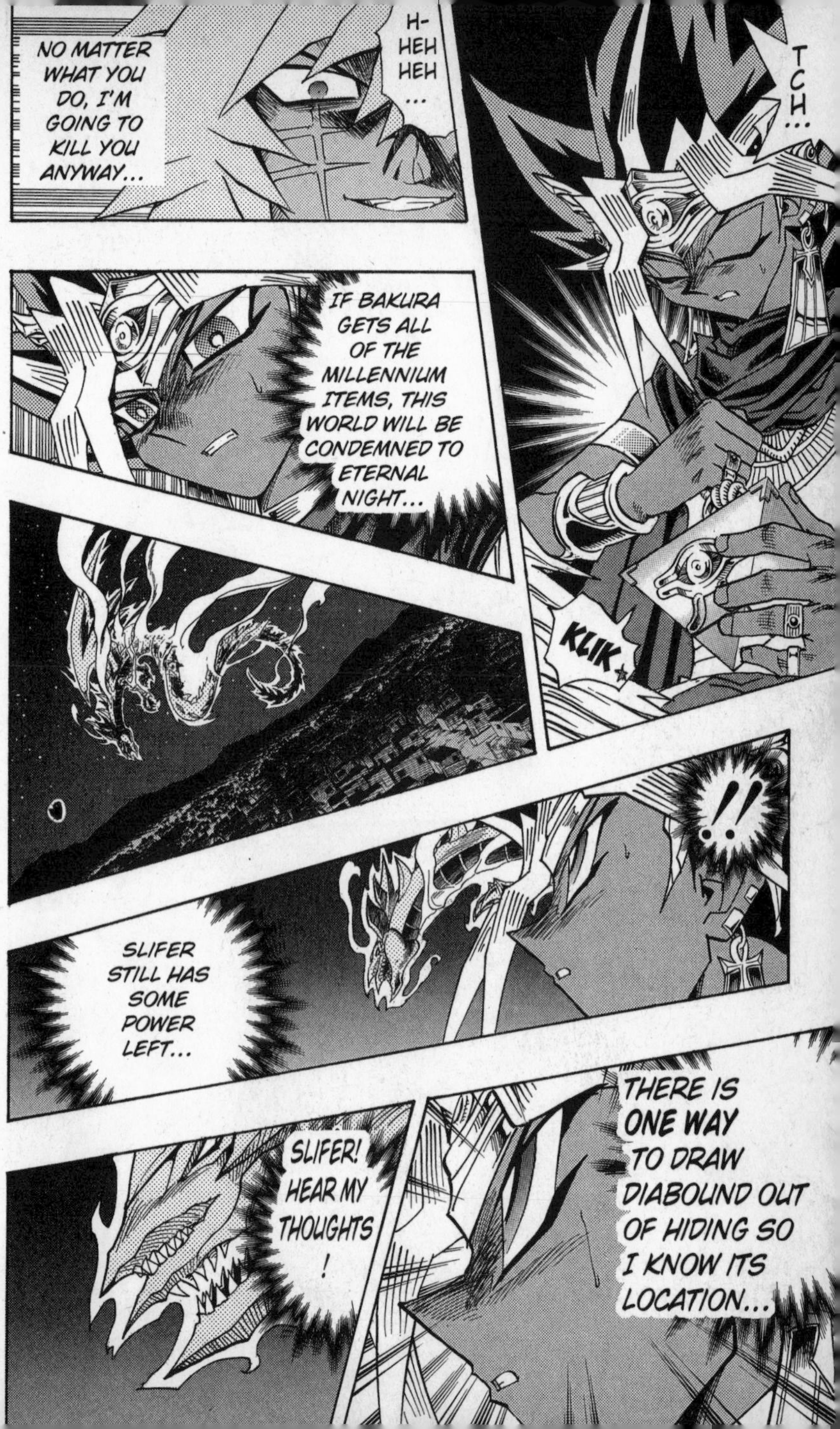
TCH...
KLIK
H-HEH HEH...
NO MATTER WHAT YOU DO, I'M GOING TO KILL YOU ANYWAY...
IF BAKURA GETS ALL OF THE MILLENNIUM ITEMS, THIS WORLD WILL BE CONDEMNED TO ETERNAL NIGHT...
!!
SLIFER STILL HAS SOME POWER LEFT...
THERE IS ONE WAY TO DRAW DIABOUND OUT OF HIDING SO I KNOW ITS LOCATION...
SLIFER! HEAR MY THOUGHTS!

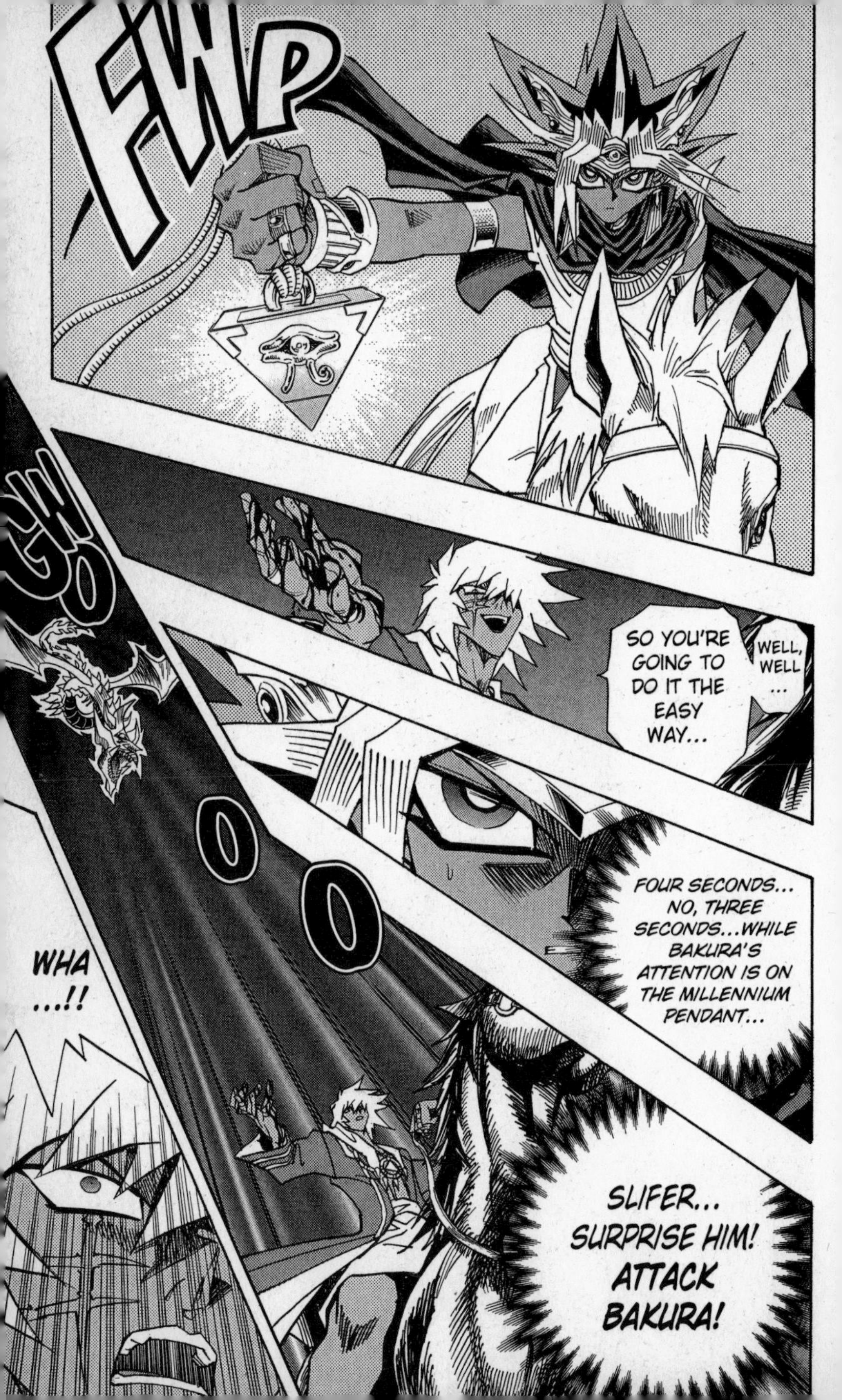

FWP
WELL, WELL...
SO YOU'RE GOING TO DO IT THE EASY WAY...
FOUR SECONDS... NO, THREE SECONDS...WHILE BAKURA'S ATTENTION IS ON THE MILLENNIUM PENDANT...
SLIFER... SURPRISE HIM! ATTACK BAKURA!
GWOOO
WHA ...!!

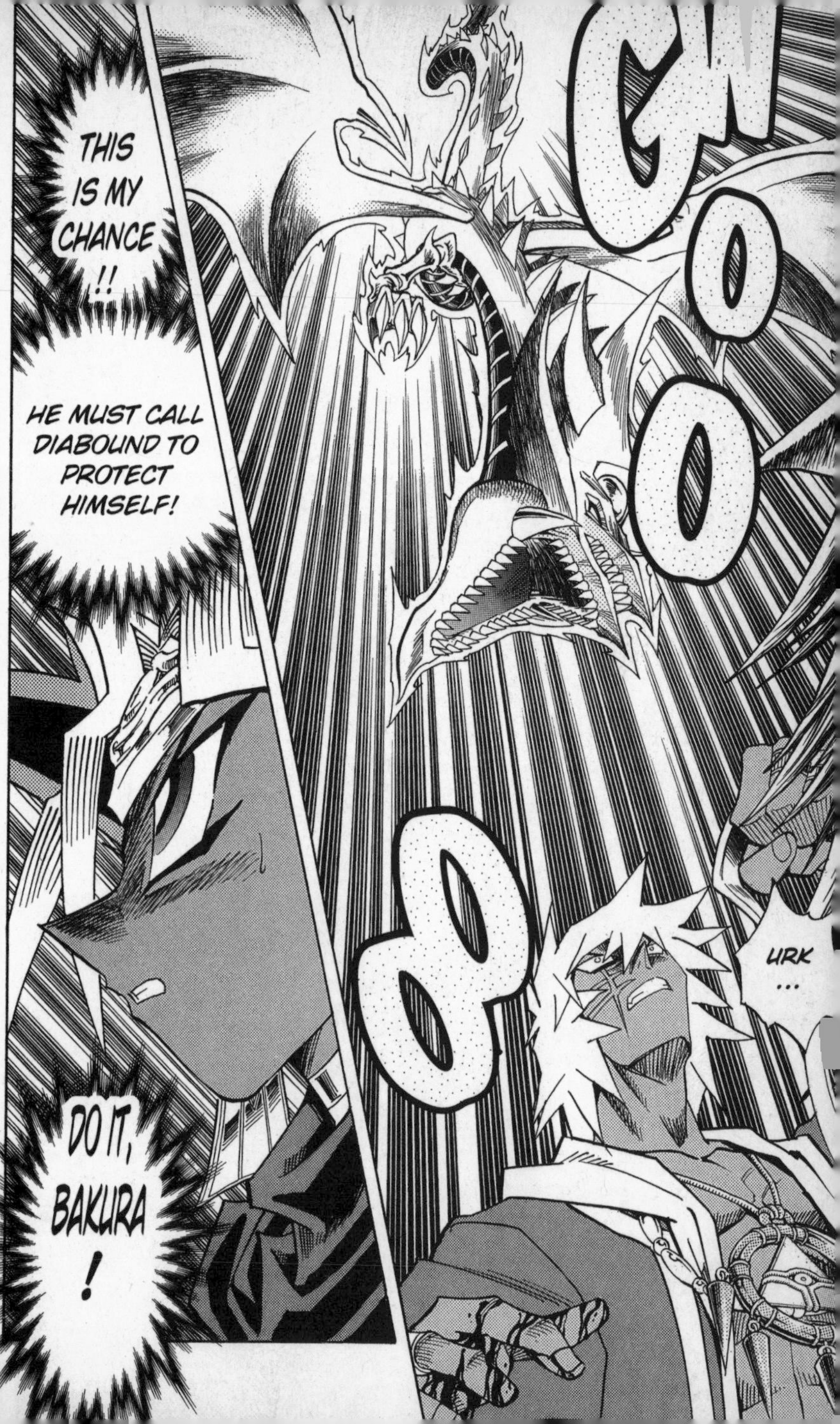
GWOOO
URK ...
THIS IS MY CHANCE !!
HE MUST CALL DIABOUND TO PROTECT HIMSELF!
DO IT, BAKURA !

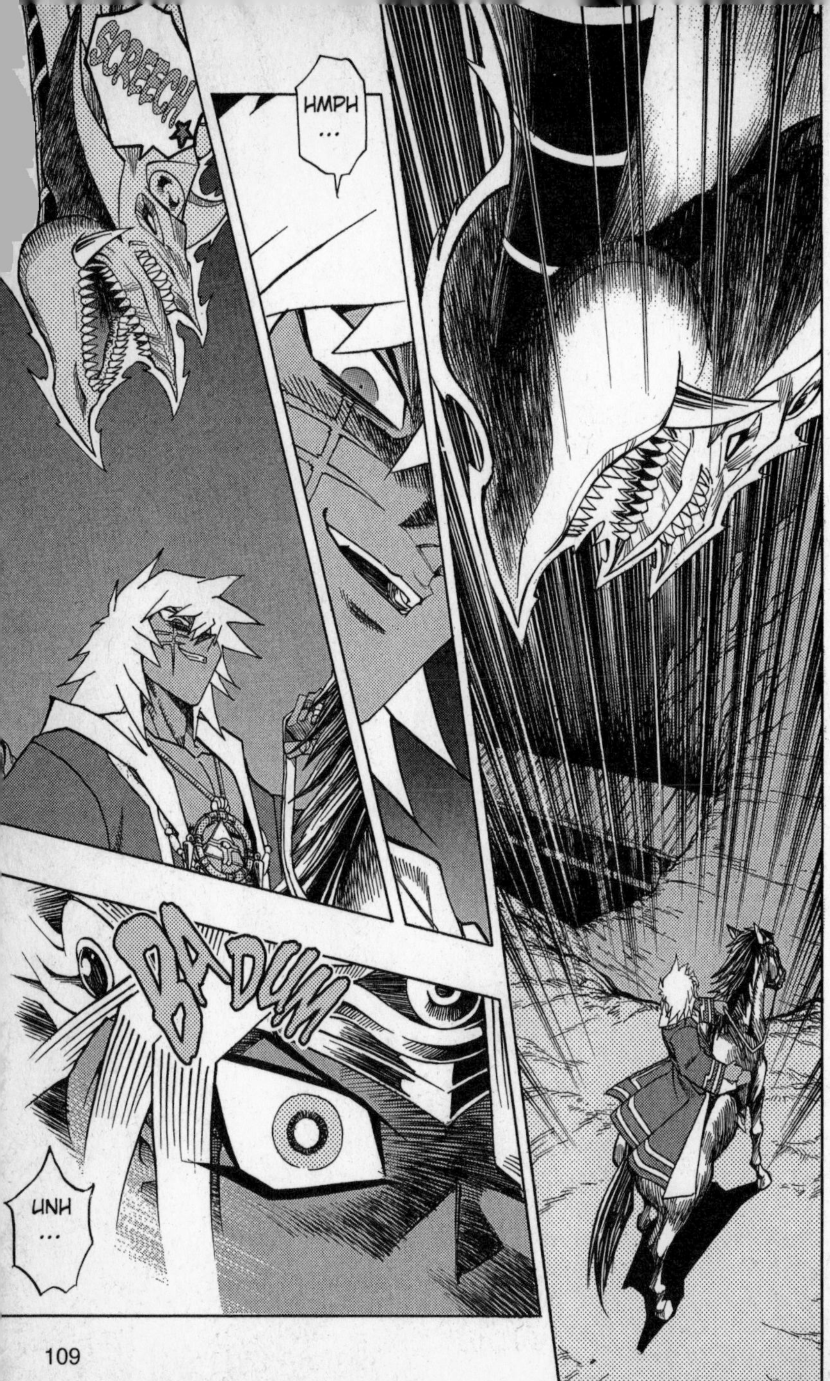
HMPH ...
SCREECH
BA-DUM
UNH ...

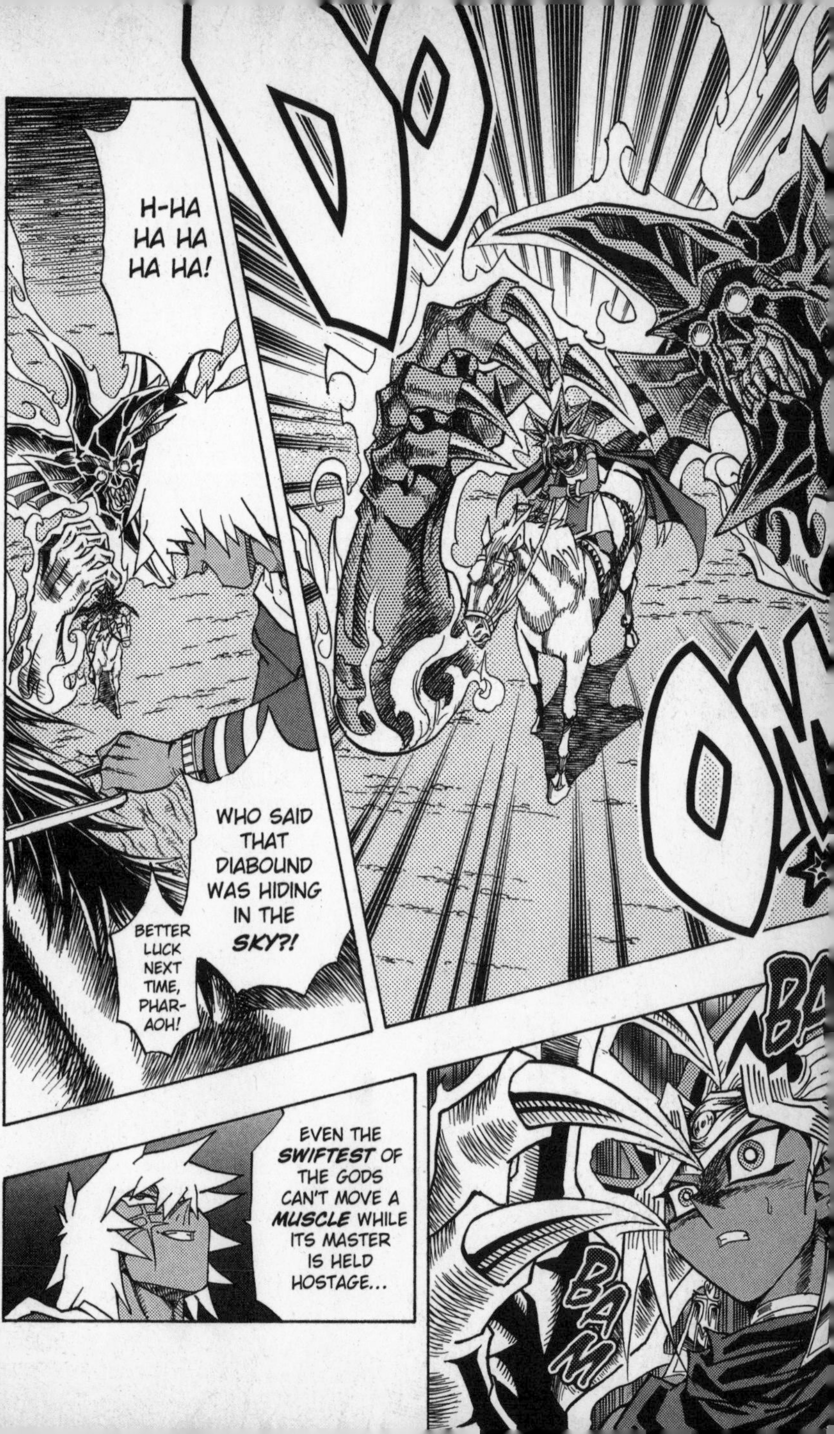

DO
OM
H-HA HA HA HA HA!
WHO SAID THAT DIABOUND WAS HIDING IN THE SKY?!
BETTER LUCK NEXT TIME, PHAR-AOH!
BA
BAM
EVEN THE SWIFTEST OF THE GODS CAN'T MOVE A MUSCLE WHILE ITS MASTER IS HELD HOSTAGE...

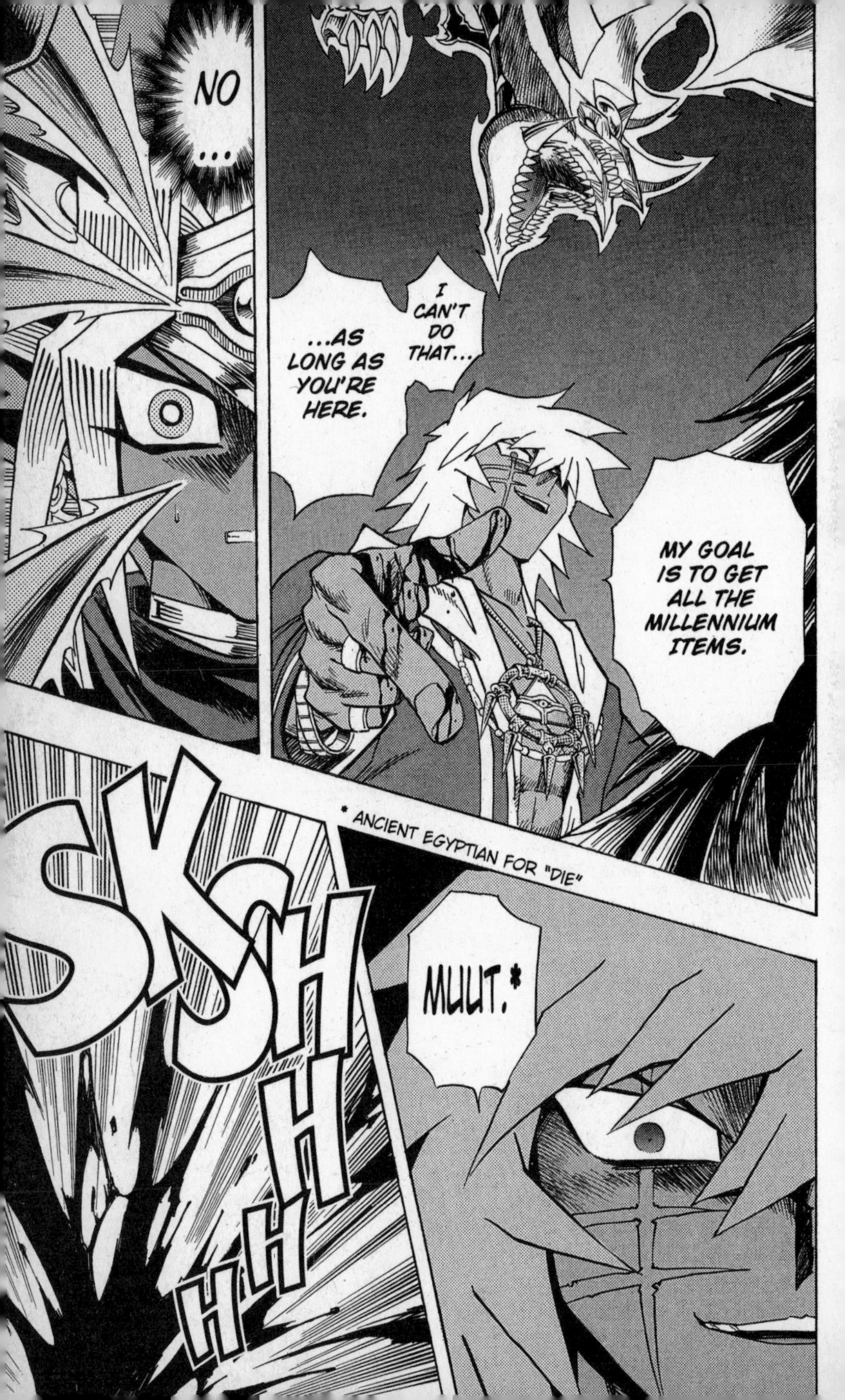
MY GOAL IS TO GET ALL THE MILLENNIUM ITEMS.
I CAN'T DO THAT...
...AS LONG AS YOU'RE HERE.
NO ...
MUUT.*
* ANCIENT EGYPTIAN FOR "DIE"
SKSHHHHH

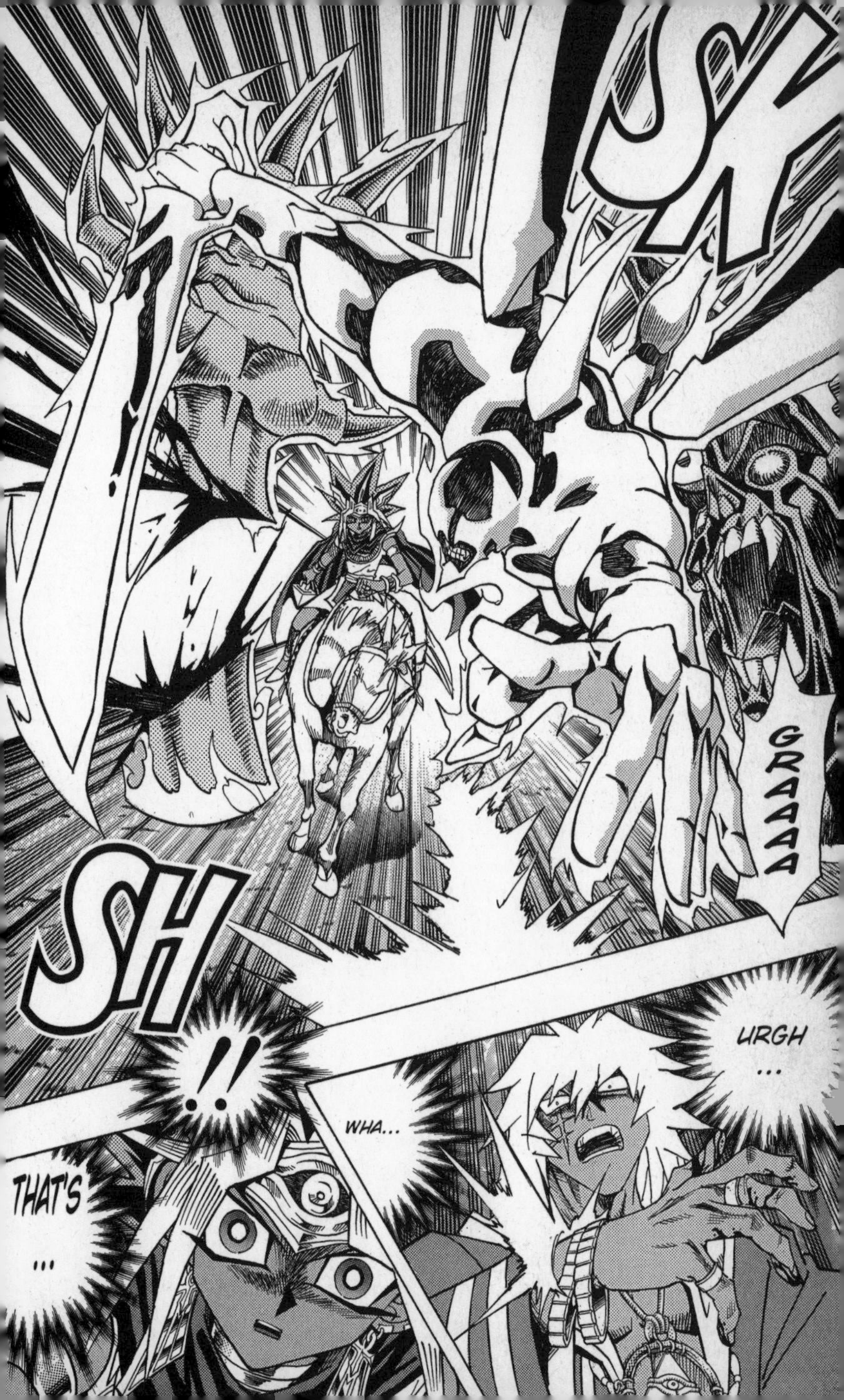
SH
GRAAAAA
SH
URGH ...
!!
WHA...
THAT'S ...

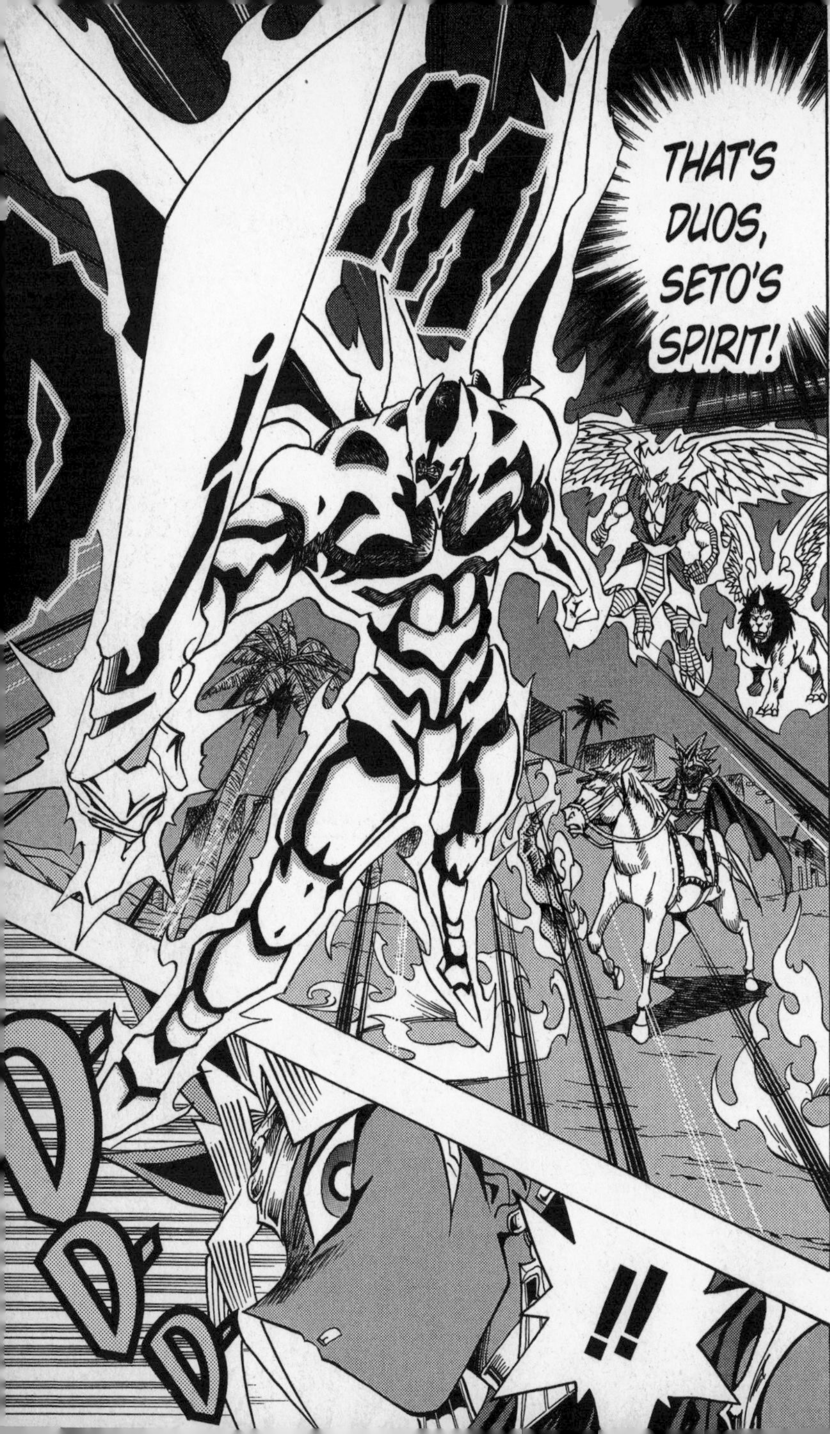
THAT'S DUOS, SETO'S SPIRIT!
!!

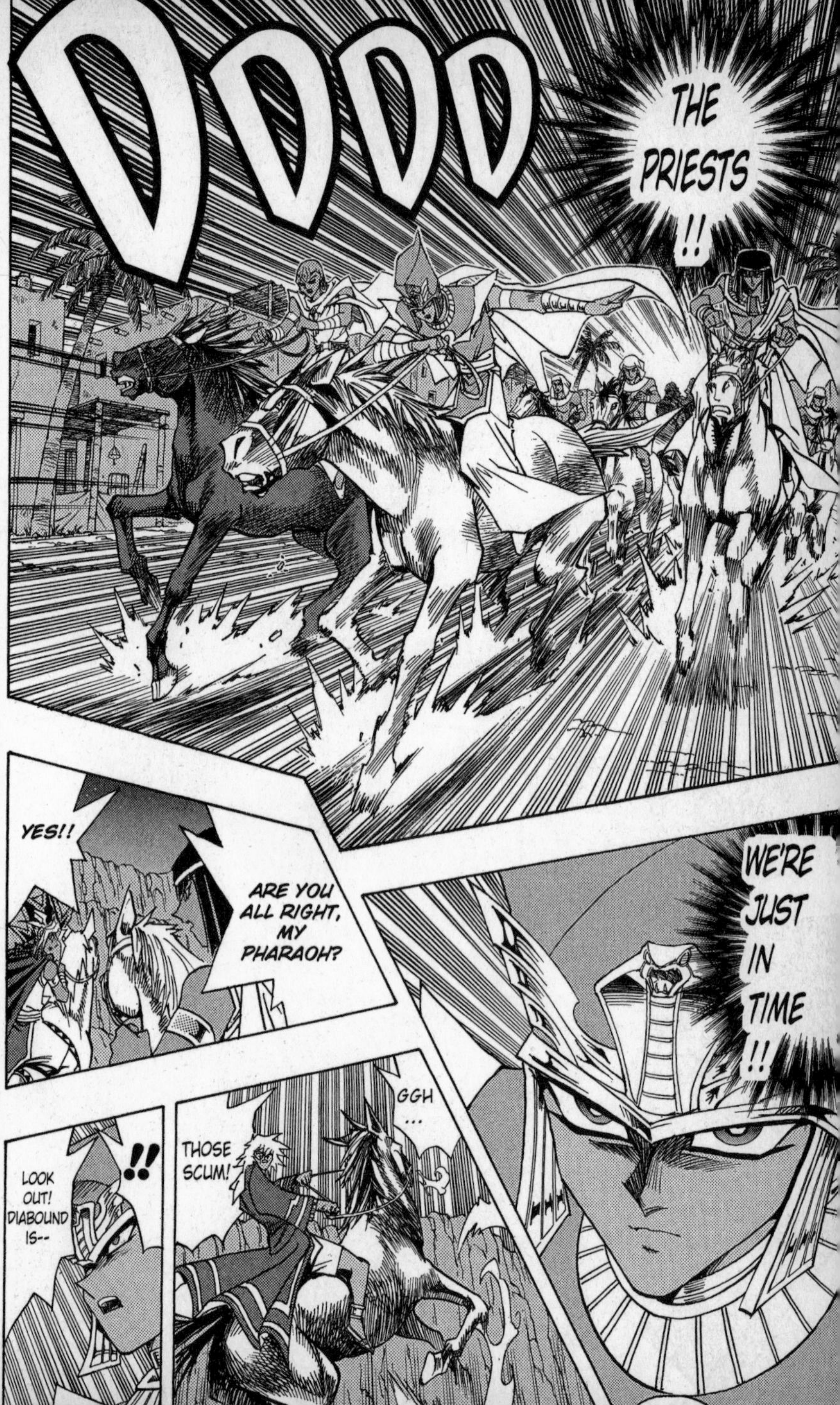
THE PRIESTS !!
DDDD
WE'RE JUST IN TIME !!
ARE YOU ALL RIGHT, MY PHARAOH?
YES!!
GGH ...
THOSE SCUM!
!!
LOOK OUT! DIABOUND IS--

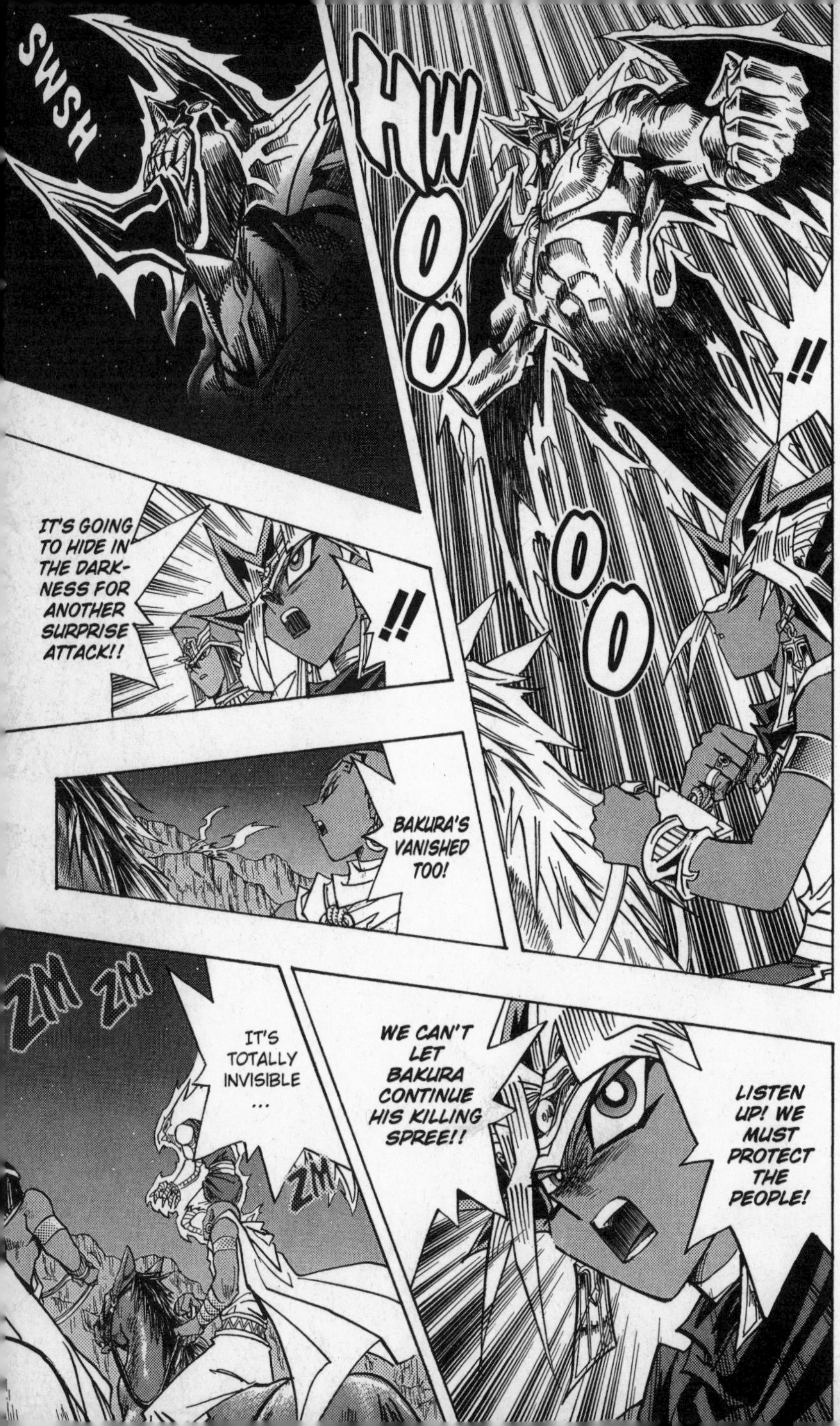
HWOOOOO
!!
SWSH
IT'S GOING TO HIDE IN THE DARKNESS FOR ANOTHER SURPRISE ATTACK!!
!!
BAKURA'S VANISHED TOO!
LISTEN UP! WE MUST PROTECT THE PEOPLE!
WE CAN'T LET BAKURA CONTINUE HIS KILLING SPREE!!
ZM ZM
IT'S TOTALLY INVISIBLE ...
ZM

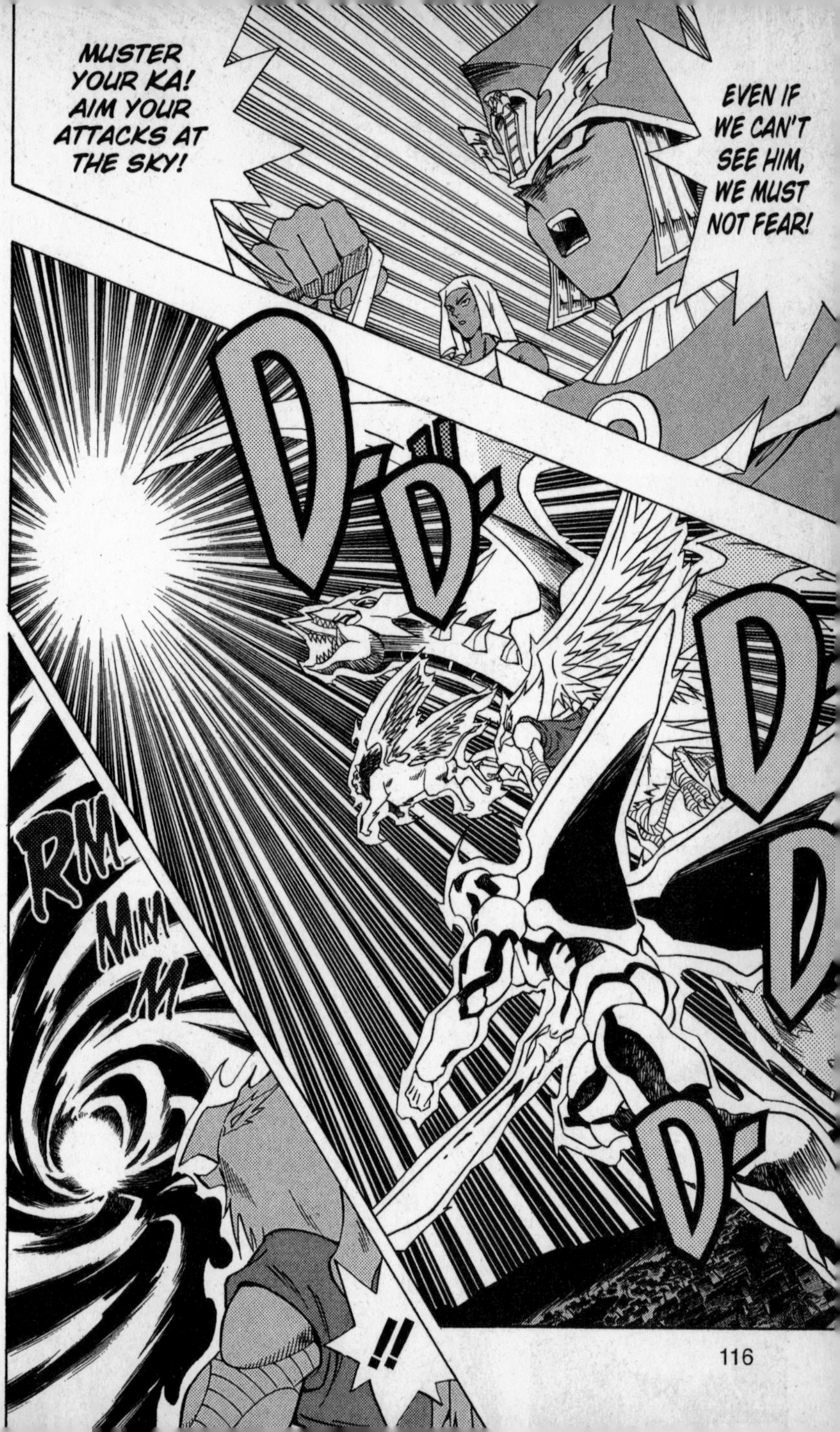
EVEN IF WE CAN'T SEE HIM, WE MUST NOT FEAR!
MUSTER YOUR KA! AIM YOUR ATTACKS AT THE SKY!
D D
D D
D
RMMMM
!!

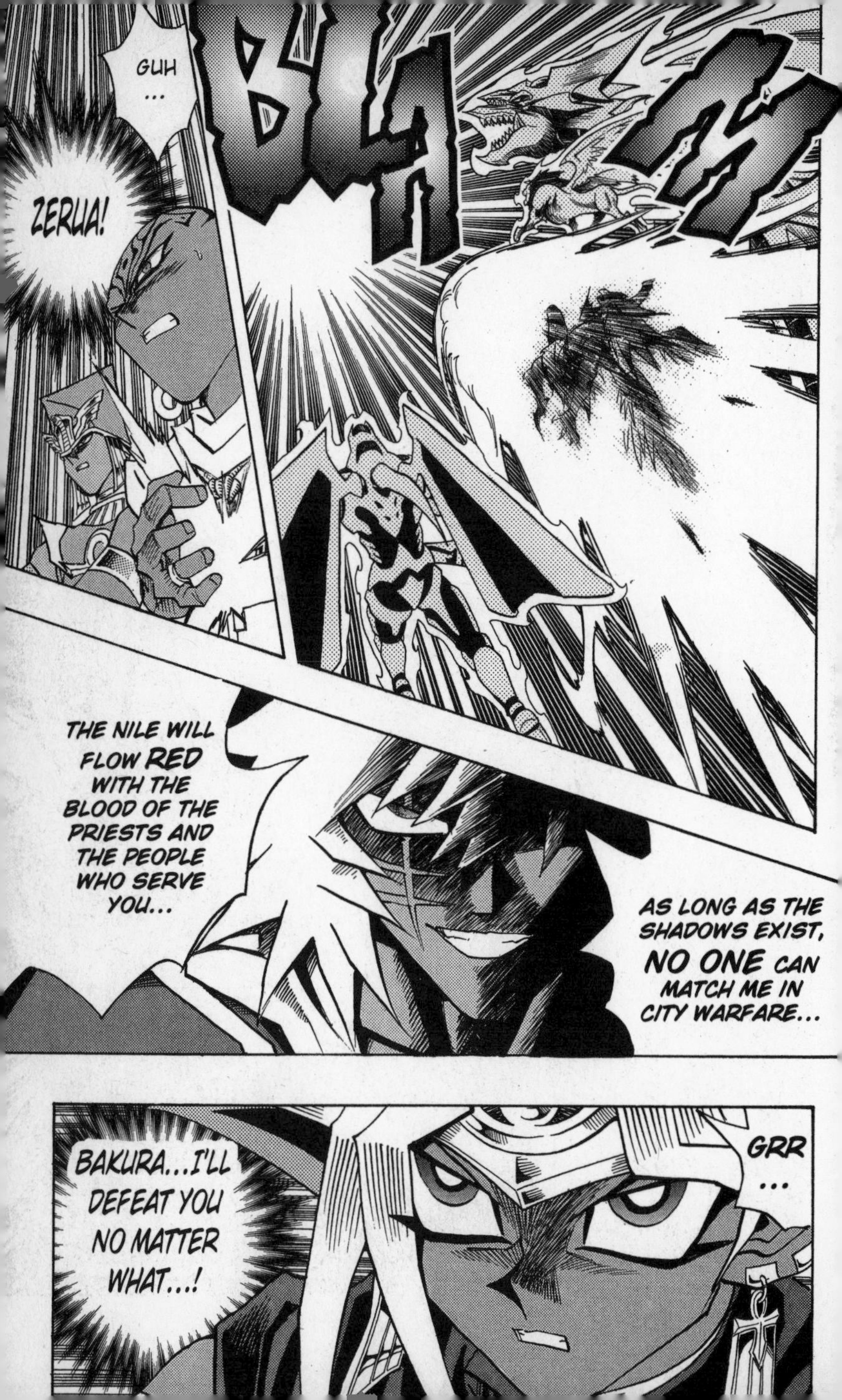

BLAM
GUH ...
ZERUA!
AS LONG AS THE SHADOWS EXIST, NO ONE CAN MATCH ME IN CITY WARFARE...
THE NILE WILL FLOW RED WITH THE BLOOD OF THE PRIESTS AND THE PEOPLE WHO SERVE YOU...
GRR ...
BAKURA...I'LL DEFEAT YOU NO MATTER WHAT...!

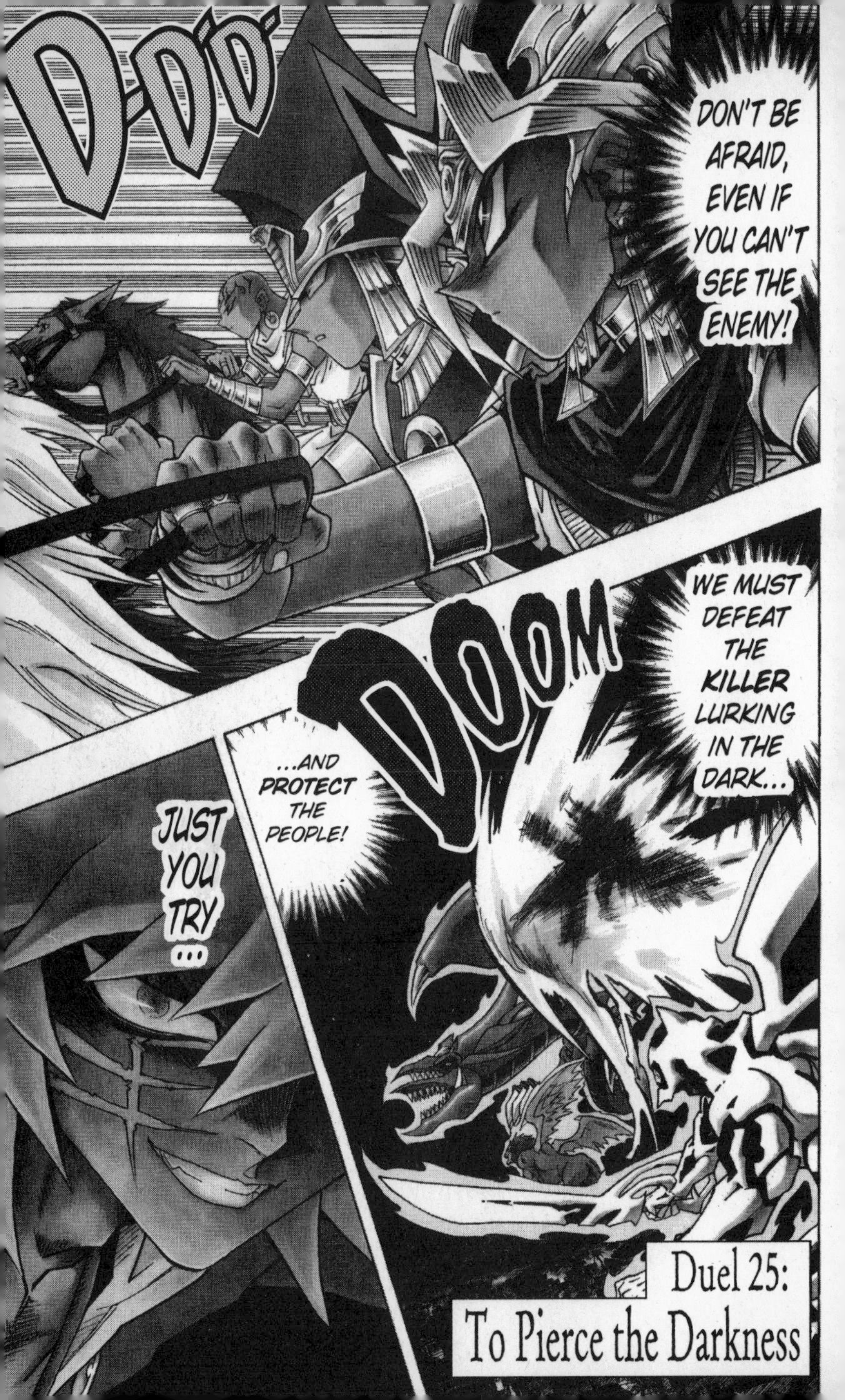
D-D-D
DON'T BE AFRAID, EVEN IF YOU CAN'T SEE THE ENEMY!
WE MUST DEFEAT THE **KILLER** LURKING IN THE DARK...
DOOM
...AND **PROTECT** THE PEOPLE!
JUST YOU TRY...
Duel 25:
To Pierce the Darkness

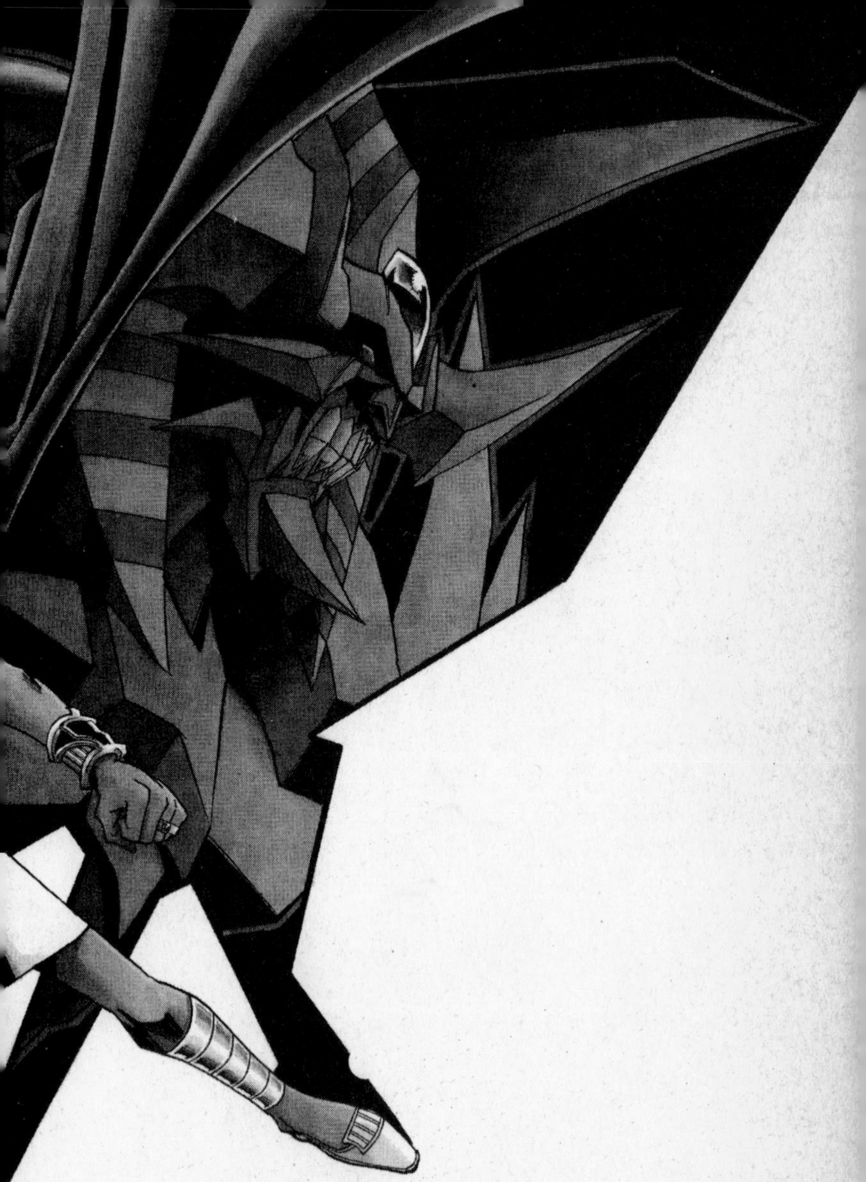

Duel 25:
To Pierce the Darkness!

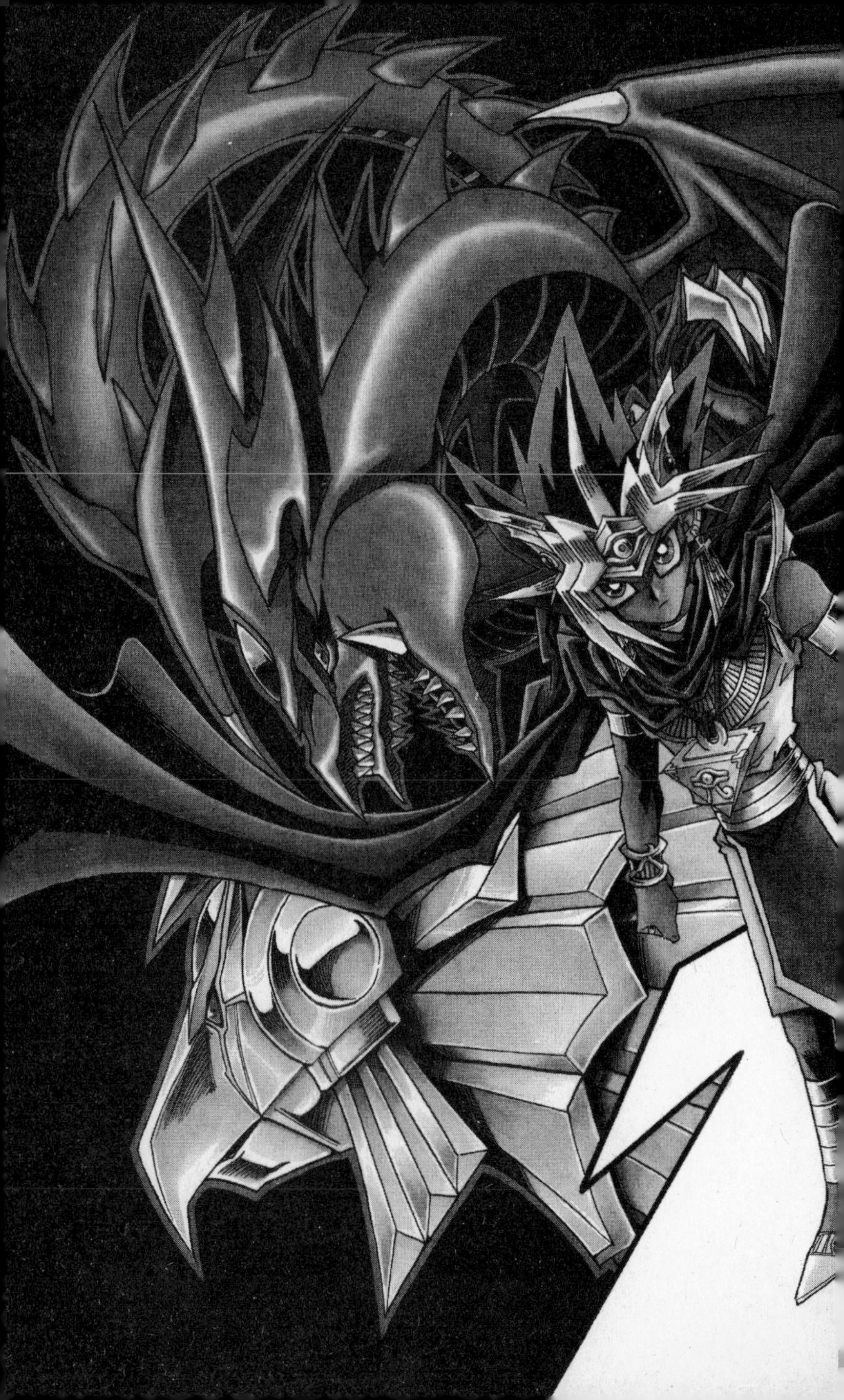

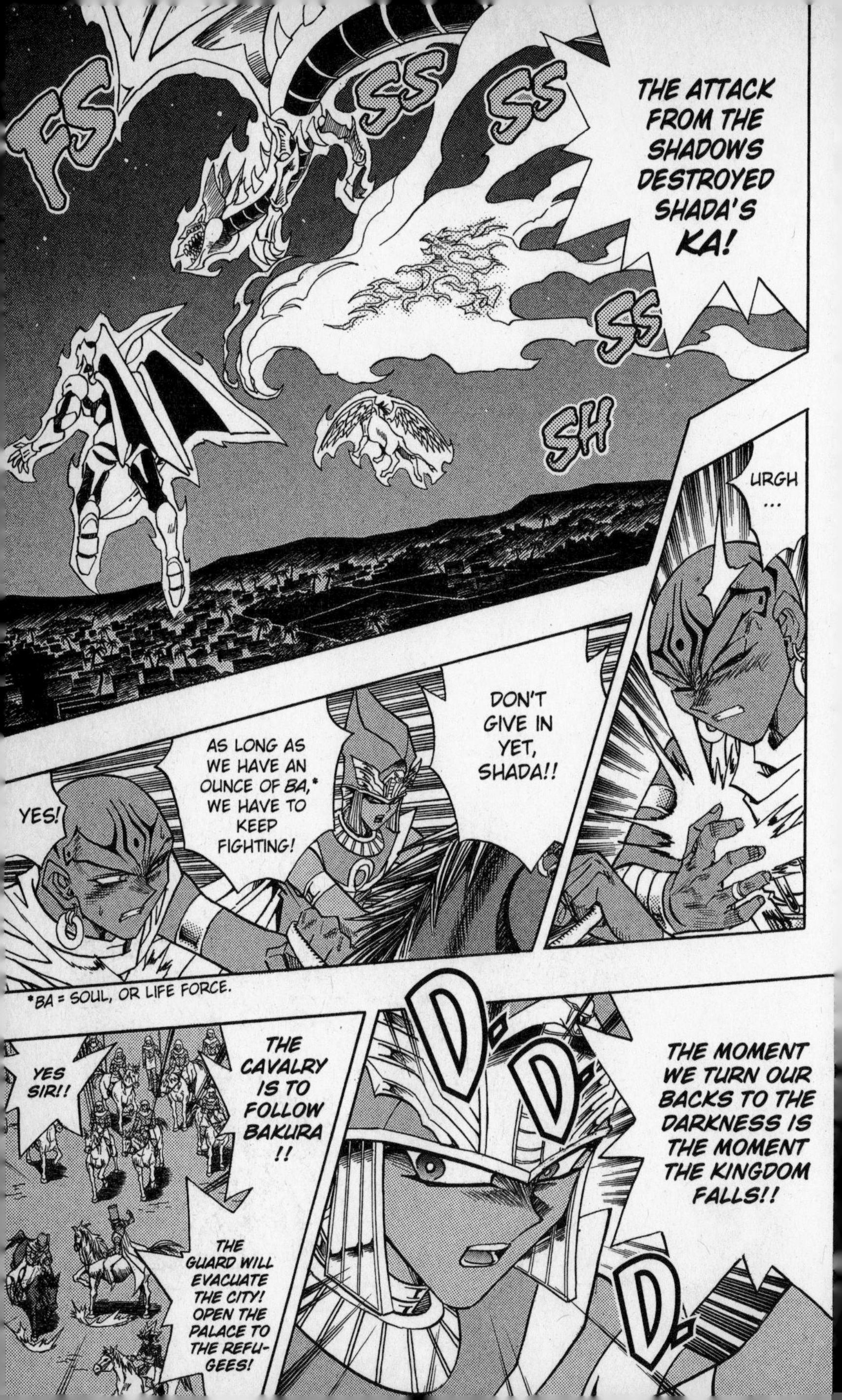
THE ATTACK FROM THE SHADOWS DESTROYED SHADA'S KA!
FSSSSSSSSSH
URGH ...
DON'T GIVE IN YET, SHADA!!
AS LONG AS WE HAVE AN OUNCE OF BA,* WE HAVE TO KEEP FIGHTING!
YES!
*BA = SOUL, OR LIFE FORCE.
THE MOMENT WE TURN OUR BACKS TO THE DARKNESS IS THE MOMENT THE KINGDOM FALLS!!
DDD
THE CAVALRY IS TO FOLLOW BAKURA!!
YES SIR!!
THE GUARD WILL EVACUATE THE CITY! OPEN THE PALACE TO THE REFUGEES!

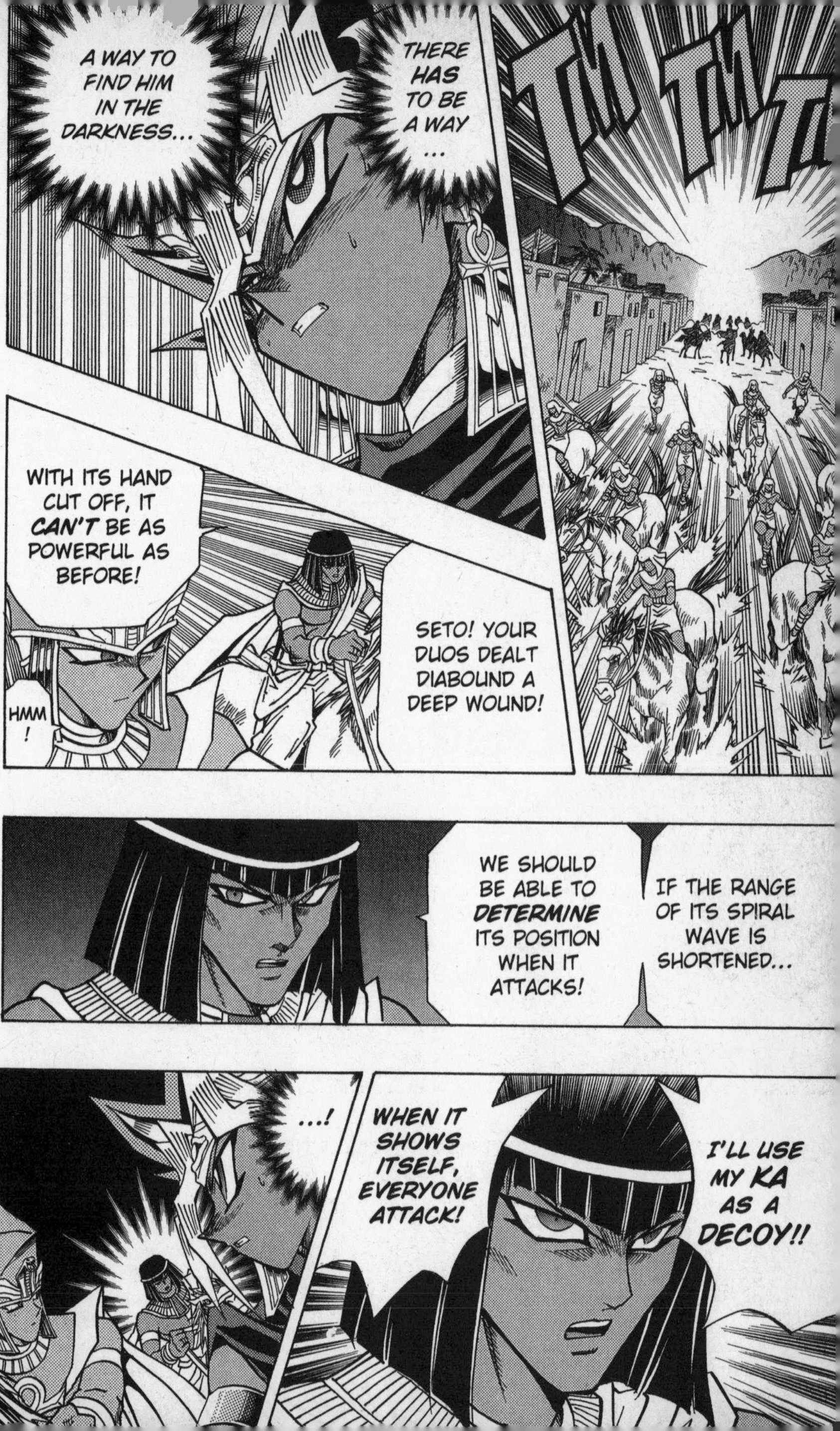
THERE HAS TO BE A WAY ...
A WAY TO FIND HIM IN THE DARKNESS...
SETO! YOUR DUOS DEALT DIABOUND A DEEP WOUND!
WITH ITS HAND CUT OFF, IT ***CAN'T*** BE AS POWERFUL AS BEFORE!
HMM!
IF THE RANGE OF ITS SPIRAL WAVE IS SHORTENED...
WE SHOULD BE ABLE TO ***DETERMINE*** ITS POSITION WHEN IT ATTACKS!
I'LL USE MY KA AS A DECOY!!
WHEN IT SHOWS ITSELF, EVERYONE ATTACK!
...!

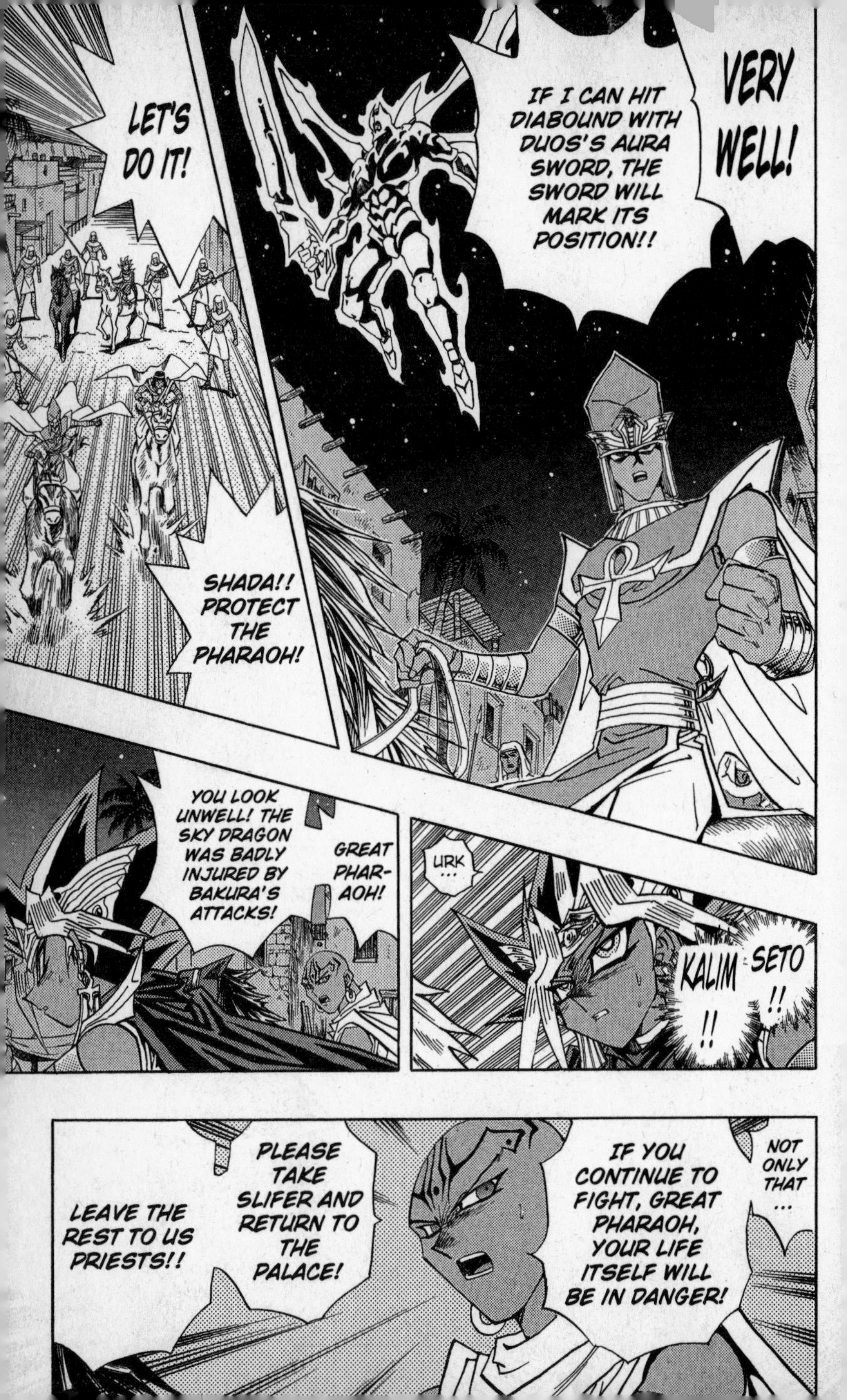
VERY WELL!
IF I CAN HIT DIABOUND WITH DUOS'S AURA SWORD, THE SWORD WILL MARK ITS POSITION!!
LET'S DO IT!
SHADA!! PROTECT THE PHARAOH!
URK...
SETO!!
KALIM!!
GREAT PHAR-AOH!
YOU LOOK UNWELL! THE SKY DRAGON WAS BADLY INJURED BY BAKURA'S ATTACKS!
NOT ONLY THAT...
IF YOU CONTINUE TO FIGHT, GREAT PHARAOH, YOUR LIFE ITSELF WILL BE IN DANGER!
PLEASE TAKE SLIFER AND RETURN TO THE PALACE!
LEAVE THE REST TO US PRIESTS!!

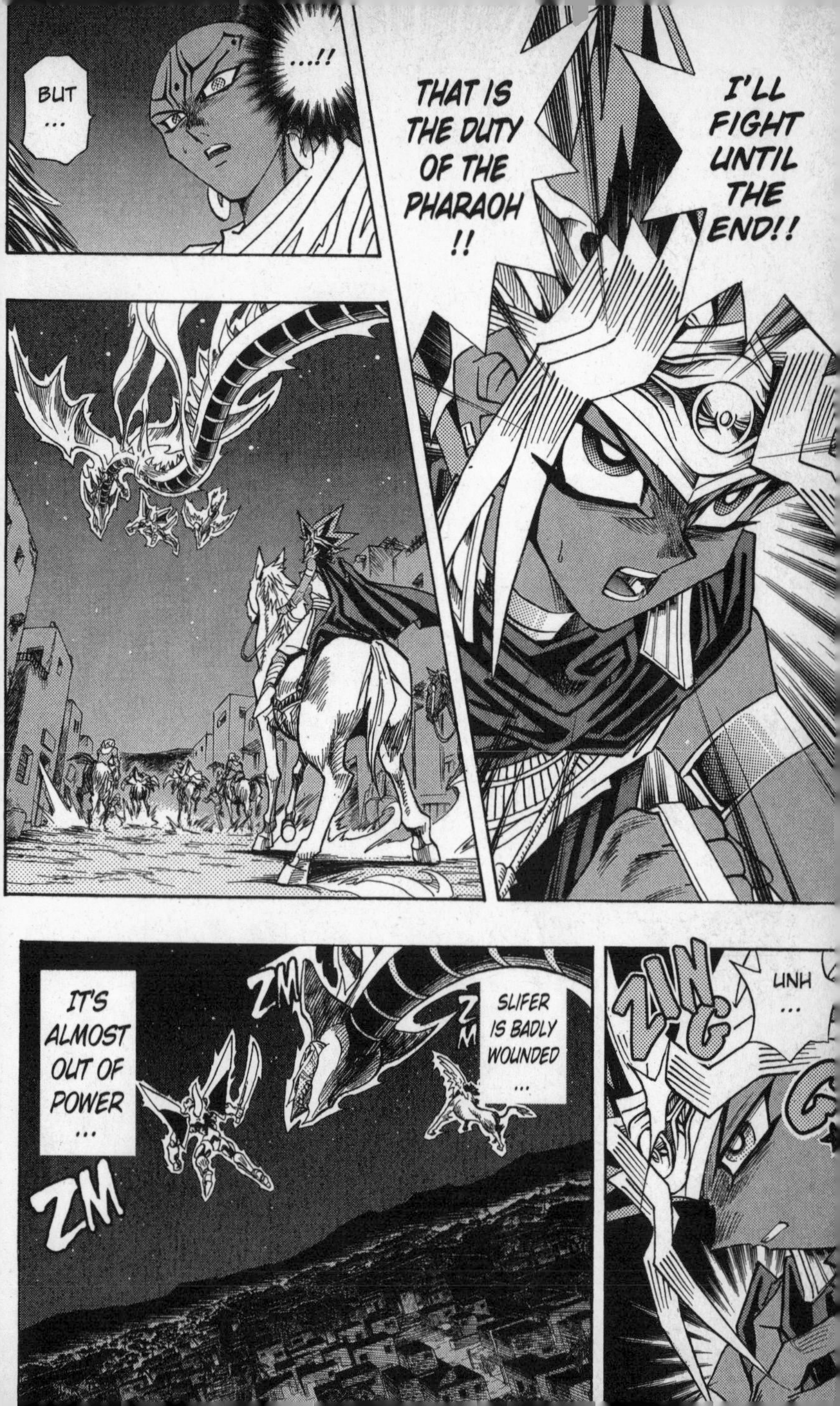
I'LL FIGHT UNTIL THE END!!
THAT IS THE DUTY OF THE PHARAOH!!
...!!
BUT ...
ZING
UNH ...
ZM
SLIFER IS BADLY WOUNDED ...
ZM
IT'S ALMOST OUT OF POWER ...
ZM

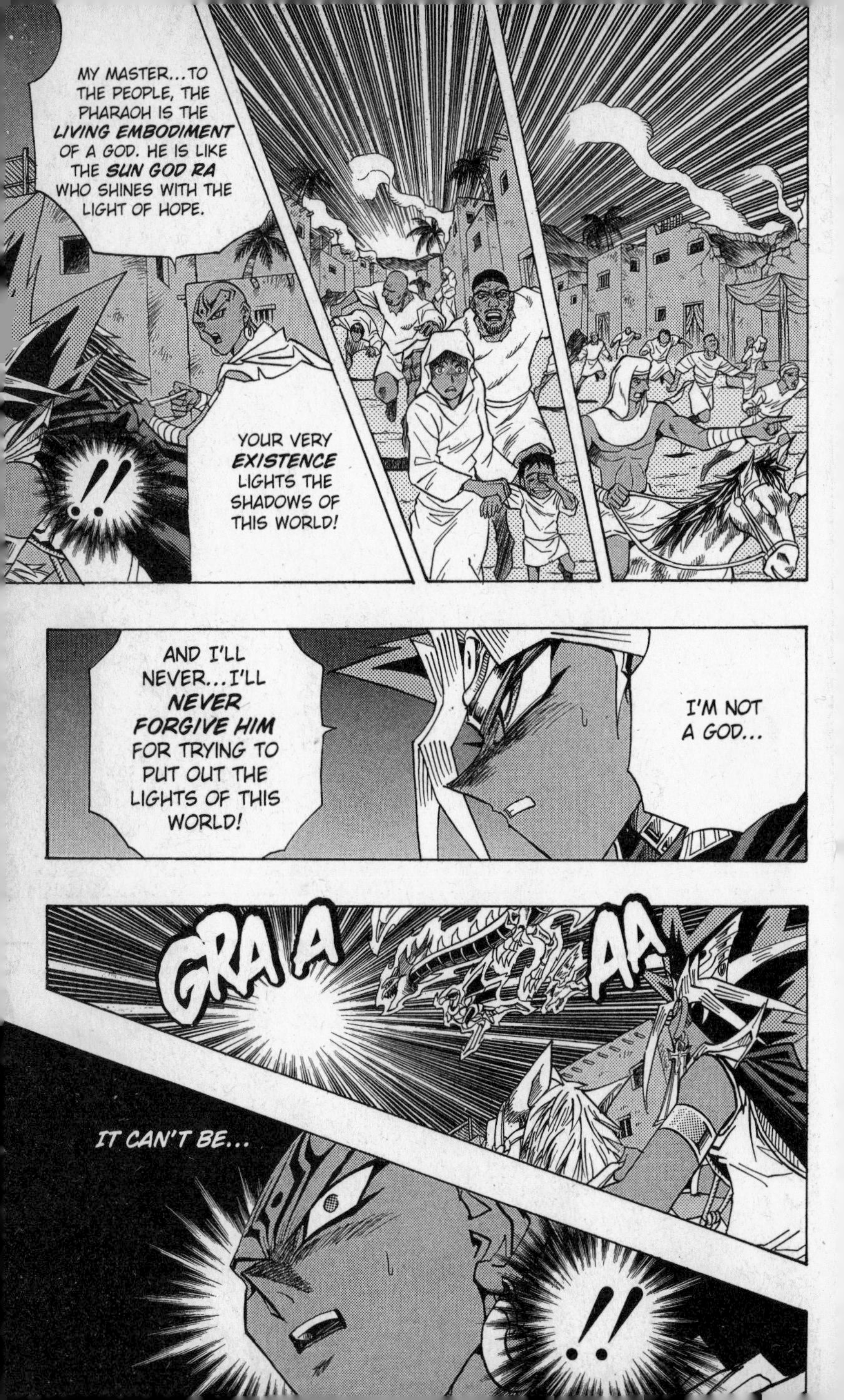
MY MASTER...TO THE PEOPLE, THE PHARAOH IS THE *LIVING EMBODIMENT* OF A GOD. HE IS LIKE THE *SUN GOD RA* WHO SHINES WITH THE LIGHT OF HOPE.
YOUR VERY *EXISTENCE* LIGHTS THE SHADOWS OF THIS WORLD!
!!
I'M NOT A GOD...
AND I'LL NEVER...I'LL *NEVER FORGIVE HIM* FOR TRYING TO PUT OUT THE LIGHTS OF THIS WORLD!
GRA A AA
IT CAN'T BE...
!!

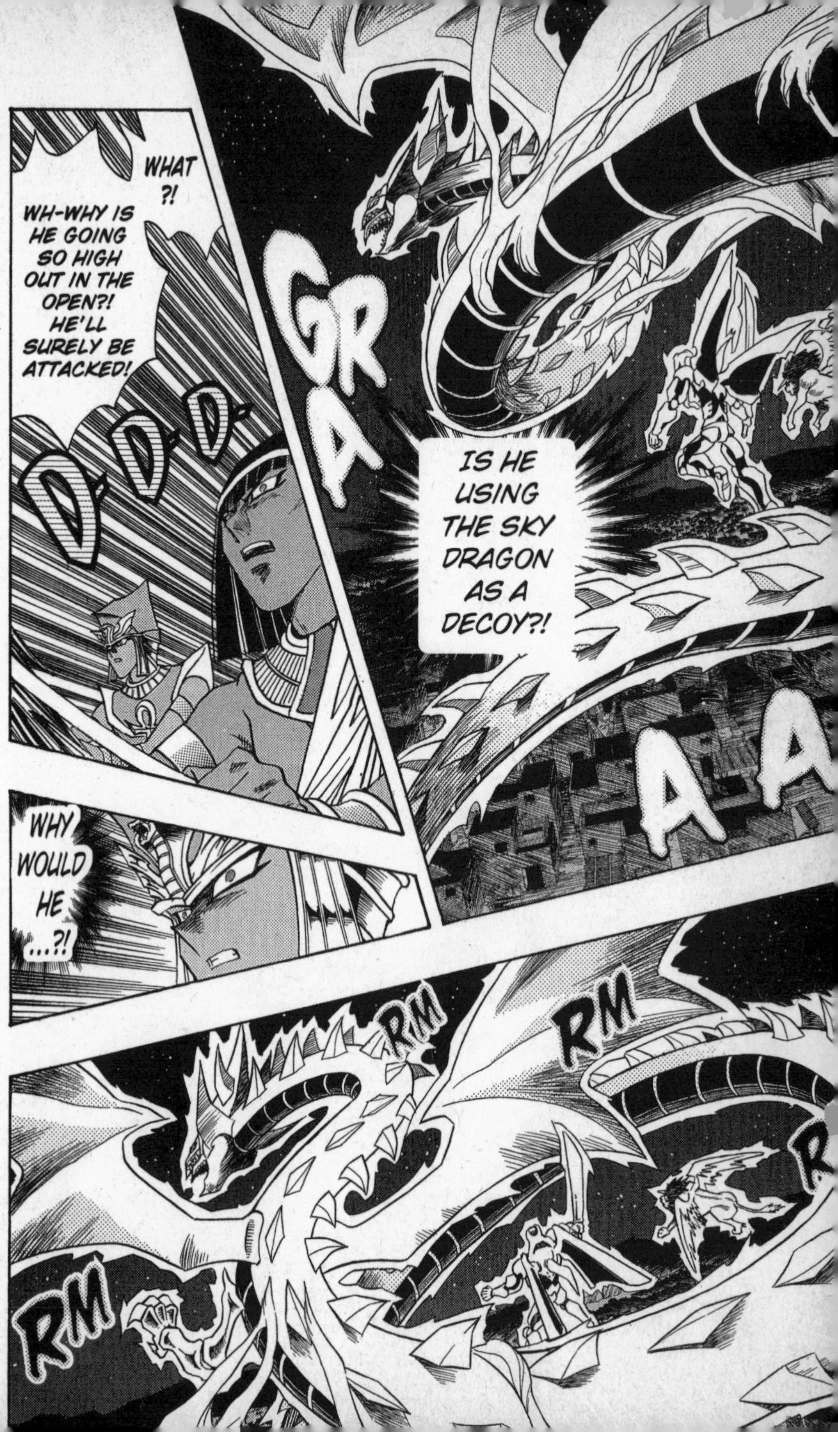
GRAAA
IS HE USING THE SKY DRAGON AS A DECOY?!
WHAT?!
WH-WHY IS HE GOING SO HIGH OUT IN THE OPEN?! HE'LL SURELY BE ATTACKED!
D-D-D
WHY WOULD HE ...?!
R
RM
RM
RM

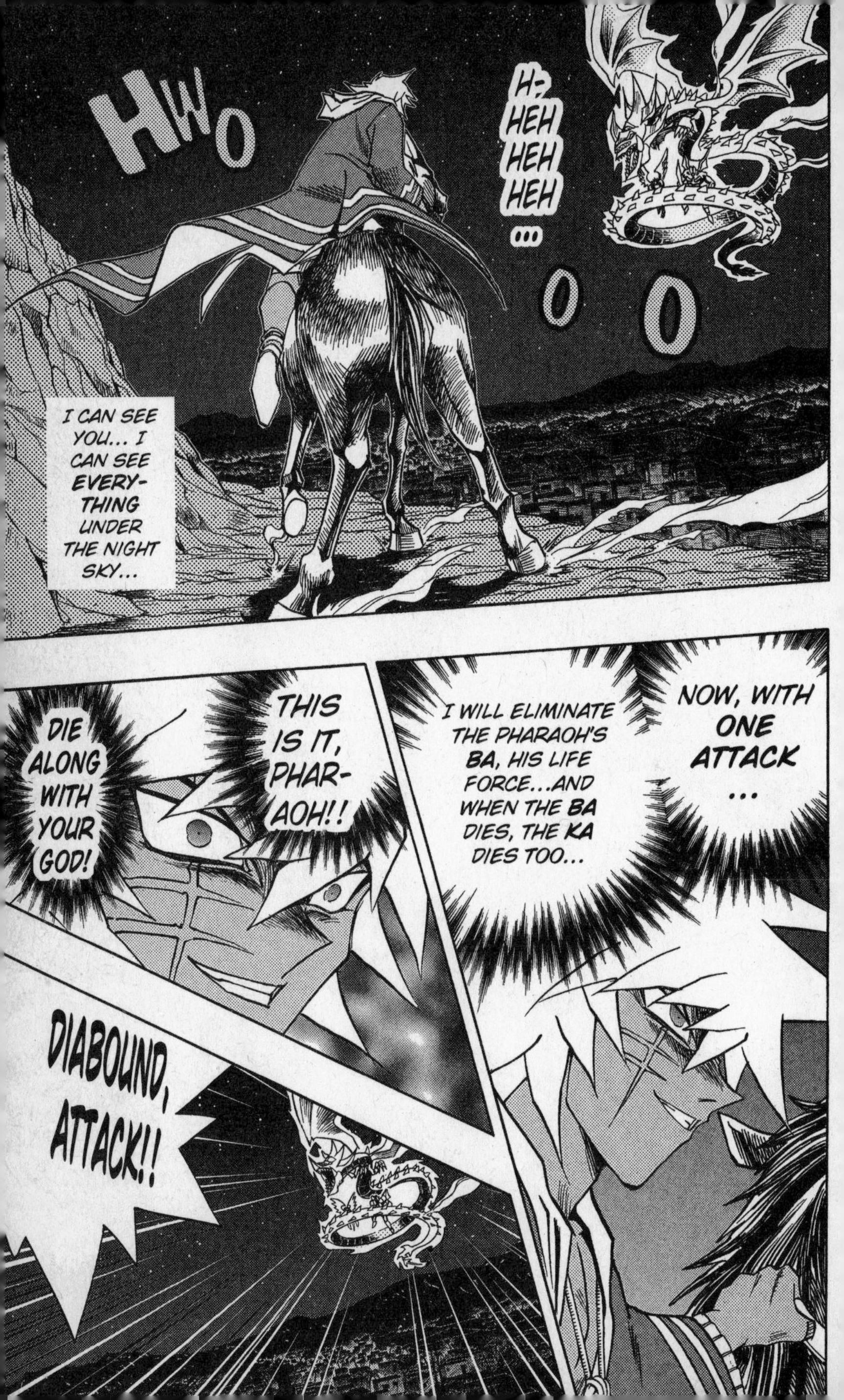
H-HEH HEH HEH...
HWOOO
I CAN SEE YOU... I CAN SEE EVERYTHING UNDER THE NIGHT SKY...
NOW, WITH ONE ATTACK...
I WILL ELIMINATE THE PHARAOH'S BA, HIS LIFE FORCE...AND WHEN THE BA DIES, THE KA DIES TOO...
THIS IS IT, PHARAOH!!
DIE ALONG WITH YOUR GOD!
DIABOUND, ATTACK!!

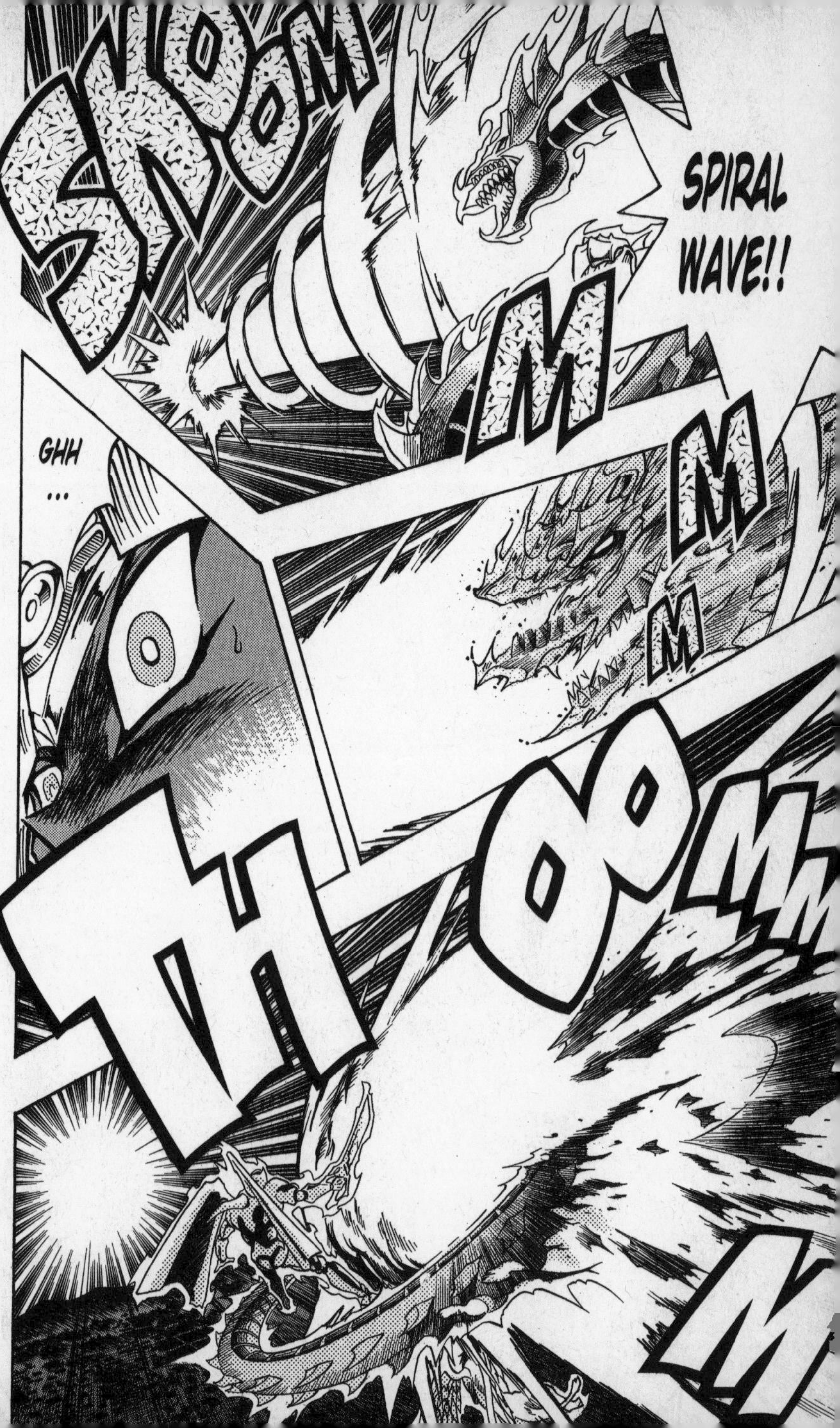
SPIRAL WAVE!!
SHOOMMMM
GHH ...
THOOMM

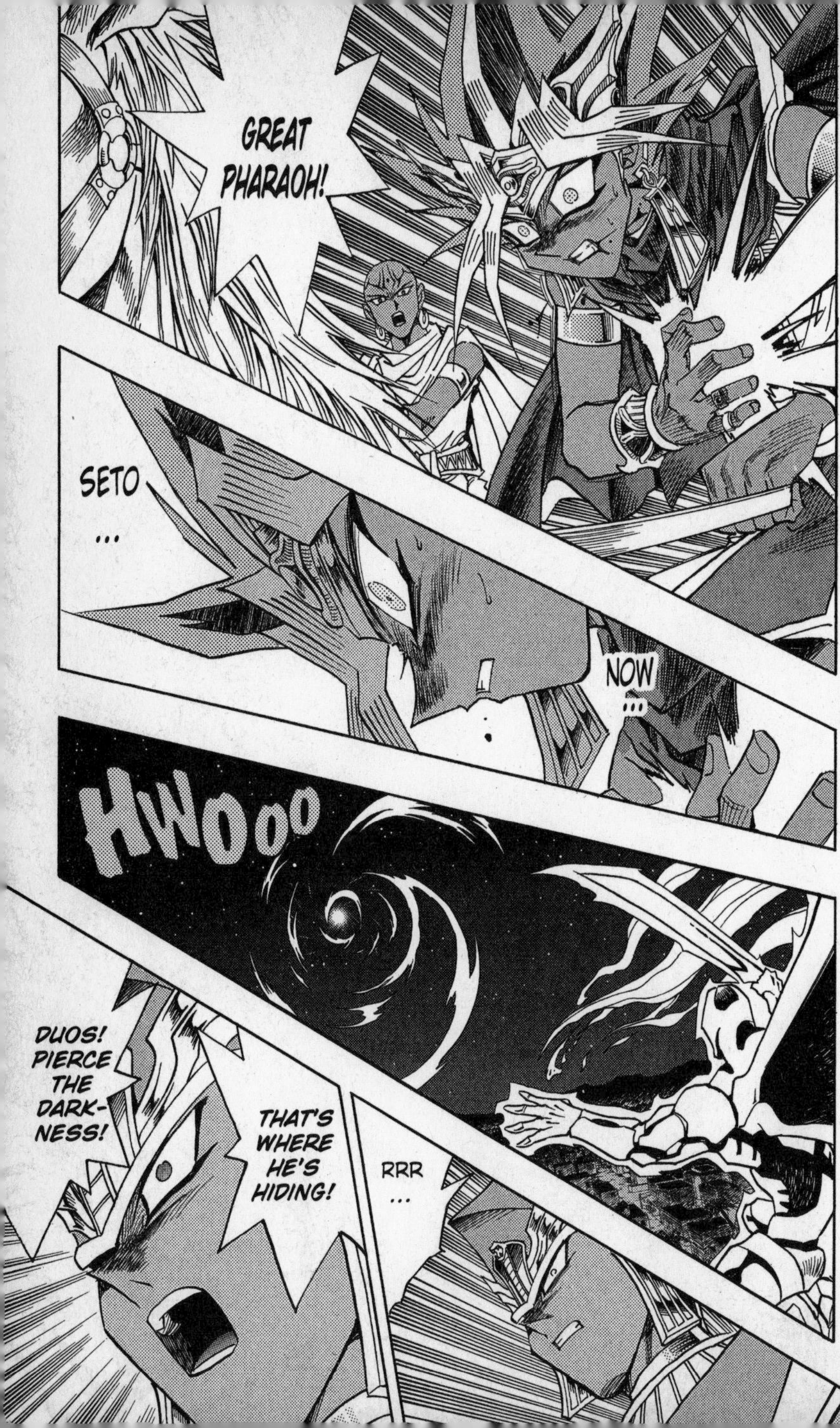
GREAT PHARAOH!
SETO ...
NOW ...
HWOOO
RRR ...
THAT'S WHERE HE'S HIDING!
DUOS! PIERCE THE DARK-NESS!

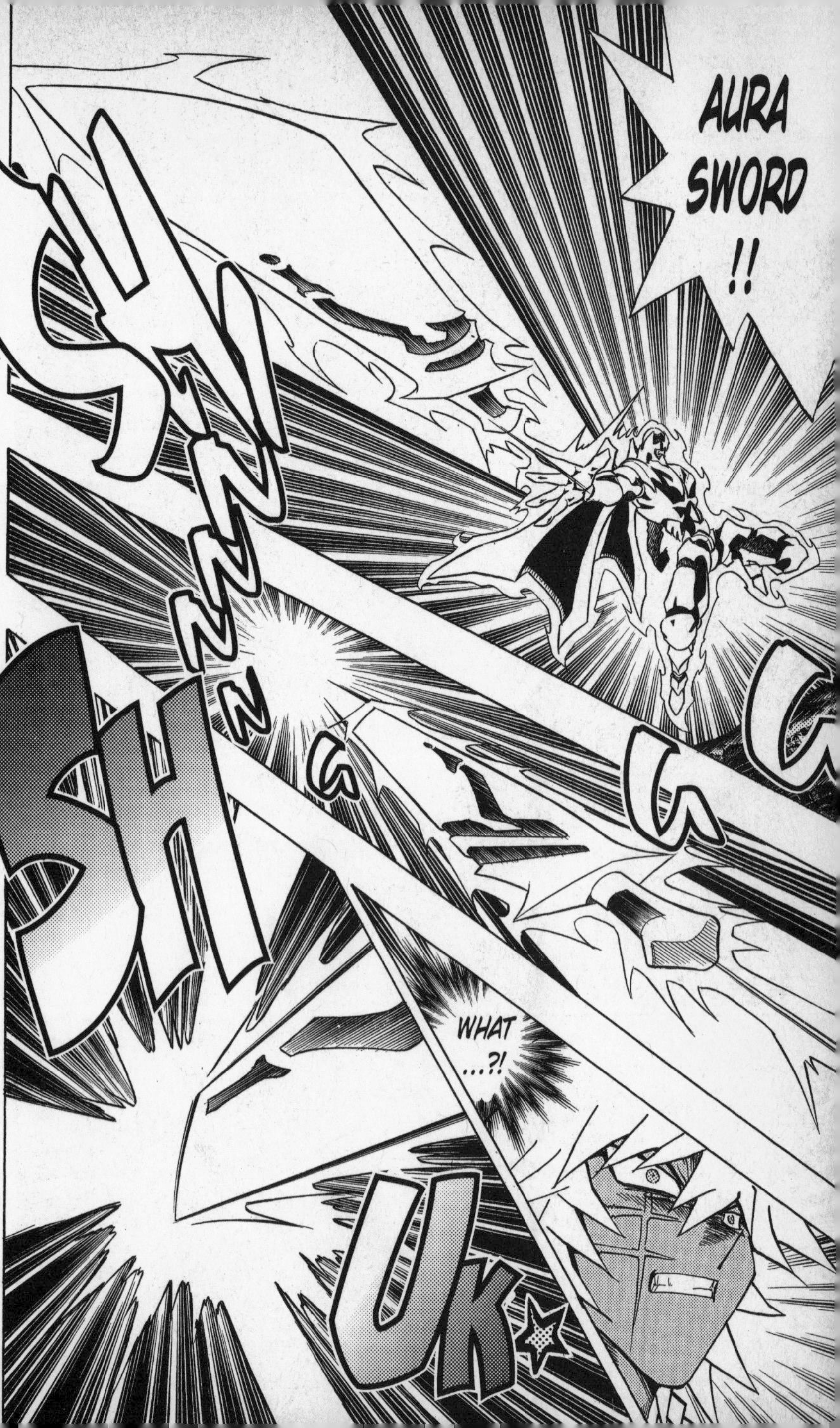
AURA SWORD !!
WHAT ...?!
SHUK

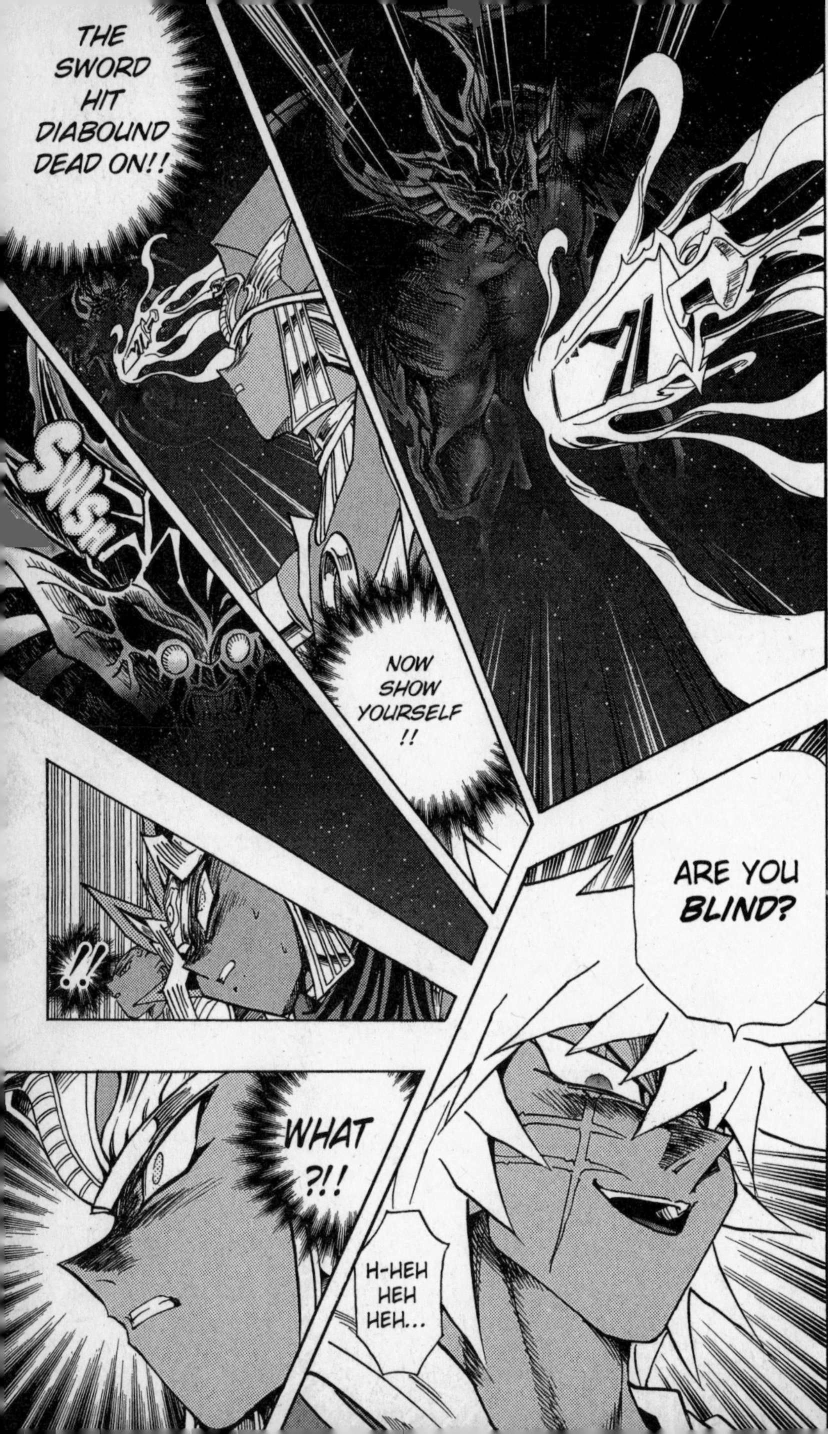
THE SWORD HIT DIABOUND DEAD ON!!
SNSH
NOW SHOW YOURSELF!!
ARE YOU BLIND?
!!
H-HEH HEH HEH...
WHAT?!!

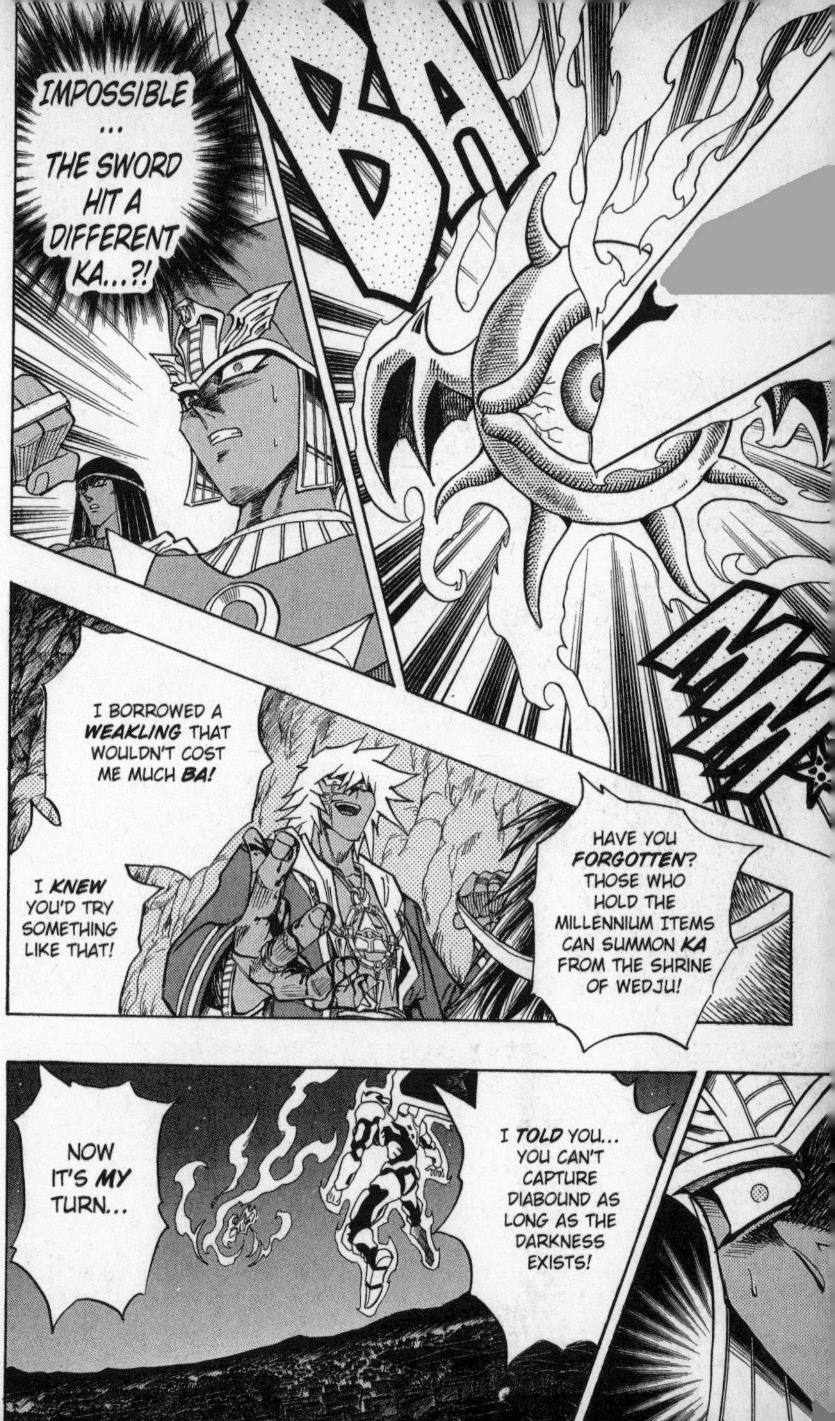
IMPOSSIBLE ... THE SWORD HIT A DIFFERENT KA...?!
I BORROWED A **WEAKLING** THAT WOULDN'T COST ME MUCH **BA!**
HAVE YOU **FORGOTTEN?** THOSE WHO HOLD THE MILLENNIUM ITEMS CAN SUMMON **KA** FROM THE SHRINE OF WEDJU!
I **KNEW** YOU'D TRY SOMETHING LIKE THAT!
I **TOLD** YOU... YOU CAN'T CAPTURE DIABOUND AS LONG AS THE DARKNESS EXISTS!
NOW IT'S **MY** TURN...

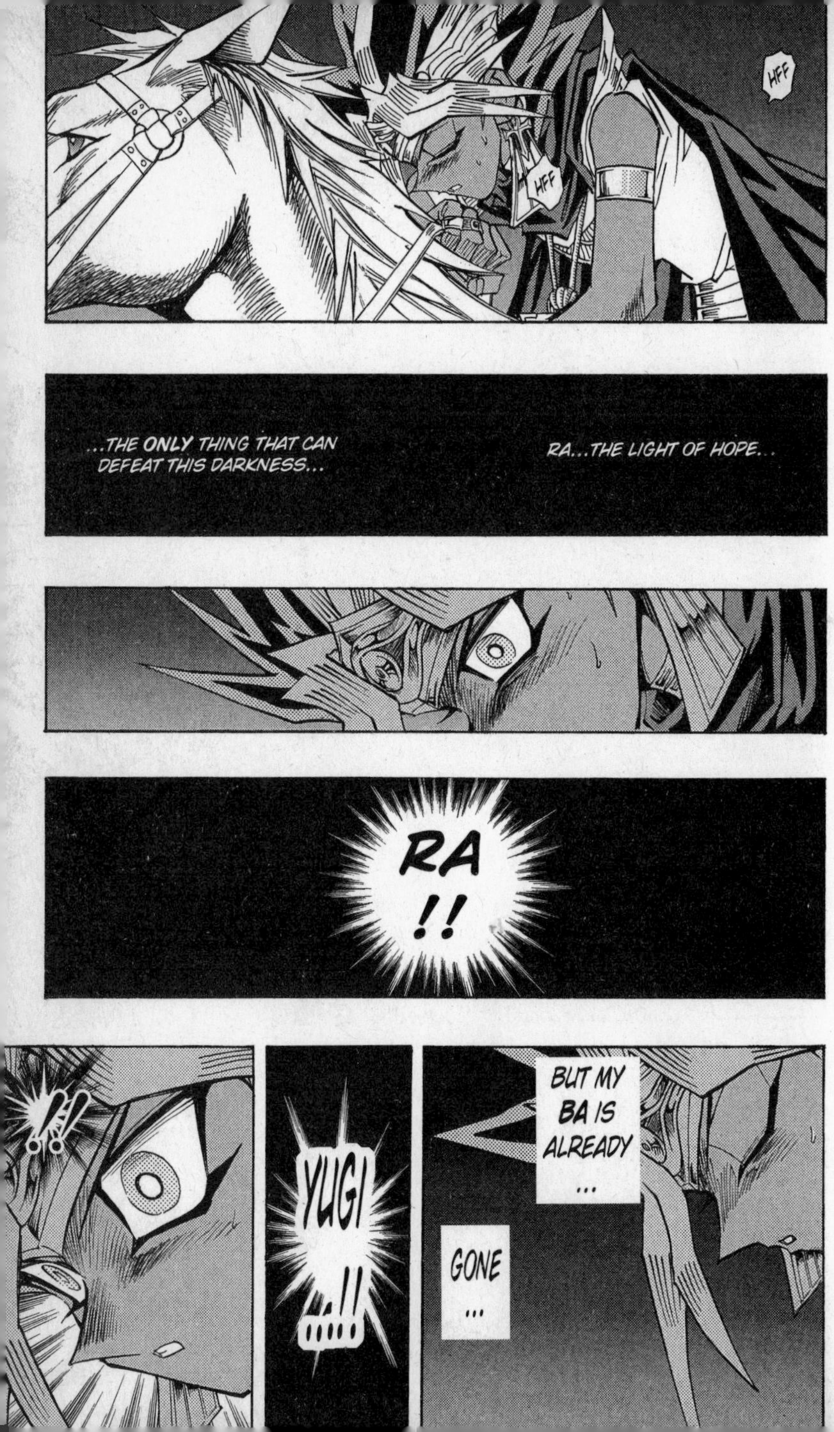
HFF
HFF
RA...THE LIGHT OF HOPE...
...THE ONLY THING THAT CAN DEFEAT THIS DARKNESS...
RA!!
BUT MY BA IS ALREADY...
GONE...
YUGI...!!
!!

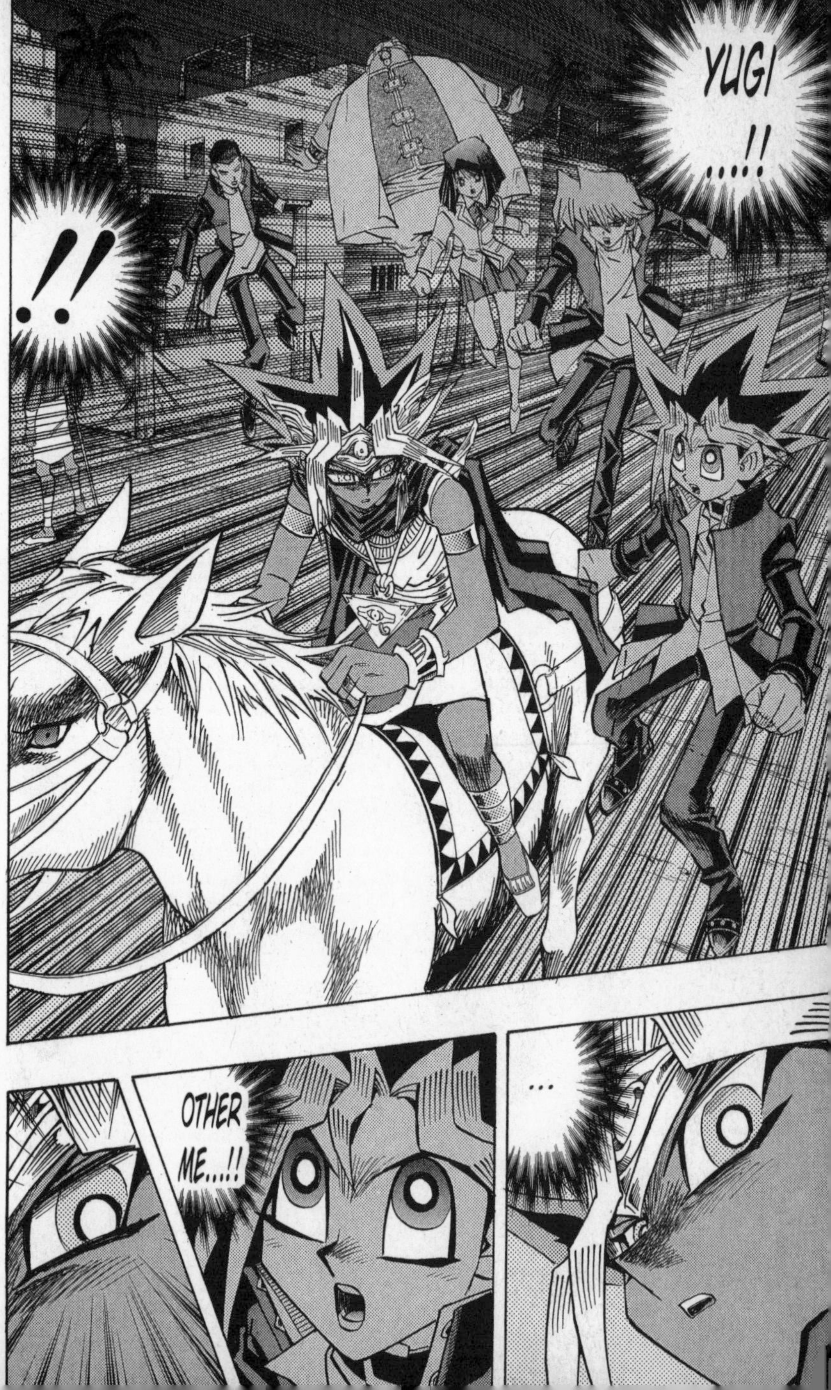
YUGI ...!!
!!
...
OTHER ME...!!

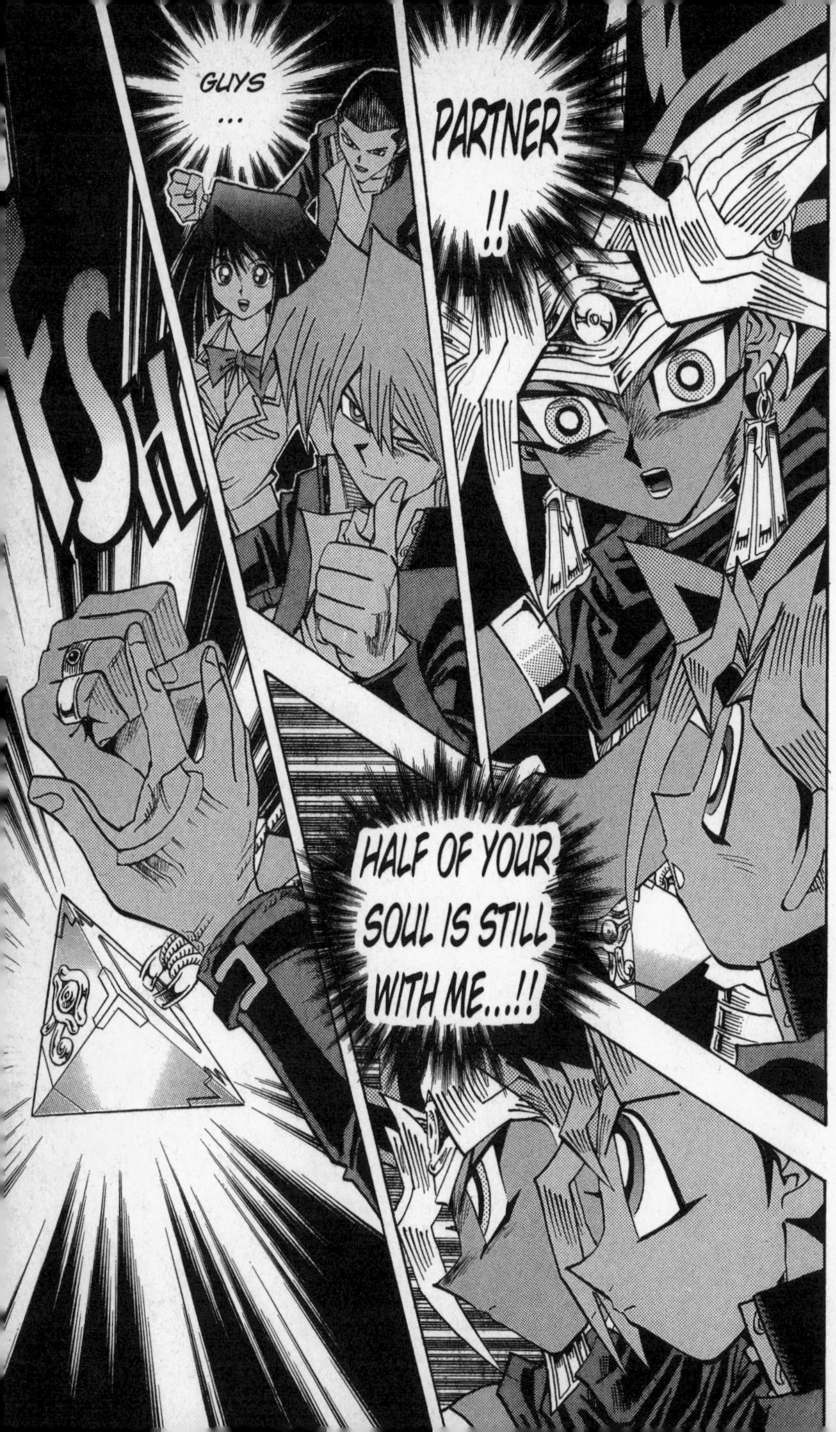
PARTNER !!
GUYS ...
HALF OF YOUR SOUL IS STILL WITH ME...!!

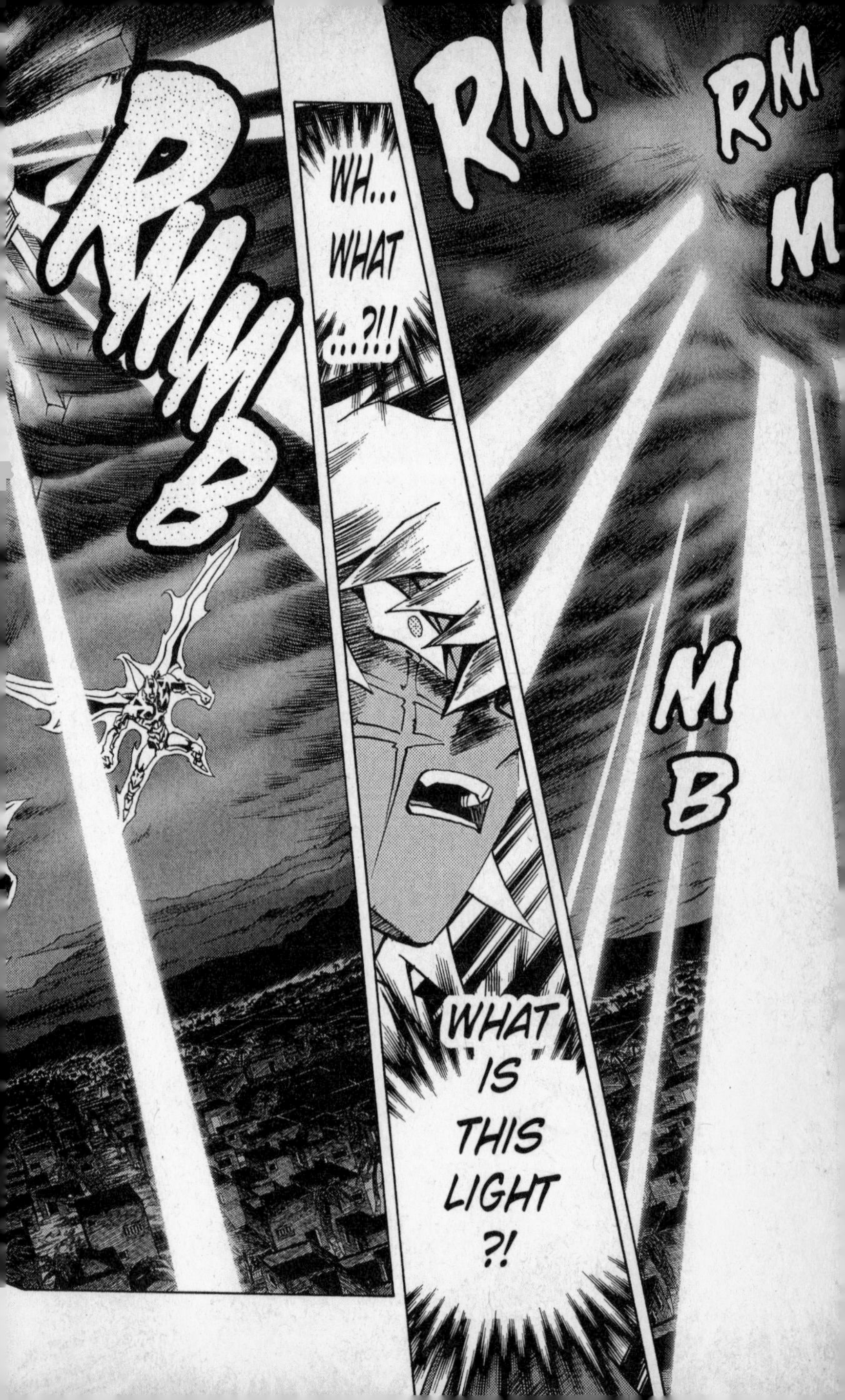
RM
RM M
M B
WH... WHAT ...?!!
WHAT IS THIS LIGHT ?!
RUMMB

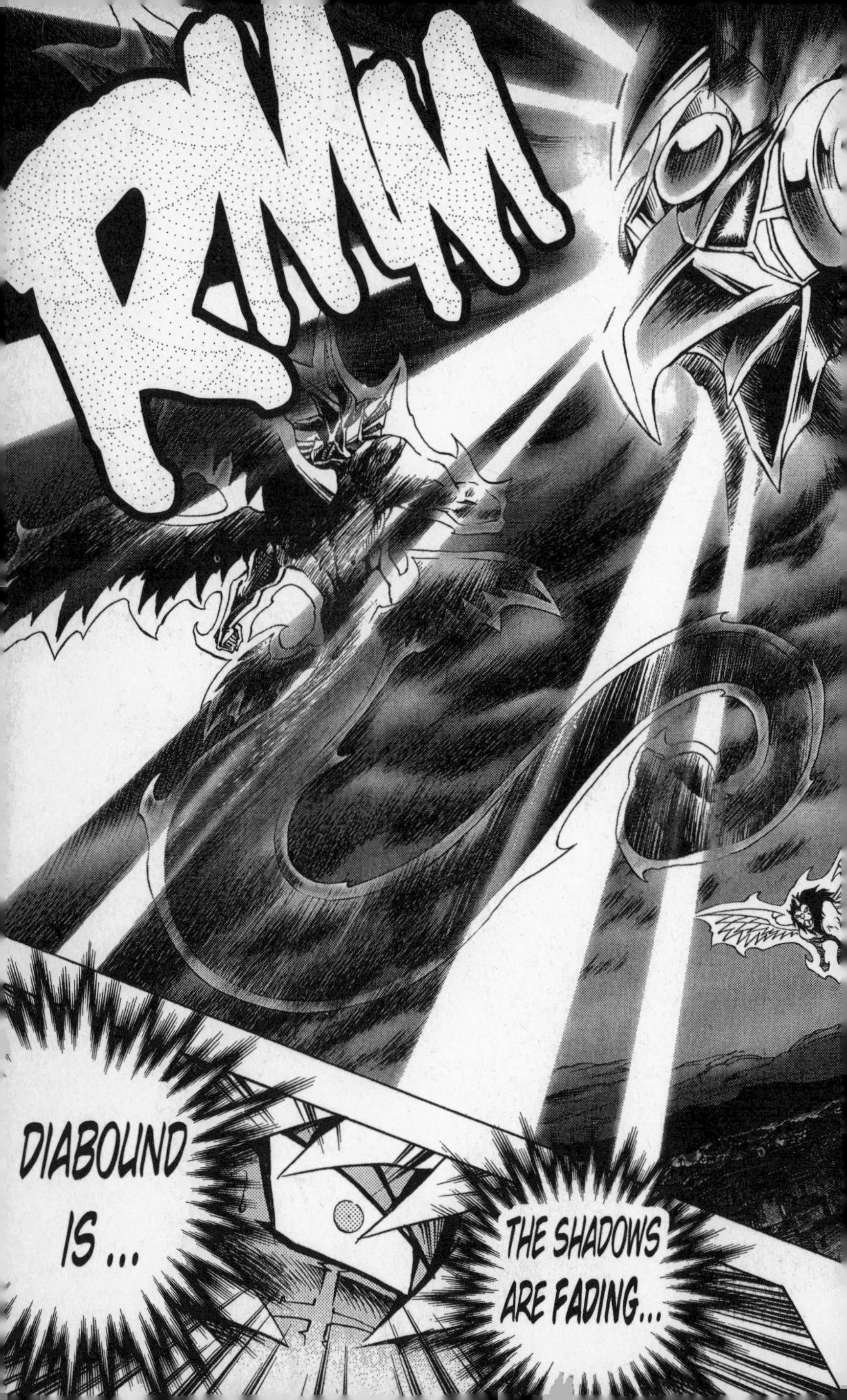
THE SHADOWS ARE FADING...
DIABOUND IS ...

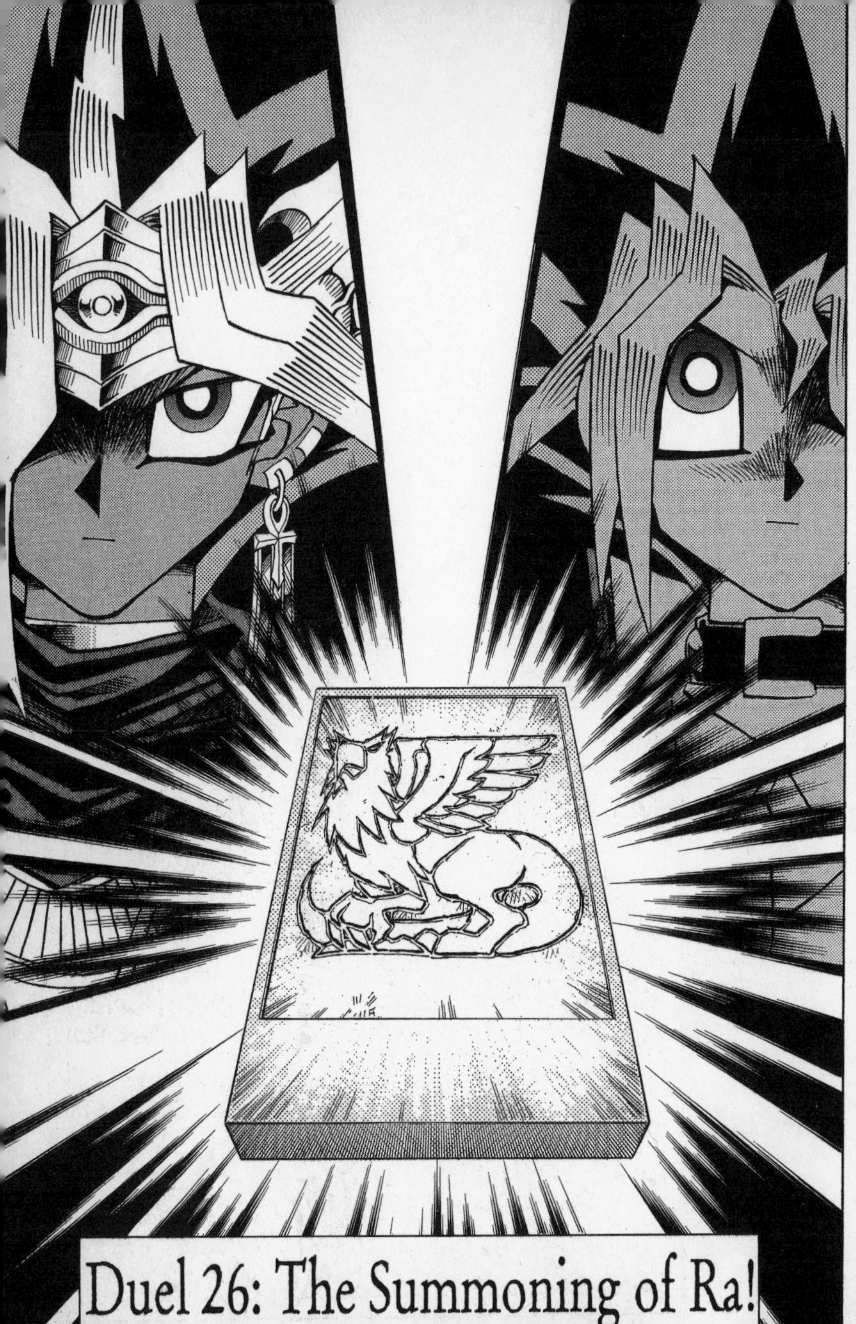

Duel 26: The Summoning of Ra!

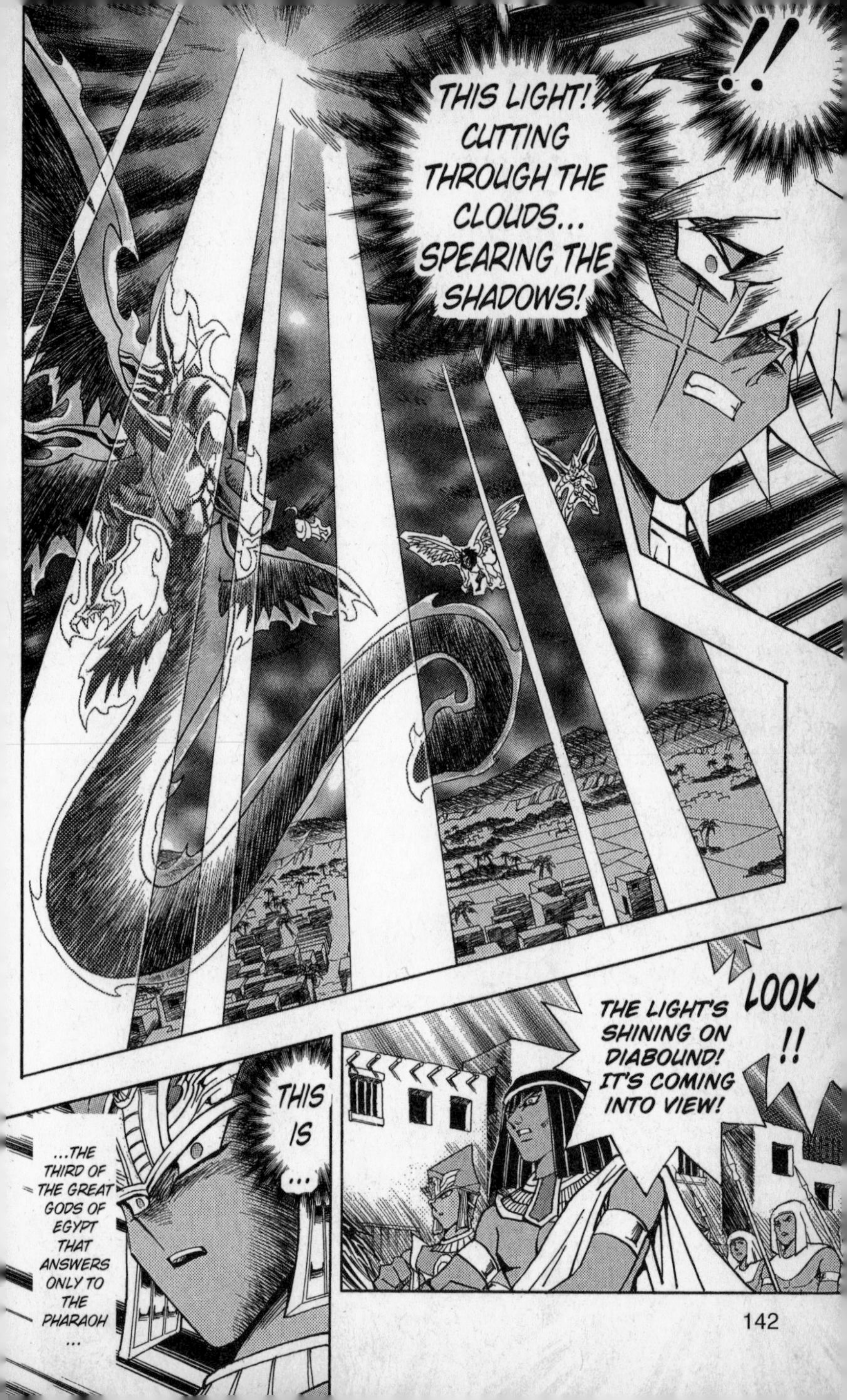
!!
THIS LIGHT! CUTTING THROUGH THE CLOUDS... SPEARING THE SHADOWS!
LOOK !!
THE LIGHT'S SHINING ON DIABOUND! IT'S COMING INTO VIEW!
THIS IS ...
...THE THIRD OF THE GREAT GODS OF EGYPT THAT ANSWERS ONLY TO THE PHARAOH ...

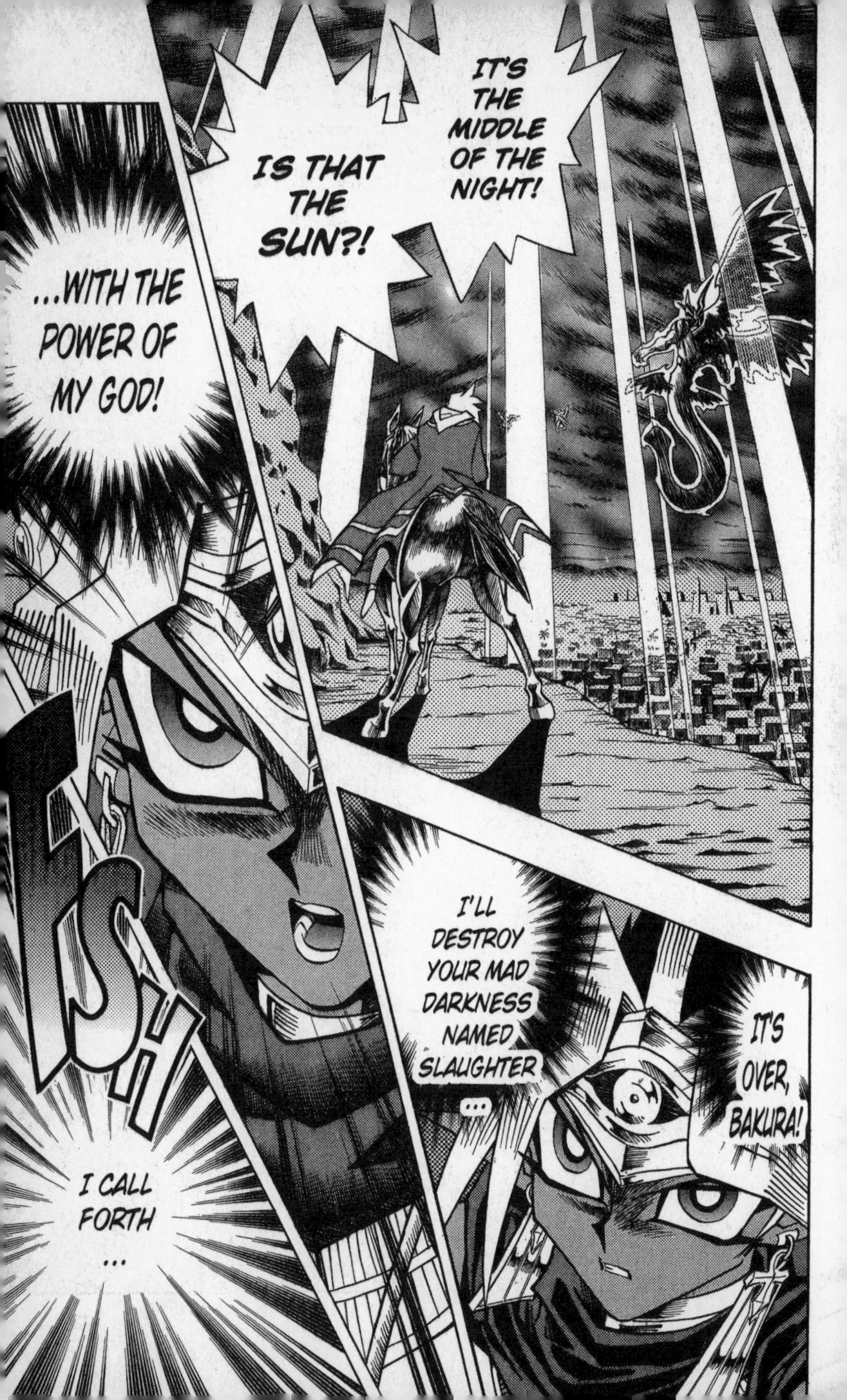

IT'S THE MIDDLE OF THE NIGHT!
IS THAT THE SUN?!
IT'S OVER, BAKURA!
I'LL DESTROY YOUR MAD DARKNESS NAMED SLAUGHTER ...
...WITH THE POWER OF MY GOD!
I CALL FORTH ...

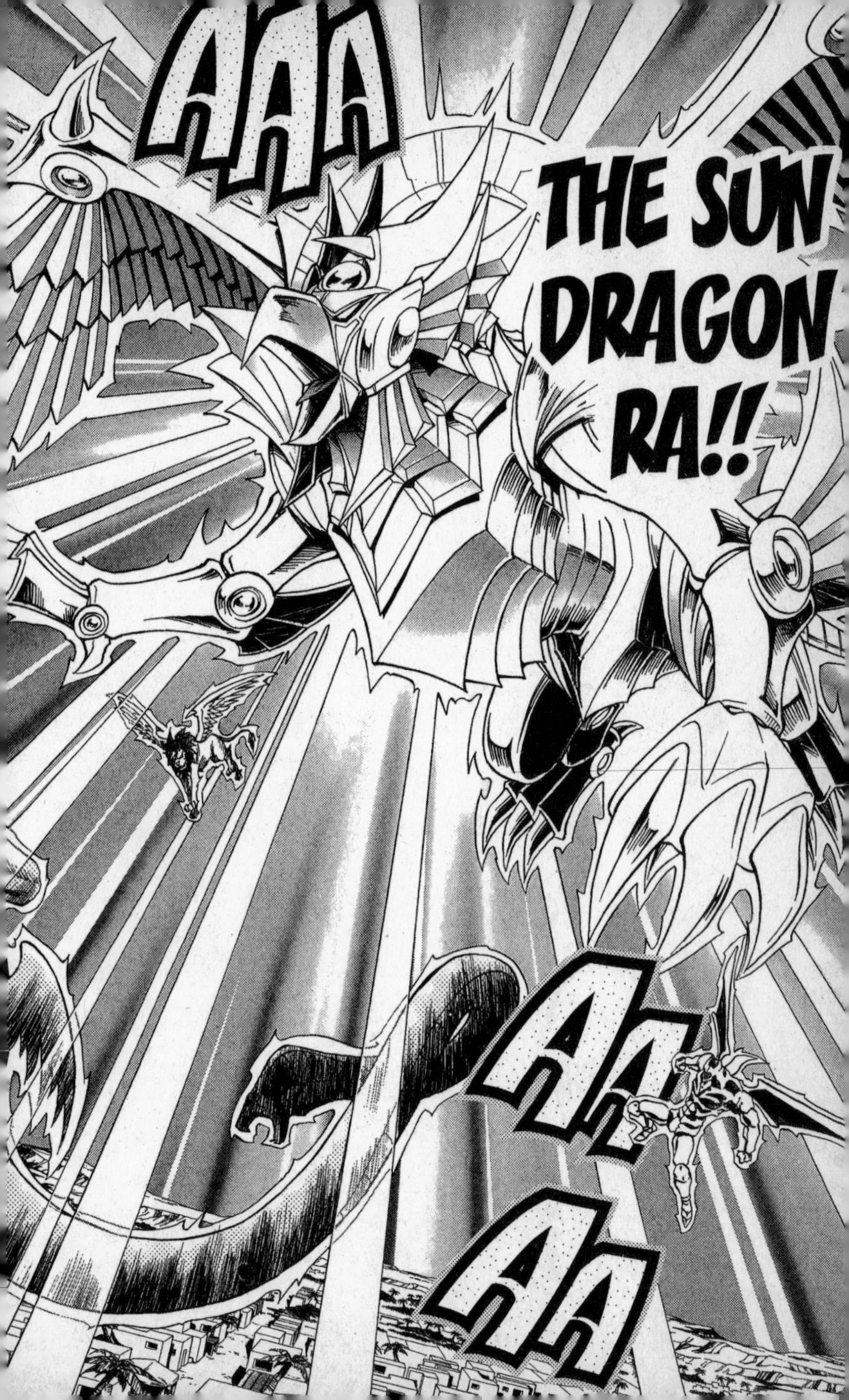
AAA
THE SUN DRAGON RA!!
AA
AA

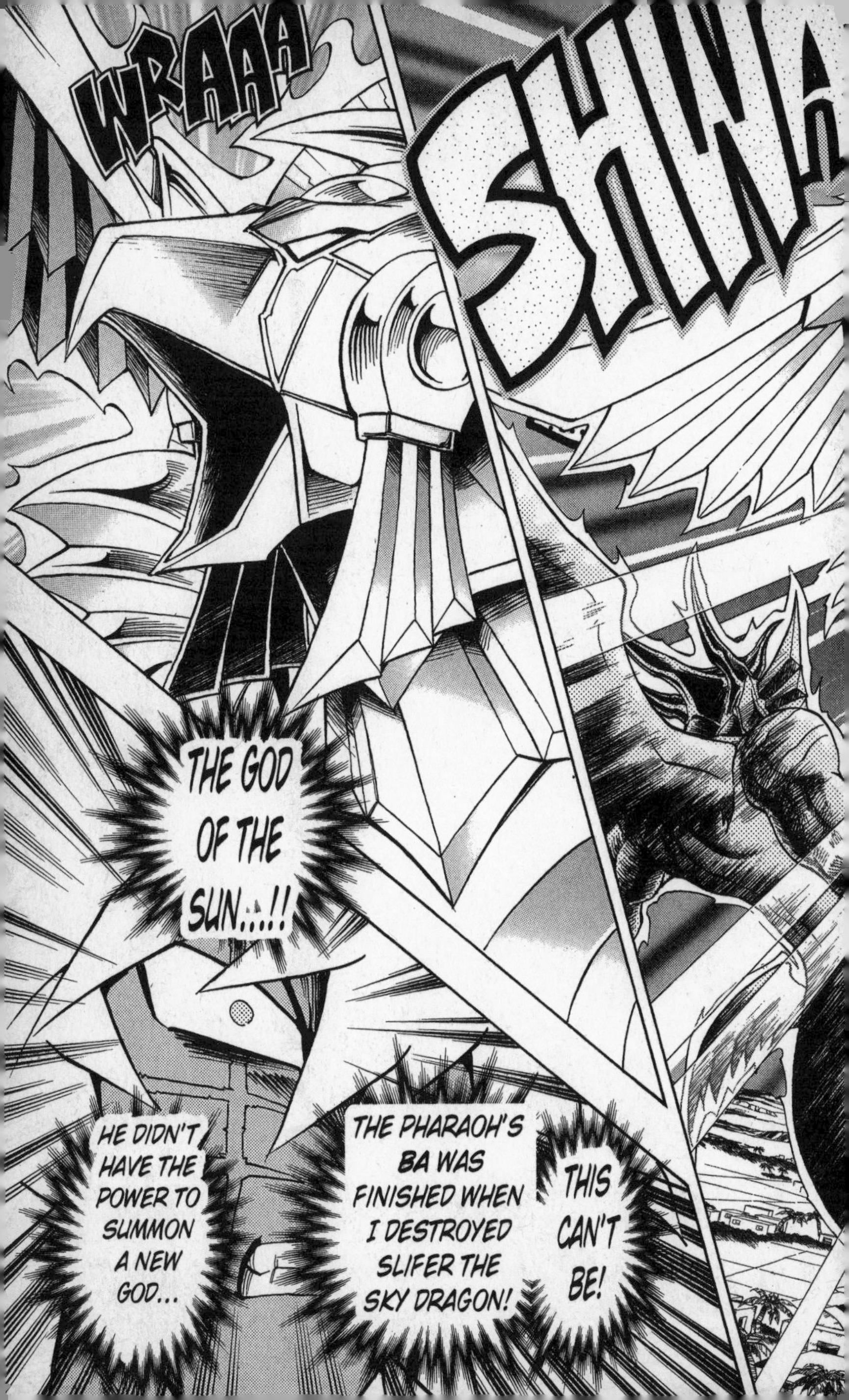
SHWA
WRAAA
THE GOD OF THE SUN...!!
THIS CAN'T BE!
THE PHARAOH'S BA WAS FINISHED WHEN I DESTROYED SLIFER THE SKY DRAGON!
HE DIDN'T HAVE THE POWER TO SUMMON A NEW GOD...

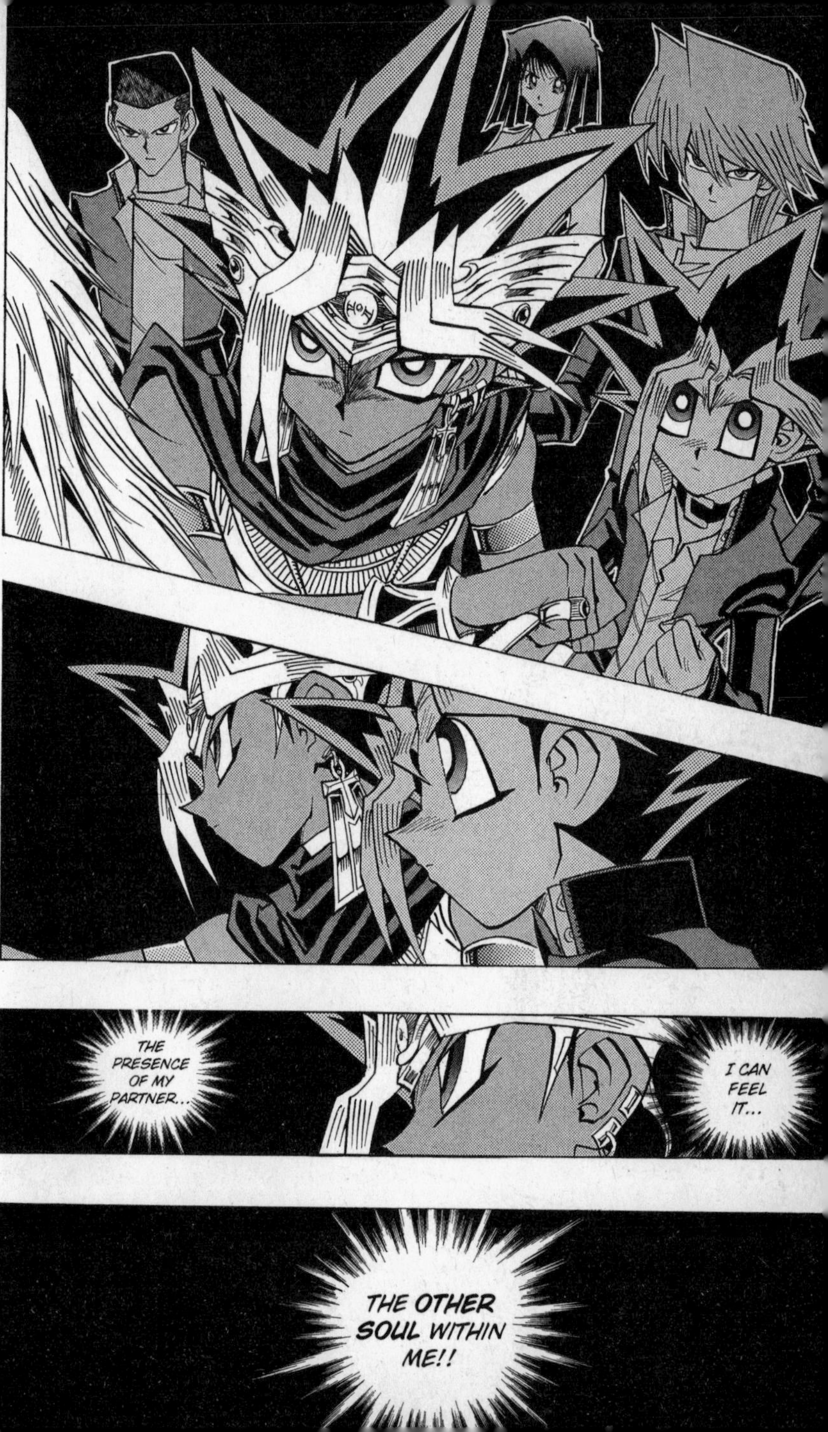
I CAN FEEL IT...
THE PRESENCE OF MY PARTNER...
THE OTHER SOUL WITHIN ME!!

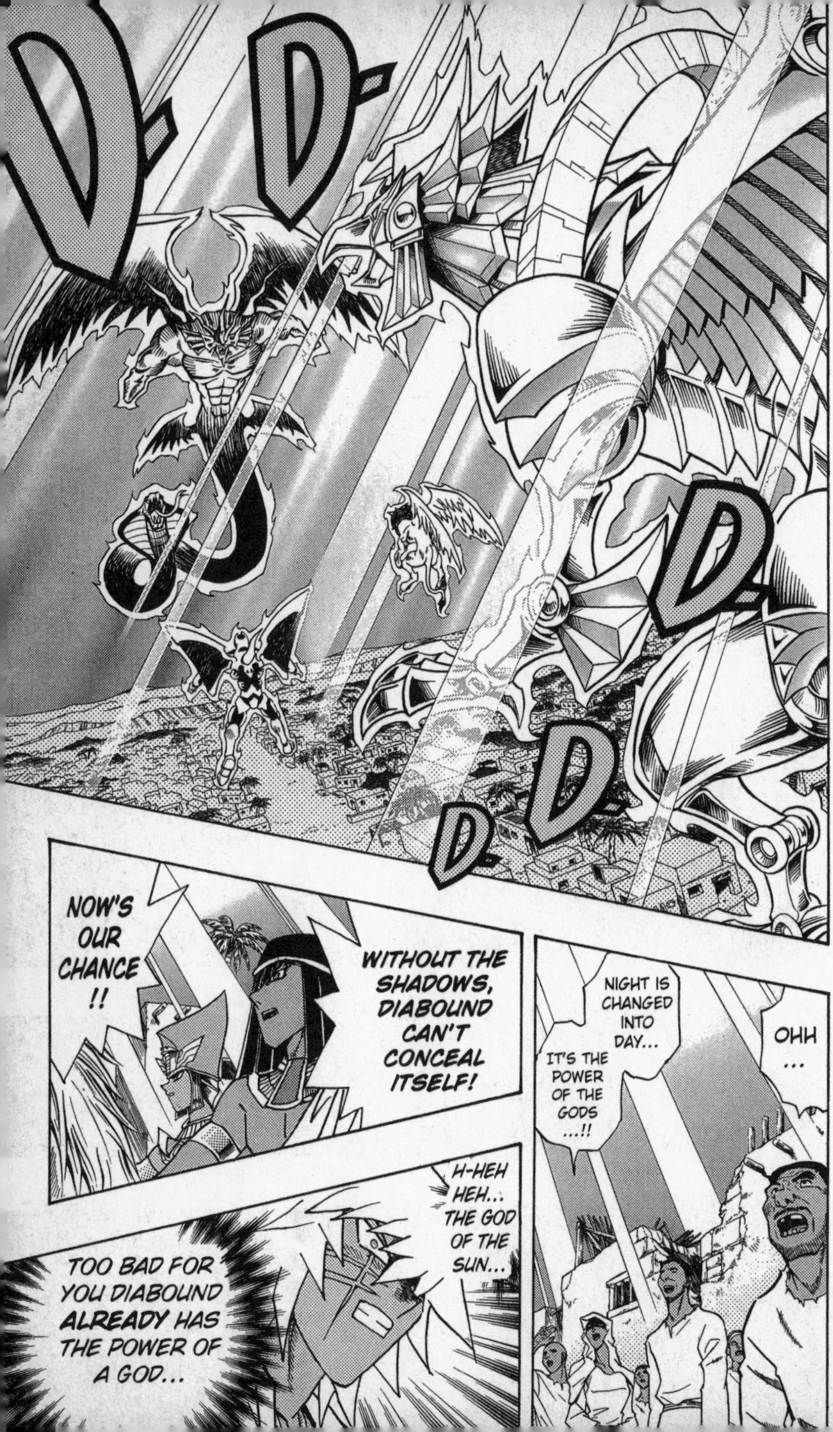
D- D-
D- D- D-
NIGHT IS CHANGED INTO DAY...
IT'S THE POWER OF THE GODS ...!!
OHH ...
NOW'S OUR CHANCE !!
WITHOUT THE SHADOWS, DIABOUND CAN'T CONCEAL ITSELF!
H-HEH HEH... THE GOD OF THE SUN...
TOO BAD FOR YOU DIABOUND ALREADY HAS THE POWER OF A GOD...

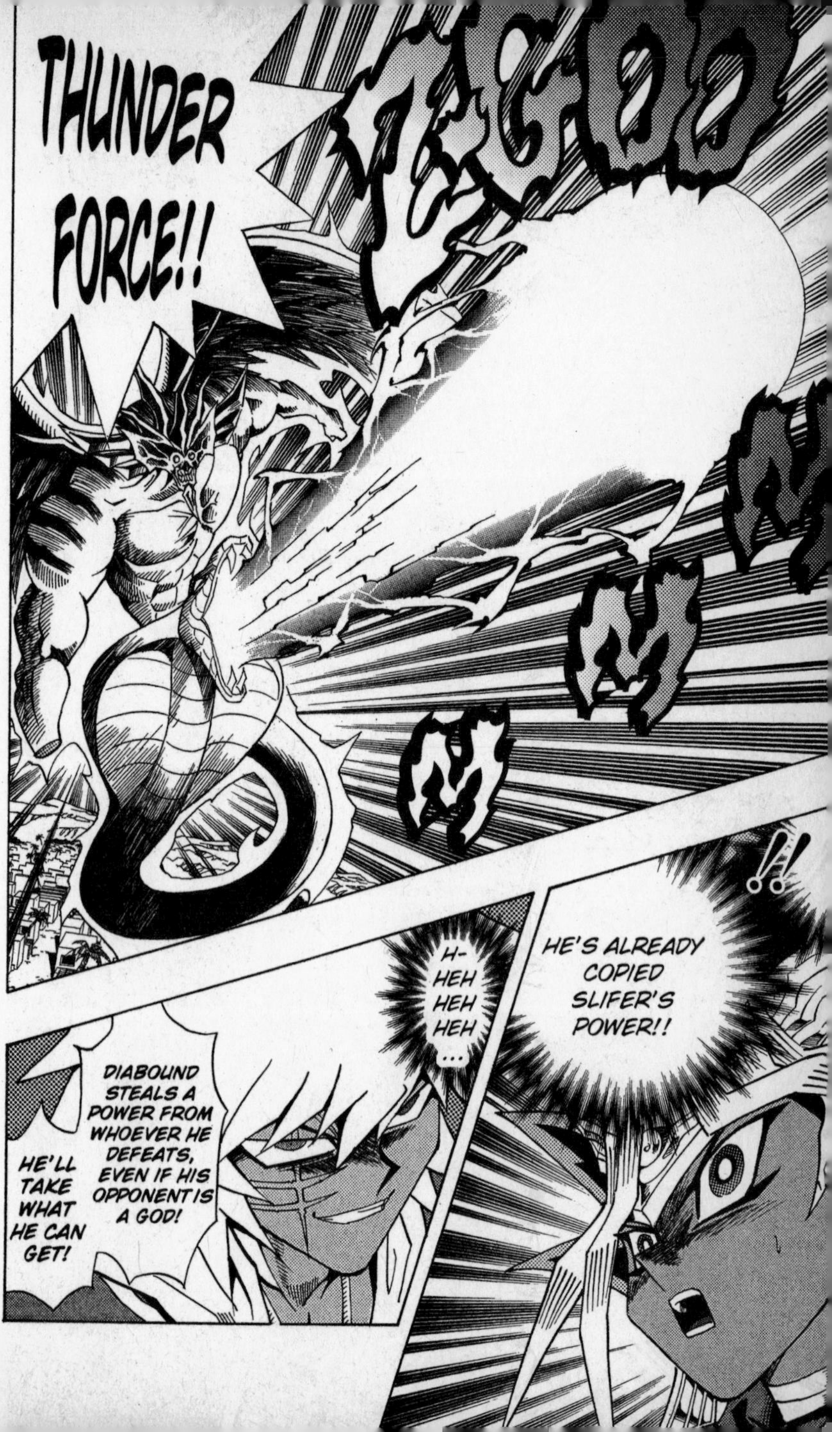
THUNDER FORCE!!
!!
HE'S ALREADY COPIED SLIFER'S POWER!!
H-HEH HEH HEH...
DIABOUND STEALS A POWER FROM WHOEVER HE DEFEATS, EVEN IF HIS OPPONENT IS A GOD!
HE'LL TAKE WHAT HE CAN GET!

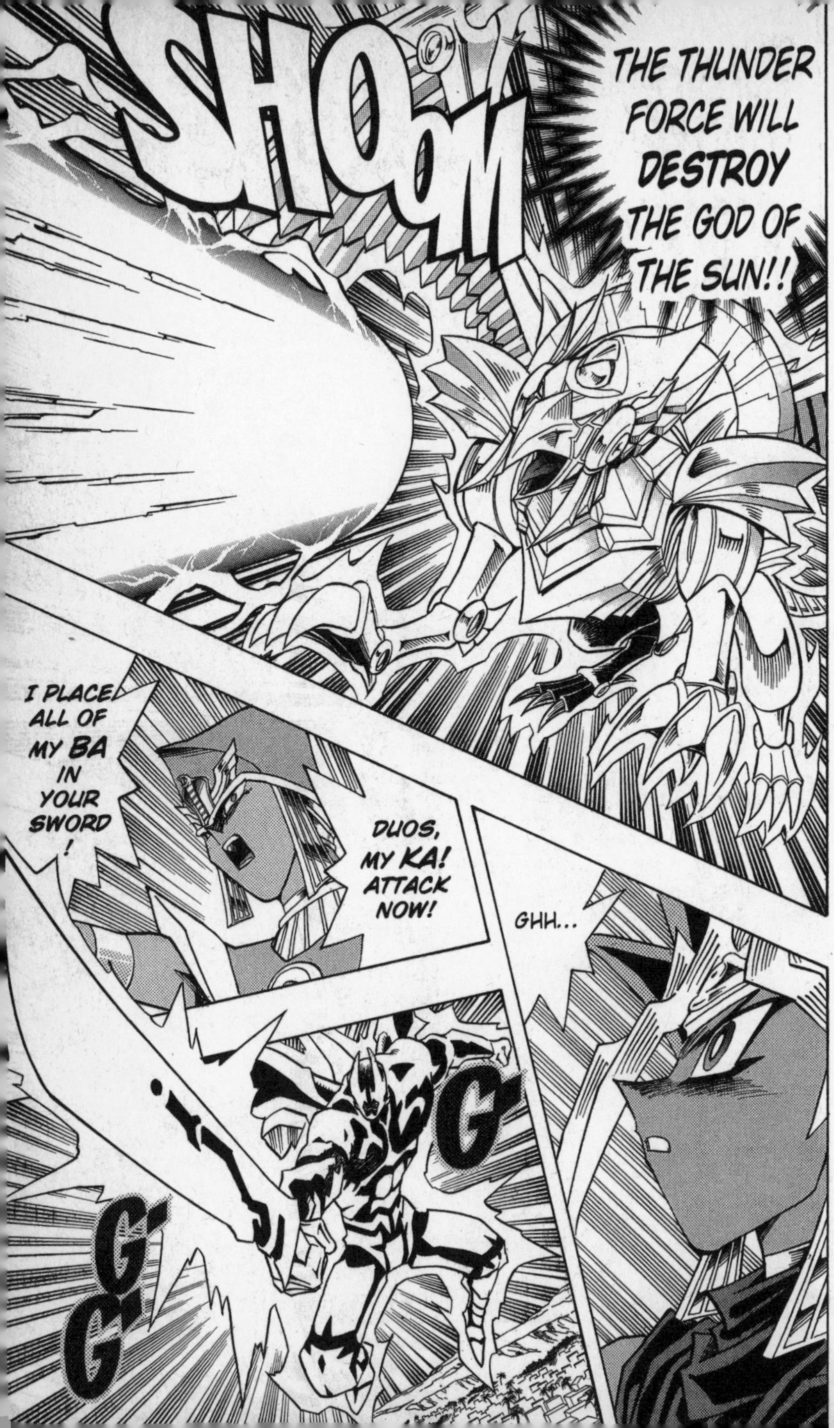
THE THUNDER FORCE WILL DESTROY THE GOD OF THE SUN!!
SHOOM
GHH...
I PLACE ALL OF MY BA IN YOUR SWORD!
DUOS, MY KA! ATTACK NOW!
G
GG

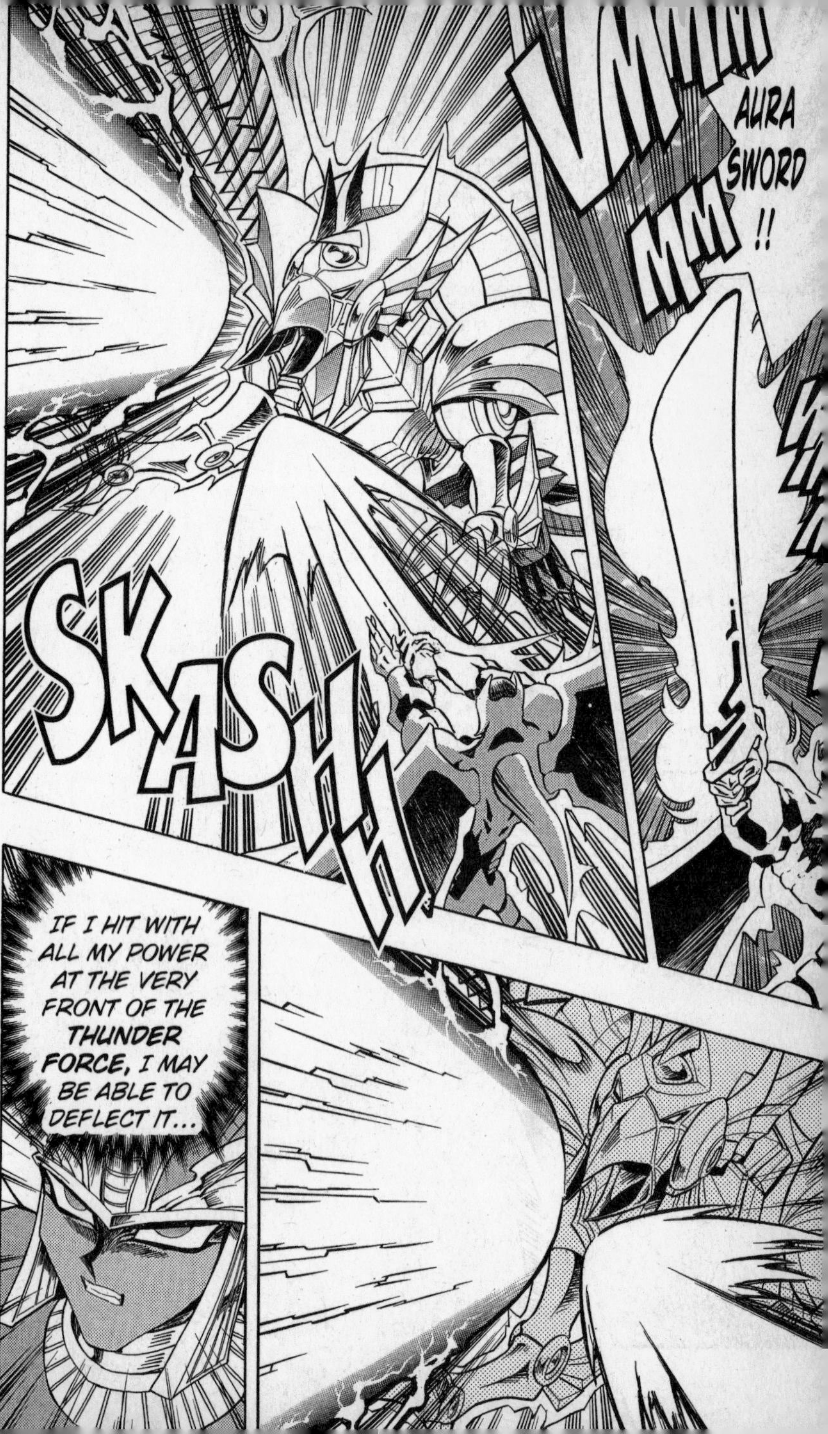
VMMMMM
AURA SWORD!!
SKASH!!
IF I HIT WITH ALL MY POWER AT THE VERY FRONT OF THE THUNDER FORCE, I MAY BE ABLE TO DEFLECT IT...

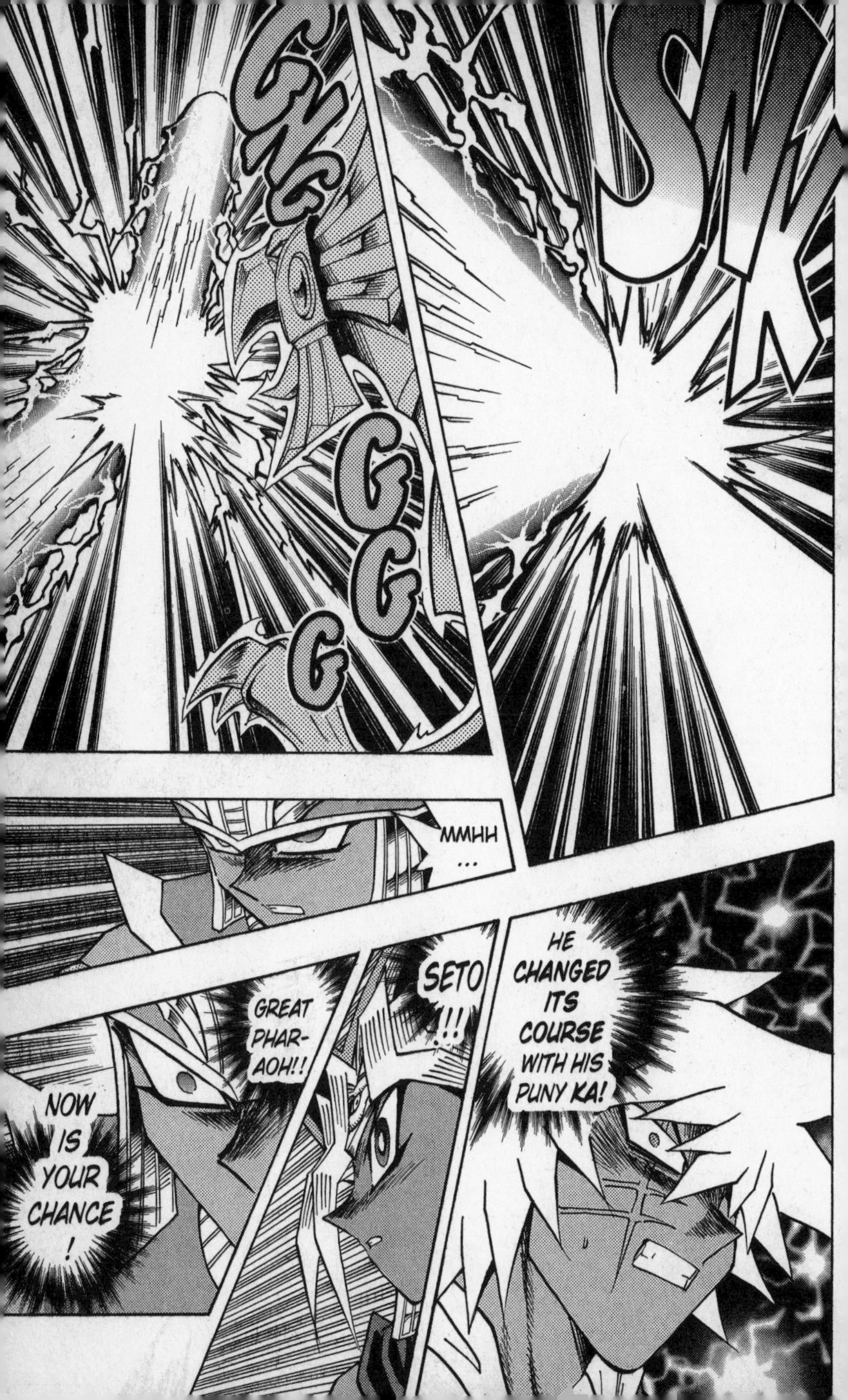
MMHH ...
HE CHANGED ITS COURSE WITH HIS PUNY KA!
SETO !!
GREAT PHAR-AOH!!
NOW IS YOUR CHANCE !

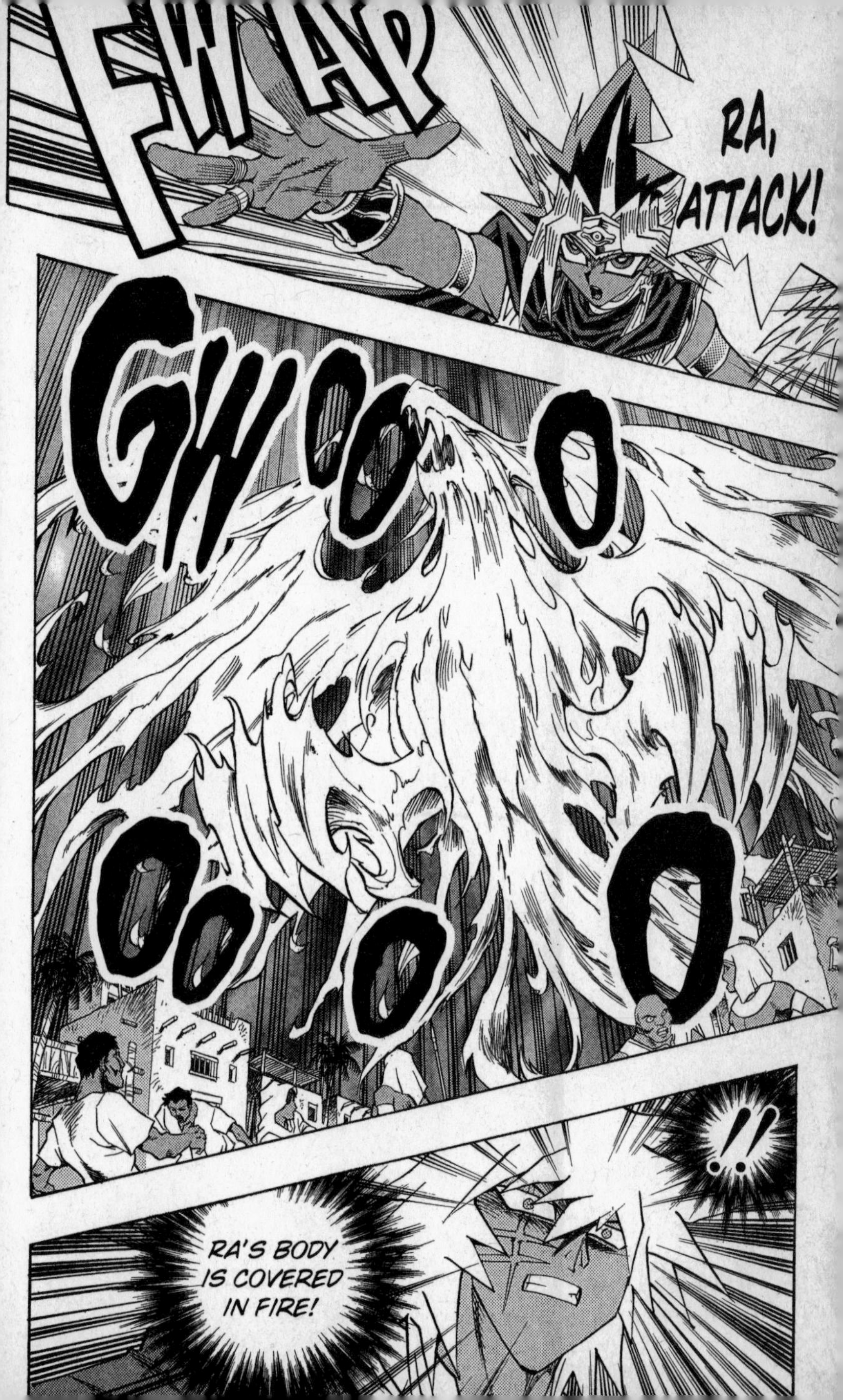
RA, ATTACK!
FWAP
GWOOOOOOO
!!
RA'S BODY IS COVERED IN FIRE!

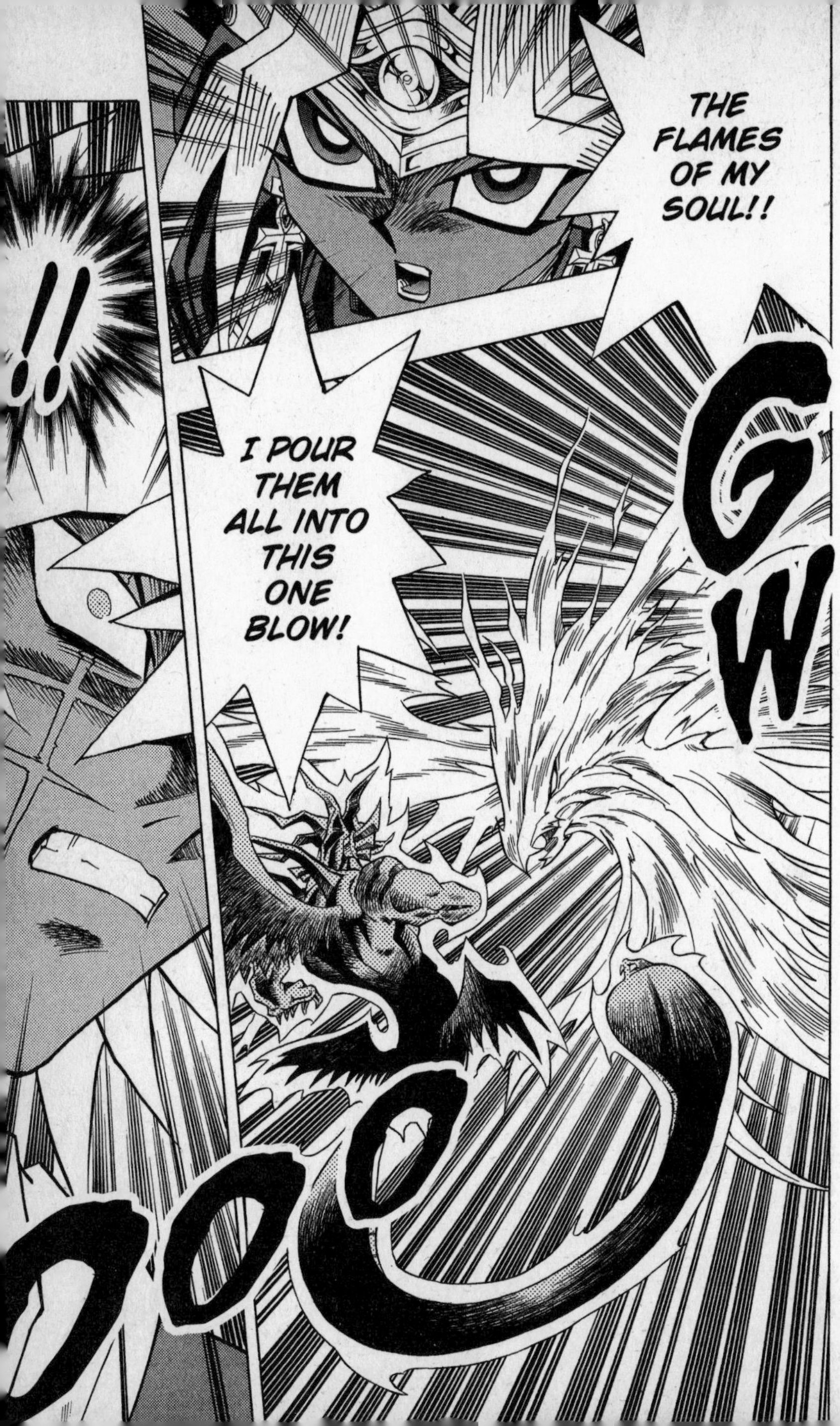
THE FLAMES OF MY SOUL!!
!!
I POUR THEM ALL INTO THIS ONE BLOW!

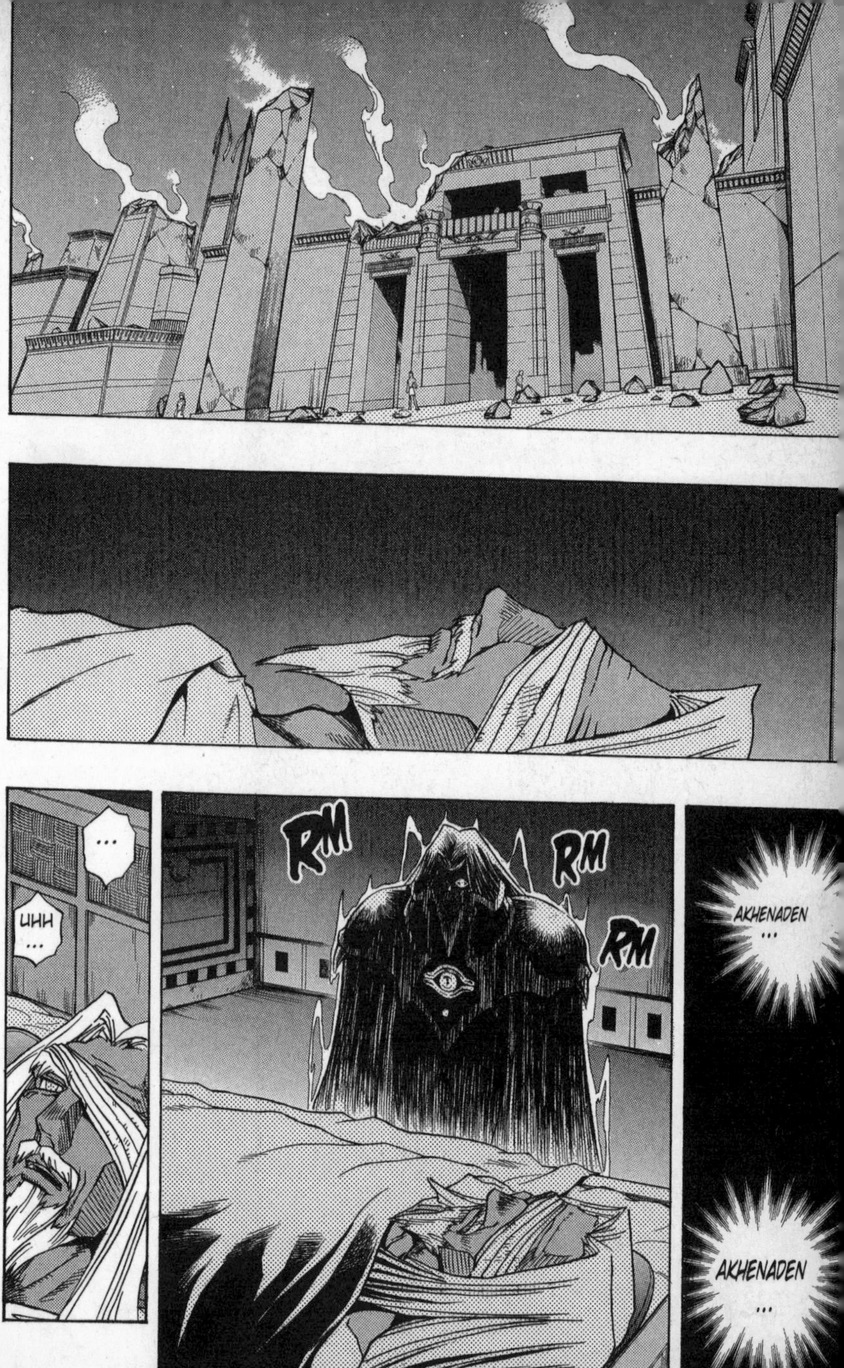
AKHENADEN ...
AKHENADEN ...
RM
RM
RM
...
UHH ...

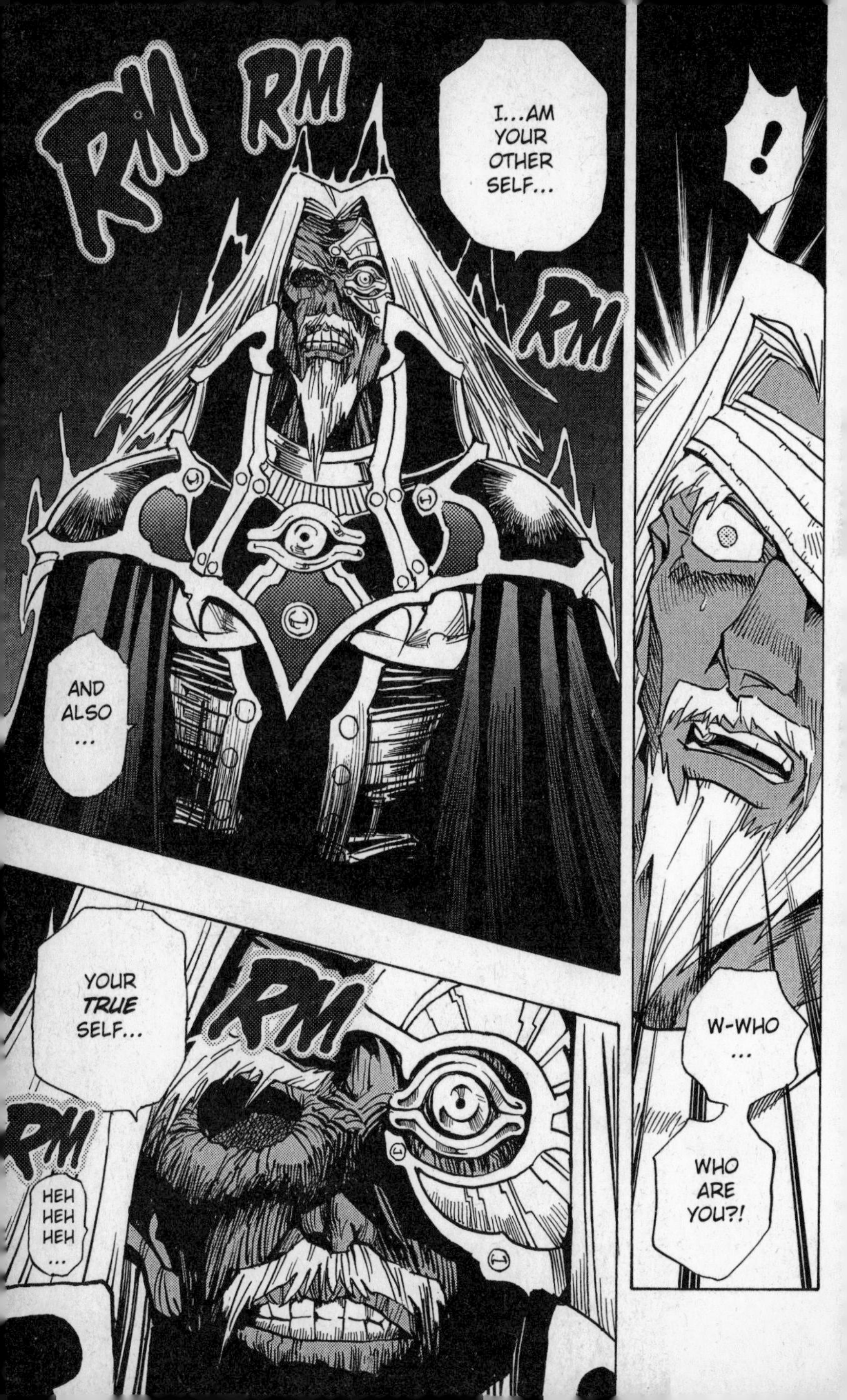
!
W-WHO...
WHO ARE YOU?!
RM RM
I...AM YOUR OTHER SELF...
RM
AND ALSO...
YOUR *TRUE* SELF...
RM
RM
HEH HEH HEH...

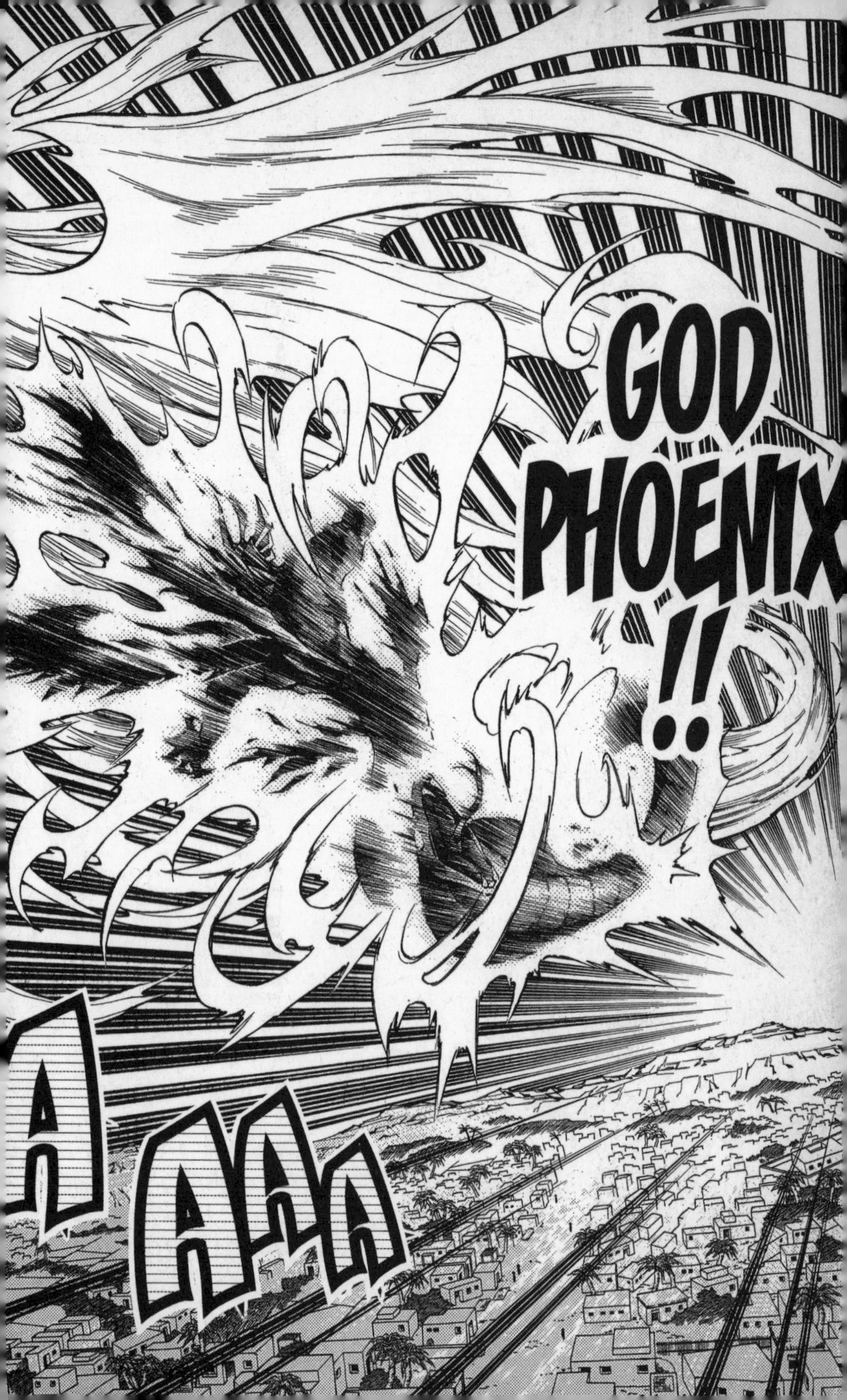
GOD PHOENIX!!
AAAAA

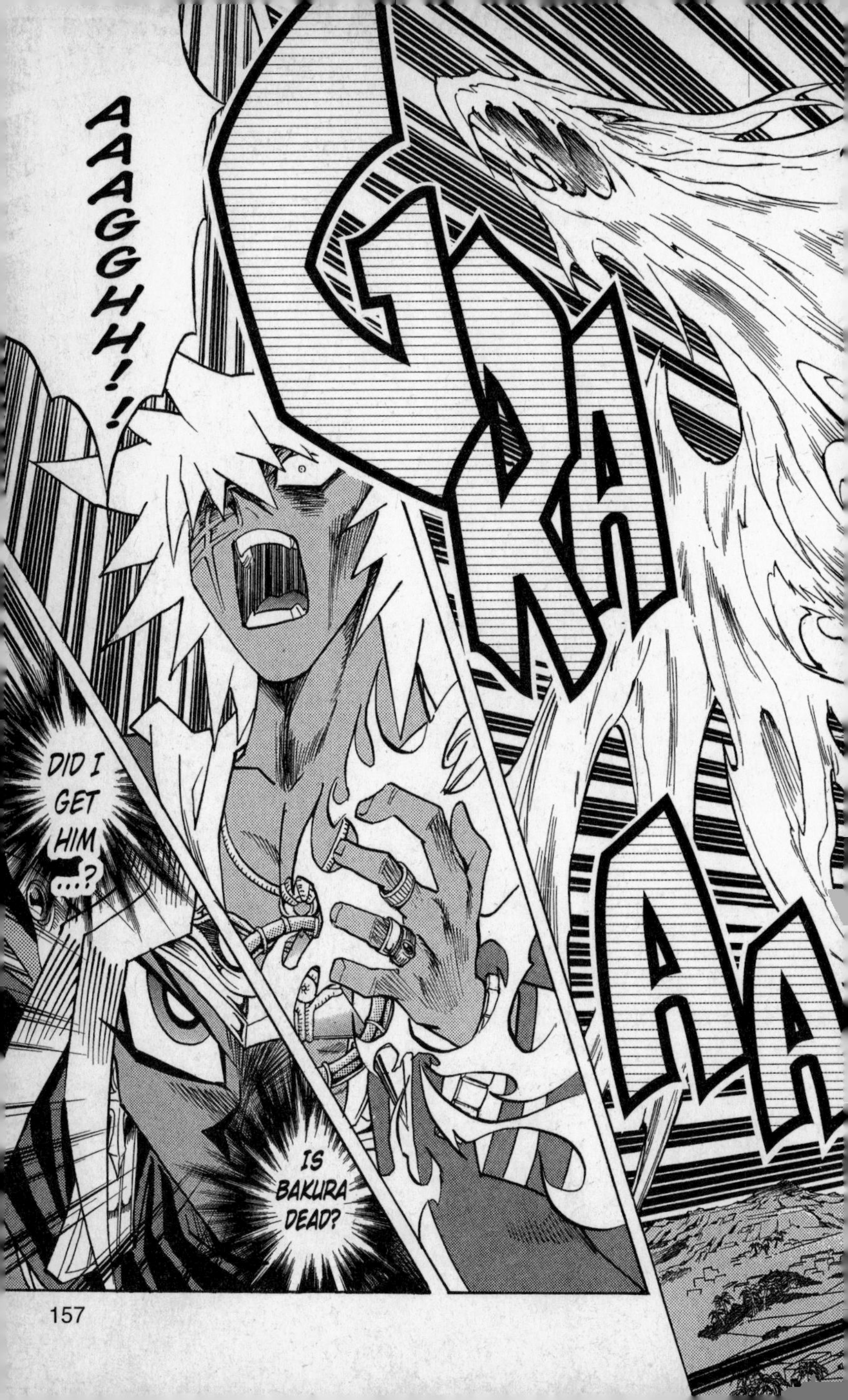
AAAAGGHH!!
DID I GET HIM ...?
IS BAKURA DEAD?

Duel 27: Ruler of Shadows!!

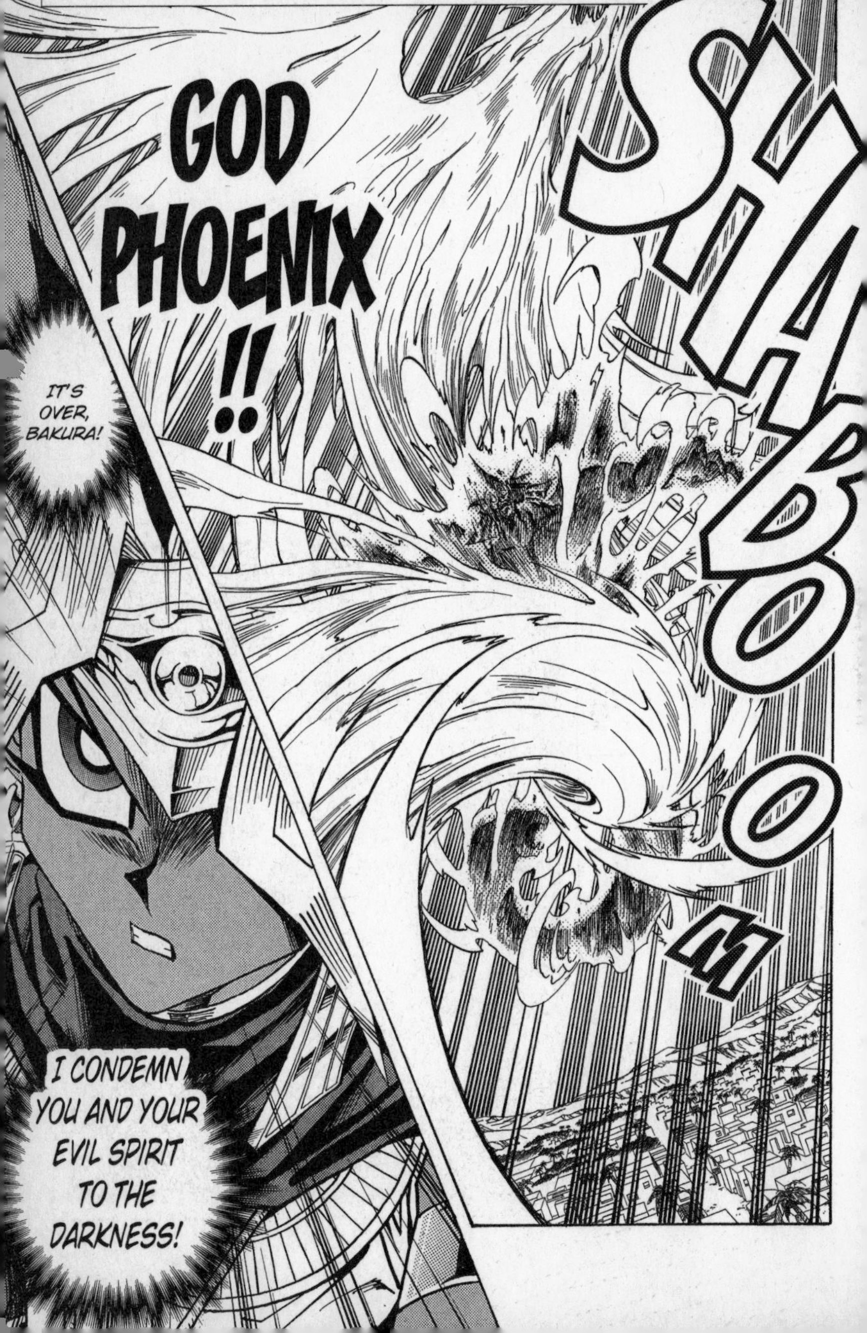
GOD PHOENIX!!
SHABOOOM
IT'S OVER, BAKURA!
I CONDEMN YOU AND YOUR EVIL SPIRIT TO THE DARKNESS!

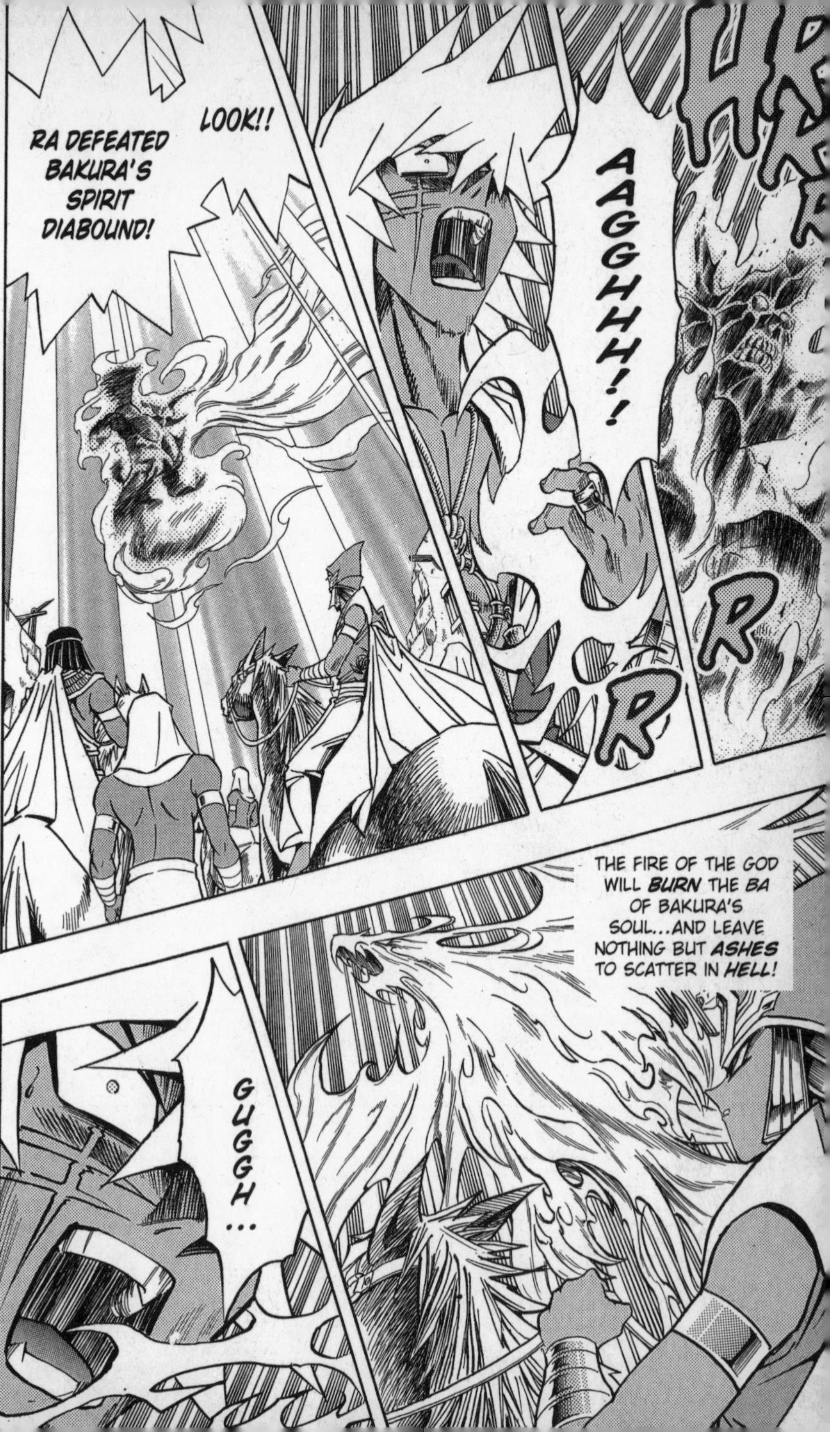
URRRR
AAGGHHH!!
LOOK!!
RA DEFEATED BAKURA'S SPIRIT DIABOUND!
THE FIRE OF THE GOD WILL BURN THE BA OF BAKURA'S SOUL...AND LEAVE NOTHING BUT ASHES TO SCATTER IN HELL!
GUGGH...

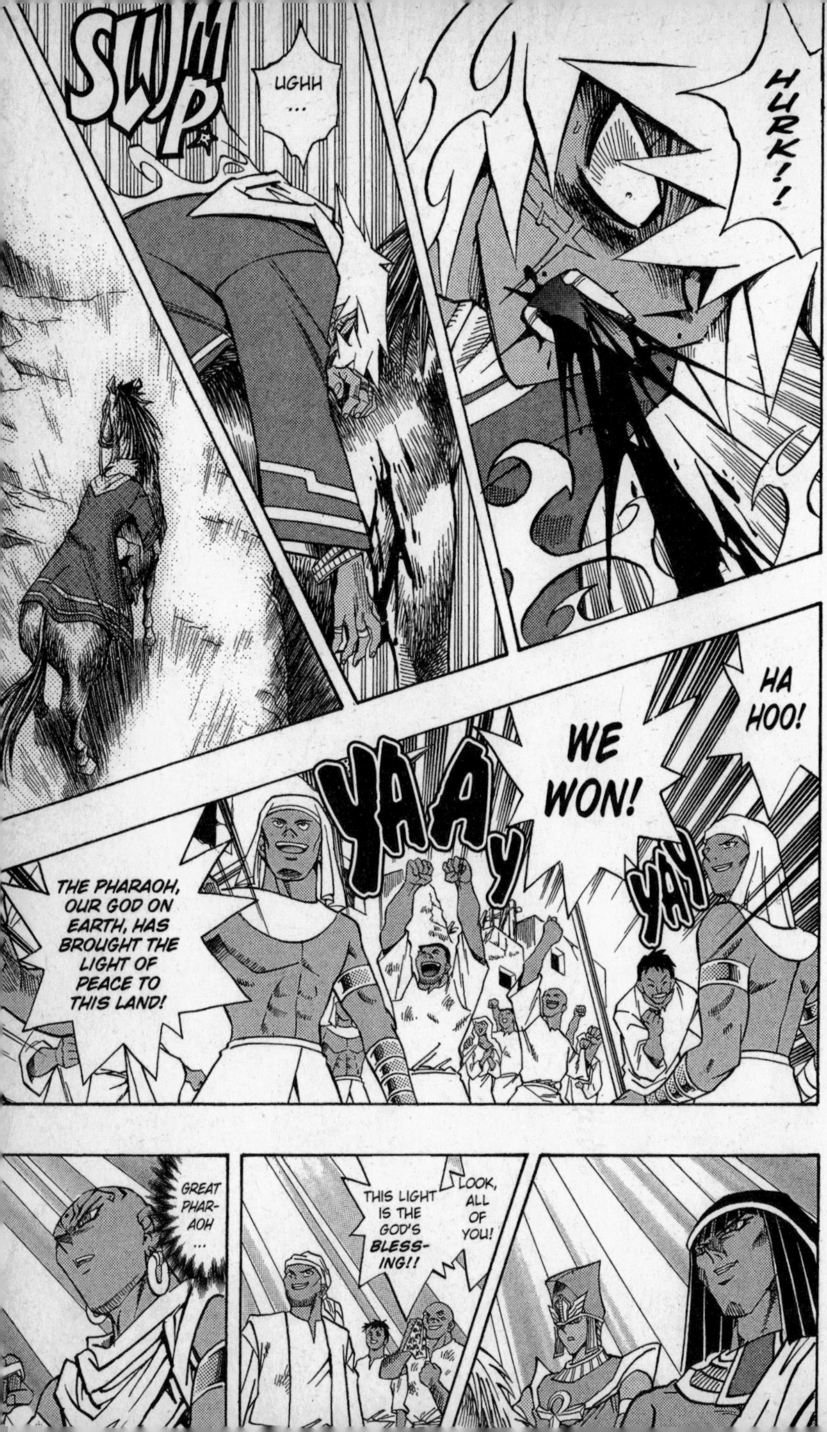
HURK!!
UGHH ...
SLUP
HA HOO!
WE WON!
YAAY
YAY
THE PHARAOH, OUR GOD ON EARTH, HAS BROUGHT THE LIGHT OF PEACE TO THIS LAND!
LOOK, ALL OF YOU!
THIS LIGHT IS THE GOD'S BLESSING!!
GREAT PHARAOH ...

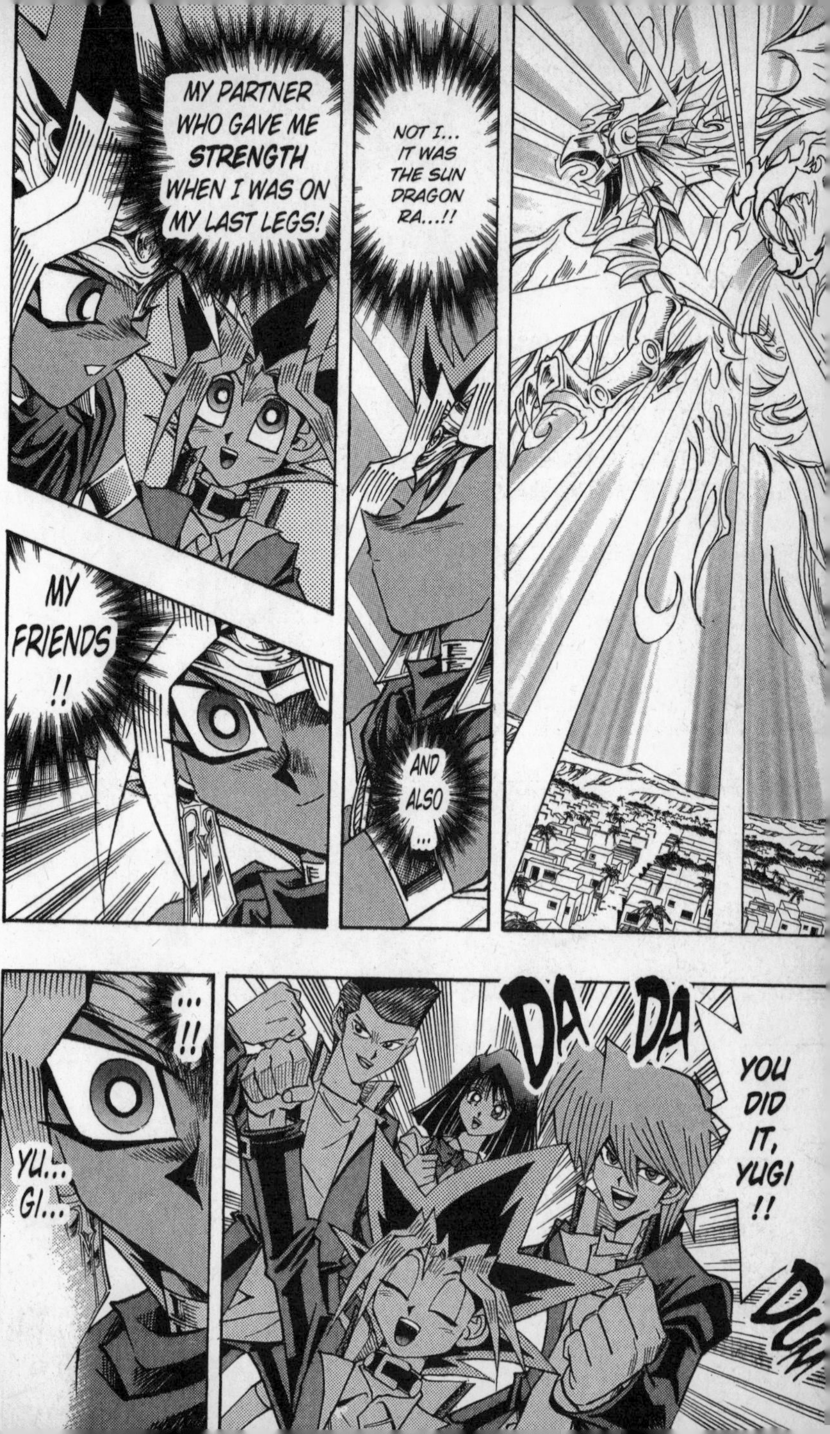
NOT I... IT WAS THE SUN DRAGON RA...!!
AND ALSO ...
MY PARTNER WHO GAVE ME STRENGTH WHEN I WAS ON MY LAST LEGS!
MY FRIENDS !!
DA DA
YOU DID IT, YUGI !!
DUM
...!!
YU... GI...

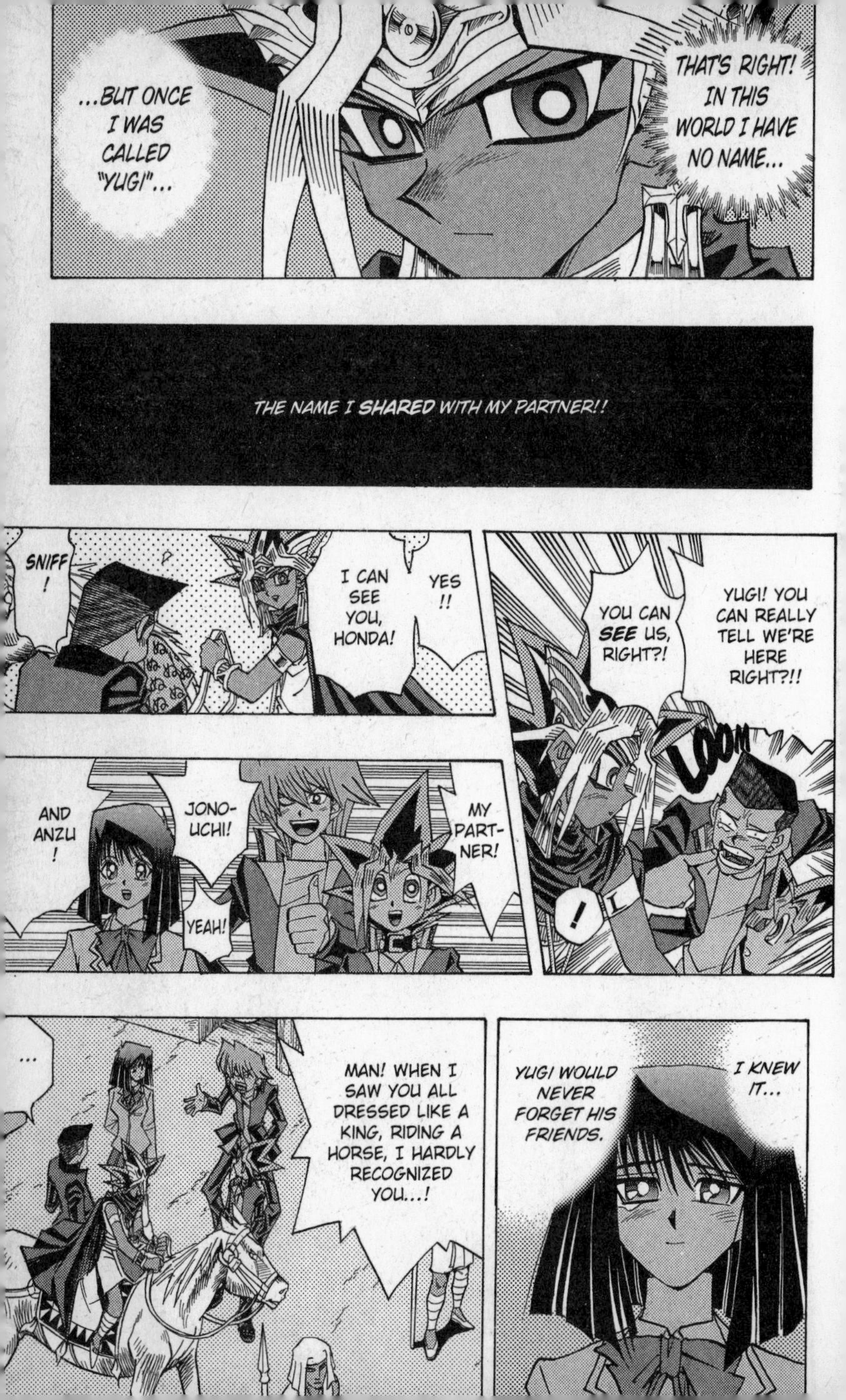
THAT'S RIGHT! IN THIS WORLD I HAVE NO NAME...
...BUT ONCE I WAS CALLED "YUGI"...
THE NAME I SHARED WITH MY PARTNER!!
YUGI! YOU CAN REALLY TELL WE'RE HERE RIGHT?!!
YOU CAN SEE US, RIGHT?!
LOOM
!
YES!!
I CAN SEE YOU, HONDA!
SNIFF!
MY PARTNER!
JONOUCHI!
YEAH!
AND ANZU!
I KNEW IT...
YUGI WOULD NEVER FORGET HIS FRIENDS.
MAN! WHEN I SAW YOU ALL DRESSED LIKE A KING, RIDING A HORSE, I HARDLY RECOGNIZED YOU...!
...

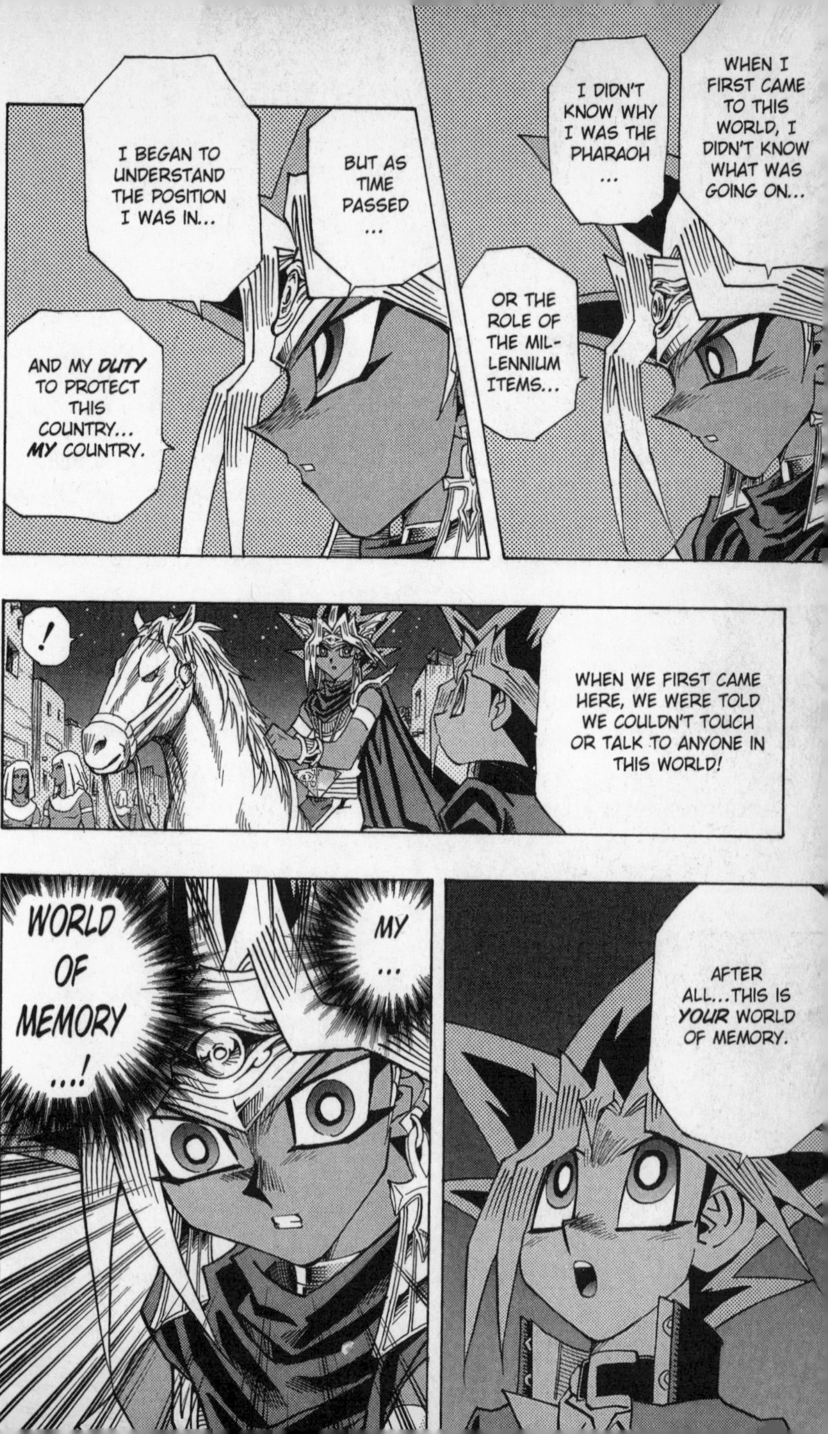
WHEN I FIRST CAME TO THIS WORLD, I DIDN'T KNOW WHAT WAS GOING ON...
I DIDN'T KNOW WHY I WAS THE PHARAOH ...
OR THE ROLE OF THE MIL-LENNIUM ITEMS...
BUT AS TIME PASSED ...
I BEGAN TO UNDERSTAND THE POSITION I WAS IN...
AND MY DUTY TO PROTECT THIS COUNTRY... MY COUNTRY.
WHEN WE FIRST CAME HERE, WE WERE TOLD WE COULDN'T TOUCH OR TALK TO ANYONE IN THIS WORLD!
!
AFTER ALL...THIS IS YOUR WORLD OF MEMORY.
MY ...
WORLD OF MEMORY ...!

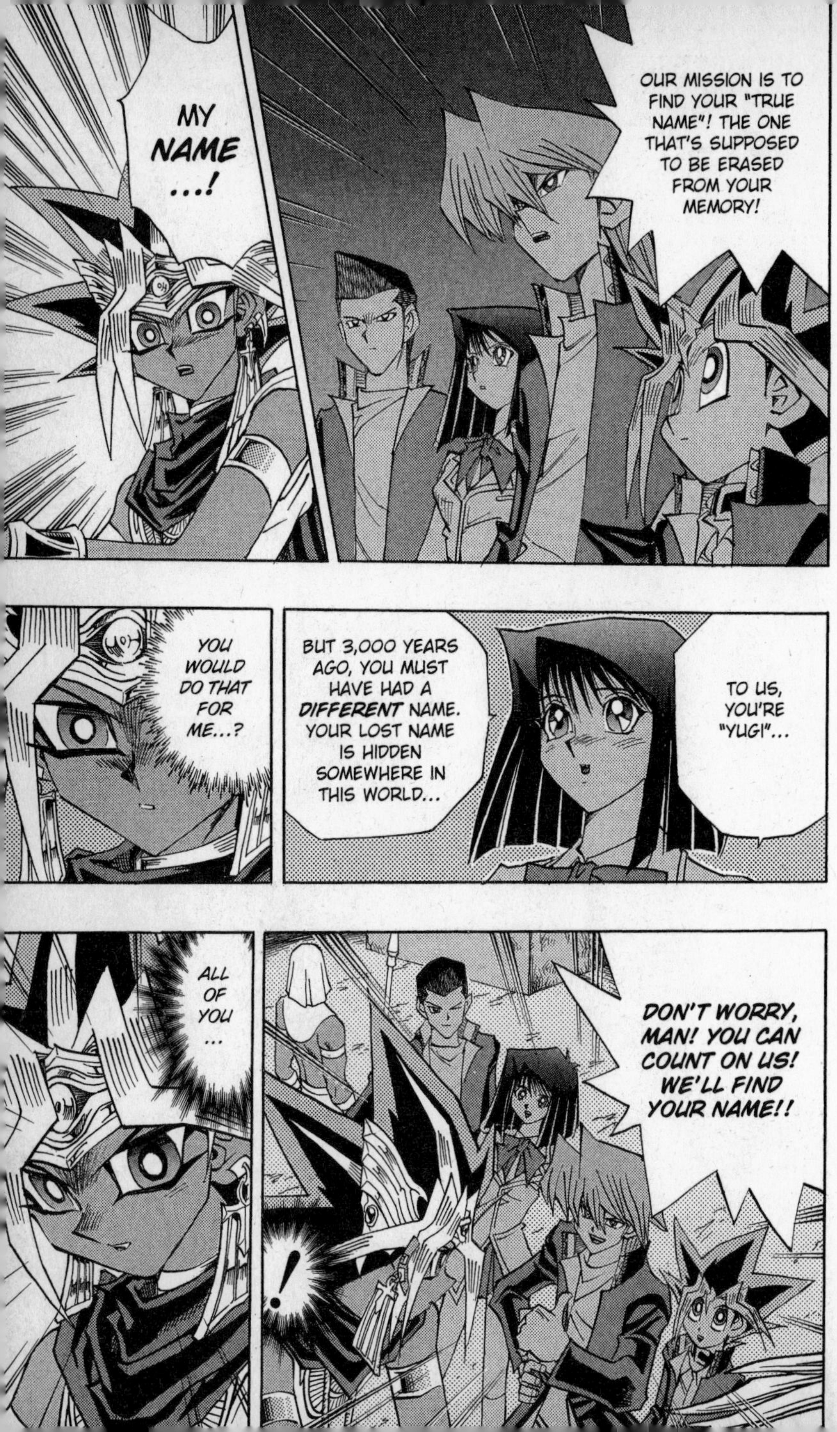
OUR MISSION IS TO FIND YOUR "TRUE NAME"! THE ONE THAT'S SUPPOSED TO BE ERASED FROM YOUR MEMORY!
MY NAME ...!
TO US, YOU'RE "YUGI"...
BUT 3,000 YEARS AGO, YOU MUST HAVE HAD A DIFFERENT NAME. YOUR LOST NAME IS HIDDEN SOMEWHERE IN THIS WORLD...
YOU WOULD DO THAT FOR ME...?
DON'T WORRY, MAN! YOU CAN COUNT ON US! WE'LL FIND YOUR NAME!!
!
ALL OF YOU ...

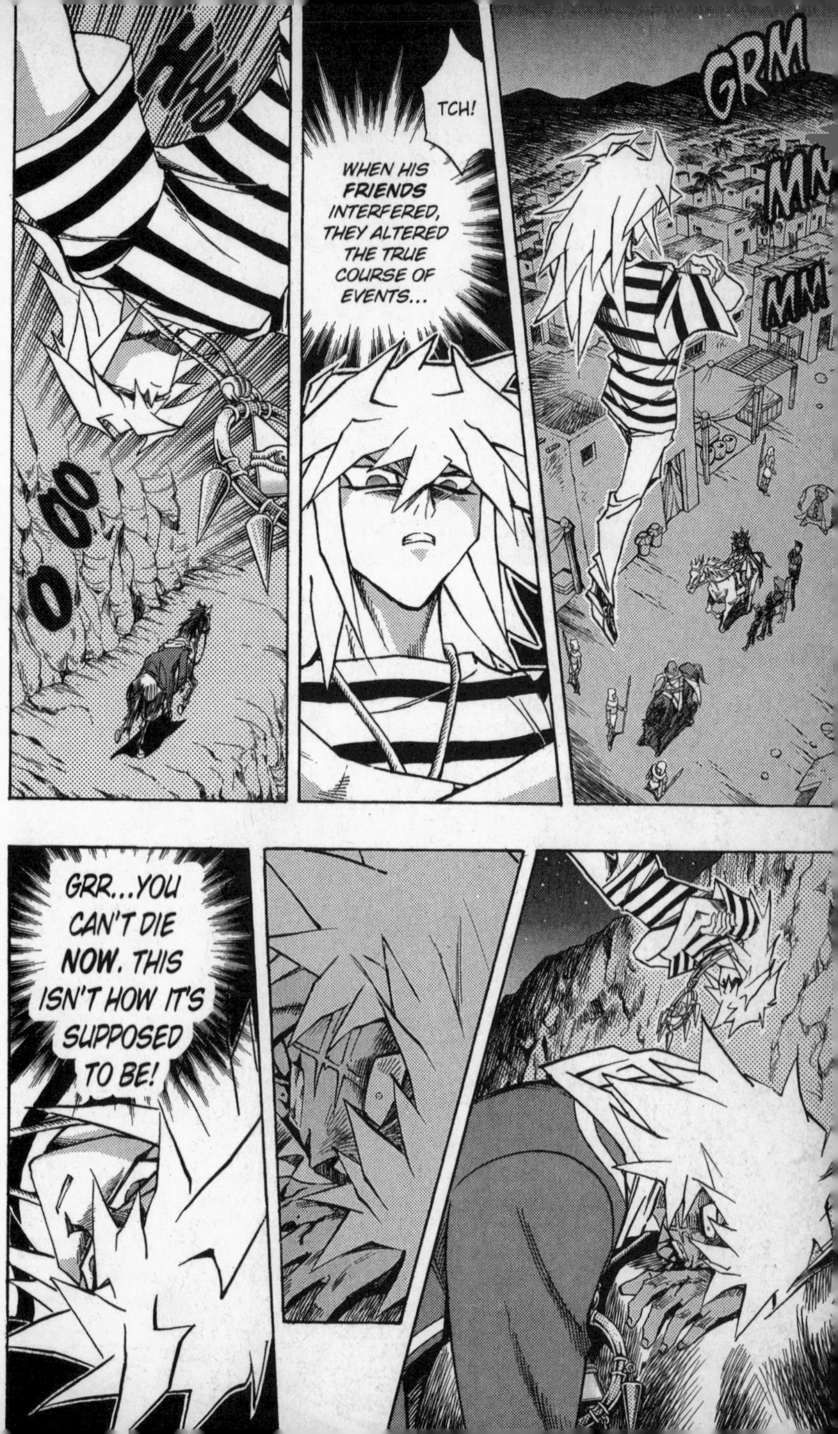
GRM
TCH!
WHEN HIS FRIENDS INTERFERED, THEY ALTERED THE TRUE COURSE OF EVENTS...
GRR...YOU CAN'T DIE NOW. THIS ISN'T HOW IT'S SUPPOSED TO BE!

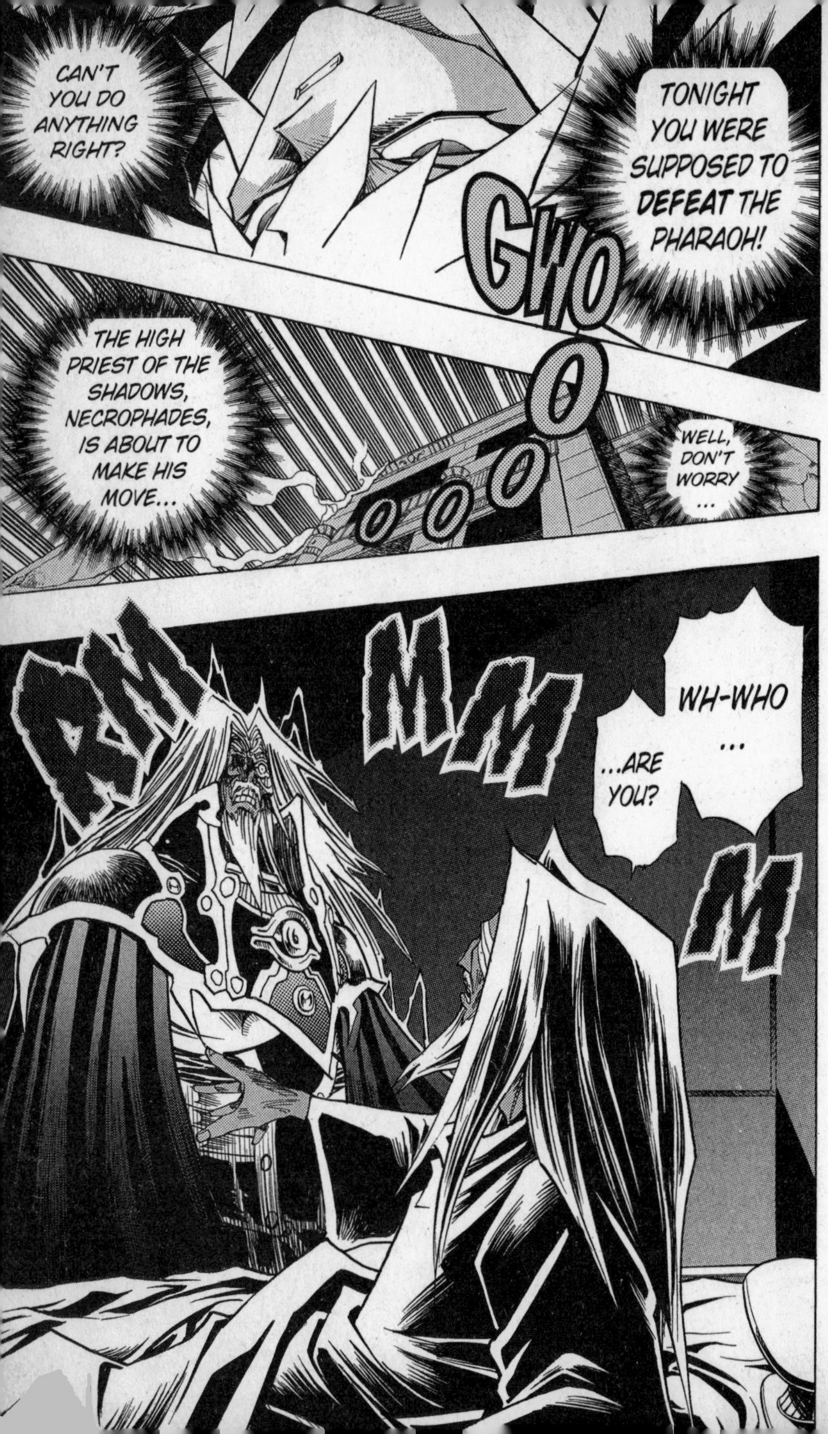
TONIGHT YOU WERE SUPPOSED TO **DEFEAT** THE PHARAOH!
CAN'T YOU DO ANYTHING RIGHT?
GWOOOOOO
WELL, DON'T WORRY ...
THE HIGH PRIEST OF THE SHADOWS, NECROPHADES, IS ABOUT TO MAKE HIS MOVE...
WH-WHO ...
...ARE YOU?
RMMMM

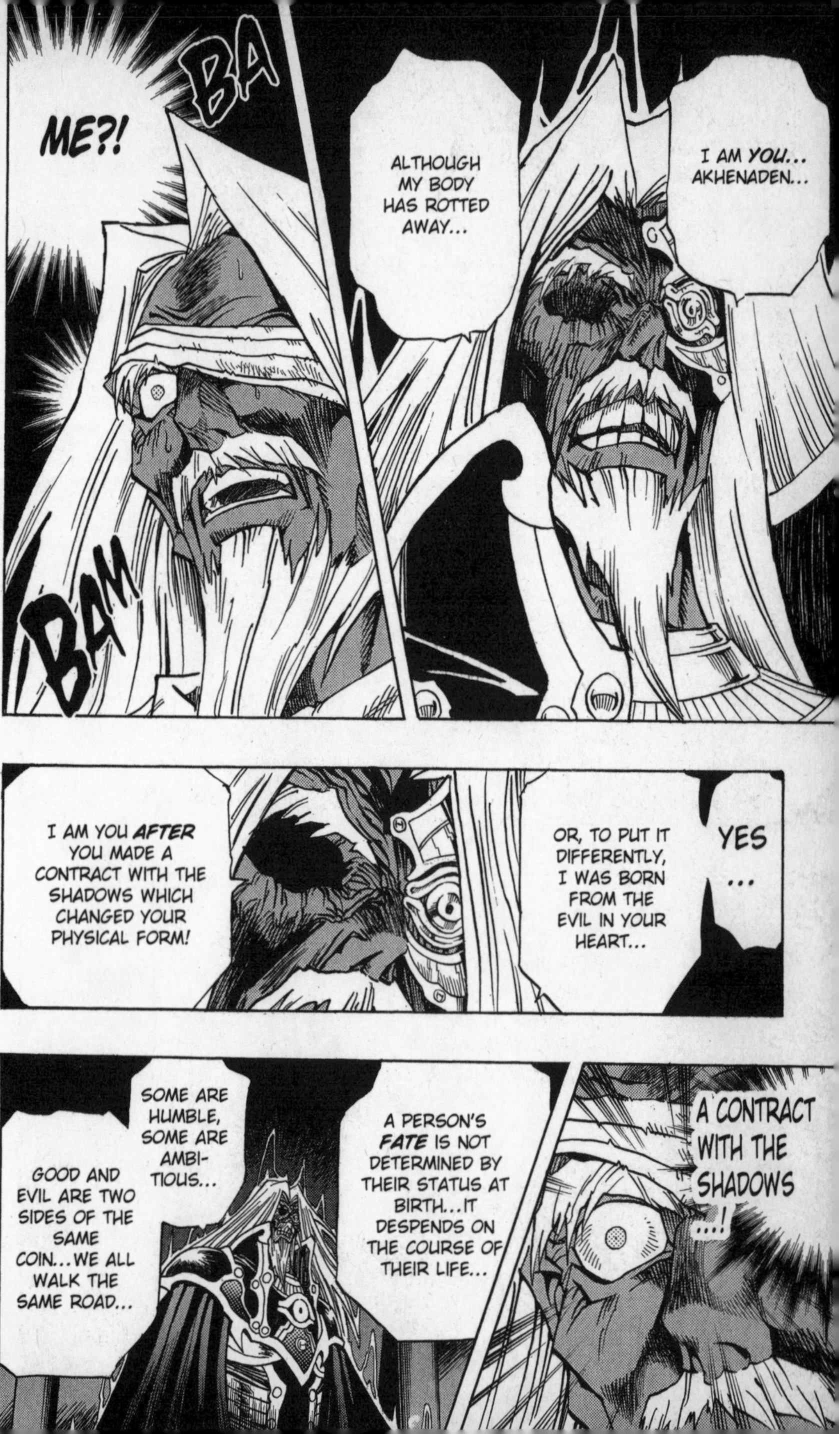
I AM YOU... AKHENADEN...
ALTHOUGH MY BODY HAS ROTTED AWAY...
BA
ME?!
BAM
YES ...
OR, TO PUT IT DIFFERENTLY, I WAS BORN FROM THE EVIL IN YOUR HEART...
I AM YOU AFTER YOU MADE A CONTRACT WITH THE SHADOWS WHICH CHANGED YOUR PHYSICAL FORM!
A CONTRACT WITH THE SHADOWS ...!
A PERSON'S FATE IS NOT DETERMINED BY THEIR STATUS AT BIRTH...IT DESPENDS ON THE COURSE OF THEIR LIFE...
SOME ARE HUMBLE, SOME ARE AMBITIOUS...
GOOD AND EVIL ARE TWO SIDES OF THE SAME COIN...WE ALL WALK THE SAME ROAD...

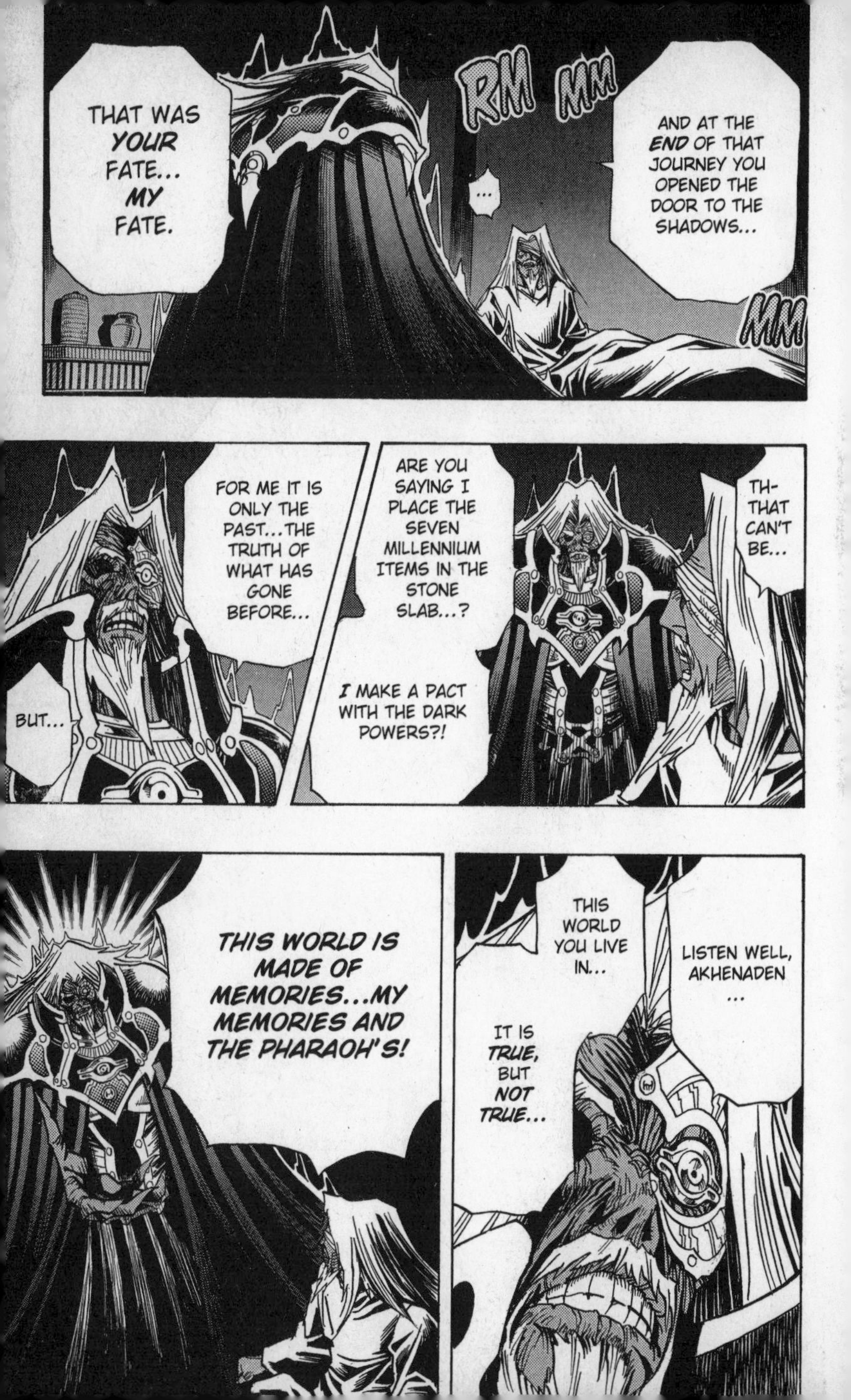
AND AT THE END OF THAT JOURNEY YOU OPENED THE DOOR TO THE SHADOWS...
RM MM
MM
...
THAT WAS YOUR FATE... MY FATE.
TH- THAT CAN'T BE...
ARE YOU SAYING I PLACE THE SEVEN MILLENNIUM ITEMS IN THE STONE SLAB...?
I MAKE A PACT WITH THE DARK POWERS?!
FOR ME IT IS ONLY THE PAST...THE TRUTH OF WHAT HAS GONE BEFORE...
BUT...
LISTEN WELL, AKHENADEN ...
THIS WORLD YOU LIVE IN...
IT IS TRUE, BUT NOT TRUE...
THIS WORLD IS MADE OF MEMORIES...MY MEMORIES AND THE PHARAOH'S!

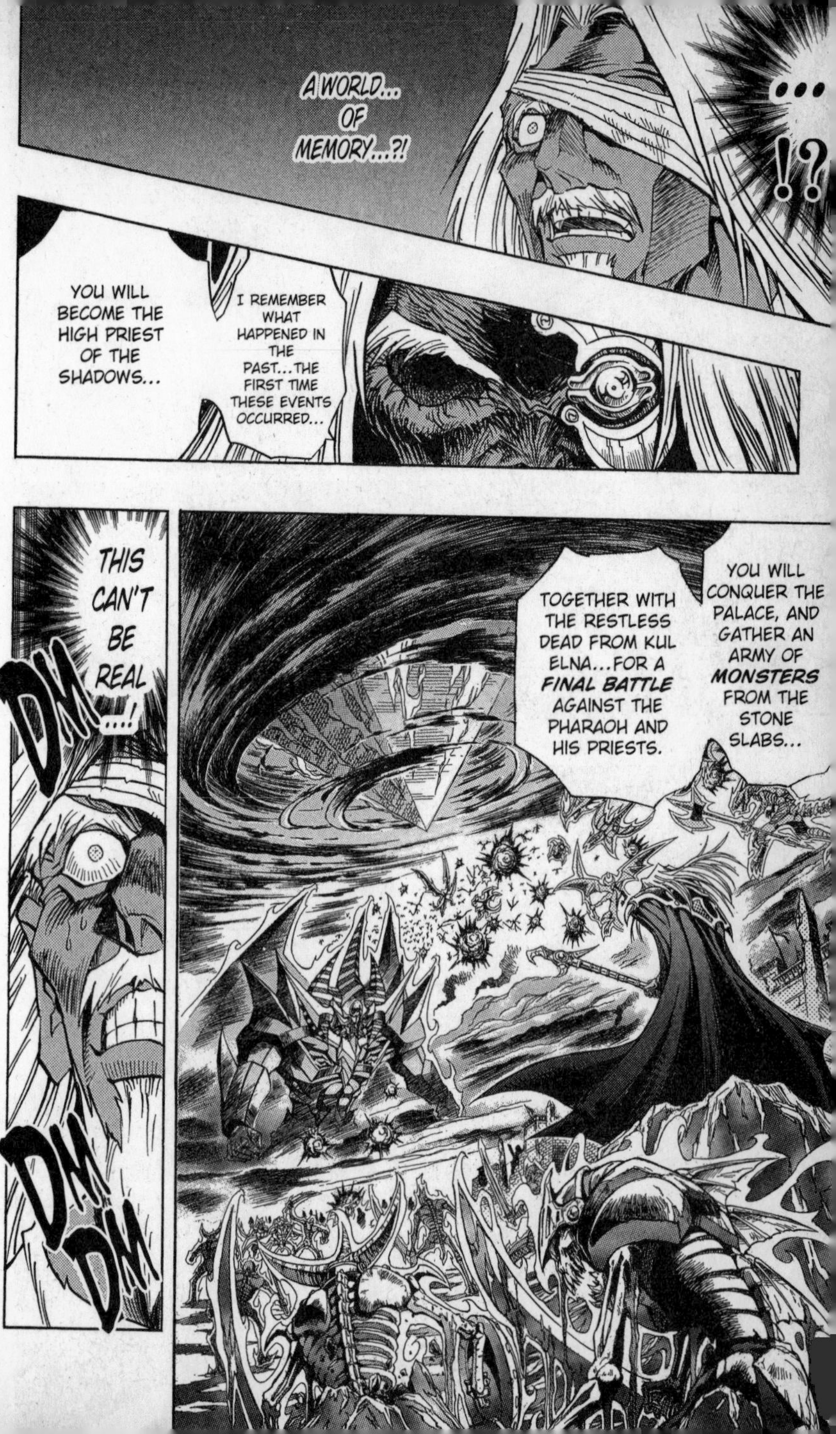
...!?
A WORLD... OF MEMORY...?!
I REMEMBER WHAT HAPPENED IN THE PAST...THE FIRST TIME THESE EVENTS OCCURRED...
YOU WILL BECOME THE HIGH PRIEST OF THE SHADOWS...
YOU WILL CONQUER THE PALACE, AND GATHER AN ARMY OF **MONSTERS** FROM THE STONE SLABS...
TOGETHER WITH THE RESTLESS DEAD FROM KUL ELNA...FOR A ***FINAL BATTLE*** AGAINST THE PHARAOH AND HIS PRIESTS.
THIS CAN'T BE REAL...!
DM
DM
DM

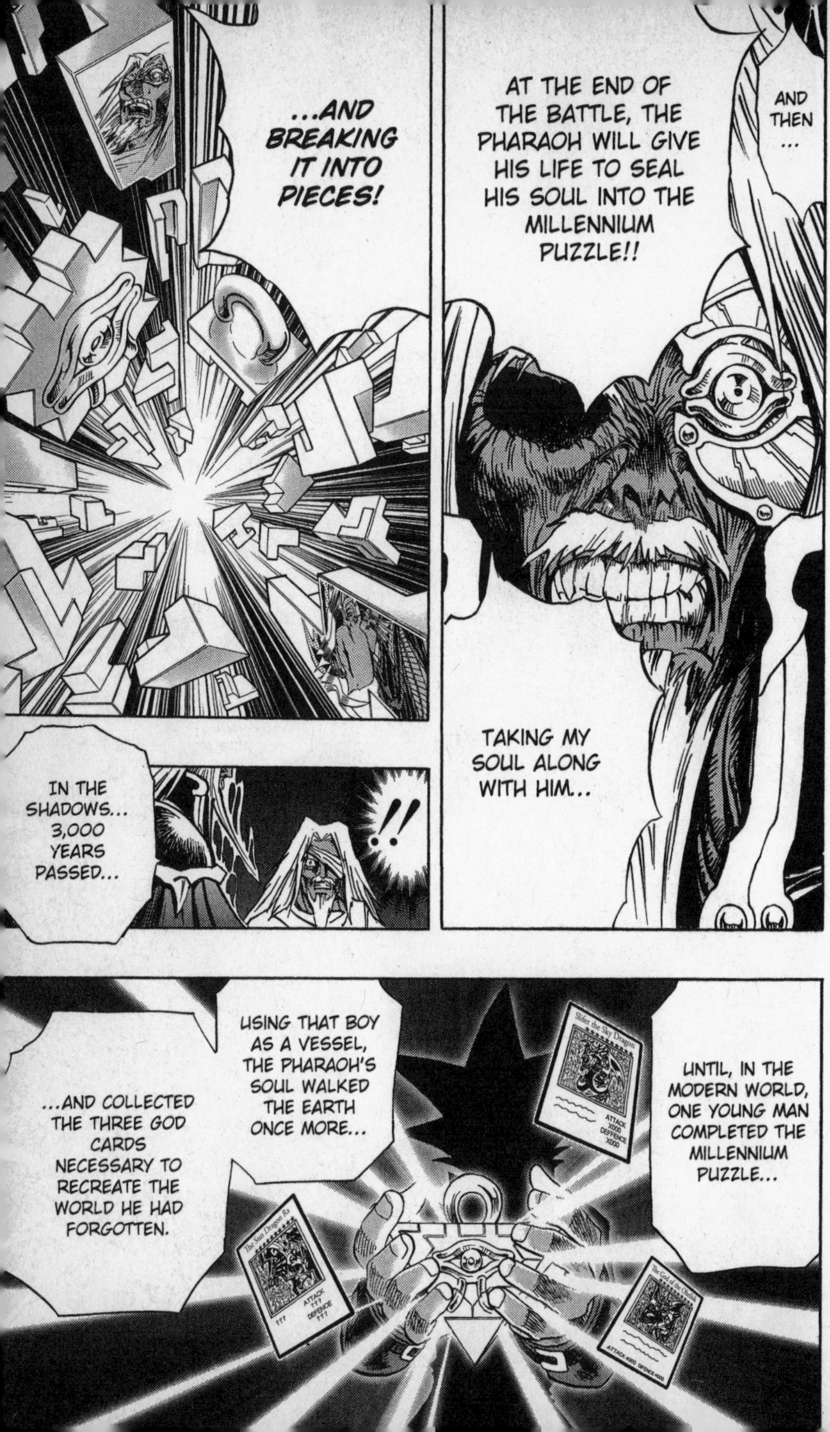
AND THEN ...
AT THE END OF THE BATTLE, THE PHARAOH WILL GIVE HIS LIFE TO SEAL HIS SOUL INTO THE MILLENNIUM PUZZLE!!
TAKING MY SOUL ALONG WITH HIM...
...AND BREAKING IT INTO PIECES!
!!
IN THE SHADOWS... 3,000 YEARS PASSED...
UNTIL, IN THE MODERN WORLD, ONE YOUNG MAN COMPLETED THE MILLENNIUM PUZZLE...
Slifer the Sky Dragon
ATTACK X000 DEFENCE X000
USING THAT BOY AS A VESSEL, THE PHARAOH'S SOUL WALKED THE EARTH ONCE MORE...
...AND COLLECTED THE THREE GOD CARDS NECESSARY TO RECREATE THE WORLD HE HAD FORGOTTEN.
The Sun Dragon Ra
ATTACK ??? DEFENCE ???
The God of the Obelisk
ATTACK 4000 DEFENCE 4000

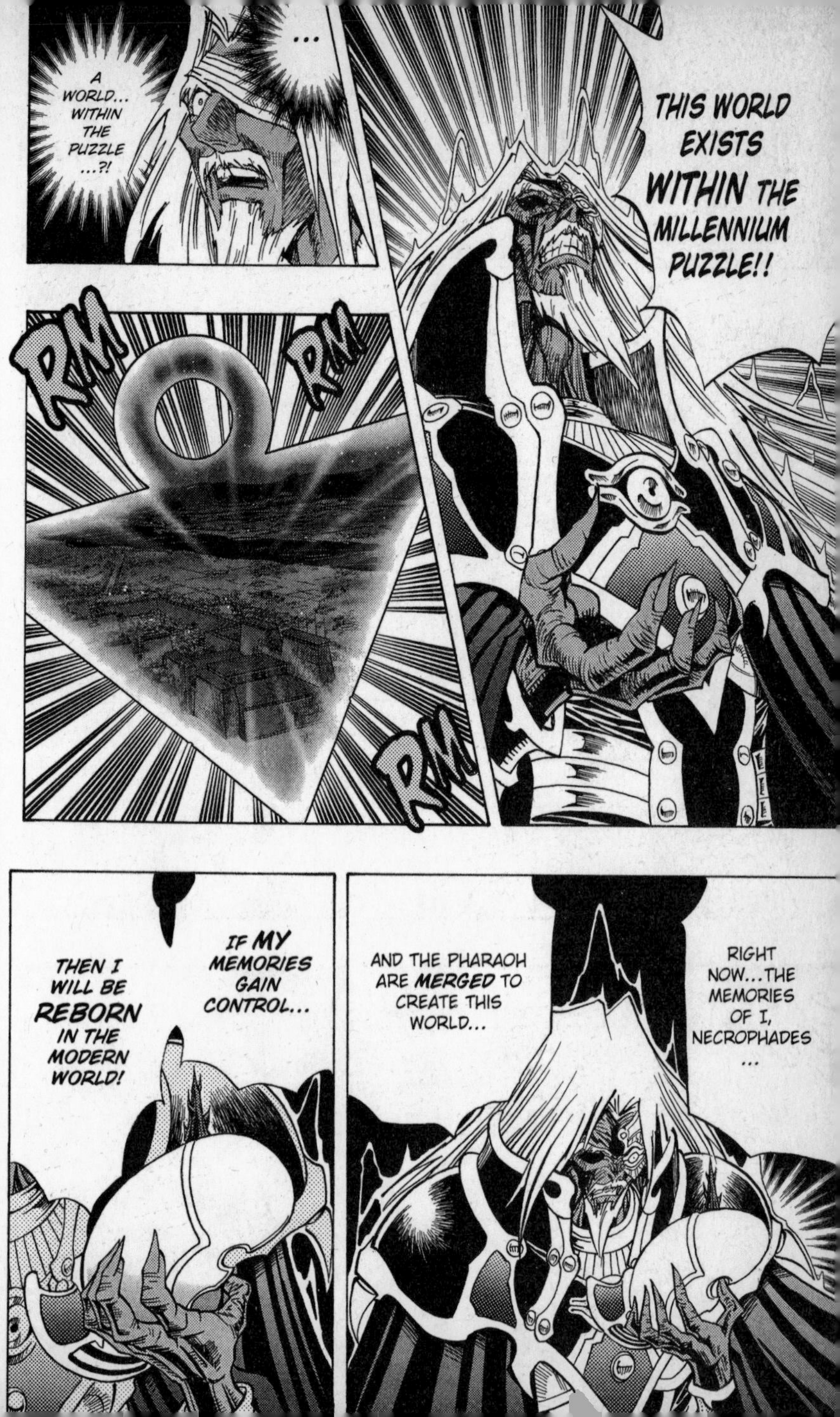
THIS WORLD EXISTS WITHIN THE MILLENNIUM PUZZLE!!
...
A WORLD... WITHIN THE PUZZLE ...?!
RM
RM
RM
RIGHT NOW...THE MEMORIES OF I, NECROPHADES ...
AND THE PHARAOH ARE MERGED TO CREATE THIS WORLD...
IF MY MEMORIES GAIN CONTROL...
THEN I WILL BE REBORN IN THE MODERN WORLD!

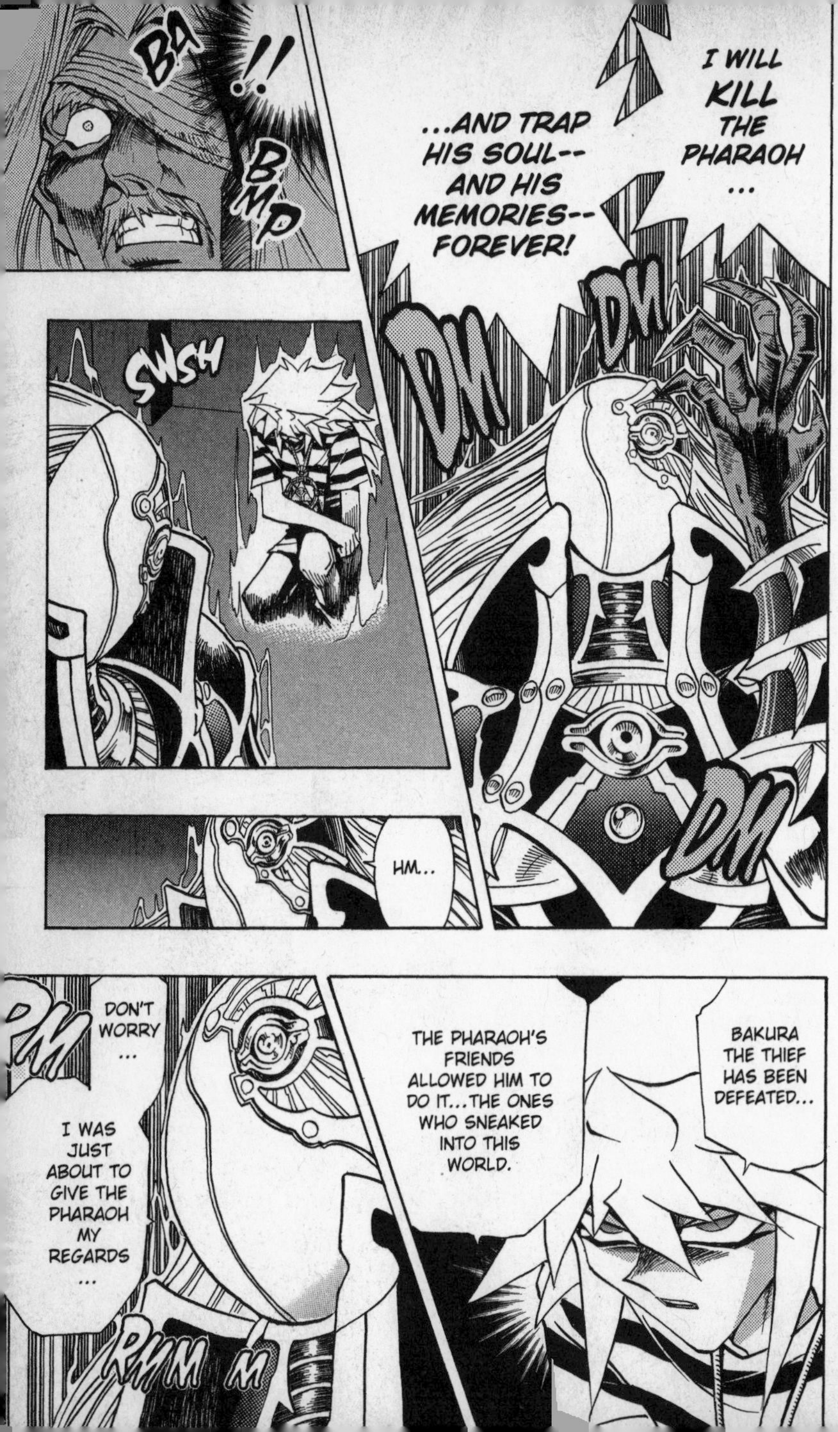
I WILL KILL THE PHARAOH...
...AND TRAP HIS SOUL-- AND HIS MEMORIES-- FOREVER!
DM
DM
DM
BA
!!
BMP
SWSH
HM...
BAKURA THE THIEF HAS BEEN DEFEATED...
THE PHARAOH'S FRIENDS ALLOWED HIM TO DO IT...THE ONES WHO SNEAKED INTO THIS WORLD.
DON'T WORRY...
I WAS JUST ABOUT TO GIVE THE PHARAOH MY REGARDS...

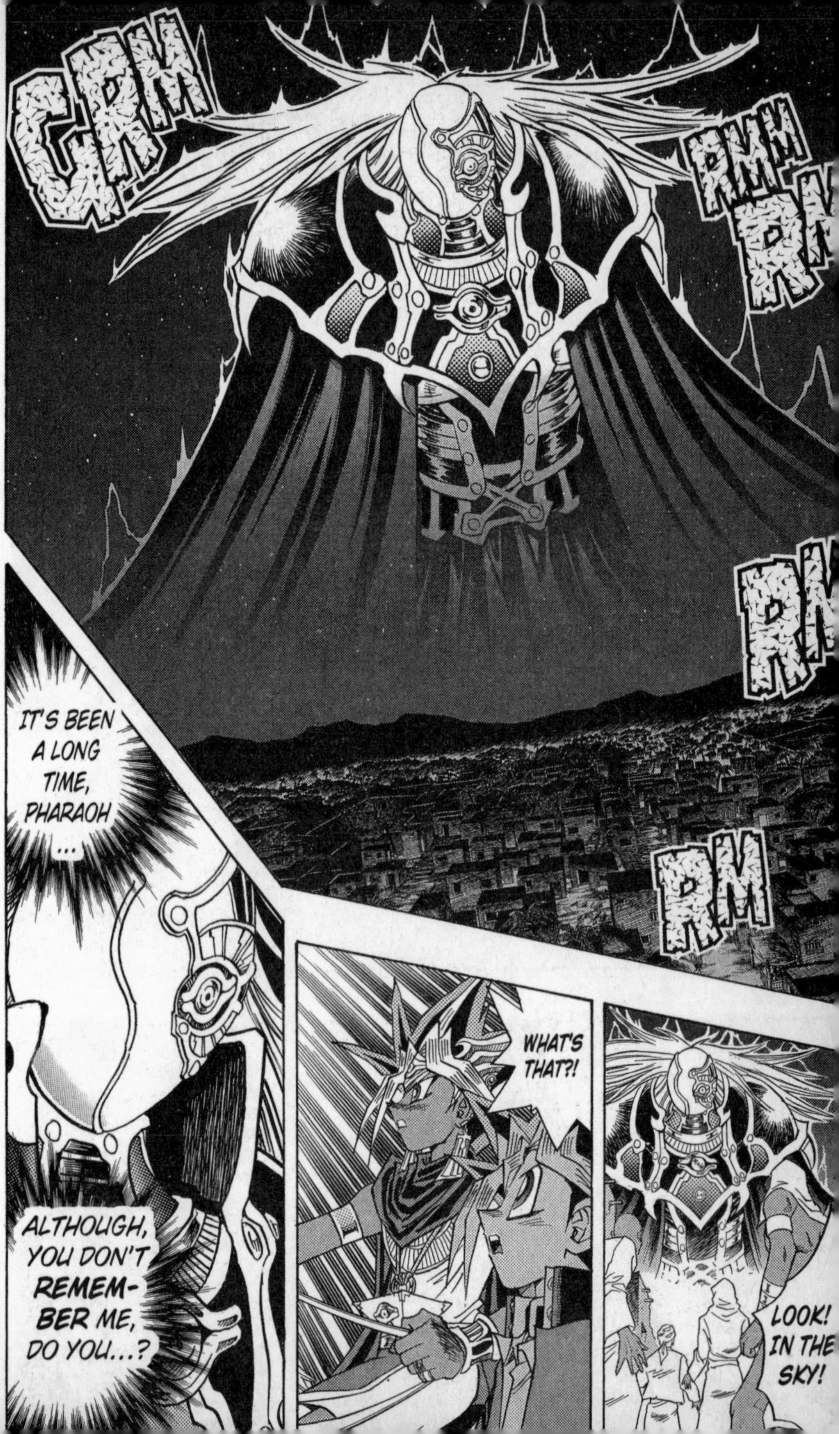
RMM
RM
CRM
RM
RM
RM
LOOK! IN THE SKY!
WHAT'S THAT?!
IT'S BEEN A LONG TIME, PHARAOH ...
ALTHOUGH, YOU DON'T REMEM-BER ME, DO YOU...?

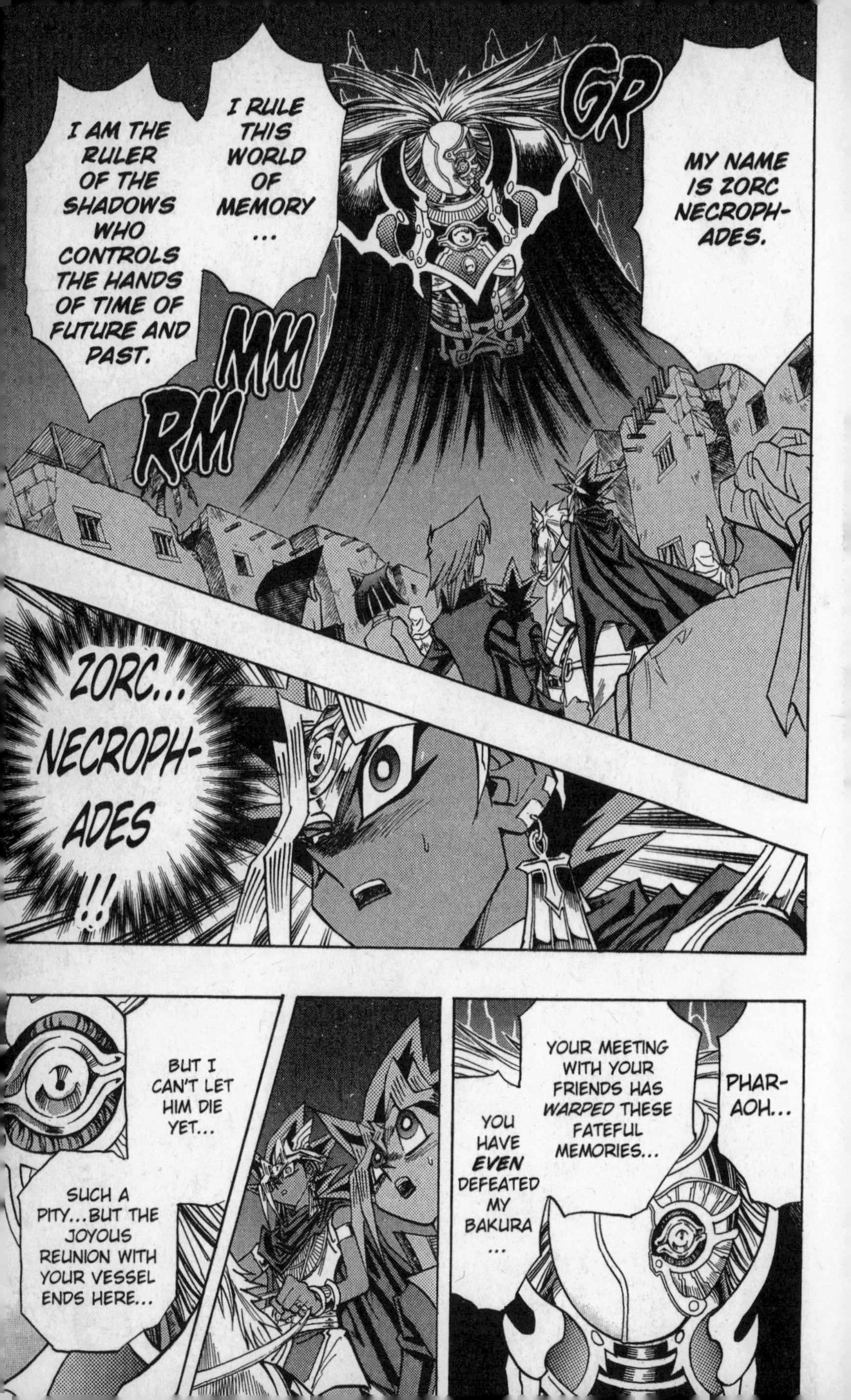
MY NAME IS ZORC NECROPH-ADES.
GR
RMMM
I RULE THIS WORLD OF MEMORY ...
I AM THE RULER OF THE SHADOWS WHO CONTROLS THE HANDS OF TIME OF FUTURE AND PAST.
ZORC... NECROPH-ADES!!
PHAR-AOH...
YOUR MEETING WITH YOUR FRIENDS HAS WARPED THESE FATEFUL MEMORIES...
YOU HAVE EVEN DEFEATED MY BAKURA ...
BUT I CAN'T LET HIM DIE YET...
SUCH A PITY...BUT THE JOYOUS REUNION WITH YOUR VESSEL ENDS HERE...

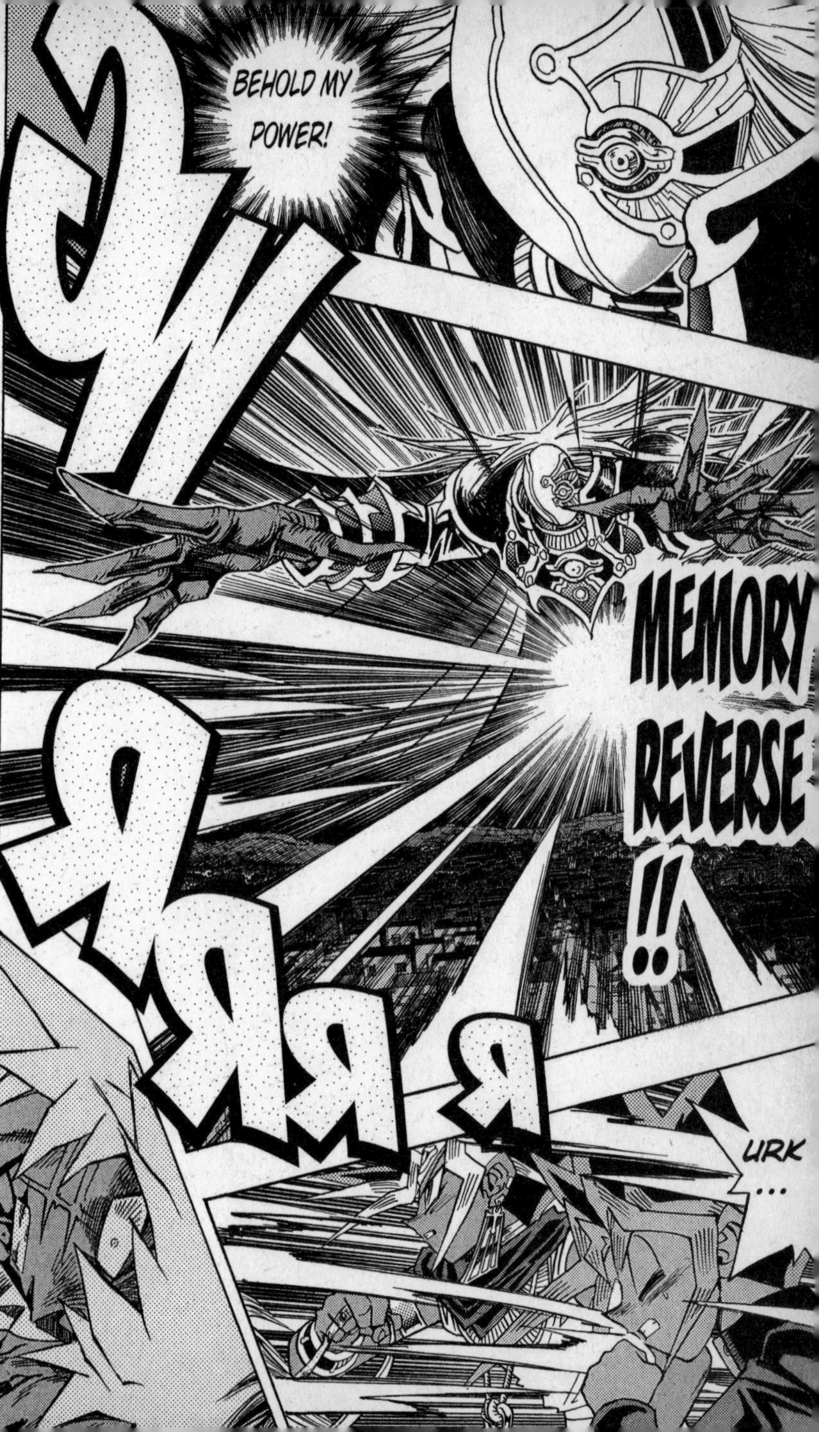
BEHOLD MY POWER!
MEMORY REVERSE!!
URK...

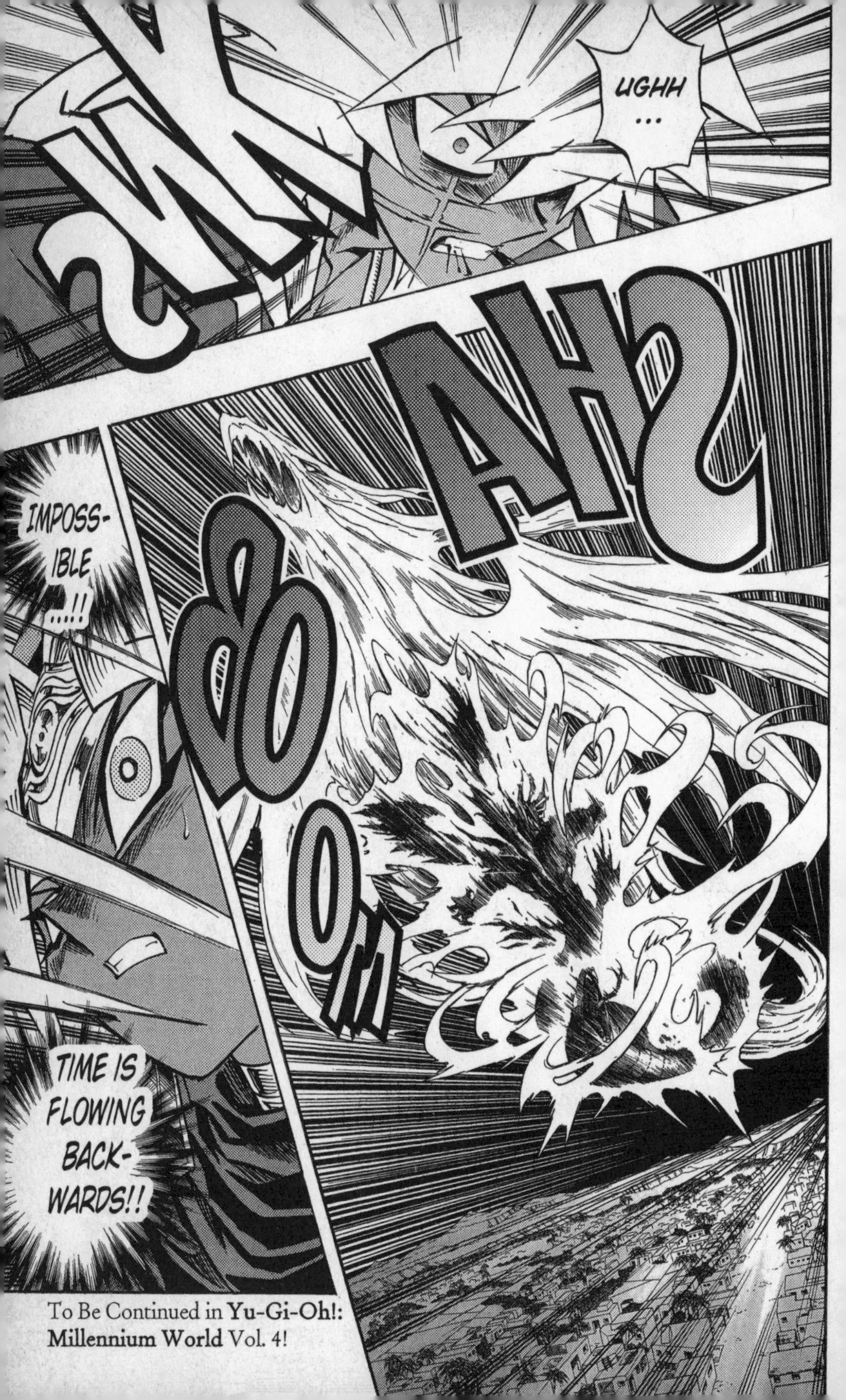
UGHH ...
IMPOSS-IBLE ...!!
TIME IS FLOWING BACK-WARDS!!

To Be Continued in **Yu-Gi-Oh!: Millennium World** Vol. 4!

IN THE NEXT VOLUME...

Time rewinds, forcing Yu-Gi-Oh to fight Bakura all over again...only this time without the Egyptian Gods! As the kingdom searches for a savior, Seto confronts the horrifying results of his *ka* experiments and awakens the awesome power of the Blue-Eyes White Dragon. Lurking in the ruins of Kul Elna, Bakura prepares to complete the dark ritual which will unleash the evil god Zorc Necrophades in the world of memories...*and the world of the present day!*

COMING AUGUST 2006!

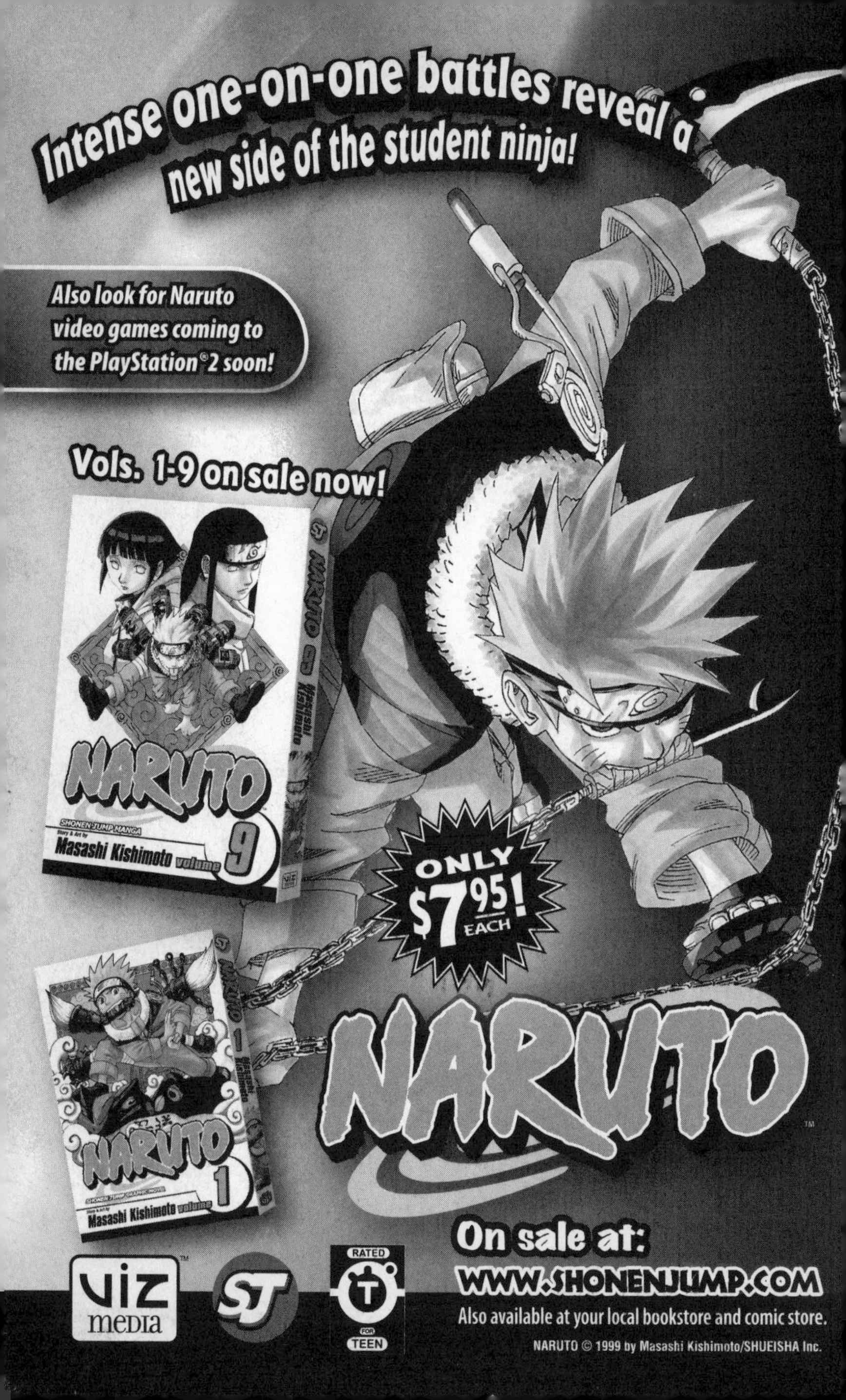
Intense one-on-one battles reveal a new side of the student ninja!
Also look for Naruto video games coming to the PlayStation® 2 soon!
Vols. 1-9 on sale now!
NARUTO
SHONEN JUMP MANGA
Masashi Kishimoto volume 9
ONLY $7.95! EACH
NARUTO
Masashi Kishimoto volume 1
NARUTO™
On sale at:
WWW.SHONENJUMP.COM
Also available at your local bookstore and comic store.
viz media
SJ
RATED T FOR TEEN
NARUTO © 1999 by Masashi Kishimoto/SHUEISHA Inc.

Tell us what you think about SHONEN JUMP manga!

Our survey is now available online.
Go to: ***www.SHONENJUMP.com/mangasurvey***

Help us make our product offering better!

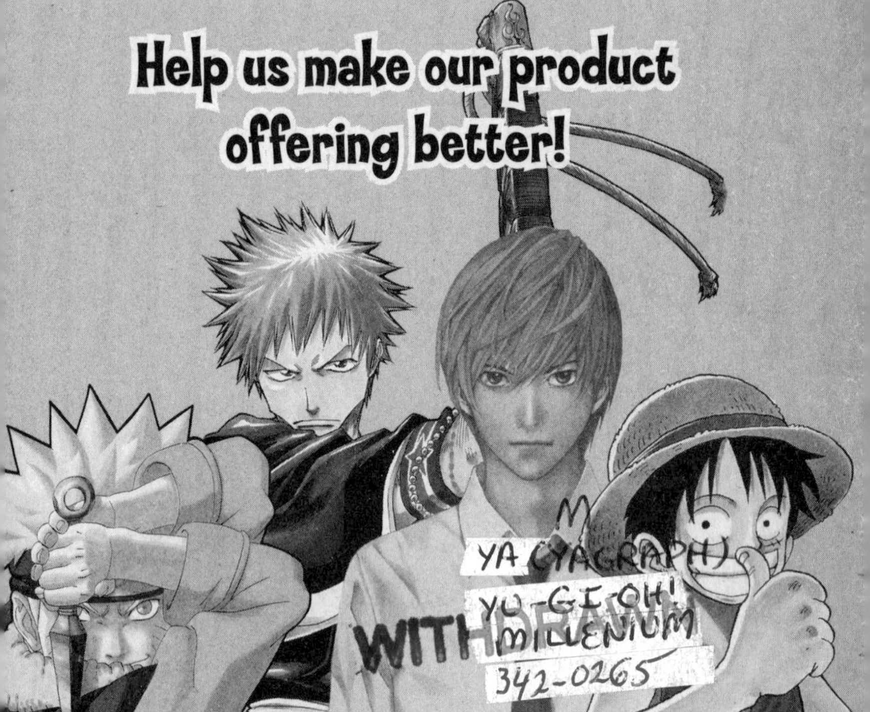

THE REAL ACTION STARTS IN...

SHONEN JUMP
THE WORLD'S MOST POPULAR MANGA
www.shonenjump.com

SJ ADVANCED

SJ

viz media

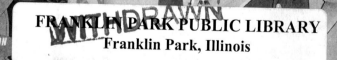